For Steven & Re.

Present at the creation,
there at the end, and
all the times in-between.

— David Prochaska

25 July 1990

Making Algeria French

This book is published as part of the joint publishing agreement established in 1977 between the Foundation de la Maison des Sciences de l'Homme and the Press Syndicate of the University of Cambridge. Titles published under this arrangement may appear in any European language or, in the case of volumes of collected essays, in several languages.

New books will appear either as individual titles or in one of the series that the Maison des Sciences de l'Homme and the Cambridge University Press have jointly agreed to publish. All books published jointly by the Maison des Sciences de l'Homme and the Cambridge University Press will be distributed by the Press throughout the world.

Cet ouvrage est publié dans le cadre de l'accord de co-édition passé en 1977 entre la Fondation de la Maison des Sciences de l'Homme et le Press Syndicate de l'Université de Cambridge. Toutes les langues européernnes sont admises pour les titres couverts par cet accord, et les ouvrages collectifs peuvent paraître en plusieures langues.

Les ouvrages paraissent soit isolément, soit dans l'une des séries que la Maison des Sciences de l'Homme it Cambridge Press ont convenu de publier ensemble. La distribution dans le monde entier des titres ainsi publiés conjointement par les deux établissements est assurée par Cambridge University Press.

Making Algeria French

Colonialism in Bône,
1870 – 1920

DAVID PROCHASKA
University of Illinois

CAMBRIDGE UNIVERSITY PRESS

Cambridge   New York   Port Chester   Melbourne   Sydney

EDITIONS DE LA MAISON DES SCIENCES DE L'HOMME
Paris

Published by the Press Syndicate of the University of Cambridge
The Pitt Building, Trumpington Street, Cambridge CB2 1RP
40 West 20th Street, New York, N.Y. 10011 USA
10 Stamford Road, Oakleigh, Melbourne 3166, Australia

First published 1990

Printed in the United States of America

Library of Congress Cataloging-in-Publication Data

Prochaska, David.

    Making Algeria French : colonialism in Bône, 1870–1920 / David
Prochaska.
      p. cm.
    Bibliography: p.
    ISBN 0-521-34303-8
    1. Bône (Algeria)—History.   2. French—Algeria—Bône—History.
I. Title.
DT299.B6P76   1990
965'.5—dc20   89-33176
                                                  CIP

British Library Cataloguing in Publication Data

Prochaska, David

    Making Algeria French: colonialism in Bône, 1870–
1920.
    1. Algeria, Annaba. Social conditions, history
I. Title
965'.5

ISBN 0-521-34303-8

For Harry,

my intellectual and spiritual mentor early on
—who better read it

and for Mohan Lal Chipa,

who for no good reason befriended me
—and who will never read it.

Contents

Tables

Tables

Maps and figures

Maps and Figures

Illustrations

Illustrations

Abbreviations

AN	Archives Nationales, Paris
AOM	Archives Nationales, Dépôt d'Outre-Mer, Aix-en-Provence
APCA	Archives de l'Assemblée Populaire Communale de Annaba (former Archives Municipales de Bône)
AWC	Archives de la Wilaya de Constantine
BNV	Bibliothèque Nationale, Versailles
PP	British Parliamentary Papers, Accounts and Papers
SGA	Gouvernement Général de l'Algérie, *Statistique Générale de l'Algérie* (Algiers: Imprimerie Algérienne, 1870–1929)
SNED	Société Nationale d'Edition et de Diffusion
TEFA	*Tableau d'Etablissements Français en Algérie* (Paris: Imprimerie Royale, 1837–66)

Preface

Albert Camus received the Nobel Prize in 1957. At a press conference afterwards, he was asked about the Algerian Revolution, then raging. *"If I had to choose between justice [independant Algeria] and my mother* [Algérie française], *I would choose my mother."* Camus was a Frenchman born in colonial Algeria, a settler or *pied noir*, to use the somewhat pejorative term. Like George Orwell in India, he was a colonial by background. *"At present the Arabs do not alone make up all of Algeria. The size and seniority of the French settlement, in particular, are enough to create a problem that cannot be compared to anything in history. The Algerian French are likewise, and in the strongest meaning of the word, natives."*

Camus's father worked as a cellarman in the wine trade. In 1913 the elder Camus was posted to Mondovi in eastern Algeria. Mondovi was located eight miles inland from Bône, the third largest port city in Algeria. The largest, Algiers, was where the Camus family came from, and where Camus set *The Stranger* (*L'Etranger*). *"Mother died today. Or, maybe, yesterday; I can't be sure."* The second largest port, Oran, furnished the locale for *The Plague* (*La Peste*). *"From dark corners, from basements, from cellars, from sewers, they [rats] came up in long tottering lines to stagger at the light, turn round and die near men."* Bône itself was situated on the site of St. Augustine's Hippo. All three of these settler colonial cities were populated by more Europeans than native Algerians.

Albert Camus was born in Mondovi in 1913. Ten years before Jérome Bertagna, the "boss" of Bône, died in Mondovi. Where Camus's background was Spanish, Bertagna's was Italian. Where the Camus were dirt-scrabbling poor, Bertagna made his fortune in colonial Algeria. Elected mayor of Bône in 1888, Bertagna was the single most powerful person in the region until his death in 1903. It was he who was primarily responsible for constructing the port of Bône through which Camus's father shipped pressed grapes to France. With his economic wealth and political clout, Bertagna created a vast 7,500-acre estate in Mondovi, 1,500 acres of which he devoted to vineyards, perhaps including the one where Camus's father worked.

Making Algeria French constitutes a postcolonial look at the colonial past of Bône-become-Annaba. The title is ironic, for the unmaking of French Algeria soon followed its making, a case of the failure of success. Eschewing earlier colonial interpretations, I view the Bône past differently, as French settler colonialism in a colonial city. Furthermore, I have employed elements of a modernist prose structure to convey a sense of my postcolonial perspective as well as to present my substantive findings. In keeping with the shape of a city, therefore, this work is multidimensional and architectonic, rather than one-dimensional and linear. To be sure, we will get from the top of the Cours – the main street in Bône/Annaba – to the port at the foot, and from one side of town to the other, but not before pausing to explore some of the side streets, and taking a few detours to point out the sights. I invite the reader, then, to take a guided tour with me through colonial Bône.

*   *   *

Given the circumstances under which this book was conceived and carried out, I am happy to acknowledge the aid of the following individuals. First of all, this study simply would not have been possible had it not been for the aid of Jean-Claude Vatin, Directeur, Centre d'Etudes et de Documentation Economique Juridique et Sociale, Cairo; R. Ainad Tabet, former director, Archives Nationales d'Algérie, who kindly granted me unrestricted access to the Algerian archives; Brahim Jatni, Secrétaire General, Assemblée Populaire et Communale de Annaba; and Nick Macris, Dravo Corporation. Also in Algeria, Prof. Louis P. Montoy of the Université de Constantine; Abdelkrim Badjadja, director of the Archives de la Wilaya de Constantine; and Prof. James Malarkey facilitated my research.

On this side of the Atlantic, I owe a special debt of gratitude to Edmund Burke and Paul Rabinow. Steven Vincent, Robert Moeller, Ronald Toby, and James Barrett read earlier versions of the study. Charles Tilly and John Modell provided valuable advice on the quantitative aspects of this project. I also wish to acknowledge the support of Rob and Val Hollister, Connie Hungerford, Rollie Guild, Steven and Rebecca Tobias, Liz Friedman, Daniel and Janet Atlan, Fryar Calhoun, Elinor Accampo, Lynn Dumenil, Irving Elichirigoity, and most of all, Sally.

A study such as this requires time and money to bring to fruition. The University of California, Berkeley, the French Government, and the Mabel McLeod Lewis Fund at Stanford provided financial support for lengthy archival research. At Berkeley I received additional support from the Institute of International Studies and the Graduate Division. At the University of Illinois, I have received extensive support from the Center for Advanced Study, the Center for African Studies, International Programs and Studies, the Faculty Research Board, and the Humanities Released Time program. My grandparents, Mr. and Mrs. C. E. Long, also provided welcome support at opportune moments. More recently, my work has been supported by the American Philosophical Society, the ACLS-SSEC, the National Humanities Center, and the Davis Center for Historical Studies at Princeton. Finally, I thank the staffs of the archives and libraries which made available the documentation utilized in this study, especially the Archives de l'Assemblée Populaire et Communale deAnnaba, Archives de la Wilaya de Constantine, and the Archives Nationales de France.

The maps and figures have been produced by James Bier. In France, Mme. Brigitte Richon kindly made copies of several photographs of colonial Bône that she had gathered in the course of her photographic research for Frederic Musso's *L'Algérie autrefois* (1976). It has been a pleasure working with the staff of Cambridge University Press, especially Frank Smith.

Earlier versions of Chapter 6 and 7 appeared as "The Political Culture of Settler Colonialism in Algeria: Politics in Bône, 1870–1920," *Revue de l'Occident Musulman et de la Méditerranée*, no. 48–49 (1988), pp. 293–311, and as "Reconstructing *L'Algérie Française*," in Jean-Claude Vatin, ed., *Connaissances du Maghreb* (Paris: Centre National de la Recherche Scientifique, 1984), pp. 65–78, respectively. Parts of Chapter 3 were published in "Fire on the Mountain: Resisting Colonialism in Algeria," in Donald Crummey, ed., *Banditry, Rebellion and Social Protest in Africa* (Portsmouth, NH: Heinemann, 1986), pp. 229–52; and a section of Chapter 5 in "La ségrégation résidentielle en société coloniale. Le cas de Bône en Algérie de 1872 à 1954," *Cahiers d'Histoire* 25 (1980): 53–74.

I take responsibility for what is wrong with this work as well as what is right.

1

Theoretical foundations:
Settler colonialism and colonial urbanism

Not one in a hundred books of colonial history is scientifi-
cally honest [scientifiquement honnête].
— Charles-André Julien[1]

There is a historiographical debate over colonial Algeria which mirrors
the personal and private one, a debate which revolves essentially around
the nature and consequences of French colonialism in Algeria. The end
of French rule and the beginning of Algerian independence are still so
close, achieved in such a violent paroxysm of decolonization and national
liberation, that the literature on Algeria suffers from the bane of so
much contemporary history: too much personal polemic and not enough
dispassionate analysis, too much in the way of historical myth and too
little historical fact, too much reading the present into the past and too
little consideration of the past on its own terms. Paradoxically, the fact
that it has proven so damnably difficult to move beyond one-sided pre-
sentations testifies not only to the strong emotions aroused but also to
the importance of the issues involved. All of which only serves to underscore the necessity for a history of colonial Algeria which transcends
ideological *parti pris*.

Colonial Algeria

As a first attempt to characterize the corpus of colonial Algerian historiography, consider the typology put forth by one scholar, who distinguishes four overlapping but discernible groups, each representing a
more or less distinct interpretive approach.[2] First, there are the colonialist historians and colonial apologists, who were virtually the only
writers on Algerian history until the 1930 centenary of French rule, and
who dominated the field right up to the end of *Algérie française*. Known
collectively as the "Ecole d'Alger" because centered at the University

1

of Algiers, this group of French humanists, social scientists, and pub-
licists included E. F. Gautier, George Marçais, Christian Courtois,
Roger Le Tourneau, Stephane Gsell, Claude Martin, Julien Franc, and
Pierre Boyer, among others. Beginning in about 1930 a second group
emerged consisting of Muslims who wrote Algerian history from a dis-
tinctly Islamic point of view: Moubarek al-Mili, Tewfik al-Madani, and
Abd al-Rahman.[3] At around the same time a cluster of French scholars
began to take issue with the dominant colonialist historiography. This
group of liberal colonialists, humanist in outlook and sympathetic to
Algerian nationalism, includes several of the most widely respected
French authorities of colonial Algeria: Marcel Emerit, Charles-André
Julien, and more recently, Charles-Robert Ageron and André Nouschi.
Lastly, there emerged during and after the struggle for independence a
number of nationalist Algerian and French Marxist writers who largely
superceded the earlier Islamicists comprising Mostefa Lacheraf, Mo-
hamed Cherif Sahli, Djilali Sari, Mahfoud Kaddache, and Yves
Lacoste.[4]

To highlight clearly the differences between these four groups, let us
examine the representative colonialist and anticolonialist viewpoints
concerning the successive colonizers of Algeria from the Phoenicians to
the French. First of all, colonialist historians stress that earlier con-
querors of Algeria – the Phoenicians, Romans, Arabs, Turks – were
exploitative, alien invaders who so disrupted Algerian society that by
1830, when the French came, no Algerian "nation" could be said to
exist (if there ever had been one). The anticolonialists counter that
Algeria was indeed a nation prior to the French invasion, a highly
developed, populous country with a high literacy rate. Moreover, they
claim that the Phoenicians and Arabs cannot be considered colonizers
in the ordinary sense of the word because the ease with which they were
incorporated into the indigenous Berber society attests to their common
racial and cultural features. The same argument of racial and cultural
similarity is applied to the Turks. Although exploitative, they at least
shared the same Islamic faith as the Arabs and Berbers they ruled.[5]

In the case of French colonialism, the debate hinges on the causes of
the Algerian war. This issue is important for two reasons. First, it led
directly to the collapse of the French Fourth Republic as a result of a
military-settler uprising and precipitated de Gaulle's return to power.
Second, the Algerian Revolution has been exported as a revolutionary
model throughout the Third World. Colonialist historians view the steps
leading up to the 1954 outbreak as a series of missed opportunities, of
failures to offer meaningful reforms in time, particularly the refusal to
accept the French-educated Muslim elite, the *évolués*, as French citizens
without restrictions. Where Julien emphasizes the proposed Blum-

Violette bill of 1936 as a key turning point, Ageron stresses the Jonnart reforms of 1919.[6] But anticolonialists such as Lacheraf and Sahli reject in toto the argument that there was ever a genuine possibility of Algerian-French rapprochement, arguing instead that the Muslims would never have accepted assimilation with France, and that independence was inevitable in the long run.[7]

The question of the potential for Algerian-French assimilation shades off into the related one of the French *oeuvre* in Algeria. French apologists and colonialist historians have been concerned primarily with French colonization rather than French colonialism, that is, with tracing the stages of French settlement, the creation of an infrastructure (roads, railroads, schools, ports, hospitals, sanitary facilities, public utilities, and the like), in short, with what the French so aptly term the *mise en valeur* of Algeria. The decades-long discussion over whether to colonize Algeria and how, the successes and failures in attracting migrants, the heroic aspects of the early colonizers in taming Algeria and the Algerians alike, the bloody campaigns waged by the French army against recalcitrant Muslim rebels – all these are characteristic colonialist themes. Inevitably the indigenous Arabs and Berbers are neglected, although ironically the sources for the history of the Algerians since 1830 consist primarily of materials collected, annotated, and translated into French by French linguists, ethnographers, archeologists, and sociologists.

The anticolonialists rebut this view, arguing that even if the French are primarily responsible for laying the groundwork for a modern society, a vastly disproportionate amount of the benefits accrued not to the Algerians but to the French. Even more important, these historians point out that the effects of the French presence on Algerian society and culture – the systematic neglect if not outright attack on the Islamic religion, the refusal to provide for Arabic education, the progressive impoverishment of the Algerian *fellah* (peasant), the expropriation and exploitation of the best arable land and forests, the destruction or cooptation of the indigenous elite –were nothing short of catastrophic. The Front de Libération Nationale (NLF) goes still further and charges that the French were guilty of depersonalization, deculturation, enforced resettlement, and in some cases even of genocide.[8]

Although more recent work mostly continues these themes and debates, there has been one significant historiographical development. In 1954, at the beginning of the end of *Algérie française*, Marcel Emerit could write that "The history of Algeria since 1830 has been based, almost exclusively, on French documents and studied from a European point of view [*dans un esprit d'Européen*]."[9] Today it could be said that the sources remain essentially the same, but the viewpoint is no longer primarily Eurocentric, that there is a greater sensitivity to the ideological

3

Theoretical foundations

biases and distortions inherent in the historical record. For parallel to the historical decolonization of the Third World has been a less sweeping decolonization of historiography about the Third World. One of the key developments here has been the rise of what can be termed the "colonial sociology of knowledge," and within the field colonial Algeria has been the focus of a disproportionately large amount of work.[10]

The colonial sociology of knowledge can be defined as a hermeneutic approach to reading the vast corpus of European writings about Third World peoples, an interpretive exegesis of colonialist bias in the sources of our knowledge about the Third World. Central to this area of inquiry are Pierre Bourdieu's conception of *champ scientifique/champ politique*, scientific field/political field, and Michel Foucault's analogous notion of power/knowledge, as filtered down through Edward Said.[11] Summarily stated, the intention of the colonial sociology of knowledge is to demonstrate how the scholar who generates knowledge and the knowledge which results are inextricably connected, that since the knower is not objective, neither is his knowledge. A good example is the historical myth propounded by the French that the Berbers were more assimilable than the Arabs. Now, a Berber is not an Arab, but it is no coincidence that by overstating their differences intellectually French scholars contributed a rationale for French administrators to practice classic divide-and-rule politics, the better to colonialize both Arab and Berber.[12] Although the colonial sociology of knowledge suggests a way through the historiographical underbrush, the actual path remains largely to be cleared.[13]

In all this historiographical discussion, one may ask where are the *pieds noirs*, the European settlers of Algeria? After all, they were the ones primarily responsible for the physical development of Algeria, they were the ones with whom the Algerians came into daily contact rather than the French of the *métropole*, and it was they who in collusion with the French army toppled the Fourth Republic. Amazingly enough, however, they have elicited little historiographical controversy from either side of the ideological barricades. It is almost as if their presence in the Algerian tragedy was a fact too big to be seen; there from the beginning of *Algérie française*, they finished by being taken for granted.

Throughout the historiographical literature the struggle for hegemony in Algeria is depicted as a two-way battle waged between the French on one side and the Algerians on the other. The polemic conducted between Xavier Yacono, author of a highly considered regional study of Algerian colonization and a convinced supporter of French Algeria, and Charles-Robert Ageron on the occasion of the publication of the latter's monumental *doctorat d'état* is indicative in this regard.[14] In his review of Ageron's book, Yacono propounds two main theses. The first

4

is that metropolitan French indifference and not simply *colon* (colonist) resistance accounts for how events turned out in Algeria. The second is that the *colons* did not form a unitary bloc, that the conflict was not simply between metropolitan French liberals and reactionary *pieds noirs*, but instead that there was a small but vociferous liberal minority among the settlers. Ageron counters that the notion that France was indifferent to the fate of colonial Algeria is simply not an "objective observation," that it is nothing but the old settler complaint that France hindered Algerian industrialization and exploited its population, both European and Muslim, and second, that in the course of fifteen years spent studying the 1870 – 1919 period he has never encountered this liberal *pied noir* group.[15]

What is striking about this exchange is the inability of either author to break out of the intellectual straitjacket which has so far constricted the debate over colonial Algeria. Yacono still mistakes isolated individuals for a cohesive, well-defined group,[16] while Ageron is still unable to see that for all the French efforts at Algerian reform the result was virtually nil, that "the history of Algeria cannot be written according to its laws: its history is the manner in which the French of Algeria have gotten around them."[17] As a matter of fact, Ageron's disclaimer that he minimized the role of the European settlers rings hollow.[18] Nowhere, for example, does he follow up his observation that French colonialism in Algeria constituted "a force of implantation rarely attained in other colonies."[19] For throughout his massive study the settlers are treated as a *donnée*, a given. They are everywhere referred to, but nowhere actually scrutinized and fleshed out.[20] And this despite the fact that the *pieds noirs* briefly occupy center stage in Ageron's saga during the key 1898 crisis, which is admittedly the climax of his entire study. In the last analysis, therefore, Ageron fails to accord the *pieds noirs* a position commensurate with the role they played in the Algerian drama.

Moreover, Algerian historians have evidenced even less interest in the settlers than French historians, for reasons which Jean-Claude Vatin explains.

Algeria is preoccupied more with denying its colonial history, in the same fashion that colonial history had denied it [Algeria] previously. [Thus,] it is not the action of the colonizer who has *determined* Algeria, it is [Algeria] which has *reconstituted* itself. . . . The history of the Algerian people, of the Algerian nation, owes nothing to anyone. In short, Algeria has become a *historical subject* by its own forces.

Retour violent du bâton. Previously the Arabs "obscured" Algeria in the eyes of the French. Now it is the French who, by their occupation, have obscured the true Algeria in the eyes of the Algerians.[21]

And among the French colonizers, who played a more important role day in and day out than the *pieds noirs*?

Yet the fact that the settlers comprise a third significant force in addition to the metropolitan French and Muslim Algerians has been recognized throughout the history of colonial Algeria, although never systematically analyzed. No less a committed colonialist than Jules Ferry, for example, criticized "*l'état d'esprit* of the *colon* vis-à-vis the vanquished people: it is difficult to make the European *colon* understand that there exists other rights besides his in an Arab land," and that "the indigenous people are not at his beck and call." Ferry concluded that France should act as an ar-biter in Algeria, in this land which was "necessarily given over to the con-flict between two rival races," and mediate between the European settlers on the one hand and the Algerians on the other.[22]

Astonishingly enough, however, Pierre Nora is the only historian to have written a study squarely focused on the *Français d'Algérie*.[23] Even his book, however, is not so much a work of history (it is not based on orig-inal research and is devoid of the usual scholarly apparatus) as a personal account written in a passionate, powerful style.[24] In Nora's view there was never any real prospect of Algerian-French assimilation. Rather, he ar-gues that in the very manner in which the settlers formed Algeria, they pre-cluded any future evolution. "What they [the settlers] wanted in Algeria was Algeria; in the two forms they saw it: land and the Arab. By that, from the beginning and spontaneously, they installed themselves counter to any current of evolution, they blocked history." Throughout their attitude was "take the land, take the people, contain history." To the extent that this conflicted with official French policy in Algeria, "The French of Algeria have fought on two fronts: Algeria and the métropole." Not simply the im-pact of a modern industrial civilization on a traditional peasant society, "the fundamental fact of the history of Algeria for 130 years [has been] the systematic if not premeditated desire of the conquering minority to not treat the traditional civilization of Algeria as a civilization, and yet for all that of taking advantage of its presence."[25]

Nora pushes his critical analysis of the *pieds noirs* so far that he has been accused of engaging in polemics and lacking any human sympathy for the lot of the settlers.[26] But one thing which he fails to do is to treat them as one of three protagonists in a context of settler colonialism.

Settler Colonialism

White men who live beside, but not among, a colored proletariat will insist that they cannot afford to deal in ethics that do not relate to that predicament. That they choose to stay in it is beside the point. They resent the social analyses that issue from a commentator's armchair, because they see in them only a menace to their own security, to preserve which is, and must always be, their first duty. – A. P. Thornton[27]

That the presence of a sizeable settler population is an important factor in determining the nature and impact of colonialism in a given colonial situation has long been recognized. Likewise, the phrase "settler colonialism" turns up time and again in scholarly discourse as well as the mass media.[28] It is surprising, therefore, that no one to date has shown exactly how settlers are significant, or established satisfactorily settler colonialism as an important and legitimate subtype of imperialism and colonialism. On the one hand, the most common distinction made between imperialism and colonialism – terms too often used interchangeably in intellectual discourse – is that colonialism entails the presence of settlers while imperialism does not.[29] On the other hand, the few studies that discuss settler colonialism as a separate category simply do not advance the discussion very far.[30] In short, settlers and settler colonialism are topics which everyone mentions but which no one pursues.

It is not in explicit discussions of settler colonialism that insights into this historical phenomenon are to be gained so much as in the literature pertaining to the plural society, internal colonialism, and to a lesser extent, the colonial situation.[31] A plural society is defined here as "one made up of a set of socially segregated subgroups sharing only the narrowest and most provisional of cultural consensuses."[32] And the single best example of a plural society, the one in which its characteristics stand out in the boldest possible relief, is colonial society in general and a settler colony in particular. That this is so follows naturally from the way in which the concept was developed. J. S. Furnivall first used the term to describe the colonial societies of South and Southeast Asia, especially Burma and Indonesia, which he observed firsthand during the interwar period. For Furnivall a plural society was one in which a European colonizing minority lived alongside an indigenous colonized majority with, in addition, intervening ethnic or racial groups which provided labor that the Europeans and natives either would or could not perform themselves.[33]

A corollary of the plural society idea is the notion that in such societies there exists a dual economy consisting of a "bazaar economy . . . in which the total flow of commerce is fragmented into a very great number of unrelated person-to-person transactions" and a "firm-centered economy . . . where trade and industry occur through a set of impersonally defined social institutions which organize a variety of specialized occupations with respect to some particular product or distributive end."[34]

7

The plural society concept was later picked up by M. G. Smith who applied it to the primarily postcolonial and mixed European, African, creole, and East Indian Caribbean society which he studied as an anthropologist in the British West Indies.[35] More recently, the concept has been extended to societies elsewhere, especially to Africa, by Smith and Leo Kuper among others.[36] Yet at the same time that the plural society idea has been applied more widely, its theoretical content has been watered down. Thus it has been argued that other societies and not simply colonial societies are plural in nature, that there is not always a foreign minority dominating an indigenous majority, and that a plural society engenders consensus rather than conflict between its members.[37] However these issues are resolved, the narrow definition of a plural society has the advantage, for my purposes, of providing a model of multiethnic and multiracial colonial societies relevant especially to settler colonies.

Internal colonialism is a second concept which bears certain family resemblances to settler colonialism. It differs from other varieties of colonialism insofar as the "colonizers" occupy the same territory as the "colonized." But whereas settler colonialism applies to an actual colonial situation, internal colonialism is used figuratively to describe situations with certain colonial features. In fact, the characteristics of an internal colony sound very similar to those of a plural society: economic and social dualism, plus what one writer calls a "cultural division of labor" in which "objective cultural distinctions are superimposed upon class lines."[38] The concept of internal colonialism was used first by Lenin and then Gramsci, but it has been elaborated more fully by writers on Latin America to account for relations between Indians and ladinos. It has been extended more recently to the relationship of ethnic, cultural, national, or racial groups within societies such as blacks in the United States and South Africa, and the Irish in Great Britain. At the same time, it has been criticized on the same grounds as the plural society, namely, that it emphasizes race and ethnicity over socioeconomic class.[39] However, the main drawback of internal colonialism for my purposes here is that it does not fit the case of colonial Algeria: although the European settlers occupied the same territory as the Algerians, Algeria was not an internal colony run by the *pieds noirs*, but a French colony ruled ultimately by France despite substantial local control by the settlers. Moreover, internal colonialism represents a diluted version of the plural society notion – colonial analogies without colonial actualities.

The closest French analogue to the plural society and internal colonialism concepts is the much less well-developed notion of the colonial situation. Georges Balandier is chiefly responsible for articulating this approach, by which he means to stress simply the primacy of the colonial

8

context itself in shaping and determining a given colonial experience.[40] Thus he diverts attention away from the colonizing country and towards the colony itself, and in particular to the relations between the various social groups in the colony. Given the bias in colonial historiography towards the *métropole* rather than the colonies and towards colonial politics and doctrines rather than colonial practice, this represents a noteworthy advance.[41] Otherwise, however, the analysis of the colonial situation corresponds almost exactly to that of the plural society narrowly defined.[42] For my purposes, moreover, the disadvantage of the colonial situation, at least in Balandier's formulation, is that he fails to distinguish settler colonial situations from others.[43] Yet clearly the colonial situation per se is even more important in settler colonies than in others. In any case, it is worth noting that no one has studied colonial Algeria from the standpoint of the plural society, internal colonialism, or the colonial situation.[44]

Now in my view settler colonialism shares certain features with the concepts of the plural society narrowly defined and the colonial situation, but it differs from them both in arguing that settler colonialism is a discrete form of colonialism legitimate in its own right. For what distinguishes it so clearly from other varieties of colonialism is that whereas in the majority of colonial situations there are two primary groups involved – temporary migrants from the colonizing country (colonial administrators, military personnel, merchants and traders, missionaries) and the indigenous people – in settler colonies the settlers constitute a third group. It is not simply the existence of settlers which makes a difference, but rather the implications and consequences which result from their presence that is significant.[45] Obviously, the chief characteristic distinguishing settlers from other temporary migrants is rooted in the life choice they have made to live in the colony. Admittedly, there is a fuzzy, borderline area here consisting of "crossovers": those agents of colonialism who come temporarily and decide to stay permanently, on the one hand, and those settlers who decide not to stay and leave rapidly, on the other. Yet this flux – one could almost say that it is inherent in the colonial situation – should not obscure for us the fundamental life choice which sets off settlers from others and from which so many other characteristic attitudes and attributes stem. For example, from the settlers' perspective we can see why land and access to it is even more important in settler colonies than in others, and also why it is so often remarked that colonial officials are paternalistic when it is a case of protecting "their" natives from rapacious, land-hungry settlers.[46]

One implication of this view of settler colonialism is that the formation of settler society – its emergence, growth, and coming to group consciousness – can be charted in the same way as that of any other social

Theoretical foundations

group. Whether we single out settler subgroups such as tea planters in Sri Lanka, rubber planters in Malaysia or Indonesia, tobacco growers in Zambia, cattle farmers in Kenya, wine growers in Algeria, or settler societies in their entirety, the particular determinants of life and work which make these individuals members of historically definite groups also implies that we can elucidate the core ideas, the underlying *mentalité*, around which they cohere and organize their existence.[47] A corollary is that to fully understand the settlers in their historical context, they need to be considered in relation to the other two main groups with which they come into contact in the colonial situation.[48]

It follows from the very manner in which a settler society is formed that stratification is based more on race and ethnicity than on socioeconomic class.[49] Furthermore, the maximum points of friction occur where ethnic and racial divisions are exacerbated by socioeconomic ones; in other words, for those at the top of indigenous society and at the bottom of settler society, or in sociological terms, for high-achieving non-Europeans and low-achieving Europeans. It is not surprising, therefore, that in the case of colonial Algeria it was the French-educated Algerian elite, the *évolués*, and the European "poor white trash," the *petits blancs*, who experienced the greatest status anxiety. To be sure, within the various ethnic and racial groupings a class-based hierarchy forms. But Marxists generally err in attributing the fact workers fail to perceive that common economic bonds transcend ethnic and racial divisions to false consciousness on the part of the working classes.[50]

In terms of historical development, I would argue that a settler colony passes through a series of discrete stages. During the period of colonization conflicts emerge between the settlers and the colonial administration chiefly over native policy, but these are generally papered over. Invariably the settlers want more land, sooner, and on better terms than the administration is willing to grant them. Likewise, those segments of the colonial administration which intervene between the settlers and indigenous population often acquire a paternalistic attitude vis-à-vis "their" natives. When it comes to the crunch, however, the colonial officials and administrators side with the settlers. In the case of colonial Algeria, for example, Nora notes the apparent paradox whereby "the *métropole* always disapproves of the *Français d'Algérie* and always defends them. Whatever they do, they are ours. . . . "[51] This is not a contradiction, I would contend, but rather inherent in the settler colonial situation. Later, however, during the period of decolonization when colonialism has bred a native nationalist reaction, the indigenous people emerge as a third force capable of driving a wedge between the settlers and the colonial power. It is precisely this three-sided conflict, therefore, which explains why decolonization is so much more violent in settler

10

colonies such as Algeria, Kenya, and Rhodesia-Zimbabwe than elsewhere.

The primary focus of the present study is the period prior to decolonization, that is, with the growth and formation of settler society, keeping in mind the indigenous Algerian population on the one hand, and the French colonial officials and administrators on the other. The geographical focus of the study, however, is not colonial Algeria in its entirety, but with a major societal subsystem, namely that of the city. Cities are more important relative to the countryside, and the European urban dwellers are more important than the European *colons* of the Algerian *bled* (countryside). Granted, the French term for colonist, *colon*, means specifically farmers and rural settlers, but it came to be applied indiscriminately to all the European settlers of Algeria. Furthermore, from an early date the locus of settler society was the city, especially the main cities of the Algerian littoral. Already by 1900, for example, over sixty percent of all the *pieds noirs* in Algeria lived in towns and cities. This urban preponderance only increased in the twentieth century as a result of slackening overseas immigration plus urban migration induced by the continuous rationalization and concentration of European agriculture. Moreover, in the major port cities – Algiers, Oran, and Bône – the Europeans actually outnumbered the Algerians and formed a majority of the population.

More significant, however, than the sheer number of *pieds noirs* in the cities is the fact that the urban centers of Algeria played a disproportionately important role in the history of the colony. It was here that settler society was first and most fully elaborated, it was here that Algerian nationalism arose and took root. In short, what went on in the cities largely determined what went on in Algeria as a whole. Whoever controlled the urban centers, especially the major cities of the littoral, controlled to a large extent what went on in the colony itself.

With its own distinctive patterns and rhythms, the colonial city is at once similar and dissimilar to the wider colonial society of which it is part. It is to the particular characteristics of such cities, then, that we now turn.

The Colonial City

> *The major metropolis in almost every newly-industrializing country is not a single unified city, but, in fact, two quite different cities, physically juxtaposed but architecturally and socially distinct. . . . These dual cities have usually been a legacy from the colonial past. It is remarkable that so common a phenomenon has remained almost unstudied. We have no real case studies of the introduction of western urban forms into non-western countries.* – Janet Abu-Lughod[52]

11

If the literature on non-Western cities is small in comparison to that concerning cities in the West, the literature on the colonial city is miniscule.[53] For one thing, social scientists have become cognizant only recently of how fundamentally different contemporary Third World cities – referred to here as "postcolonial" cities – are from their Western counterparts. The phenomenon of "primacy" (the tendency for the largest city, usually the capital, in any given country to be several times larger than all others), the combination of "preindustrial fertility and postindustrial mortality," the ubiquity of squatter settlements, and most importantly, the fact that industrialization and economic growth have not accompanied urbanization – these and other factors clearly distinguish the Third World urban experience from that of the West.[54] In particular, the failure of Third World cities to industrialize rapidly has led to a reassessment of their colonial antecedents in an effort to determine why they have evolved in a different fashion.

However, it has proven easier to say what colonial cities are not than what they are. By now it is clear that they do not conform to Western models of urbanization, such as those proposed by Weber, Wirth, Redfield, or Sjøberg. "Increasingly we find that models or theories developed in the context of Western industrial urbanization do not fit the majority of cities in the non-Western world and particularly, the 'colonial' or 'postcolonial' cities of Asia and Africa."[55] That the colonial city – like settler colonialism– is however a valid analytical construct rooted in historical reality is attested to by the literally innumerable references scattered throughout the literature.[56] Yet we have no thoroughly articulated model of colonial urbanism, no extended treatment of the colonial city in time or in space – extremely few studies in fact of particular colonial cities.[57] In what follows, therefore, I shall offer my own formulation of the colonial city, incorporating the insights of others where relevant.

Let us begin by defining the colonial city simply as the urban form which results when two societies intersect, the link "in the interaction of two civilizations."[58] Accordingly, cities as disparate as the Roman settlements in North Africa, Chinese treaty ports, Norman cities in Wales, and the cities the Chinese "rented" in Indonesia from the East India Company – all these urban settlements may be considered colonial cities.[59] But this is a terminological distinction having little to do with historical reality; it obfuscates more than it illuminates, because the differences between these urban agglomerations are greater than their similarities. For the term "colonial city" to be analytically useful and historically valid, therefore, it will be used in this study to describe only those cities where colonialism had a visible, marked impact. All cities which have at one time or another existed at the interface between two cultures will be termed "protocolonial," "colonial," or "postcolonial," but only those cities which have been transformed fundamentally will be called "colonial."[60]

Clearly, the emphasis is on the sheer power of colonialism to transform, to create, and to destroy: on the *dureté*, as the French say, of colonialism in an urban context. Colonialism – the hegemony of one human group over another – is, therefore, the key explanatory variable here, with all the implications of power and domination and exploitation which it connotes. We should amend our definition above then by saying that a colonial city is the concrete manifestation, the form which colonialism takes in an urban environment. Since in this definition colonialism is an independent variable, the characteristic features of a colonial city are derived from it and not vice versa. The colonial city is, in other words, a subsystem of colonial society.

Now, obviously, colonialism is not a constant, with an equal impress everywhere and at all times, just as the societies colonized are not alike and their responses to colonialism are different. More important than the parent European (in this case) society, more important than the parent native society, is the ground on which they meet, the colonial situation itself; for what characterizes the colonial city is the relationship, the relative difference, between the colonizers and the colonized.

Cities fundamentally transformed by colonialism need to be distinguished from cities only affected by colonialism, that is, colonial cities must be differentiated from protocolonial and postcolonial ones. The key question here is "how much transforming does a transformation have to be?"[61] It is clear that the greater the difference between colonizer and colonized, the greater the disparity in power, the more impact colonialism is likely to have, and the more likely that a full-fledged colonial city will result. Historically, the greatest disparity in power between societies on a worldwide scale opened up as a result of the Industrial Revolution in Europe, beginning in the latter half of the eighteenth century. This is not to say that white Europeans are inherently or intrinsically more colonialistic or imperialistic than peoples of color, for example. It is to say that in historical terms the technological gap generated by the advent of the Industrial Revolution created a potential for colonialism – and the colonial city – on a scale and with an impact qualitatively greater than previously. Likewise, the period of decolonization coincided with the narrowing of the technological gap. By and large, therefore, the colonial city is a phenomenon which can be generally – but by no means always – associated with European expansion into Asia, Africa, and Latin America between roughly 1750 and 1950. Thus, the protocolonial city occurs in a situation of cross-cultural contact prior to the mid-eighteenth century, full-blown colonial

13

cities are a phenomenon of the period 1750–1950, and the postcolonial city is a former colonial city where colonial structures and patterns still persist to a large extent. A variation of this proposed model would include those areas colonized at a later date, such as Morocco, where the stages of protocolonial, colonial, and postcolonial cities can be discerned but are foreshortened and compressed into a considerably shorter time period. Also, the colonial impress is by no means uniform throughout a given colony or area, with the result that within the same colony more than one kind of colonial city can often by observed at any given time, for example, colonial port cities in the coastal regions and protocolonial cities in the interior.[62] Each of these three urban forms will now be examined in turn.

Since my concern in this study centers on a French colonial city, the focus in this section will be on protocolonial cities created by Europeans in Asia, Africa, and Latin America, and will leave aside cities created by non-Europeans.

The main wave of European-founded protocolonial cities began around 1500 when the leading maritime and commercial powers of northern Europe – preeminently the Dutch, Spanish, and Portuguese – ventured beyond the Mediterranean and north Atlantic for the first time. Leaving aside a discussion of the technological innovations which enabled the Europeans to achieve control of the leading long-distance trade routes, we can simply say that the Europeans were interested first and foremost in commercial trade – this was the era of mercantilism – and were desirous of procuring tobacco, sugar, copra, tea, spices, and the like. Already by 1511 the Portuguese had founded Goa on the western coast of India, south of Bombay, and had conquered Malaka in what is today Malaysia. The Portuguese took over Macao in 1519, the Spanish founded Manila in 1570, and the Dutch had settled in Batavia (today Djakarta) by 1619.[63]

Intent on trade, European settlements assumed different forms. In some cases, European factories and trader residences were established in the vicinity of indigenous cities. Sometimes all-European garrisoɴ and trading settlements were built. Finally, full-fledged cities were also founded, such as Batavia and Manila.[64] Local variations should not blind us, however, to the features which these urban agglomerations shared in common. In the first place, most of these protocolonial European settlements were ports. To be sure, the exigencies of maritime trade required a coastal location, but the primary reason was that the not insignificant power of indigenous states was concentrated in the interior. In South and Southeast Asia, for example, the chief cities were administrative and commercial centers of agrarian empires located inland, which overshadowed by far the European coastal beachheads. One of

14

the main differences between protocolonial and full-blown colonial cities was the lack of formal, direct political control, if not over the city itself, then over the territory of the state in which it was situated. The existence of these colonial outposts – many of which later evolved into important colonial cities – must not obscure for us the fact that everywhere at this time it was the native societies and not the European intruders who were dominant. In India, for example, the Mughal Empire did not begin until 1526, which was fifteen years after the founding of Goa; the Ming dynasty was to last until 1644 – more than 100 years after the Portuguese had arrived in Macao.[65]

Such European settlements linked productive hinterlands overseas to Europe via the major sea routes. As such they acted as funnels or transfer points of goods primarily, but also of values.[66] In these protocolonial cities Europeans were only one among many ethnic and racial groups involved in trade. In addition to local native traders and Europeans in Asia, for example, Arabs, Malays, Chinese, and Gujeratis (from the region north of Bombay) had engaged in maritime commerce for centuries. It was the mix of such disparate peoples, especially in colonial ports, which led to the creation of the plural societies of South and Southeast Asia.

Already in these protocolonial cities signs can be detected of a distinctive urban morphology. In some cases, urban European forms simply coexisted alongside indigenous ones. As in preindustrial cities everywhere, well-defined quarters and residential segregation were the norm, so that side by side with the native districts resided foreign commercial groups. Typically, European architectural forms were only noticeable in the factories and forts they built. Elsewhere, however, cultural contact had begun already to transmute "parent" urban forms. Batavia is a case in point. Originally planned as a replica of a Dutch city in Indonesia, "complete with canals and stuffy, tightly packed and many-storyed houses," the exigencies of the colonial situation led to the creation of a quite different city partly based on the aristocratic Javanese home and suburb consisting of "country villas – roomy, airy and cool – surrounded by extensive gardens."[67] Dutch Batavia appropriated, therefore, forms which were more expressive of the hierarchical, colonial society the Dutch were forming.

In the political sphere as well these European beachheads of colonialism differed significantly from both the parent European society and the native society. Representative institutions developing at that time in Europe were never transplanted entirely to these colonial outposts. Politics in Dutch Batavia, for example, was autocratic rather than democratic; the center of government was, significantly, not the town hall but the Governor-General's castle.[68]

15

One crucial difference distinguishing these protocolonial cities from each other seems to be which European country colonized them. More important than whether indigenous cities existed prior to European contact, more important than what kind of physical settlement the Europeans built are the different intentions of the colonizing powers. In this regard, the case of Spanish cities in Latin America and the Philippines is noteworthy, because the intensity of the Spanish impact is such that these cities exhibit both colonial and protocolonial features, and thus constitute a case apart from other protocolonial cities.[69]

On the one hand, the organization and control of urban life within the city transformed these Spanish settlements to such an extent that they must be termed colonial cities. Of crucial importance here is the preeminent role the Spaniards assigned to urban settlements in their schema of colonization, whereby the creation of a network of primary urban centers and secondary towns provided a backbone for their colonial domination. "Essential instruments of territorial occupance, economic exploitation, regional administration, and religious conversion," it is "no exaggeration to say that Spain's sprawling empire in the New World was secured by an urban keystone."[70] To this end, the Spanish drew up a highly detailed series of instructions for the founding of cities called the Laws of the Indies, which had been completed already by 1523 and which were revised several times thereafter. Thoroughgoing resettlement was carried out both to protect the Spanish from the native inhabitants and to settle the indigenous peoples close enough to utilize their labor. Morphologically as well, these Spanish cities were already colonial in form. A central rectangular plaza, a grid layout, and the general absence of walls – all these features of colonial Spanish urbanism were applied first in the colonies and only later transplanted to Spain.[71]

On the other hand, the transformation of the hinterland, although important, differed substantially from the changes wrought by railroads and the introduction of steam power in the periphery of colonial cities after 1800. Rather, the Spanish aim was to extract the mineral and agricultural wealth quickly, efficiently, and completely. Part colonial and part protocolonial, these Spanish cities and towns can be described best, therefore, as a case apart from European protocolonial cities found elsewhere during the early modern period.

The colonial city is distinguished from the protocolonial city first of all by formal political control. The potential for thoroughgoing transformation inherent in direct political control is obvious. Although the Europeans achieved such control at different times in different places, it can be argued that it was increasingly the case in the post–1800 period. At about the same time cumulative changes occurring in the rural hin-

16

terland areas altered fundamentally the socioeconomic structure. Gradually a subsistence peasant economy was transformed into a commercial agricultural one, and in the process the indigenous elite and mercantile groups were subordinated. The peasant economy was monetized, new and in particular cash crops were introduced (cocoa, for example, in West Africa), and the entire economy became oriented increasingly towards international trade channeled through the colonial port cities. The introduction of two key technological inventions – the railroad and steamships – mark significant turning points in what had been previously a long, drawn-out process of incremental change. From the midnineteenth century onwards railroads to transport mineral and agricultural goods to the coasts, and steamships to ship these same goods overseas drastically altered the physiognomy of hinterland areas in Asia, Africa, and Latin America.[72]

Changes occurring in the countryside had important repercussions in the cities. For one thing, the economies of rail transport and the rising construction costs of technologically advanced port facilities engendered the growth of so-called primate cities, which dwarfed in size and importance surrounding towns and cities. Thus, a combination of functional obsolescence and economies of scale stimulated the growth of outsized colonial cities.[73]

In addition, the commercial as opposed to industrial nature of colonial cities, especially colonial port cities, was accentuated even more than previously. This commercial function of the colonial city reflected its role as the transfer point through which agricultural and mineral goods (coffee, cocoa, cotton, minerals) were funneled to Europe, and European manufactured goods (cloth, kerosene, sewing machines, bicycles) were channeled to the colony. (The French word for market, *débouché*, is apt.) In colonial cities "long, ugly tin warehouses replaced the industrial smokestacks of the industrial towns of Europe."[74] Concomitant with the commerce-oriented economy, the occupational structure of the colonial city is marked by a lopsided, "warped" development of the tertiary or service sector.[75]

Politics in the colonial city mirrors this commercial orientation insofar as politics tended to matters of administration and bureaucracy rather than popular participation in formal political bodies. The requirements of running a colonial economy and governing the colony entailed the creation of both a colonial administration and extensive business staffs. In both cases the individuals involved were to a great extent temporary residents in the colony, and their attention was focused largely on Europe rather than the colonies. Given the commercial and bureaucratic orientation of the colony and the dearth of divisive issues among this colonial elite, it is little wonder that politics, especially municipal politics, was rudimentary, perfunctory, and lagged far behind conditions prevailing in Europe.

Perhaps the single most characteristic feature of the colonial city is its plural nature, the fact that it is comprised of a mixture of ethnic and racial groups.[76] It is almost as though technological developments provided greater opportunity for Europeans to come into contact with other cultures than previously. Yet it was clear from the first that Europeans would not emigrate in sufficient numbers, especially to the tropical colonies, to occupy fully all the social and economic niches created by colonialism. Instead, other ethnic and racial groups present or close at hand – in many cases earlier colonizers themselves – were both willing and able to fill those roles in the colonial city which the Europeans either could not or did not want.

Now there is a difference between intermediate and so-called "stranger" groups in a plural society.[77] Intermediate groups occupy positions midway between the European colonizers and indigenous inhabitants in socioeconomic status. The best examples of such intermediate groups are those of mixed descent such as creoles and mestizos in Latin America, and the so-called coloreds in the West Indies and the coloureds in South Africa. Stranger groups also occupy intermediate positions in colonial society, but they are set off to a greater extent from both natives and Europeans by a combination of ethnicity, race, religion, and culture. Examples are the Jews in North Africa, the Chinese in Southeast Asia, and the Indians in the West Indies, East Africa, South Africa, and Southeast Asia.

These several ethnic groups comprising the plural society tend to specialize in specific trades and to deal in specific commodities. Thus, in addition to vertical occupational stratification according to ethnic and racial criteria, there is functional occupational specialization along ethnic and racial lines. This is linked in turn to the economic dualism characteristic of the colonial city. It is sociologists of development, in particular, who have proposed any number of models to account for the workings of such economies. These range from the dual economy to the enclave economy, from the informal sector to the segmented market.[78] Yet no single model has been agreed upon; no single model corresponds exactly to what I term the colonial city. On the one hand, these models differ on how to characterize the sectors of the urban economy, on whether or not the segments are linked to each other and if so how – not to mention how they articulate with the larger world economy. On the other hand, they all tend to agree that there is a radical bifurcation of the urban economy into such dualities and halves, sectors and seg-

18

ments. As part of the sociology of development literature, such approaches have been developed primarily for what I call here postcolonial cities, but it can be shown that the bifurcation found in the postcolonial economy corresponds by and large to an earlier division of the colonial economy into a "traditional" sector identified primarily with colonized Third World peoples and a "modern" one associated with European colonizers.

In terms of urban morphology, spatial layout, and land use patterns, the dual nature of the colonial city is also evident. Here again the key terms are segregation and differentiation. For one thing, there is an uneven spread of city services and amenities – roads, recreational space, water, electricity, sewers, not to mention housing, shopping areas and hotels – between the Western and non-Western sections of the colonial city. Moreover, decreasing density gradients outward from the city center (in conformity with the negative exponential rule), and faster population growth in the urban periphery than in the city center, although generally true of the colonial city as of the Western city, vary significantly according to the size, duration, and location of the particular ethnic and racial communities.[79]

Any catalogue of the component parts of the colonial city would have to include a Western-style central business district, a corresponding indigenous and stranger retailing district, residential neighborhoods segregated along class and ethnic or racial lines, and military or police quarters (forts, cantonments, barracks). The diverse manner in which these sectors of the colonial city are combined to create quite different-looking cities should not obscure the fact that they are essentially variations on the same basic colonial urban forms. Thus, planned colonial cities, "transplant" cities (colonial cities in which European urban forms are transferred relatively intact and predominate to a large extent), and "grafted" cities (colonial cities in which European urban forms have been grafted onto preexisting indigenous settlements) all contain the same essential urban ingredients, only the mix is different. For purposes of classification only, therefore, we may distinguish the following varieties of colonial urban morphology: new cities founded by the Europeans in the colonies (for example, Abidjan, Kinshasa, and Nairobi in Africa); European towns set alongside and often dwarfing preexisting indigenous settlements (Bombay, Tamil Nadu, Calcutta in South Asia; Lagos, Douala, Kampala in sub-Saharan Africa; Algiers, Tunis, Cairo, Casablanca in North Africa); and physically separate but connected European and indigenous cities (New and Old Delhi, Hyderabad-Secunderabad, Bangalore in South Asia; Kano, Zaria, Fès in Africa).[80]

One of the most important features of the colonial city is residential segregation along ethnic and racial lines – another reflection of the plural society in the urban environment. Not all residentially segregated cities are colonial, but all colonial cities (as defined here) are segregated residentially. In fact for at least one commentator, segregation is the quintessential characteristic of the colonial city: "The colonial city is that urban area in the colonial society most typically characterized by the physical segregation of its ethnic, social and cultural groups, which resulted from the processes of colonialism."[81] Furthermore, non-Europeans tend to be segregated within their neighborhoods according to ethnic and racial origin, religion, and culture, whereas Europeans are segregated within the Western residential districts along class lines. Because of residential segregation, therefore, the colonial city represents not so much a melting pot as a meeting ground where both ethnic and socioeconomic groupings can be discerned.[82]

Demographically, the population groups of the colonial city differ significantly according to whether they are temporary migrants or permanent settlers. By and large the Europeans are temporary residents with little stake in the town. There is a dearth of women and children in what is a preponderantly male society, and a clustering occurs in the productive age categories between fifteen and fifty because of the relatively few old people and children. There are accordingly few schools, nurseries, hospitals, and, conversely, an abundance of recreational facilities. Those non-Western ethnic and racial groups who are more properly permanent residents exhibit a corresponding age, sex, and family structure. However, a large proportion of the indigenous urban population consists of males who migrate to the cities in search of work. Already sizeable in the nineteenth century, this migratory stream really accelerated only in the twentieth century and is a major cause of current overurbanization.[83]

Finally, social stratification in the colonial society is determined more by ethnic and racial factors than by class. Classes do form but within the overall racial structure, much as residential segregation by class occurs, especially in the Western community, but within an overarching framework of ethnic and racial segregation. The consequences of such stratification for collective activity, ranging from labor strikes to anti-colonial movements, need not be stressed. A related issue is the extreme importance attached to creating and maintaining social distance between ethnic and racial groups. This is evident most clearly in social stratification and residential segregation, but to a lesser degree also in social etiquette and suburbanization. In the case of the latter, the growth of suburbs in the West occurred as a result of improved transport technology, whereas suburbanization in the colonial city took place relatively earlier due to the desire of the European colonizers to preserve their social distance from the colonized population.[84]

With the coming of political independence as a result of decolonization, colonial cities have been transformed into postcolonial cities, the contemporary cities of the Third World. Although exhibiting several features in common with colonial cities, the fact that formal colonial rule has ended clearly distinguishes postcolonial cities from their colonial antecedents. Undoubtedly, there has been a weakening of colonial structures and institutions, but what is striking about the postcolonial city is not so much how it differs from the colonial city as how much it continues to resemble it.[85]

Although the European component of the plural society no longer exists, for all intents and purposes, the several indigenous and stranger ethnic and racial groupings remain, the result of which is "the persistence of the plural societies in the great cities."[86] In fact, the key here is persistence in general, and especially the persistence of those elements of the colonial city attributable to its plural nature. Thus, the tertiary sector remains overdeveloped. The "patterns of ethnic occupational concentration still persist."[87] The alien stranger communities are still clustered in commercial, financial, industrial, and artisanal occupations, whereas indigenous groups occupy the lower and upper rungs of the occupational scale – unskilled service and domestic occupations on the one hand, and government positions and the liberal professions on the other hand. Residential segregation primarily by ethnic and racial origin has been replaced by segregation according to socioeconomic rank where the indigenous nationalist elite has moved into the residences vacated by the former colonial elite.[88] In short, the persistence and continued importance of colonial structures in the postcolonial city attest to the fundamental changes wrought by colonialism in the colonial city.

The settler colonial city

> *The colonial world is a world cut in two. . . . The zone where the natives live is not complementary to the zone inhabited by the settlers. . . . The settlers' town is a strongly built town, all made of stone and steel. It is a brightly lit town; the streets are covered with asphalt, and the garbage cans swallow all the leavings, unseen, unknown and hardly thought about. The settler's feet are never visible, except perhaps in the sea; but there you're never close enough to see them. His feet are protected by strong shoes although the streets of his town are clean and even, with no holes or stones. The settler's town is always full of good things. The settler's town is a town of white people, of foreigners.*
>
> *The town belonging to the colonized people, or at least the native town,*

21

> *the Negro village, the medina, the reservation, is a place of ill fame, peopled by men of evil repute. They are born there, it matters little where or how; they die there, it matters not where, nor how. It is a world without spaciousness; men live there on top of each other, and their huts are built one on top of the other. The native town is a hungry town, starved of bread, of meat, of shoes, of coal, of light. The native town is a crouching village, a town on its knees, a town wallowing in the mire. It is a town of niggers and dirty Arabs. The look that the native turns on the settler's town is a look of lust, a look of envy; it expresses his dreams of possession – all manner of possession: to sit at the settler's table, to sleep in the settler's bed, with his wife if possible. The colonized man is an envious man.*
> – Frantz Fanon[89]

The intensity and impact of settler colonialism at a societal level leads to a qualitatively different colonial city at the urban level. The settler colonial city thus forms a variant or subtype of the colonial city in which all the features of the colonial city are intensified and exacerbated. It is here that the parent European society is most fully replicated.

First of all, there is the sheer number of settlers. On the one hand, only two percent of the population of colonial Delhi was European in 1921, five percent of colonial Cairo in 1897, and twenty to thirty-five percent of colonial Casablanca between 1913 and 1952. On the other hand, a full seventy-five to eighty percent of colonial Algiers in 1881 and 1926 was European, there was a European majority in Oran throughout the colonial period, and in colonial Bône the Europeans were in the majority until 1954.[90] At the deepest, most fundamental level, what this means is that the more the Europeans predominated in the settler city, the less scope there was for indigenous and intervening population groups. Due to the European impress, the indigenous urban society contracted vis-à-vis the Europeans, that is, the indigenous social structure was compressed, and a "bunching"occurred at the lower levels of the urban hierarchy. The European colonial sector, on the other hand, underwent an increase in population, an expansion of its economy, and an articulation and elaboration of its social structure.This greater complexity of urban society is evidenced in the greater propensity in settler cities for there to develop parallel structures (the structural separation of ethnic and racial groups within the same organization in combination with interethnic and interracial contact and cooperation at various supervisory levels and effective control by the politically dominant ethnic or racial group), and intercalary structures (those structures inserted or forming between ethnic or racial groups which serve both to separate and coordinate their activities).[91]

At the same time, those features of the plural society discussed in terms of the colonial city apply with all the more force to the settler colonial city. In fact, the settler city constitutes the colonial urban form of the plural society par excellence. The chief demographic difference between a colonial city and settler city is that whereas the European colonizers tend to be temporary migrants in the former, they tend to be permanent residents in the latter. Ironically enough, in the colonial city of the settlers it is the Europeans who tend to reside permanently, whereas the indigenous people, who come to the city in search of work, tend to dwell there temporarily. Whereas in the colonial city European age pyramids bulge in the productive age categories, males predominate by far over females, and household structure is skewed towards single males residing in groups, in a settler colonial city these and other demographic characteristics approximate more closely those found in the parent European society. In addition, this more settled population creates for its own use an infrastructure of schools, nurseries, and hospitals modeled after metropolitan lines.

In terms of the urban economy, the fact that there are relatively more positions filled by Europeans and correspondingly fewer by the indigenous and intervening groups entails a compression of the indigenous occupational structure. To be sure, the colonial urban economy generates a demand for labor but at still lower skill levels than generally in colonial cities. Domestics, and in colonial Bône, dock workers, proliferate. In analogous fashion, control of the rural agricultural economy by Europeans eliminates jobs and functions filled elsewhere by indigenous peasants and farmers. For example, the demand for food generated by the urban economy is met mainly by European farmers producing primary foodstuffs for the urban market and cash crops for export, whereas the indigenous cultivators still engage by and large in subsistence agriculture.[92]

Residential segregation and social distance are even more pronounced in a settler city than in other colonial cities. It has been pointed out that "Where there was no entrenched settler element, there were fewer and weaker forces making for the confrontation of two homogeneous and mutually exclusive social categories identified by racial signs."[93] Also indicative of the extreme social distance prevailing in a settler city generally is the absence in colonial Algeria of a counterpart to the hill stations found throughout colonial South and Southeast Asia. Hill stations function as resorts and retreats where the Europeans cool off away from the humid plains regions and at the same time get away from the indigenous population for months at a time during the hot season.[94] Granted, there were few suitable locations for hill stations in colonial Algeria. Yet colonial Bugeaud (now known as Seraidi), located in the hills immediately outside Bône, would have been geographically and climatically ideal. The fact that it was simply a small year-round European community instead of a true hill station suggests that the *pieds noirs* of Bône were so well ensconced in Bône itself that they felt no need to escape, as it were, from the Algerians and reside part of the year elsewhere.

It is perhaps in the realm of politics that the colonial city of the settlers diverges most from others. In contrast to colonial situations of direct or indirect rule, settler colonialism engenders a panoply of settler political organs which sometimes act in unison and sometimes compete with the official colonial political bodies. On the municipal level, settler politics takes the form of either bona fide settler political forums, or agitation for the creation of bodies to fulfill such functions. Where local settler-politics is developed, ties are formed with broader-based settler institutions and lobbying groups in both the metropolitan government and colonial administration. Everywhere the quintessential problem of settler politics is to legitimate rule of the colonized majority by the colonizer minority. This is the central issue in all colonial government, of course. But it is rife with difficulties in settler colonies both because it is literally a life-and-death issue for the settler community, and because the settlers are faced with the dilemma of how to coerce the colonial administration into granting them representative government while at the same time denying it to the indigenous population.

The primary means by which this gap or discontinuity between the colonial political and social structure is bridged is through the creation of parallel and intercalary structures. The main example of such parallel structures in the political sphere is two-college institutions which keep the indigenous people separate from and unequal to the European settlers.[95] The single best example of intercalary political structures in a settler context is politics based on patronage, on patron-client relations. After all, patronage politics constitutes by definition an informal political structure inserted in the interstices of a formal political structure. It is this very quality which permits patronage politics to bridge so effectively the gap between the colonizers and the colonized, between the political and the social structure in a settler community. "Clientage, the institutionalized association of men of sharply different status in contexts of political competition, has often served to integrate the members of differing social sections in plural societies."[96] In the case of colonial Bône, duly elected Algerian municipal council members formed the official Algerian political elite, but it was the *adjoint indigène* (appointed Muslim representative) who wielded real power in the Algerian community by virtue of his position as a broker, a liaison between the Muslim and European communities.

At the same time, the existence of settler political bodies espousing a well-defined settler viewpoint tends to retard and atrophy indigenous

24

politics. On the one hand, indigenous politics are tightly reined and short-circuited by parallel and intercalary political structures. On the other hand, the existence of a settler community in uneasy alliance with the colonial administration means that there are correspondingly fewer political posts for the indigenous population to fill. Therefore, mediating roles and the avenues of collaboration are restricted where they are not eliminated altogether.[97]

The last and ultimately most important difference between a colonial and a settler city is the formation in the latter of a definite settler viewpoint indicative of a shared consensus on fundamental issues. The preconditions for the development of such a group feeling or consciousness seem to be, first, a minimum number of permanent settlers – a critical mass, one could say – and second, sufficient time spent in the colony to acquire a recognizably settler outlook. One way to estimate the period of time required is by the time of arrival; a useful measure is the median date of arrival, that is, the date by which one-half of all immigrants had arrived.[98] Another measure is the date by which half of the settler population was born in the colony rather than emigrating to it. For example, beginning in 1896 more *pieds noirs* were born in Algeria than in Europe and elsewhere. In a more impressionistic vein, it is generally argued that the disparate European national groups (French, Spanish, Italians) had fused to form an identifiably *pied noir* community some time between the turn of the twentieth century and the outbreak of the First World War.[99]

Deconstructing *L'Algérie Française* and Making Algeria French

> *The dead zone [of research on North Africa] corresponds exactly to what could be called the European present. We have heard very little ... about the settlers [colons], the colonial officials, the rural and urban workers who are in North Africa a living and fragile Europe. Nevertheless, even given the perspective of our disciplines, European Africa is worthy of intellectual interest and surpasses Roman or Byzantine Africa in practical utility. ... North Africa is not only a museum. I wonder what the image that a conscientious reader in a university, let us say American, could have of this distant land. – Fernand Braudel*[100]

In what follows I combine these perspectives on colonial Algerian historiography, settler colonialism, and the colonial city to reinterpret the history of Bône/Annaba between 1830 and 1920 as a case of settler colonialism in a colonial city. Although I focus primarily on the European settlers, I incorporate the metropolitan French and the native Algerians into the story at relevant points. This study seeks to redress, therefore, the disproportionate historiographical attention paid to the

25

metropolitan French by analyzing the historical importance of the European settlers of Algeria. Much historiographial work has been devoted also to the Algerians in general, and Algerian nationalism in particular. Ultimately, it is only by discussing the relationship between European colonizers and Algerian colonized that the historical significance of the colonial city of Bône can be fully elucidated. To render justice to the Algerians in Bône, however, requires an extended treatment which cannot be attempted here.

The history of French colonialism in Bône can be divided into three distinct periods. In Chapter 2, I describe the European presence in a protocolonial city not so much from the perspective of Bône and the French as from Annaba and the Algerians on the eve of the French conquest in 1830. Between the French invasion of 1830 and the replacement in France of the Second Empire by the Third Republic in 1870, Bône can be termed a fully fledged colonial city. In Chapter 3, therefore, I discuss the first forty years of French hegemony by delineating the expropriation of land and buildings within the city and of land outside the city; the first attempts to exploit the cork oak forests and extract the abundant iron ore and phosphates in the hinterland; and the peopling of Bône by Europeans.

Between 1870 and Algerian independence in 1962, Bône can be analyzed as a settler colonial city. The advent of the Third Republic in France has usually been treated as a shift from military to civilian rule in Algeria. But the argument I develop in Part II goes considerably further, for I show that a settler society formed between 1870 and 1920. In making Bône a European city in the nineteenth and early twentieth centuries, moreover, the settlers blocked social evolution, attempted to contain history, and precluded thereby any genuine rapprochement with the Algerians in the twentieth century. "From 1914 to 1962, Algeria, like the other countries of the Maghrib, and to an even greater extent, went through several phases of tension and apparent relaxation."[101] Yet no fundamental shift in power occurred between the metropolitan French, European settlers, and the Algerians before the outbreak of the Algerian Revolution. Therefore, this study concentrates on the period 1870–1920.[102]

Chapter 4 delineates the main features of the Bône economy: first, the development of the tertiary or service sector over and against the secondary or manufacturing sector, and second, the existence of economic dualism in a colonial urban economy. Chapter 5 examines the social structure and social stratification of colonial Bône through an analysis of residential segregation, vertical occupational stratification, and functional occupational specialization in which the major ethnic and racial groups – the native and naturalized French, Italians, Maltese,

26

Jews, Arabs and Berbers – are analyzed systematically. In Chapter 6 I
show that the primary features of the political culture of colonial Bône
were patronage politics and political corruption. Patronage relationships
characterized both the municipal elections in which candidates were
elected, and the municipal administration to which officials were appointed, and were characteristic, therefore, of settler political power in
Bône and elsewhere in colonial Algeria. Finally, Chapter 7 demonstrates
the creation of a settler colonial culture between 1890 and 1914 through
an examination of street names and picture postcards, as well as language
and literature.

*   *   *

A different approach to a subject merits a different stylistic treatment.
In *Change at Shebika* by the French sociologist Jean Duvignaud, for
example, two sorts of changes occur.[103] Young, Western-oriented social
scientists from the capitol of Tunis gradually comprehend that concepts
of economic development which originate in the West and which they
import to villages like Shebika relate little to the villagers' collective
values and actual needs. Even more important, change occurs at Shebika
once the villagers realize they must become the active architects of their
collective fate rather than the passive recipients of economic aid from
Tunis. The book climaxes when the villagers refuse to quarry rock for
a new government building and launch a de facto sitdown strike, when
what they really need is government support to repair their own houses.
Thus, Duvignaud renders problematic his own position as well as that
of his Tunisian coworkers by showing clearly how the social enquiry
they conduct, the intellectual categories they employ, and the questions
they ask cause the Shebikians to rethink the view Tunis – and by extension the West – has of them.

Making Algeria French entails more than one kind of making as well.
On one level, it demonstrates how the settlers formed a colonial society
and in the process made Algeria French, at least before the rise of
Algerian nationalism. On another level, the book is about the decon-
struction of the colonialist conception of Algerian history epitomized in
the term *Algérie française*, and about the construction of the particular
interpretation of colonial Algerian history which it sets forth. As such,
it exemplifies certain recent trends within the so-called "new social history." For what Lawrence Stone terms the "revival of narrative" marks
a shift in emphasis within the field of social history from long-term
changes in social structure to case studies of what the French call *mentalité*, or cultural outlook, from an interest in historical sociology to a
fascination with cultural anthropology.[104] This shift in intellectual con-

cerns is part and parcel of a larger movement within the *sciences humaines* away from what Clifford Geertz calls a "laws and instances" approach and towards a "cases and interpretations" one.[105]

The point to be made here is that the turn to interpretation has engendered a renewed interest in theory. The more social historians concern themselves with *mentalité*, with culture broadly construed, the more they draw on the literary theory of Barthes, Burke, and Derrida as well as the social theory of Kuhn, Bourdieu, and Foucault. And at the heart of this concern with theory is the problem of representation: how is it possible to write about another culture, about the Other in a colonial situation, and to present such a representation of three-dimensional, flesh-and-blood people in the pages of a two-dimensional text? It is no wonder, therefore, that one avenue taken by practitioners of this hermeneutic, or interpretive approach, has been to produce a spate of texts commenting on texts, of self-reflexive works.[106]

Agreeing with those who argue that what we say is inescapable from the way we say it, I have attempted here to make explicit the contingent nature of my position as author of *Making Algeria French*. But where others engage informal discussions of theory, I have chosen instead to employ a series of literary devices with the aim of underscoring the interpretive nature of my study. Historians tend to adopt an impersonal but omniscient, third-person narrative point of view to write linear, chronological accounts which move in a straightforward, causal manner from point A to point B. However, such narrative structures tend to express a fixity of vision which corresponds neither to my experience of nor my reading about the Third World. The problem is that such compositional modes tend implicitly to smooth out the historical record, to emphasize historical continuities over discontinuities, and to privilege the authority of the historian/narrator. Rather than the omniscient third-person author narrating the text from a single, all encompassing viewpoint, I have interjected at various points my first-person point of view and presented a series of multiple and often clashing perspectives. Rather than a smooth, linear chronology, I have purposely interrupted the narrative with a series of cinematic-style jump cuts copied from the modernist, stream-of-consciousness novel to create a nonlinear account. In this manner, I argue my case regarding settler colonialism and colonial urbanism, and situate it simultaneously within a specific intellectual discourse.

PART I

From precolonial Annaba
to colonial Bône, 1830–1870

2

Annaba on the eve of the
French conquest

The Algerians called Bône, *bled al-Aneb,* or Annaba, which means in
Arabic "land of the jujubes," because of the large number of jujube
trees that used to grow in the vicinity. My aim in this chapter is to
describe what Annaba was like in its own terms prior to the coming of
the French. "In its own terms": this is something the French never sought
to do, preoccupied as they were with making the city French. In two
earlier local histories, for example, the reader searches in vain for information about Muslim Annaba in the midst of which lived a handful
of Europeans.[1]

The sources used in this chapter are varied. They consist of Arabic
sources collected primarily by Europeans. Biased though they are, we
can also use contemporary European travelers' accounts.[2] Some recent
social scientific research can be drawn upon although it applies more to
the present than to the past. There is more, however. In much the same
way that Napoleon's 1798 invasion of Egypt engendered the first pain-
staking, systematic study of that society, so the 1830 invasion of Algeria
unloosed a veritable swarm of surveyors, geologists, geographers, archeologists, botanists, zoologists, painters, and protosocial scientists
who sized up and took the measurements of the Barbary Coast recently
become *l'Afrique du Nord.*[3] Weberian rationalism run rampant in the
service of colonialism? The scientific appropriation of one culture by
another? Perhaps. But keeping in mind the insights of the colonial
sociology of knowledge, this mass of post–1830 documentation can be
mined to imaginatively reconstruct Annaba before it became Bône and
Algeria before it became French.

Therefore, I combine here contemporary European travelers' accounts used selectively, post-1830 French documents read backwards,
and anthropological insights applied retrospectively to describe what
Annaba was like in 1830, surveying in succession geography, population,
economy, society, politics, and religion.

31

Illustration 2.1   View of Bône (Bibliothèque Nationale Cabinet
d'Estampes).

Geography

Algeria can be divided into three major climatic and geographical belts
from north to south: the coastal region, the high plains of the interior,
and the Sahara (Fig. 2.1). Annaba forms part of the Algerian littoral
which extends inland an average of 100 kilometers. The area is Mediterranean in climate. Temperatures are slightly warmer and it is more
humid than on the other side of the Mediterranean, but otherwise it is
not unlike, for example, the southern coast of France.

The primary geographical features of the Annaba region are the
Edough mountains and the plain of Annaba (Figure 2.2).[4] The plain
surrounding Annaba has been renowned since antiquity when it formed
part of the North African territory termed the "granary of Rome."
Actually, the plain consists of two plains, a small one immediately outside the city, which the French later called the *petite plaine*, and a larger
one which extends from twenty-five to forty kilometers into the interior.
The *petite plaine* lies between the mountainous Edough and Djebel Bou
Kanta west and southwest of Annaba, and the knoll known as the Ras
Bou Hamra to the south. It covers approximately 10,000 hectares, and
corresponds roughly to the boundaries of the future French *commune*
of Bône. Part of this plain, especially northwest of the city gates and

32

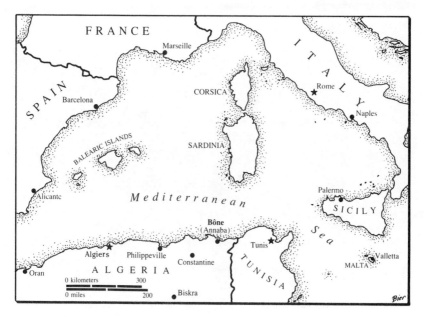

Figure 2.1   Map of Europe and the Maghrib.

amidst the ruins of Hippo, consisted of orchards where Algerians grew olives and mulberry trees, lemons and oranges, almonds and jujubes.

The plain of Annaba properly speaking encompasses an area more than 100,000 hectares in extent. From Annaba it extends in an arc west and southwest along the mountainous spine of the Edough to Guerah Fetzara (Lake Fetzara), and then moves east, stopping only at the foot-hills in the south, the forest of the Beni Salah in the southeast, and the Mafrag River and sand dunes in the east. It is the presence of this plain combined with its relatively easy access from the sea which is no doubt the chief reason why there has been continuous human settlement in the Annaba region for two millennia.

The Edough mountains are located immediately north and northwest of Annaba and extend north and west along the coast. A second im-portant forest area is that of the Beni Salah situated at the southern edge of the Annaba plain. None of these mountainous areas is partic-ularly high – the highest peak in the Edough range is that of Bou Zizi at 1000 meters – but the weather is markedly cooler and wetter than on the plains. Oak, especially cork oak, and pine trees are plentiful. In 1763 one traveler who journeyed the length of the coast between Ta-barka (just over the border in Tunisia) and Annaba saw enough oak forests to "furnish wood for construction for all the commercial cities of the Levant."[5] Animals abounded, including wild boar and monkeys,

33

Figure 2.2   Map of Annaba region. *Source:* Baude, *L'Algérie* (1841).

lions, tigers and leopards, hyenas and jackals. (Today the tigers have long since disappeared, but Europeans still relish boar hunting.) Physical access to these areas in 1830 was difficult and potentially dangerous. Yet the hamlet the French later established in the Edough, for example, lay only 13 kilometers from the center of Annaba.

It was on the fertile plain, however, that the bulk of the people in the Annaba region lived. Where the plain meets the Mediterranean, a flat, low-lying delta formed which consisted of sand dunes, marshes, stagnant pools, and meadows. Two rivers irrigated the plain, the Boudjimah and the more important Seybouse. The Seybouse originates in

34

Illustration 2.2   View of Bône after Rouargue frères (Léon Galibert,
L'Algerie [Paris: Furane, 1844], between pp. 364–5).

the mountains south of Annaba, flows the length of the plain, and
empties into the Mediterranean just south of the city. However, it is
not navigable far inland because it tends to overflow its banks and silt
up. Nor is it suitable for a port because it tends to change course. At
the time St. Augustine was archbishop, for example, Hippo was located
on the Seybouse, but by 1830 it was some distance inland. Therefore,
the port of Annaba, called Mersa Mania by the Algerians, was situated
immediately east of the city. Unfortunately, it could be used only from
mid-May to mid-September because of the lack of shelter from the
prevailing winds. Thus a second anchorage, called Mersa Ibn al Albiri
by the Muslims and Fort Génois by the Europeans (after the Genoese
who had built it in the fourteenth century for their coral-fishing boats),
and located nine kilometers north of the city, served as Annaba's port
during the remainder of the year. As we shall see, the location and
construction of an adequate port is one of the key concerns in making
Bône a colonial city.

In the Annaba region in 1830 there were no roads which had been
constructed and which were maintained regularly. Instead, the paths,
trails, and roads which did exist varied in size simply according to the
amount of use and terrain. There was only one functioning bridge, later
called the Pont d'Hippone by the French, and it had been built by the

35

Romans across the Boudjimah River a short distance outside Annaba on the way to Constantine city in the interior. There was no bridge which spanned the Seybouse, although a makeshift ferry was apparently available. There were a number of *qūbba-s*, or tombs of Muslim holy men, throughout the city and region which served as physical landmarks. Perhaps the most noteworthy was that of Sidi Brahim situated at the point where the Pont d'Hippone crossed the Boudjimah.

There were also no fixed settlements as such. In the countryside people lived either in tents or *gourbis*. Tents were made from pieces of cloth woven from wool and goat hair supported by wooded poles; *gourbis* were constructed of wood and thatch. Some 1740 tents and 72 *gourbis* were in use on the plain, and 1500 tents and 430 *gourbis* in the Edough mountains. In addition, there were three *zawiyas*, or lodges of Sufi brotherhoods, two on the plains and one in the mountains.[6]

No roads or bridges were built by the Muslims, yet the region was dotted with the ruins of roads, bridges, aqueducts, dwellings, cisterns, and tombs built by the Romans. In addition to the bridge over the Boudjimah, there were vestiges of a Roman road which had led east along the coast all the way to Carthage outside modern-day Tunis, and a second one which had connected Hippo with Constantine. Moreover, there were ruins of two defunct aqueducts which had brought water to Hippo, one from the Edough mountains and one across the plain. The main Roman ruin was, however, Hippo itself – literally, since it was excavated only later by the French. Muslims referred to it as the city of St. Augustine, but in 1830 little of it was visible because it was overgrown with bushes and shrubbery and planted with well-tended orchards. In fact, the entire plain of Annaba was covered with considerably more vegetation than we would imagine from the sparse amount of trees and shrubs found today.

The city of Annaba itself was surrounded by walls in 1830, but that did not mean that the country stopped abruptly at the gates or that the city did not extend into the countryside.[7] Orchards and gardens adjacent to the city were cultivated by townspeople. Cemeteries were located beyond the walls: the Muslim cemetery between the city and the Casbah to the northeast, the Jewish cemetery considerably farther away to the southwest, and even a European cemetery situated east of the Casbah and northeast of the city proper. Furthermore, the Casbah or fort was located outside the city walls. Built in the fourteeth century, it looked down on the city from a strategic vantage point on a nearby hill. Another fort, which the French later called Fort Cigogne, was perched on the southeast corner of the city and surveyed approaching ships.

Annaba in 1830 was a small city; it took no more than five or ten minutes to walk across (Figure 2.3). It had been walled shortly after

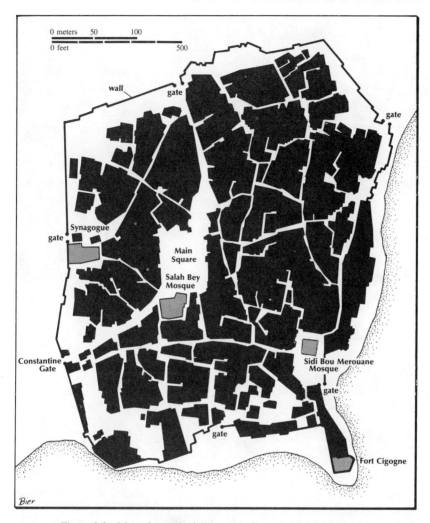

Figure 2.3   Map of precolonial Annaba. *Source:* After Maitrot, *Bône militaire*, between pp. 496 and 497.

1058, mainly to guard against marauding Arab tribes then invading the Maghrib from the east. The walls were punctuated by six gates, with the chief one, the *Bab al-Costantina* or Gate of Constantine, located at the southwest corner of the city. From the gate a road led by the *marabout* (tomb) of Sidi Brahim across the Pont d'Hippone and continued approximately 200 kilometers southwest to Constantine, the capital of the province.

Inside the gate a street led to a square in the center of town, the

37

Illustration 2.3   Mosque of Salah Bey (Bibliothèque Nationale Cabinet d'Estampes).

largest open space in the city. On the south side of it was one of Annaba's two main mosques, the Djemaa al-Bey or mosque of Salah Bey, Bey of Constantine between 1771 and 1792, built at his initiative. But the main mosque was that of Sidi Bou Merouane, the tallest building in town and situated on the eastern edge of the city overlooking the Mediterranean. According to an old Arabic manuscript, it had been built in

38

1033 by one Muslim saint, Sidi Bellit, and later named after a second one, Sidi Bou Merouane, who had come to Annaba in 1087 and died there in 1111.[8] There were numerous other mosques in Annaba in 1830, in various states of repair, although certainly fewer than the 37 which is the figure usually cited.[9] For example, the mosque called the Romanets was nearly in ruins and did not even have a *muezzin*, the Muslim who called the faithful to prayer. We do know that there were 91 *ahbas* (singular, *habus*; Frenchfied as *habous*) properties which were either land or buildings which had been donated by pious Muslims for religious purposes.[10] Some of these properties must have been used as Koranic schools attached to the city's mosques; *medersas*, Muslim secondary schools; and *zawiyas*, lodges where members of Sufi brotherhoods met and studied. There were two of these *zawiyas* in Annaba city in 1830. But other *habus* properties were in a state of disrepair, disuse, or had been simply abandoned due to insufficient revenue and neglect.

Annaba can be divided into three discernible areas in 1830, a commercial section, residential neighborhoods, and the Jewish quarter. The commercial center was located in the southern half of the city between the gate of Constantine and the Sidi Bou Merouane mosque. As in Islamic cities elsewhere, artisans practicing the same craft and merchants specializing in the same goods worked and sold their merchandise in the same area, usually on the same street, in sûq-s (Fenchified as *souks*) or markets. In Annaba there were the following *souks*:

> *souk al Djiarine*, the masons, at the gate of Constantine
>
> *souk al Hadadine*, ironsmiths, and *souk al Kharrazine*, the cobblers on the lower or southern half of the street, running from Constantine gate to Sidi Bou Merouane mosque
>
> *souk al Haouka*, the burnous merchants, on the upper or northern half of the above street
>
> *souk al Fakharine*, the potters, and *souk al Nedjarine*, the woodworkers, on a side street to the east of the above street
>
> *souk al Attarine*, the perfume sellers and druggists, on the main street leading from Constantine gate to the main square
>
> *souk al Dezzarine*, the butchers, on the street leading from the main square to the Jewish quarter
>
> *souk al Hadjamine*, the barbers, on the street leading east from the main square along the mosque of Salah Bey.[11]

These were all Muslim *souks*. In addition there were Jewish craftsmen who specialized in producing jewelry, cloth, and tailored goods. These goods were produced by Jewish artisans and their families and were marketed in the Jews' own *souks*. All of these latter *souks* were clustered in or around the Jewish quarter in the area between the Constantine gate and the main square and on the street leading from Constantine gate to the Sidi Bou Merouane mosque. The only other commercial establishment in Annaba in 1830 was the warehouse, or *comptoir*, of the French trading company, the Compagnie d'Afrique, where goods were stored while waiting to be either shipped to France or sold to the Muslims.

The second main part of Annaba was the residential area, for Muslims in Annaba as elsewhere did not live where they worked. This residential area covered most of the northern half of town. Just as the commercial section was divided into *souks*, so the residential half of the city was divided into neighborhoods. Each neighborhood was largely autonomous and more or less physically isolated from other urban areas. Neighborhood solidarity was based on kinship, ethnicity, and regional origin; family members from the same region or ethnic group tended to live in the same area of town. Neighborhoods were often named after the principal building in the vicinity. The neighborhoods of Annaba included Kouchat al Assafri, al Agba, Hammam al Kaid, and Bir Djerada. Hammam al Kaid was named after the Turkish bath or *hammam* frequented by the *caid* or governor of the city; Bir Djerada after a woman by the name of Djerada of Constantine who had donated a well which she owned to the city.[12]

The streets themselves were "very narrow, filthy, muddy, unpaved, and always full of muck and cow dung."[13] "This mud [in the streets]," wrote another, "is caused by the droppings of the oxen and cows which the inhabitants feed and house in their homes."[14] Houses opened off these streets, which were often little more than alleys and cul-de-sacs. A blank facade on the outside, the rooms were arranged in a rectangle on the inside which opened onto an interior court. Homes were rarely more than one or two stories in height, but the roofs were generally flat and used by the family, especially in the hot season. Houses were built of stone, brick and earth, and whitewashed on the outside. Certain rooms were set aside for cooking, others for the ubiquitious goats and sheep, and still others for slaves' and servants' quarters (in well-to-do households). Interior decoration varied according to the owner's wealth. Rooms used by the family were covered with mats and rugs, but the walls were generally bare. Often the family cultivated small garden plots either inside the family compound or on vacant patches of land inside the city walls.

40

Turkish baths or *hammams* were scattered throughout town. They were sexually segregated, open to the men in the morning and the women in the afternoon. They were one of the primary places where men and especially women met and socialized. An adequate supply of drinking water was always a problem. Most families trapped rainwater in cisterns in their homes. In addition, there were 17 fountains in town, and a pottery conduit brought water from a stream, the Oued Forcha, north of town to a tank outside the city gates.

The Jewish quarter or *mellah* was located in the northwest part of the city between the main square and the town walls and was called Sidi Abra or Houma la Yaoud. A small, nondescript Jewish synagogue was situated along the city wall in a Moorish-style building with ramparts. Jewish residences were strictly segregated from Muslim residences, and clustered in the streets between the synagogue and the main square.

Demography

The inhabitants of the plains and mountains surrounding Annaba were Arabs and Berbers. Some past observers have argued that the Arabs were nomads who lived on the plains in tents, whereas the Berbers were sedentary people who lived in the mountains in *gourbis* made of wood and thatch; that the Arabs spoke Arabic and practiced Islam, whereas the Berbers spoke Berber and were more resistant to Islamic culture.[15] By and large, these global generalizations are not accepted by scholars today. The primary distinction between Arab and Berber boils down to a linguistic one. Arabic and Berber belong to different language families, and in fact Berber has never evolved a written language. The point here is that Arab-Berber differences revolve ultimately around the question of the degree of acculturation which has occurred over the last thousand years. For the Berbers of today are descended from the original inhabitants of North Africa, and the Arabs migrated west from Egypt and Asia Minor a millennium ago. The first Arabs were nomadic, and the Berbers retreated from them in large numbers to the less accessible mountain areas. Hence the stereotypes. Yet long centuries of intermingling have broken down in large part these original distinctions.

Whether Arab or Berber, the people who lived in the Annaba region in 1830 were few in number and widely scattered. Of a population estimated at three million for the whole of Algeria in 1830 and at 1,200,000 for the province, or *beylick*, of Constantine, some 25,000 lived in the area surrounding Annaba.[16] The rural population of the Maghrib was divided into what the French later somewhat misleadingly termed "tribes."[17] In turn, tribes were divided into settlements or camps consisting of groups of tents known in Algeria as *duwar-s* (Frenchified as

41

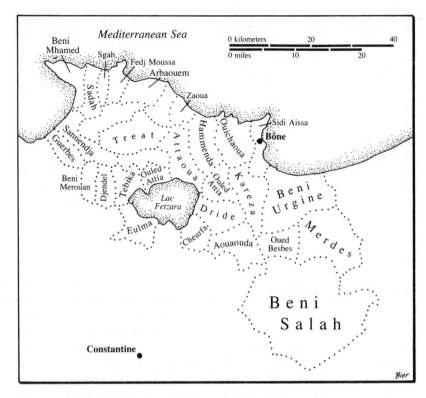

Figure 2.4   Map of social groups in Annaba region, ca. 1850. *Source:* After AOM, Subdivision de Bône. Carte indiquant la délimitation des territoires, civile et militaire; and Tomas, *Annaba*, p. 137.

douars), which were further subdivided into families. The following four tribes are representative of the tribes in the Annaba region: the Merdès and Beni Urgine on the plain, the Senhadja in the Edough mountains, and the Beni Salah in the forest of the same name along the southern edge of the Annaba plain. Together they numbered roughly 8,500 people (Table 2.1).[18]

Considering the entire plain of Annaba, children under the age of 18 comprised 36.5 percent of the population. Population density was between 9 and 12.1 persons per square kilometer. For the Edough Mountains alone, it was slightly higher at 14.4 persons.[19] This is equivalent to one person every ten hectares, which is a very low density. This places the population density of the Annaba region midway between the sparsely inhabited southern zone of Algeria bordering on the Sahara, on the one hand, and the more densely populated area of the high plains

Table 2.1. *Population of selected tribes in Annaba region, ca. 1830*

Tribe	Population
Merdès	1,695
Beni Urgine	2,611
Senhadja	2,400
Beni Salah	1,805
Total	8,511

Source: TEFA 1844–5, pp. 400, 403, 422–3, 426.

and Kabylia (the area roughly between Algiers and Constantine where the Berbers predominated) on the other.

How and under what conditions the Arabs and Berbers had settled in the Annaba area is largely unclear. In theory, each member of a tribe traced his or her descent from a common ancestor who was often a *marabout* or holyman.[20] In practice, families and the tribes to which they belonged migrated for any one of several reasons: to escape contact with the Turks; on account of climatic changes, disease, or famine; as a result of conflicts with tribal members; or as a result of disputes with neighboring tribes.[21]

Consider, for example, how the Merdès tribe came to establish themselves on the plain.[22] In the last half of the sixteenth century, an Arab by the name of Khaleb ben Mihoub left his home in Tunisia with his family and eleven followers "no doubt as the result of some disaster." He sought refuge with the Oulhassa tribe outside Annaba, who allowed him to settle on part of their very sizeable territory on the left bank of the Bounamoussa River. Pressured by his son Nasseur ben Ali to expand his territory, Khaleb enlisted on his side everyone who came to settle "for one reason or another" along the river. At last feeling strong enough, Khaleb attacked both the Oulhassa and the neighboring Beni Salah as well. The struggle continued for several years; five of Nasseur's seven grown sons were killed. Exhausted, the Beni Salah ceased fighting. Finally, the Merdès and Oulhassa agreed to a final, winner-take-all combat using only four-year-old horses. However, the Merdès cut their horses' manes and tails to make them appear younger than they in fact were. As a result of this chicanery, the Merdès won and Nasseur, who had meanwhile succeeded his father as tribal leader, named one of his sons *shaykh* or chief of the Oulhassa. In the nineteenth century, therefore, the six Merdès tribal fractions traced their descent in the following manner.

Ouled Hassan Heleymin	descendants of the conquering family
Mdeinia Gheiria	descendants of an individual named Ahmed ben Mohammed and another unknown warrior who had joined Nasseur ben Ali
El Feid El Mehareb	comprised of outsiders who had joined Nasseur ben Ali after the first battles with the Oulhassa

So much for the idealized notion of descent from a common ancestor.

Turning to the city itself, no one knows for sure how many people lived in Annaba in 1830.[23] Estimates range from 3,000 to 12,000; a figure of 4,000 seems most likely. Admittedly this is small, but then towns were small – Algiers had declined to 30,000–35,000 in 1830 – and at most five percent of the Algerian population lived in towns at this time.

The people of Annaba were extremely heterogenous, and varied ethnically, racially, and by religion. No fewer than six different groups may be distinguished. The majority of the population were Moors. They were descended largely from Spanish Muslim refugees who had migrated to the Maghrib at the end of the Reconquista in the fifteenth century. Moors comprised the core of the urban Maghribi population from Algiers to Tunis. Generally they made their living as merchants, shopkeepers, craftsmen, and market gardeners.

The Turks in Annaba were recruited in the Levant, where they had been trained as janissaries. Exclusively male, they served as troops and were garrisoned in three barracks in town plus the Casbah. Of 10,000 Turks in all of Algeria, there were less than 100 stationed in Annaba. The Turks were further differentiated from the other townspeople insofar as they spoke Turkish and adhered to the Hanifi legal rite of Islam, whereas the other Muslims spoke Arabic and observed the Maliki rite. The offspring of Turks and Moors were termed *koulouglis*, and constituted a distinct group. Probably as numerous as the Turks, they enjoyed Moorish social status combined with Turkish pecuniary advantages.

From the surrounding plains and mountains came Arabs and Berbers, few in number, seeking work primarily as temporary migrants. Mostly they came from the tribes closest to the city, namely, the Merdès, Beni Urgine, Kharezas, and Senhadja.

The last major population group were the Jews, who numbered "several families" in the late eighteenth century. The Jews, had fled from the Iberian peninsula at roughly the same time as the Moors, but they were scarcely better treated on the southern shore of the Mediterranean than they had been on the northern. In Annaba they were "very despised, and crushed by tributes and *corvées*."[24] In certain cities of the Maghrib, such as Tunis and Algiers, Jews who had migrated to Leghorn in Italy and from there to North Africa formed something of an elite within the larger Jewish community. It is unclear whether there were any Jewish immigrants from Leghorn in Annaba, but it is certain that there were commercial relations between the two cities because it was to Leghorn that the majority of the coral fished off the coast went.[25]

Finally, there was a smattering of other peoples living in Annaba in 1830. There were a number of black Africans mostly from the Sudan, who were primarily household slaves in the homes of the well-to-do. There were a few Mozabite merchants who had migrated from the Mzab in the Sahara. Whereas both the Turks and other Muslims were Sunni Muslims, the Mozabites were Ibadites, adherents of a small, ascetic Islamic sect. There was a handful of Europeans including foreign consuls, "renegade" Christians who had been captured in pirate attacks and had apostasized, and the employees in the Compagnie d'Afrique warehouse. None of these latter groups was sizeable; the Compagnie employed one agent and four or five lower officials at the end of the eighteenth century.

We know somewhat more about the number of people in Annaba and the region than about the rate at which the population was either rising or falling, that is, about fertility and mortality. Given the nature of preindustrial society, we can surmise that in general there was a high birthrate and an equally high death rate so that the population was stabilized at a fairly low level, or perhaps increasing gradually. It is a society which would be prone to the kind of periodic demographic crises so ably described for *ancien régime* France by Pierre Goubert: two or more years of crop failures followed by famine and starvation together with a higher incidence of disease, resulting in a sharp rise in mortality.

In the Algerian case, little information exists on famines due to crop failure. In 1805 there was famine throughout the Regency of Algiers, and people starved to death in the province of Constantine. In Annaba itself, there was a poor harvest in 1817. Somewhat more is known concerning illness and disease. The people of Annaba were prone to certain illnesses continuously: fevers, intestinal disorders (diarrhea, dysentery), which were common especially in the fall; pulmonary ailments (bronchitis, pneumonia) prevalent during the cold season. Epidemics of typhus and cholera occurred frequently enough that they must be considered endemic. In this regard, the swampy marshland of the *petite plaine* functioned as an ideal breeding ground for insects and microorganisms. As a result of the "pestilential exhalations," the area was "very unhealthy, little populated."[26]

Yet the most dreaded disease – and for that reason the one we know most about – was the plague, which occurred right up to the end of Turkish rule. In the Annaba region, there were cases of plague every

45

year between 1785 and 1793 and between 1817 and 1819.[27] In 1785 Turkish troops formed a *cordon sanitaire* in an attempt to prevent the plague from spreading from the tribes in the region to the city. In vain, for the plague broke out in the city the following year. But the plague was spread chiefly by Muslims returning from the pilgrimage to Mecca. One could chart how the plague spread east to west across the Maghrib with a murderous consistency as boat loads of returning pilgrims docked at each port. Of the devastating effects there can be no doubt. A European traveler who was in the Annaba area during the plague in the 1780s wrote,

The ravages of the plague are so considerable in all this land... that in the midst of these sad solitudes, I see almost nothing but graves, and instead of aromatic odors I smell only the emanations spread far and wide by the bodies buried in shallow graves. These lugubrious depots of the remains of humanity, placed here and there in solitary spots, sadden my imagination, and offer only a tableau of our destruction.[28]

And during the 1818 outbreak, an inhabitant of Annaba wrote, "One perceives painfully the ravages that the plague has made here when one considers that two-thirds of the houses of the city are closed."[29]

At such times economic activity virtually ceased and the social fabric threatened to unravel altogether. During the plague in the 1780s, for example, so many died that the tribes no longer brought their grain and cloth to market in Annaba. In the city the poor died at such a frightful rate that property owners offered half of their wheat and barley crop in exchange to anyone willing to harvest it – and still they had trouble attracting sufficient labor.

The level of material culture no doubt contributed to the high mortality during such crises.[30] I have already described the rudimentary housing prevalent in the region, namely tents and *gourbis*. Clothing was mostly lightweight and better suited to the hot season than the cold. The main garments were the *haik*, a long, commodious cotton overgarment worn by the women, and the *gandoura*, a long linen garment worn by the men. Moreover, the diet was starchy and often lacking in sufficient protein. The main dish was and is *couscous*, which is made from cracked wheat. The same name is applied to the grain and to the dish which is garnished with meat, broth, and vegetables. *Couscous* constitutes a more than adequate meal when it is prepared with a fair amount and variety of meat and vegetables, but it is doubtful that this was generally the case. The diet was supplemented with unleavened bread made from wheat or barley, and with fruits, vegetables, and olives when available and depending on a family's wealth. However, some of the people all of the time and many of the people some of the time

46

subsisted on flour made from acorns. Particularly common in the mountain areas, the effects of this diet were graphically described in a series of sayings current among the Berber Kabyles.

> I ate it [acorns] fresh,
> It gave me diarrhea;
> I ate it with legumes,
> It gave me colic;
> I ate it with bouillon,
> It set my body on fire;
> I ate it straight,
> My guts swelled up;
> I ate it with sour milk,
> It burned my insides;
> I ate it with mallow leaves,
> My belly became bloated;
> I ate it with oil,
> I spent the night on my left side;
> I ate it with butter
> I stank like a dog.[31]

Economy

The Arabs and Berbers of the Annaba region, whether plains-dwellers or mountain inhabitants, practiced both sedentary agriculture and stock-breeding.[32] Generally half of a tribe's land was used for pasture and the other half was cultivated. One-third of the arable was cropped in any given year.

There was no regular transhumance in the region, but animals moved freely about on unfenced tribal land from pasture to pasture, and grazed regularly on the stubble left over after the harvest. Animals were prized possessions; their products ranged from food (meat, milk, fats) and woolen cloth to hides. Table 2.2 gives an idea of the number and kind of animals owned by the tribes in the area.[33] In terms of the land available, this is equivalent to slightly more than two head of livestock per hectare, again a relatively low figure.

Although the older view that nomads on the plains raised livestock and mountain dwellers engaged in sedentary agriculture is an oversimplification; a distinction should be made between intensive agriculture found typically in the mountainous areas and extensive cultivation which prevailed on the plains. Cereal crops characteristic of extensive cultivation – wheat and barley – predominated on the plain. In addition, vegetables, olives, and fruits were also grown. In 1845, 9,567 ha. were cultivated on the plain, including 384 ha. belonging to the Merdès and 327 ha. belonging to the Beni Urgine.

Table 2.2. *Animals of selected tribes in Annaba region, ca. 1830*

Tribe	Cattle	Sheep	Goats	Horses	Mules
Merdès	8,000	5,000	150	400	105
Beni Urgine	4,780	9,640	130	470	289
Beni Salah	6,200	11,000	2,300	675	500
Senhadja	4,000	5,000	1,500	250	400
Total (for Annaba region)	53,532	85,990	13,871	4,671	4,016

Source: TEFA 1844–5, pp. 400, 403, 422–3, 426; Nouschi, *Enquête*, pp. 135–6.

Agricultural tools and techniques were rudimentary. The primary – and in many instances the only – tool was a simple wooden plow fitted either with an iron blade or a wooden one. Such a plow was virtually the same one used by the Romans centuries before. The only other common implement was a wooden harrow. There was virtually no wheeled transport.[34]

The agricultural cycle began by clearing the fields at the end of the summer. If sufficient stubble or grass remained, it was burned. The field was sown after the first autumn rain. Sometimes it was plowed prior to sowing, other times the field was plowed only afterwards to turn the seed under. After harrowing, the peasant or *fellah* had little to do before harvesting the crop at the end of May or beginning of June. No fertilizer was used (aside from the dung of animals which had strayed onto the field); no irrigation was performed; and there was no protection from pests or diseases. The bulk of the harvest went to current consumption. Some was set aside for use as seed the following year, some went to pay taxes, and the rest – if there was any surplus – was either stored or marketed.

In the mountain areas cultivated land had been carved literally out of the forest. Arable land was at a premium, and it was cultivated in a meticulous, careful, and labor-intensive manner. In 1845 the Senhadja in the Edough cultivated 1,906 ha., and one tribal fraction of the Beni Salah, the Beni Salah Ouled Ahmed, raised crops on 370 ha. in the Beni Salah forest. The forest was cleared by burning, known as *kçar*, which consisted in burning the lower branches of trees and using the cinders as fertilizer. After the harvest, the reclaimed land was left fallow for three years, and then the entire cycle started over. The same plow was used in the mountains as on the plains, except that the mountain plowshare was made more often of iron. Furthermore, the soil was fertilized more rigorously in the mountains, and the small truck gardens of cantaloupes, watermelons, squashes, onions, and turnips were irrigated in a rudimentary fashion. Cereal crops were raised but generally in insufficient amounts, so that vegetables were traded for grain at market. Moveover, cereals were rotated with nitrogen-fixing legumes, including peas, lentils, and green beens, to increase yields.

In addition, the forest itself was "farmed" intensively. Wood was used for tent poles, and leaves and branches from oak, pine, and cork-oak trees were employed to build *gourbis*. Charcoal was prepared and utilized as fuel for heating, cooking, and to forge iron plowshares. Wood was transported to market for city- and plains-dwellers and wood was used to make tools and implements ranging from beehive cages to plates and spoons to fencing for the fields. Tannin was utilized in making leather from animal hides. And acorns, of course, were a source of food.

These various land uses entailed different forms of land tenure and ownership.[35] There were four recognized categories of property in Annaba and the rest of Algeria in 1830. In the first place, *habous* was land given by individuals for religious purposes and administered by an ad hoc private institution. *Habous* land was used by mosques, by *marabouts*, or rented out. Landholdings could be quite considerable. In addition to 91 *habous* properties in Annaba city in 1830, another 881 ha. belonged to a single *zawiya*, or Sufi lodge, on the plain.

Second, beylical lands were controlled by the Bey of Constantine. Such land was obtained most commonly by outright confiscation as punishment of a tribe. The Bey then either had the land worked by forced labor, had it share-cropped (*khamisat*), or let it out to officials or tribes as payment of their services. The *'azl-s* (Frenchified as *azels*) holdings, for example, covered 7,394 ha. in the plain of Annaba; the *azel* of the Oued Besbès amounted to 3,645 ha. alone. The latter had been expropriated from the Merdès tribe around 1740 when the Bey at the time was trying to force the Merdès to submit to Turkish suzerainty. Originally given in appanage to a high beylical official in exchange for an annual payment, part of it was taken back later and distributed to several individuals "who had distinguished themselves by their courage and piety."[36]

The third form of land, *'arsh* (Frenchified as *arch*), was neither exactly common land nor individual private property, but combined features of both. *Arch* certainly looked like common land with its open, unfenced fields, lack of trees and any kind of irrigation system. But the key characteristic of *arch* – and what differentiates it from common land – is that the organization of work was by family and not by tribe. To be sure, people shared tasks and took account of when and where their neighbors planted their crops and grazed their animals, but the same family used the same land from generation to generation.

The fourth and final form of land, *milk* (Frenchified as *melk*), resembled more closely private property. Whereas *arch* was typical of the area of extensive cultivation, *melk* was prevalent in the area of intensive cultivation. Again, however, what distinguishes it from true private property is that *melk* was rarely bought and sold. Instead, land was imbued with value by labor. It did not exist as a commodity in this essentially precapitalist society. To speculate in land thus ran counter to the entire weight of communal tradition, which stressed conservation of the family patrimony.

In return for allowing access to the land, the Turks required the Arabs and Berbers to pay four types of taxes: the *'ushr* (Frenchified as *achour*), a ten percent levy on everything produced – crops, animals, olive oil; the *hokor*, special to Constantine province, a land tax applied to *azel* and *arch* lands; the *gharam*, which was collected from tribes who, although submitting nominally to Turkish rule, remained strong enough to refuse payment of the *achour* and *hokor*; and the *lazmah*, which was assessed on those tribes outside Turkish control. This was a market tax; when the tribe brought its goods to market, the Turks were there to tax the ensuing transactions.[37]

Clearly, the taxes collected varied according to the Turks' ability to enforce payment.[38] The question of the extent of Turkish authority will be discussed below. Generally speaking, all the tribes in the Annaba region paid taxes although the amount varied over time and from tribe to tribe. The tribes in the mountainous areas paid less and less frequently than did the tribes on the plain. The Senhadja in the Edough mountains, for example, lived "almost independently" of the Turks. The Beni Salah only came under Turkish rule definitively during the reign of the last Bey of Constantine. On the plains, the Merdès resisted Turkish hegemony for a long period, and the Turks launched several punitive expeditions, or *razzias*, against them.[39]

Given such a situation, it is clearly impossible to gauge precisely the fiscal burden weighing on the peasants. Generally scholars concur that the tax burden was relatively light. Moreover, most argue that the standard of living in this agrarian society was fairly high. The impression of the contemporary observer who described Constantine province as "rich because it produces an abundance of wax, honey, linen, oil, butter and other similar products which are loaded for shipment especially to Bône [Annaba]" is typical.[40] But such evidence tells us nothing about the fiscal impact on different individuals, or about the impact at different periods, for example, during an economic slump. Now the Algerian economy as a whole was undergoing just such an economic decline in the period prior to the French invasion. The decline of piracy in the late eighteenth and early nineteenth centuries had pinched severely the fiscal resources of the Regency of Algiers, although the proportion of state revenue contributed by pirate booty has generally been overestimated. "Deprived of the profits of piracy, Algiers turned to exploitation of the country."[41] The tax burden was increased simply by assessing the amount to be paid not at harvest time but while the crop was still in the fields – a maneuver which always resulted in higher taxes. The repercussions were severe. Regrettably, we have no details, but the result in the Annaba region has been described as a "mass migration" of the tribes on the plain to the Regency of Tunis.[42] However moderate the tax burden may have been in normal times, in this instance the tribes voted with their feet.

*   *   *

The city and region of Annaba existed in a symbiotic economic relationship, but whereas the rural hinterland could – and at times did – manage to do without the city, the city could not have survived long without the countryside. Economic interdependence was engendered by a variety of economic ties between urban and rural inhabitants. Arabs and Berbers labored on orchards belonging to urban dwellers. Peasants agreed, tacitly or verbally, to market their goods with particular merchants. Properties were exploited jointly by wealthy peasants and urban landlords. But the most important transactions between country and city occurred where the two met, namely in the marketplace. It was to the Annaba market that the Arabs and Berbers brought their surplus animals and crops. Mountain tribes traded their fruits and vegetables for the cereal grains they lacked. Berber Kabyles supplied the bulk of the city's wood. The Bey constrained certain tribes to market their produce in Annaba in lieu of tax payments made to the treasury in Constantine. Thus the Merdès brought their grain where the Bey's agents then turned it over to European traders. More than 30 tribes frequented the Annaba market in 1842–3, and there is certainly no reason to think there were any fewer in 1830.[43]

In exchange for their surplus food and animals, the Arabs and Berbers bought goods produced by the Moors and Jews and sold in the city's *souks*. The craftsmen of Annaba processed agricultural products and manufactured goods for everyday use: rugs, cloaks, saddles, shoes, cloth, and simple agricultural implements. They also provided services found typically in an urban center: grocers, barbers, bakeries, baths, and cafes. Table 2.3 suggests the number and variety of Moorish artisans and businessmen in Annaba.[44]

The nature of work in Annaba was artisanal. Workshops were small; masters labored side by side with a few journeymen and apprentices from the same ethnic group if not the same family. In Annaba at least

51

Table 2.3. *Selected occupations of Moors in Annaba, 1833–4*

Occupations	Year	
	1833	1834
Wholesale merchants	22	15
Commercial agents	2	2
Restauranteurs	2	3
Building contractors	1	1
Cloth merchants	21	18
Grocers	29	28
Ironworkers	3	1
Stationers	1	1
Sweet sellers	0	2
Woodworkers	2	11
Bakers	2	9
Butchers	3	5
Tobacconists	9	11
Total	97	107

Source: AOM, E 73 (1): Rapport du Directeur des Finances, 1834. Reprinted in Chollet, "Bône," pt. 6, chap. 2.

there were no large workshops, no nascent capitalist enterprises. There was little specialization and little division of labor, since the person who made an object sold or exchanged it as well. Likewise, there was much less distinction between merchants and artisans in terms of wealth and social status at this time than later. The same or similar goods were found on the same street in the same *souk* and were made by the same ethnic group. Goods were bartered or exchanged more frequently than bought since there was little need for money and little money in circulation. Although there seems to have been no formal corporation or guild structure similar to that found in early modern Europe, there was a modicum of quality control exercized by the *muhtasib*, or market inspector, who also arbitrated labor disputes.[45]

The Moors and other inhabitants of Annaba had to pay taxes just as the Arabs and Berbers in the countryside. We do not know exactly how much the shopkeepers and merchants paid in 1830, but it has been estimated that the businessmen of Constantine city, for example, paid 10,000 francs annually.[46] The Jews were definitely taxed much more heavily in proportion to their Muslim counterparts. And we know that every six months the *caid* or governor of Annaba was responsible for leading a caravan with taxes and tribute to the Bey in Constantine. At the end of the eighteenth century this caravan with the *caid* at the head and accompanied by Turkish troops consisted of 2,000 cattle and 100 horses. No doubt such a considerable procession served to reinforce the ruler's hegemony in the eyes of the populace among whom it traveled.[47]

In addition to internal trade with tribes of the region, Annaba played a key role in external trade with Europe.[48] Just as Constantine city acted as an entrepot and redistribution center between caravans coming from the Sahara and the coastal cities of Tunis, La Calle, and Annaba, so Annaba served as a transshipment center between Constantine and the rest of eastern Algeria and Europe. This trade was comprised of two strands, one connecting Annaba to the Jews in Leghorn and one to the French in Marseilles.

Italian Jews in Leghorn carried on an active trade with their confreres in the Maghrib, especially in Algiers and Tunis. Moreover, the coral fished off the coast of eastern Algeria went primarily to Leghorn, where it was refined, polished, made into jewelry and amulets, and reexported. We do not know the extent to which the Jews of Annaba participated in this trade, but economic transactions were clearly facilitated by contacts with Jewish communities elsewhere in the Mediterranean. To fully understand the Annaba economy in 1830, therefore, the role played by the Jews as creditors, commercial intermediaries, as well as artisan producers, must be taken into account.

The second trade link between Annaba and Europe was that with Marseilles. Generally speaking, raw materials – grain, hides, coral, linen, oil, wax – were exported from Algeria via Annaba, while luxury and manufactured goods – sugar, coffee, spices, cotton, linen, silk, metal goods – were imported. As we have seen earlier, this trade had been organized and run primarily by a succession of trading companies chiefly from Marseilles. The best known and most profitable company was the Compagnie d'Afrique, which reached its apogee between 1741 and the Revolution of 1789. Although the Compagnie was active all along the coast between La Calle to the east of Annaba and Collo to the west, the bulk of its trade went through Annaba. Coral fishing was its raison d'être, but in fact the Compagnie engaged primarily in the export of Algerian agricultural products legally when possible and illegally when not. Every year the Compagnie paid the Dey of Algiers 100,000 *livres tournois* plus two chests of the finest quality coral for the monopoly or coral fishing alone. In addition, the Compagnie paid the Bey of Constantine a ten percent tax on all goods exported except coral, plus a number of other taxes, fees, and export licenses, not to mention bribes. It has been estimated that given the various taxes, fees, and the inflated prices at which the Bey sold the goods – in large part the surplus left over from the *achour* tax paid by the peasants – his profit amounted to no less than 100 percent.[49]

As surprising as it may at first appear, Annaba may have surpassed

Algiers in commercial importance before 1789 due to its volume of external trade. There is no question that it was "the *rendez-vous* of all the commerce engaged in by the Compagnie Française d'Afrique."[50] During the French Revolution, however, the Compagnie collapsed and the volume of external trade – and with it Annaba's commercial activity – fell off considerably.

Society

To gauge precisely the tax burden on the peasants of the Annaba region, to measure the economic clout of the countryside relative to the city, to ascertain exactly the role of internal trade with Constantine to the south and external trade with Leghorn and Marseilles to the north – these are tasks which remain largely to be done due both to the paucity of sources and the lack of research in those available. Paradoxically, however, this very lack of empirical research has engendered a veritable florescence of theoretical speculation. The primary theoretical emphasis has been to elaborate a model of the mode of production in precolonial Algeria, which would be applicable of course to Annaba as well. This theoretical concern reflects a more general trend in studies of the Third World, at least among Marxists, to comprehend the economic and social formations of precapitalist societies outside Europe.[51] In the case of Algeria, the lead has been taken by René Gallissot, who terms the precolonial mode of production "command feudalism," which he defines as the relations of internal Algerian production and exchange engaged in by the peasantry and "the dominant class complex," which included the landed aristocracy, merchants, and Turkish military elite.[52] For my purposes here, however, the main flaw with such theory is just that – it is theory, which is no substitute for an actual description of what was going on in the Annaba region.[53]

The question of the mode of production of precolonial Algeria shades off into the related issue of social structure, that is, the whole question of what constitutes the basic building blocks, the primordial groupings of Algerian and Maghribi society. Consider first rural Algerian society. One leading scholar structures rural society in the following rough-and-ready fashion: large landlords at the top who exerted enormous influence in local affairs, followed by rich landlords but with less influence, then a host of middle and small peasant proprietors, and at the bottom of the social scale, the shepherds and sharecroppers (*khammès*).[54] Although by no means an egalitarian society, the consensus of scholars is that compared at least to colonial Algeria, precolonial Algerian society was not highly stratified, that, for example, property was distributed relatively equally.[55]

54

The problem of urban social structure is more intractable due to greater ethnic diversity and division of labor. Muslims themselves – or at least the learned ones who wrote down their views – divided the urban population into elites and masses. At the top of the social pyramid was the Turkish military elite, *al-khassa*; and the so-called notables, *al-ayan*, consisting of the *'ulama* or religious leaders, leading officials, rich merchants, and well-to-do artisans. The masses were divided in turn into the common people, *al-amma*, including respectable shopkeepers, artisans, and petty officials; *as-sifla*, riffraff or members of lower social groups; and *al-barraniyin*, recent rural in-migrants as opposed to more settled urban dwellers (*al-hadariyin*).[56] An empirical albeit schematic study of social structure in Constantine city appears to corroborate this view. The urban elite comprised fifteen to twenty percent of the total population, and was based on a combination of wealth (the commercial middle class, well-off artisans), birth (rural landholders who lived in the city), and office (beylical officials).[57]

In fact, however, social structure constitutes another area in which theoretical speculation has outstripped by and large empirical investigation. And here the lead has been taken by anthropologists. The contrast in views between anthropologists can be seen most clearly in the debate between Ernest Gellner and Clifford Geertz. Gellner is the leading contemporary exponent of the view that Moroccan society – and Algerian, plus a good many others as well – is organized along the lines of lineage segmentation. Based on the principle "I against my brother; my brother and I against my cousins; my cousins and I against the outsider," segmentation claims to explain how societies are segmented into ever smaller units, yet which "nest" together to form alliances when threatened by other segments of roughly equal number and complexity.[58] Segmentation theory itself has a long and illustrious, if a somewhat obscure and tortuous, lineage. Moreover, it purports to explain nothing less than how stateless societies the world over can unite temporarily in powerful coalitions, which collapse as rapidly as they are formed.[59]

Clifford Geertz seeks to revise classic segmentation theory. His argument, badly stated, is that segmentation is a fiction, a collective ideology whereby naive anthropologists have been led astray by accepting their informants' views at face value.[60] Whereas the ideal may be confederations aligned symetrically into segments, reality is rarely so neat. Instead, the basis of Moroccan and by extrapolation Algerian society is individuals who form dyads to accomplish specific, limited goals. Geertz substitutes dyads, therefore, for such primordial groupings as tribe, lineage, Sufi brotherhood, and the extended family favored by other scholars. Such dyads can agglomerate in turn to form increasingly large human groupings which may resemble in fact the segments of classic theory,

55

but Geertz' main emphasis is on the shifting nature of such transitory alignments, on the gap between what native informants say happens and what happens in reality.

One key advantage to Geertz' argument is the way in which it links up at least implicitly with other streams of Mediterranean anthropology, especially patron-client relations and social networks. In its simplest form, after all, a patron and client constitute a dyad. Larger and more complex skeins of patrons and clients form social networks, which consist at base of individuals who ally with one another for mutually beneficial purposes, ranging from economic cooperation to godparenthood to marriage. In this regard, the frequency of first-cousin marriages among Arabs and Berbers is noteworthy; it has been observed often that there is a high incidence of both godparenthood and first-cousin marriage among Mediterranean peoples.[61]

Social networks facilitate access to scarce material resources; participating in them constitutes a hedge against hard economic times. For a client in one relationship can be a patron in another and vice versa. Individuals commonly participate in more than one network. Thus, social networks can be viewed as agglomerations of dyads which are linked via family and kinship groups to larger social groupings based on ethnicity, neighborhood, and occupation. Whereas mode of production analysis stresses "horizontal" class relationships, both lineage segmentation theory and patron/client relations emphasize "vertical" ties which unite people occupying different socioeconomic positions in the social hierarchy. What is missing, of course, in discussions of such alleged Mediterranean-wide social characteristics, is a demonstration that, on the one hand, differences between people of the Mediterranean – for example, that between Christians and Muslims – are less important than their similarities, and on the other hand, that such features are more pronounced in the Mediterranean than elsewhere in the world.

Such considerations, however, lead us further afield from Annaba than it is necessary to journey. What we know about Annaba is that in 1830 two main families dominated: the Benyacoubs and the Boumaizas. The Benyacoubs were the predominant family of the Dreid tribe located on the plain of Annaba. Moreover, they were closely linked to the Bey of Constantine. The Boumaiza family was of maraboutic origin, and even claimed descent from one of the Prophet Muhammad's four companions. They controlled extensive land in the Tobeiga area of the Edough bordering on Lake Fetzara. They too were allied with the Bey of Constantine. Both of these families sought to attract the largest possible number of relatives, friends, and friends of friends. They literally divided Annaba and its region into two competing clans in their quest for leadership of the Muslim community both before and after 1830.[62] Since the available sources describe two and only two families arrayed in opposing *çuff-s* (Frenchified as *çoffs*), or clans, it would appear we have here a classic case of segmentation. Considering that they sought to organize together as many relatives and friends as possible, they could also be said to form competing social networks consisting at base of dyads. It is not possible to proceed further than this, because the historian – the present interpreter of the past – cannot penetrate beyond the representations in which others couched their depictions of the past.

Politics

In Annaba in 1830 the Turks held a monopoly of political power; the ultimate basis of their authority was military power. Most of the 10,000-odd Turkish troops in Algeria were stationed in garrisons scattered throughout the country. In Annaba, eighty troops, commanded by an *aga*, were garrisoned in the Casbah and three barracks within the city walls.

To a large extent, the Turks ruled through intermediaries who were held responsible for those whom they represented. In the countryside tribal leaders or *shaykhs* represented their respective tribe in dealings with the Turks. The *shaykhs* together with the Turks surveyed the land to assess taxes, and it was the *shaykhs* who were responsible for seeing that the taxes were paid. In Annaba itself a *caid*, generally but not always a Turk, held sway. The *caid* in turn relied on *amins*, leaders of the respective ethnic and religious communities to maintain order and settle internal disputes. The *caid*'s chief responsibility was to collect taxes and pay tribute to the Bey of Constantine.

Virtually no social services were provided by the Turkish state. Such services that existed were organized and run by private individuals, usually notables of the community. Alms donated by citizens were distributed to the poor through a poor relief agency, the *Beit al Mal*. The use of *habous* properties for religious purposes was determined by an ad hoc private administration.

Religious authority was concentrated in the hands of the *'ulama*, the guardians of Islamic orthodoxy. From their ranks came the officials who ran the mosques and the Koranic schools attached to them, and the *qadis*, the judges who adjudicated legal disputes according to Islamic law.

The Regency of Algiers has been described variously as a piratical kingdom, protonation state, military oligarchy, and quasicolonial state.[63] In theory dependent on the Ottoman Empire, in fact it was virtually independent of Constantinople. Questions regarding the nature of the political order ultimately revolve around the makeup of the social order. On the one hand, the Turks differed from the Algerians insofar as they were foreigners who spoke a different language, observed a different school of Islamic law, and never assimilated as much as the Turks in neighboring Tunisia. On the other hand, both the Turks and the Algerians were followers of Islam, and compared to the French later they intermarried to a much larger degree, forming unions typically between Turkish men and Algerian women whose offspring were known as *koulouglis*.

The Turks ruled through a combination of force, intimidation, and shrewd diplomacy. Given their small numbers, they could not – and did not – hesitate to employ force. At the same time, the Turks proved adept at a policy of divide and rule, co-opting some tribes to use against others, exploiting divisions between clans, playing off one Sufi brotherhood against another, and manipulating disputes between ethnic and religious communities to their advantage. "Here a real chief, there a nominal chief, governing the one, controlling the second, allied with a third, nearly unknown to the last one, the power holder in Algeria was at the junction point of an ensemble of relays, as diverse in their nature as decentralized in their effects."[64] As a result of such ties between a foreign military elite and indigenous *notables*, power was diffused rather than concentrated. The political patchwork reproduced, therefore, the ethnic and social heterogeneity of the country.

Thus, the Turks struck a tacit social compact with the Algerians: in exchange for paying taxes and tribute, the various communities were left largely alone. The range of Turkish power, however, varied considerably. Greater in the cities than in the countryside, it was greater also among the tribes of the plains than the tribes in the mountains. In fact, it has been argued that the Turks' effective authority extended to no more than one-sixth of contemporary Algeria.[65]

Furthermore, Turkish power was declining in 1830 and had been for sometime.[66] As indicated above, the decline in revenue from piracy led the Turks to increase the tax burden primarily on the peasants. This attempt to compensate for lost revenue had important repercussions. In the Annaba region it precipitated a mass exodus of the tribes on the plain to Tunis. Elsewhere in Algeria it led to a spate of tribal revolts. It led Sufi brotherhoods to contest actively Turkish power. And it led to a general decline in urban life. In Annaba itself, piracy had declined earlier so that by the end of the eighteenth century Annaba no longer had a pirate fleet. External trade, especially that conducted by the Compagnie d'Afrique between Algeria and France, had fallen off precipitously. As a result in Annaba the economy stagnated and the population leveled off.

Religion

Religion permeated virtually every aspect of life in Annaba in 1830. The Islamic world view provided a philosophical and practical mode of conduct which encompassed all aspects of daily life and which suffused them with a veneer of religious practice. From the ban on eating pork and drinking alcohol to the injunction to pray five times a day, Islam prescribed a minute regulation of life. Generally it is argued that the Arabs of the countryside were more Islamicized than the Berbers, and the Moors of the towns more so than the Arabs of the country.[67] According to another interpretation of Maghribi religion, Islam has oscillated historically between an ecstatic, hierarchical "Right," and a puritan, scripturalist, and egalitarian "Left."[68] What this so-called "pendulum swing" theory of Islam fails to explain, however, is the changing social basis underlying such presumed swings in attitude. Yet another view contrasts a formal Islam interpreted by the *'ulama* primarily in towns with a popular Islam based on local holy men and Sufi brotherhoods in the countryside. However, such dichotomous views are giving way increasingly to a view of Islamic belief and practice as a spectrum along which are ranged formal and folk elements. For example, it has been pointed out that "the general category of holy or learned man could in many cases embrace being *'alim* [singular of *'ulama*] and Sufi and curer and teacher and mediator all at once without any sense of contradiction."[69]

For purposes of discussion, we can say that formal Islam was based on the Koran and the body of Islamic law. The people of Annaba were Sunni Muslims, the dominant division in Islam, and adherents of the Maliki legal rite, the most puritanical and conservative of four rites. The Turks were Sunnis also, but followed the Hanifi legal rite, while the tiny minority of Mozabites were Ibadites, the most ascetic major division of Islam. To lead a good Muslim life in accordance with the will of Allah as revealed in the Koran included, among other things, praying five times daily and attending mosque on Fridays, observing major religious holidays, giving alms, and making the pilgrimage to Mecca. Five times daily faithful Muslims were called to prayer by the caller or *muezzin*. Devout Muslims tried to make the pilgrimage to Mecca, or *hajj*, once in their lifetime. The main holidays celebrated in Annaba – Ramadan, Aid al-Kebir, and Achoura – represent a combination of local and universal Islamic practice. During the month of Ramadan, Muslims everywhere fasted from sunrise to sunset. At the conclusion of the month, there was a three-day-long fete in Annaba. The first day sheep were slaughtered, and the two following days were devoted to games and competition, many involving horsemanship, held outside the main gate of town. Aid al-Kebir was also marked by the ritual slaughter of sheep, and commemorated the willingness of Abraham to sacrifice his son Isaac. On the other hand, Achoura was a holiday special to the province of Constantine; it honored the memory of Salah Bey, bey of Constantine in the late eighteenth century.[70]

Islam in Annaba was interpreted and applied in daily affairs by the body of learned men known as the *'ulama*. There was no formal training which led automatically to *'ulama* status, nor was it hereditary. Instead, the *'ulama* were recognized and accepted as such by other *'ulama* and the community at large after lengthy religious study. The *'ulama* earned their living as *qadis* or Muslim judges, officials in the mosques, and as teachers.[71]

Koranic schools were attached to mosques and *zawiyas*, lodges of Sufi brotherhoods. There were both primary and secondary schools, or *medersas*, in Annaba, but the actual number is unknown. Moreover, it was fairly common for families in the same neighborhood to collectively hire a *thaleb* to teach their children the alphabet and instruct them in the basics of religion. The literacy rate, however, was low.

The Sufi style of Islam was based on the veneration of *marabouts*, or holy men. Certain individuals by dint of pious acts or recognized virtue came to be considered as possessing *baraka*, grace or blessing. When these *marabouts* died, their *qūbba-s*, or tombs, often became places of pilgrimage, where people came to obtain blessings and stage commemorative festivals. Some *marabouts* were thought to bring rain or good weather, others to help find husbands for women or make women pregnant. There were *marabouts* scattered throughout the city and region of Annaba. On the territory of the Merdès alone, for example, there were four: Sidi Abd al Aziz, Sidi Cheikh, Sidi M'barek, and Sidi Muhammad Boukhara.[72]

On the basis of the teachings of these Muslim holy men, Sufi brotherhoods, or *tariqa-s*, were founded to spread their knowledge by instructing disciples. Sufi lodges or *zawiyas* were built, *habous* land was obtained, and educational facilities were provided. Certain of these brotherhoods achieved wider renown and in turn formed branch lodges. The Sanusi order of Libya, for example, was founded early in the nineteenth century by an Algerian, Muhammad 'Ali al-Sanusi. Later, it led the anticolonialist struggle against Italy (1911–42), and supplied the kings of Libya until overthrown in 1969 and suppressed by Colonel al-Qadhafi.[73] In Annaba city in 1830 there were two *zawiyas*, that of Sidi ben Abderrahmen and Sidi Abd al Kadir. In the surrounding countryside there were an additional three: Sidi bou Beida among the Ouichaoua tribe in the Edough, Sidi Denden among the Beni Urgine on the plain, and Sidi Ahmida at Dréan on the plain towards Constantine.[74]

Conclusion

What I have presented in the preceding pages is a portrait of a peasant society which shared many features in common with other such societies, including early modern France: a population stabilized at a low level, subsistence agriculture, a small degree of division of labor, and a social structure based on personal ties and social networks. More than one observer of the Maghrib has remarked on the apparent equilibrium of this society, of the tendency for there to be a place for everything and for everything to be in its place.[75] If overcrowding occurred in one forest area, for example, people simply moved and cleared another. If cultivation was extensive in one place, few animals were raised and vice versa. Certain ethnic and religious groups supplied certain goods and services. Even the rudimentary plow was an equilibrating factor, since a heavier, stronger plow simply would have exhausted the soil sooner.

Yet this snapshot of Annaba in 1830 should not lull one into committing the fallacy of the "anthropological present," that is, of considering this a "steady-state" society devoid of change, movement, progression. An outbreak of plague could turn the social order upside down, *de fond en comble*. The decades-long economic decline prior to 1830, precipitated by a drop in profits from piracy, led to an increase in the tax burden with severe social repercussions. In short, if Annaba appears in a state of equilibrium, it is an optical illusion produced by the contrast with the rapid, drastic, and fundamental transformations which occurred after 1830.

3

Bône during the first decades of French rule, 1830–1870

The biggest single difference between protocolonial Annaba and colonial Bône was who called the shots. Before 1830 it was the Turkish bey sitting in Constantine, who ruled Annaba ultimately through the Turks garrisoned in the Casbah. And the French? The French constituted a tiny commercial presence on the coast in Annaba. After 1830 the tables were reversed: Ahmed Bey was chased from Constantine, and political and military power shifted for a while to Bône.

The French invasion of Algeria in 1830 is usually treated as an attempt by Charles X to deflect internal discontent in France by engaging in an external adventure in Algeria, using as an excuse the fact that the French consul in Algiers had been slapped in the face by the Dey of Algiers with a fly swatter, literally losing face in the process. No matter that powerful Jewish grain merchants in Algiers colluded with officials in Paris to defraud the Dey, that the French used the Dey's refusal to submit to demands to rationalize a naval expedition to Algiers. All to no avail in any case since Charles X was overthrown in the revolution of 1830.[1]

The takeover of Annaba in 1832 is usually treated as "the most beautiful feat of arms of the century," whereby a handful of French soldiers scaled the Casbah under cover of darkness, overwhelmed the Turkish defenders, and from there assaulted the city below. No matter that an invasion two years earlier had failed, that the Muslim populace was divided between French and Turkish sympathizers, and that caught in a three-way cross fire between the French attackers, the Turkish garrison and Ahmed Bey's Arab troops, the inhabitants of Annaba fled en masse. No matter that the Casbah takeover was a small-scale operation, and that one of the main leaders, Yusuf, was not even French. No matter because the French were in charge, Annaba was now Bône, and a potent historical myth had been engendered which became part of the nascent colonial ideology.[2]

In 1832 Bône was primarily a beachhead, a military base and jumping off place, first, for subjugating – or "pacifying" as the French termed

Illustration 3.1   Arab Bureau of Bône by F.-J. Moulin. From left to right: Mohammed Sammard (*khodja*), Salem Marsaoui (*chaouch*), Lavondez (sous lt.), Guyon Vernier (chef), Lt. Marcourt (stagiaire), Chidiar (interprète) (Bibliothèque Nationale Cabinet d'Estampes).

it – the Algerians on the plain and in the nearby hills, and secondly, the point from which an attack on Ahmed Bey in Constantine was launched. It took five years and two attempts before the French conquered Constantine, the capital and leading city of the province located 150 kilometers inland, but by 1837 they were successful. They now controlled the urban centers, and had forced many of the Algerian tribes to come to terms either through force, cajolery, or a combination of both, although sporadic resistance continued for decades.

After subduing the native inhabitants of Bône, the next step in creating a colonial city was to seize the land and take control of the natural resources. During this next stage in the history of colonial Bône, the French practiced on the Algerians the sort of booty capitalism the Spanish had performed earlier on the Indians in Latin America. Booty, plunder, the extraction of minerals and other wealth easily obtained

63

gave way only overtime to the kind of patient, stolid, back-breaking colonization entailed in farming and town-building; road, railway, and port construction; in short, to the kind of colonial exploitation the French like to call *mise en valeur*. Yet what is striking about the early history of colonial Bône is, first, the rapidity and thoroughness with which the French exploited the city and surrounding region, and second, the virtual unanimity among the military, and even early socialists – notwithstanding their squabbles and disagreements – regarding the expropriation of the Algerians.

Takeover

First, the French occupied the buildings of Bône. In a preindustrial society land is the single most valuable commodity, and the French viewed Algeria after 1830 as a place where land was virtually for the taking. That it was taken at the expense of the Algerians was simply of no concern. In Bône such a situation as existed after 1832 is usually described euphemistically as "fluid." After all, beachheads operate according to snafus, not law. Most everything is ad hoc; what is determinative is the fait accompli. So it was in Bône. Land transactions occurred faster than they could be recorded, administrative procedures and practices were applied after the fact, corruption was rampant as bribes exchanged hands, and the law did its best to cloak the proceedings in a veneer of legitimacy. In short, there is simply no way to sort out in any precise manner the volume or chronology of land sales in such a situation.

What is clear is that the French army in Bône commandeered lodgings and quarters where they found them. The army and European businessmen simply occupied houses and buildings which they found abandoned, exercising a sort of "right of the conqueror." Thus, the leading mosque of Annaba, Sidi bou Merouane, was transformed into the military hospital of Bône. What with the destruction of the invasion plus the necessity to clear narrow streets of rubble, the number of buildings in Bône actually declined between 1833 and 1836 from 674 to 604. Of these the military had taken over 288, or nearly half; of these 288, 266 were used for barracks and only 22 for civilian services.[3]

The reason so many buildings were abandoned, of course, was because most Annabis had fled the invaders. This made it easier for the French to co-opt their homes and businesses at first, but after the situation settled down somewhat the Annabis returned to claim their property. When they found their properties occupied – possession must have constituted ninety-nine percent of the law at this time in Bône – they chose to sell them, usually for a pittance, to native Jews, or European speculators and officers, rather than contest their expropriation. Then they

64

promptly left again. By 1840 Europeans possessed 358 buildings and Algerians only 191; Europeans ran 202 business establishments and the Algerians only 56. The biggest single expropriation by the French of the Algerians in Bône occurred, therefore, at the very beginning of French rule.[4]

Land Grab

First, the French occupied the buildings of Bône. Second, they grabbed the land on the plain outside Bône. Accompanying the army into Bône in 1832 was a horde of camp followers, speculators, riffraff, and others. These hangers-on may have been despised but they came in handy. They supplied goods and services, first and foremost hay and feed grains. And it required no particular intelligence to realize that if they controlled the land directly on which the hay was produced rather than buying it indirectly from a landowner, more profit could be made. Thus was formed one group of land speculators.

But it is General Monck d'Uzer who best exemplifies how Algerian land passed into French hands, for even while general of the Bône region d'Uzer developed land speculation into a fine art. Already in 1832, just two years after the fall of Algiers, even the French military began to have second thoughts about what one procolonialist Bône historian called "the scandalous speculations undertaken by unscrupulous people" which were taking place.[5] In 1832, therefore, the French put into effect a decree banning property transactions between Europeans and Algerians. But military commander d'Uzer objected on the grounds that it inhibited civilian colonization, and after his strenuous lobbying the military decided in 1833 not to apply the decree to Bône.

Now, d'Uzer set the tone for what happened in Bône; his career there is exceptional only in the scale and audacity of his undertakings. For after preventing the application of the 1832 law to Bône, d'Uzer promptly became one of the biggest landowners in the area by buying up no less than 2,000 acres for 30,000 francs plus 1,200 francs in rent. And the manner in which he obtained the property was more scandalous still, for it was alleged that he colluded with "his" Algerian agent, one Mustapha ben Kerim – who just happened to be the chief of police for the Algerians of Bône – to hoodwink the Algerians into selling their land. In other words, d'Uzer was engaging in precisely the sort of speculation that the 1832 land law attempted to halt. That was one black mark later used against him. Another was the manner in which he had his land worked. There were relatively few settlers in Bône at this time, but there were a great many soldiers – all under his command. So, d'Uzer simply co-opted his soldiers to work his land. "The soldiers prefer this work to the inaction and idleness of the barracks," or so he claimed.[6] Paid by the army, soldiers worked d'Uzer's land for free. Decades later, that other grand seigneur of the Bône region, Mayor Jérome Bertagna, would use convict labor provided free of charge by the state to work his estate. Relative to the land available, skilled labor was in scarce supply, but the *grands colons*, the big landowners, managed and managed quite well.

Unfortunately for d'Uzer, however, the scale of his activities was too large for even the army to ignore, and in 1836 he was recalled to Paris and his command revoked. But sacking d'Uzer did not stop him. He promptly returned to the Bône region and after more adroit lobbying the general commanding Algeria appropriated money to construct a small village just outside Bône, Duzerville. Not only was Duzerville named after d'Uzer, but nearly all the land belonged to him as well. Here the former army officer lived and worked as a settler until he died in 1849.

> *The doyen of historians of colonial Algeria, Charles-André Julien, distinguished between two kinds of colonists – the mostly impoverished riffraff, and the so-called "colonists in yellow gloves," those with enough financial resources to avoid manual labor by and large.[7]*
>
> *François-Marc Lavie was definitely one of the latter. Lavie emigrated from Alsace-Lorraine; his family had been ruined financially during the 1789 Revolution. In 1834 he showed up in Bône to make his fortune, and he succeeded so well that the Lavie family became one of the four or five richest in eastern Algeria. François-Marc came prepared. He brought four sons, two cabinet-makers, and two wheelwrights; plows, harrows, other agricultural implements, an oil press, and a flour mill. Perhaps most important, he came with a personal letter of recommendation from the Minister of War.*
>
> *Lavie arrived in Bône two years after General d'Uzer had been appointed commander of the Bône region. D'Uzer promptly took in the entire family for three weeks, fed the whole entourage, and allowed Lavie to set up his flour mill on land next to the barracks. Having "arrived in Bône with . . . several letters from the Minister [of War], I thought it was my strict duty to support and favor M. Lavie," the disingenuous d'Uzer wrote. "Four colonists like M. Lavie would assure the success of the colony; they cannot be encouraged too much."[8]*
>
> *Originally, Lavie was slated to receive "an important concession of land" in the plain of Bône. In 1840, however, Lavie was in the city of Constantine, where he set up the first flour mill in the city. In 1848 he moved to Heliopolis between Bône and Guelma, where he obtained a large amount of property. By the time he died in 1863 François-Marc Lavie had firmly established his family throughout the province. His son Pierre took over the family's operations in Constantine. His son Louis took over the family business in Guelma and added a printing shop. The third generation was no less suc-*

cessful. One grandson continued the family business in Constantine, and became one of the leaders of the Opportunist Republican party there. Another grandson was a manufacturer in Bône and married the daughter of one of the city's twentieth-century mayors.[9]

Perhaps some of the Lavie success rubbed off on Jérome Bertagna. When he left the state administration in the 1870s to go into commerce, the young Bertagna went to work for Lavie as a commercial agent specializing in flour milling and selling wheat. He must have learned a good deal, because when Bertagna quit he went into business for himself and made his fortune when he won the government contract to supply the French army during the takeover of Tunisia in 1881. Seven years later he became mayor of Bône.[10]

Military men, speculators, and assorted hangers-on are not the only ones who got in on the act of colonizing Algeria – socialists did as well. Marx branded such early nineteenth-century socialists as Fourier, Saint-Simon and their epigonic "utopian socialists," and the label has stuck. By "utopian,"Marx meant to denigrate their grandiose schemes as impractical, and at the same time score propaganda points for his more "scientific" brand of socialism. As a matter of fact, Marx's epithet hit only part of the target since the Fourierists and Saint-Simonians demonstrated that they were more in tune in some respects with the sort of producer-cum-cooperative association schemes favored by skilled artisans throughout much of the nineteenth century – but that is another story. What is important here is that early socialists played a disproportionately large role in the early colonization of Algeria.

The heyday of these self-styled socialist communes was the 1840s when a large number were created all over the Western world. Brook Farm (1841–46) is probably the best-known due to the intellectual glitter lent it by such literary luminaries as Nathaniel Hawthorne, but there were also Fourierist phalansteries founded in Rumania, as well as the scheme of Victor Considerant, Fourier's chief lieutenant, for a settlement in Texas. Saint-Simonians and Fourierists alike viewed Algeria as another propitious location for their communal experiments. After all, part of the allure of colonies in general and Algeria in particular was the availability of land. In France the land was mostly spoken for, but in Algeria it was considered more or less for the taking – from the Algerians.

In western Algeria, a group of Fourierists from Lyon wrangled 7500 acres from King Louis Philippe in 1846 to found a phalanstery. The July Monarchy conceded the land, but did little else to support the colony. Disease and lack of resources took their murderous toll; plans to establish a true phalanstery were given up and much of the concession was rented back to the Algerians from whom it had been taken. Seven years later in 1853 the communal experiment collapsed when it was simply abandoned. It had outlived Brook Farm by one year.

Sometimes it is hard to see what was socialist about these socialist ventures. For example, the administrator of the colony in western Algeria, Jules Duval, went on to become one of the "four evangelists of Algerian colonization." More significantly, these would-be socialist colonists viewed their land concession as a gift from the King above rather than the Algerians below. In a profound sense, the fact that the land had been expropriated from the Algerians and handed to them, the fact that it was not empty but populated by Algerians, simply failed to enter into their socialist vision.[11]

In eastern Algeria, the preferred area for socialist experimentation was the region around Bône, and the main group conducting the experiments were Saint-Simonians. In fact, the Saint-Simonians wanted to make Bône an "Algerian Saint-Etienne."[12] The first Saint-Simonian of note in Bône was a justice of the peace named Marion. As early as 1842 Marion published a pamphlet which demonstrates clearly what would become of the Algerians' land under a Saint-Simonian regime. Marion argued that private land existed only in the towns, that the Algerians enjoyed only use rights to rural land, and that such rural land belonged ultimately, therefore, to the state which could dispose of it as it pleased. Marion provided a pseudolegal rationalization, therefore, for the expropriation of the Algerians' land in order to parcel it out in concessions to Saint-Simonians, among others.[13]

This was only the beginning, however. The leader of the Saint-Simonian's after Saint-Simon's death, Père Enfantin, made a lengthy tour of Algeria in 1839–41 and again in 1844–5, but was inspired particularly by what he saw in the Bône region. Enfantin not only stayed with Marion in Bône, but he borrowed Marion's arguments, and disseminated them widely. As the historian of the Saint-Simonians in Algeria puts it, "Enfantin was very interested in this theory [of Marion's]: Thus, the State, in Algeria, could take everything! What a perfect setting for a social experiment!"[14]

Enfantin's book on the colonization of Algeria appeared in 1843, and in it he propounded the idea that state lands recently expropriated from the Algerians could be used to create complete villages which would consist not of a small number of large property owners, but of large numbers of properties run by small owners. Furthermore, Enfantin proposed that the first such village, which would also function as the *école normale de la colonisation*, was to be located not far from Bône itself.[15]

Although neither the schemes of Marion nor Enfantin were ever put into effect, others were, and what they all shared in common was the same tendentious interpretation of Algerian land tenure systems. The problem in every case was how to rationalize seizing Algerian land for the purposes of colonization; only the means of colonization – whether civilian or military, Fourierist or Saint-Simonian – differed. We shall meet other Saint-Simonians interested in Bône shortly.

The primary difference between settlers like Lavie and Gabriel François was that François did not have the resources Lavie did, but he was not impoverished and certainly not riffraff. When the Revolution of 1848 broke out, Gabriel was making ten francs a day as a carpenter, top wage in his trade. He lived in the Faubourg St. Antoine, the leading working-class "red" neighborhood of Paris, with his wife who earned five francs a day laundering clothes, his daughter Rosine, who sold fruit on the rue Saint Jacques, his daughter Augustine, an embroideress who had made a pair of pants the previous year for King Louis Philippe himself, and his young son Eugene. After the Louis Blanc-inspired National Workshops had been closed down, and the workers put down in the June Days mainly by officers and soldiers recalled from Algeria, the government cast about for some means of getting the workers off the streets and starting up the economy again. The establishment of colonies agricoles *in Algeria was one partial solution. The government offered to pay transportation, give each family free land recently expropriated from the Algerians, and supply necessary tools, equipment, and draft animals. Landless workers would receive the land they had always wanted, and would colonize Algeria in the process.*

In November 1848 the François family left Paris, traveled on barges to Marseilles which took one month, sailed to Bône which took five days, and journeyed to Mondovi which took another couple of days, although it was only eighteen miles from Bône. In fact, there was nothing in Mondovi; the François family were the village founders. Now winter in Algeria can be cold, wet, and miserable. Luckily, the family had time to put up army tents before it started raining, because it rained for the next four months. It was when the rains stopped that the cholera epidemic began. On June 7, 1849, daughter Augustine died, June 19 Gabriel's wife, June 25 daughter Rosine's new husband. The Mondovi villagers consumed great amounts of quinine; they were told to stay active and macabre soirees of marathon dancing were organized, a sort of reactivated medieval dance of death. When it was over, 250 people had succumbed, twenty to twenty-five percent of the village total. The mortality rate was as high in the other colonies agricoles, *as high as it had been among the army in the earliest days of the conquest.*

Gabriel François renounced his concession and returned to France with his son Eugène. Days after arriving he died from exhaustion, but friends put Eugène back on the ship for Bône, where he was reunited with his sole surviving sister. Since his father had given up the family's concession, Eugène went to work as an agricultural laborer on the farm known later as Guébar. In 1859 he left Mondovi to work as a foreman on another farm owned by an early mayor of Bône. He quit a few years later and bought some land in the nascent Colonne Randon. But two-thirds of it was ex-

69

> *propriated by right of eminent domain without compensation in order to lay out streets. It was not until 1884 at the age of forty-five that he requested and finally received a concession of land in a newly created village in the plain of Bône.*
>
> *What you sow you do not always reap. Eugène François was almost an exact contemporary of Jérome Bertagna. The farm in Mondovi called Gué-bar, which Eugène left in 1859, was later bought by Jérome Bertagna, who made it into one of the biggest vineyards in Algeria. And ten years after Bertagna died in 1903, a Spanish charwoman and a French cellarman in the wine trade at Mondovi had a son, Albert Camus.*[16]

D'Uzer and Marion, Lavie and François were all interested in obtaining land in Bône. The case of d'Uzer exemplifies one sort of land-grabbing practice which occurred in the Bône region after 1832. And there were others. In the first place, sacking d'Uzer did not stop land speculation in Bône. Far from it. When d'Uzer was removed from his command in 1836, the 1832 land decree prohibiting sales between Europeans and Algerians was applied once again to Bône but not to the region around Bône where it counted, that is, where the large landholdings were concentrated. And concentrate them the French did. Within a matter of months in 1832, twenty-six individuals following d'Uzer's land-buying lead had acquired no less than 7,222 hectares in the plain of Bône. The single biggest deal occurred around 1850 when the Nicolas brothers of St. Etienne acquired 10,000 hectares.[17]

Secondly, many of the deals concluded so rapidly between Algerian and French were fraudulent on both sides. The French got land for a pittance, only to find out later that the same piece of land had been sold many times over to different buyers, that the boundaries of the parcel varied substantially, that the title deeds were worthless or fradulent. There were horse traders among the Algerians, too.

Thirdly, the discordance between Muslim and European doctrines pertaining to property opened up gaps in interpretation which the French were quick to exploit. Two examples are the *azel-s* and *habous* lands. *Azel-s*, it may be recalled, were parcels controlled nominally by the Turkish state (see Chapter 2). As sucessor to the Turks, the French state simply confiscated this land. Result: 161 hectares within the walls of Bône alone. *Habous* were privately controlled holdings used for religious purposes and charity under the Turks. The French rationalized that the French state provided welfare services that the *habous* authorities did, and according to a decree of 1843 they too were simply appropriated. Result: 4,142 hectares in the Bône region. This amounted to forty-seven percent of all the *habous* expropriated in the province of Constantine. To further compound the misdeed, the French then allowed the land to be parceled out rather than held by the state.[18] After

Napoleon III came to power, moreover, forests in Algeria were declared "vacant" – which they certainly were not – and therefore state property, free to be conceded, as we shall see shortly.

Finally, given the unbridled speculation which the decree of 1832 halted only partially, the administration was forced to set up a mechanism whereby title deeds could be verified. This was done in ordinances of 1844 and 1846, which brought some order to title deeds. But as soon as it had, the French opened up more land for colonization by simply decreeing into existence a *banlieue*, or suburb on the outskirts of Bône of no less than 40,000–50,000 hectares, and which embraced "a part of the Edough, the valley of the Kareza, the plain of Dréan, the course of the Seybouse up to the Beni Salah of the mountain, the plain which extends between the Seybouse and the Oued Bou Namouça."[19] In other words, the Algerians inhabiting the plain of Bône were to be expropriated in order to open up the Bône outskirts to colonization. Elsewhere on the plain of Bône, the practice varied only slightly. Thus, to create European villages, the surrounding land belonging to Algerian tribes was simply defined as part of the villages. This administrative legerdemain resulted in 1,656 hectares for Mondovi, 2,316 hectares for Barral, 2,274 hectares for El Hadjar, 800 hectares for Duzerville, and 1,400 hectares for Penthièvre.[20]

As a result of these and other practices, the biggest and best farm lands in Bône and the surrounding region were parceled out rapidly after 1832: the intensive exploitation characteristic of settler colonialism had begun. By 1850 French officials listed 556 properties on the plain of Bône, and had verified 425 of them: 53 European properties totaling 12,793 hectares, and 372 Algerian properties totaling 16,634 hectares. In the mid-1850s the most important farms on the plain were "those of MM. de Lutzow, Bouchet, Dubourg [a future mayor of Bône], Calbayrac, Begue Joseph, Vincent Dedies, Pionnier, Badenco, Begue Bertrand."[21] And this enumeration did not include the land belonging to the orphanage of Bône, or the estates of Gazan, Chapeau de Gendarme, St. Paul, Sidi Hameida, St. Charles, and Guébar, which had been formed from the enormous 10,000 hectare Nicolas concession. Guébar later became the estate of Mayor Jérome Bertagna. In short, "large European properties were constituted so rapidly after 1832 that the government had to give up projects of official colonization in the plain of Bône – the major part of the land already belonged to the Europeans."[22]

Capitalizing on the forests

First, the French occupied the buildings of Bône. Second, they grabbed the land on the plain outside Bône. Third, they took over the nearby forests.

At the crest of the Edough mountains just minutes from downtown Annaba, the French built a small settlement, part hamlet, part resort, which they named Bugeaud and which the Algerians have renamed Seraidi. Most people head straight for the expensive new tourist hotel just outside Seraidi designed by a French architect in mock-Moorish style, and which is already showing signs of wear and tear, unless they are passing through on their way to the almost inaccessible beaches or setting off on a neocolonial boar hunt. Meanwhile back at the hotel, the menu says Continental, the service is excruciatingly slow, and the prices are steep. But if you want a simple, solid meal, you would do better at the old French auberge *in the old settlement of Seraidi itself. To dine on straightforward country fare in the patio of the* auberge *may be to step into a colonial time warp, but the food is good and the price is right.*

Today it takes only minutes to drive from downtown Annaba to Seraidi at the top of the Edough, at nearly 3,000 feet altitude. In the 1830s and 1840s, however, there were no roads. The first step in exploiting the Edough, therefore, was to build a road to reach it. This was accomplished by General Randon, who commanded Bône after d'Uzer from 1841 to 1847, and whom the settlers liked to call the "father of Bône." Randon, a nephew of the French revolutionary Barnave, went on to become Minister of War in 1851 during the last year of the Second Republic, and Governor-General of Algeria during the 1850s when his most notable accomplishment was the subjugation of the Berbers of Kabylia, the same Berbers who not long afterward began migrating to colonial Bône, among other places.

But what is interesting about Randon's road is again how military and settler interests could dovetail, how the "pacification" or subjugation of the Algerians could pave the way for European settler colonization. For what happened was that in 1841 when Randon assumed command of the Bône region, Berber Kabyles from the mountains continued to raid European farms and fields on the plain and even up to the gates of Bône with impunity. Randon realized that to safeguard and extend the area taken over for colonization it was necessary to do something about the tribes in the Edough other than mount sporadic expeditions against them, which were only effective temporarily at best. Thus, Randon convinced the military to build a road twenty kilometers long from Bône to the heart of the Edough forest. The road was built by one thousand men under Randon's command in three months in 1842.

Construction of the road had several consequences. First, farms outside Bône were made safe for settlers by driving the Berbers further into the forest interior. Second, it literally paved the way for the expansion of Bône into the area of town contiguous to both the old and new cities called later, appropriately enough, the Colonne Randon.

Third, the road made possible the commercial exploitation of the Edough forest, and in the process later upset completely the political economy of the Berber peasant agriculturalists.[23]

French capitalists wanted to exploit commercially the Edough and Beni Salah, another forest in the Bône region, because these forests consisted in large part of cork oak trees. Like the Turks, the French state claimed legal ownership of the forests; unlike the Turks, the French conceded vast tracts of these state lands to private individuals to exploit commercially. Where the Algerians based their entire political economy on forest products and uses, the French wanted the forests primarily so they could use the cork oaks to make products such as bottle corks. Here is where the forests in the Bône region were so important, because the Edough and Beni Salah forests contained such a high proportion of cork oaks. The Bône region became, therefore, one of the leading centers in Algeria for the commercial production of cork oak, and Algeria became in turn one of the leading exporters of cork not only in the Mediterranean but in the world.[24] Who knows, perhaps Marcel Proust's cork-lined bedroom, in which he wrote *A la Recherche du Temps Perdu*, was made from Algerian cork, maybe even cork from the Edough. . . .

To glimpse what was going on in the forests, let us tag along with the English consul to Algeria on a trip he made by horseback to the Edough in 1868.

Being obliged to visit Philippeville [a port west of Bône], I thought it right to make a tour through the province of Constantine to acquaint myself with the actual state of the country. . . .

"La Safia" [in the Edough mountains] . . . three years ago was a magnificent forest of cork oak, interspersed with rich valleys more or less cleared for cultivation, and covering an area of 6,500 acres.

A concession of this forest was originally given to a French gentleman for a period of 40 years, subsequently extended to 90 years. In terms of this he was to enjoy the right of stripping the cork trees over the whole extent; and of cultivation and pasturage over about 225 acres of cleared land. From the latter portion the Arab occupants were ejected, much against their inclination, though not, I presume, without some sort of compensation. Subsequently, the right of pasturage over the whole forest was assumed by the *concessionnaire*, the claims of the Arabs were ignored, and they were only permitted to pasture their flocks within the forest on payment of rent to the *concessionnaire*.

Such was the state of things when, in 1865, this concession was purchased by the London and Lisbon Cork Wood Company for the sum of 12,000 pounds.

What I have described as having taken place at La Safia was going on all around. . . .[25]

That the forests around Bône consisted largely of cork oaks is the primary ecological fact which explains why they were exploited com-

Table 3.1. *Division of forest concessions in Constantine province, 1862*

Area of concession (ha.)	Number of concessions per ha.	
Less than 1,000	1 concession occupying	30
1,000–2,000	1 concession occupying	1,635
2,000–5,000	16 concessions occupying	52,465
5,000–10,000	6 concessions occupying	34,343
10,000+	4 concessions occupying	55,320
Total		143,793

Source: Nouschi, *Enquête*, p. 326.

mercially. But the form this commercial exploitation took reflects the colonialism practiced by the Second Empire of Louis Napoleon. Not only were the forests declared "vacant" and therefore property of the state. For even so, the lands could have remained in the hands of the state to either exploit or hold in trust. Instead, Napoleon chose to concede vast tracts to wealthy individuals, notables, cronies, and others with access to him and his court primarily in the 1850s and 1860s. As soon as General Randon's road revealed the extent of cork oaks in the Edough, therefore, powerful individuals clamored for a piece of the action. Charles de Lesseps, brother of the Suez Canal builder and member of the Emperor's entourage, obtained some 7,000 acres in the Beni Salah forest. The original French *concessionnaire* of the La Safia forest described by our English consul was a leading *colon*, or settler of Algeria, by the name of Cès-Caupenne, whose father was a high Napoleonic official.[26]

What de Lesseps and Cès-Caupenne received, however, were no more than meager plots compared to what other favorites obtained. The facts speak for themselves. The very first concession was granted in 1848 to a Parisian businessman named Lecoq. Twenty-one additional lots were leased between 1852 and 1860, which added up to more than 200,000 ha. Of this total, nearly 150,000 ha. were located in Constantine province; of 34 total concessions in Algeria, 28 were in Constantine province. Originally leased for 40 years, in 1862 the 40-year leases were lengthened to 90 years across the board.[27] And make no mistake: these were large concessions as Table 3.1 demonstrates.

Not only were three-fourths of all concessions situated in Constantine province, but half of those were located in the Bône region. Besides 10,000 ha. of the Beni Salah forest, more than 50,000 ha. in the Edough mountains had been parceled out as Table 3.2 shows.

In order to concede this land to a tiny number of French individuals

Table 3.2. *Major forest concessions in Edough Mountains, 1862*

Concessionaire	Area of concession (ha.)
Berthon-Lecoq	6,654
Martineau des Chenetz	5,972
Besson	17,824
Gary, Bure	6,773
Duprat	5,418
Cés-Caupenne	2,656
Lucy, Falcon	11,245
Total	56,542

Sources: AN, F 80 1785, Gouvernement Gènèral de l'Algèrie, *Mesures à prendre à l'occasion des incendies de forêts* (Algiers: Bastide, 1866); TEFA (1859–61), pp. 273, 275; TEFA (1862), pp. 311–15; SGA (1867–72), p. 363; SGA (1879–81), p. 129.

it had been necessary to take it from a much larger number of Algerians, as the English consul pointed out above. It is not possible to say precisely how much forest land was taken from each group of Algerians and exactly how much was given to each concessionaire.[27] We do know, however, how much forest was taken from seven of the dozen-odd ,groups of Algerians living in the Edough and Beni Salah forests (see Table 3.3). The Beni M'Hamed lost the least, 971 ha. of 13,077 ha., or seven percent of their total holdings. At the other end of the scale, the Ouichaoua lost more than 80 percent of their 29,183 ha., the single highest proportion, and the Reguegma segment of the Beni Salah lost a whopping 26,744 of 34,699 ha., the highest absolute amount.

Then in the 1860s disaster struck the concessionaires, or so it seemed at first. Fires broke out during the hot season in 1863 which affected 22,000 ha. Even more severe fires broke out again in 1865. Led by the Edough concessionaires, the concessionaires were quick to blame the Algerians, and even quicker to seek redress from the government. When Napoleon visited Algeria in 1865, the concessionaires took the occasion to complain about the 1863 fires. Napoleon had just concluded his visit when the 1865 fires began; they were not yet extinguished when concessionaire Cès-Caupenne – of La Safia – journeyed to the Emperor's Biarritz hideaway to complain personally. Duprat wrote a report. Martineau des Chenetz was hardest hit; he lost nearly 75 percent of his concession. Hard hit also were Lucy et Falcon (37 percent lost), Duprat (26 percent) and Cès-Caupenne (53 percent).[28]

The government formed a commission to investigate, and the concessionaires formed their own commission to investigate. Headed by de Lesseps, the concessionaires' panel included also Besson and Martineau des Chenetz. Where the concessionaires blamed the fires on the

75

Table 3.3. *Algerian land concessions to forest concessionaires in Bône region*

Algerian group	Total holdings (ha.)	Private concessions (ha.)	State forests (ha.)	Comments
Beni Merouan	3,472	2,674	—	To London/Lisbon and Senhadja & Collo.
Beni M'Hamed	13,077	971	—	All to Besson.
Beni Salah Ouled Serim	30,654	8,317		Includes both state and private forests.
Beni Salah Reguegma	34,699	26,744		Includes both state and private forests.
Fedj Moussa	11,020	4,335	3,375	2,093 ha. to Besson, 2,242 ha. to Gary, Bure.
Ouichaoua	29,183	23,749	2,129	Divided between Berthon Lecoq, de Noireterre, and Societé des Hamendas et de la Petite Kabylie.
Ouled Attia	23,052	15,513	—	All to Besson.
Tréat	13,630	10,992	—	4,081 ha. to Gary, Bure and 6,910 ha. to Besson.

Sources: AOM, M 90 (165) [Beni Merouan]; M 83 bis (158) [Beni M'Hamed]; M 78 (275), 8 H 6 [Beni Salah]; M 78 (276), 21 KK 11, 8 H 6 [Djendel]; M 78 (282), 21 KK 12, 8 H 6 [Dramena]; M 83 bis (55) [Fedj Moussa]; M 97 (259) [Ouichaoua]; M 84 (75) [Senhadja]; M 98 (267) [Tréat]; 21 KK 16, 8 H 6 [Talha]; Nouschi, *Enquête*, p. 335.

"religious fanaticism" of the Algerians, the government concluded that *kçar*, the Algerians' method of setting controlled fires to clear away brush to facilitate grazing, was the cause. Where the government fixed the concessionaires' losses at two million francs, the concessionaires claimed 18 million lost. Although the government and the concessionaires did not see exactly eye to eye, therefore, the government proposed what can only be termed a generous settlement in 1867. The concessionaires were to receive any burned area for free, plus one-third of their remaining concession for free, plus the option of purchasing the remaining two-thirds for a low 225–325 francs per hectare. This offer the concessionaires refused on the grounds that it was insufficient! Finally in 1870 the Second Empire rewarded the concessionaires with even greater largesse: they still received their burned land plus one-third of their unburned land free, but now the purchase price of their remaining two-thirds was lowered to a paltry 60 francs per hectare. To convey an idea of what these terms amounted to, let us note that the purchase price of 60 francs per hectare was equivalent to the cork produced by a single tree for 20 years, but that 120 to 150 cork oaks could grow on each hectare, each producing for 60 years. The concessionaires knew a good deal when they saw one – they accepted the government's 1870 terms.

Thus, the government gave away government land, and the concessionaires "made out like bandits." But the real losers were the Algerians. For where the government and the concessionaires may have disagreed on details, what they did agree on was despoiling the Algerians. How they lost out will be detailed later, but for now let us note simply the conclusion of the foremost authority on this question: "In actuality, the Second Empire put the Algerian forests up for auction. . . . Thus the forest fires revealed themselves to be an occasion of exceptional profits for the concessionaires; but for the mountain tribes or forest-dwellers, it was a catastrophe."[29]

Mining and Minerals

First, the French occupied the buildings of Bône. Second, they grabbed the land on the plain outside Bône. Third, they took over the cork oak forests. Fourth, they mined the area for minerals.

> *It is necessary to take along your own lodging, your provisions, your baggage, and often to cover a large amount of ground in order to reach a rich deposit [un bon gîte], that is to say, a spring that provides a little water. . . . You are completely on your own; you are simultaneously your own guide, in charge of your transportation, your hotel keeper, and all this under a burning sun, in the midst of tribes whose friendship is sometimes doubtful, whose apparent zeal is often suspect, and whose defiance is always certain. –Henri Fournel*[30]

Minerals – copper, lead, and especially iron – had been mined in the Bône region since antiquity, in particular by the Romans. The Edough mountains were composed primarily of gneiss, but where the mountains met the Bône plain, clumps of schist formed, and it was in the schist that at various points could be found outcroppings of iron ore – magnetite, hematite, and limonite. Most of these outcroppings of iron ore were not very extensive, but they were high in iron content.

After the invasion of Annaba but before the "pacification" of Bône was complete, geologists and prospectors began their search. And leading the way were again the Saint-Simonians, this time in the person of Henri Fournel. A geographer and historian as well as mining engineer, Fournel reconnoitered the area, "discovering," or rather rediscovering, iron at Bou Hamra, Belelieta, and particularly Ain Mokra, and lead at Ain Barbar and Kef Oum Teboul – all future mines that were to make the fortune of the Bône region. Fournel was the first, and one of the best. He conducted his searches between 1843 and 1846; he was so early that when he queried the Algerians he was accompanied by an armed military escort. The articles and books he published, the maps he made were definitely high grade, and the resulting mining fever proved contagious. Fluent in Arabic, at once geologist, geographer, historian,and engineer, Fournel merits a new look as an early de facto ethnographer and observer of colonial society.

Once rediscovered, the mines could be conceded. And they were, much as the forest. Two distinct waves of mining activity occurred in the Bône region, each linked to waves of colonization – the period 1845–63 when the Mokta el Hadid iron mine enjoyed its boom years, and the period 1890–1903 when the phosphates of the Tebessa region and the iron ore of the Ouenza led to scandals which reached from Mayor Bertagna in Bône to the National Assembly in Paris (see Chapter 4). During the first wave of mining concessions, however, things at the mines looked much as they did in the forest. To begin with, the Bône region was blessed with a plethora of rich mines compared to the rest of Algeria, much as it was with cork oak forests. The three iron mines closest to Bône alone produced three-fourths of all the iron ore extracted in Algeria. Moreover, a number of these mines were located near enough to Bône that transportation costs were relatively low. It should come as no surprise, therefore, that even before the redoubtable M. Fournel was through with his reconnaissance the first mines were conceded in the Bône area.

Fournel had mapped the mines of Bou Hamra, Meboudja, Kareza, and Ain Mokra in 1843, all of which were located within 20 miles of Bône. All were conceded in 1845, and except for one additional mine, they were the only mine sconceded in all Algeria before 1848. Three of the mines passed into the hands of the Talabot family, while the fourth mine went to a Marquis de Bassano. Here is where it gets interesting. On the one hand, the Talabot family along with their arch rivals, the Péreires, were the leading Saint-Simonians of the French Second Empire, and on the other, the Marquis de Bassano built a blast furnace to process his ore in an attempt to produce iron in Algeria rather than exporting the iron ore overseas.

Consider Bassano's blast furnace first. The historiographical context is provided by Third World dependency theorists from André Gunder Frank and Celso Furtado to Immanuel Wallerstein and Theotonio Dos Santos who have argued that the Third World as a whole has failed to industrialize because during the colonial era the Western nations "underdeveloped" these regions by the economic policies and practices they pursued. Looked at from this standpoint, the case of Bône raises some intriguing questions, for there was a moment at the beginning of French

Illustration 3.2   Marquis de Bassano's blast furnace at L'Allelick, 1847
(Bibliothèque Nationale Cabinet d'Estampes).

colonialization when some people thought the industrialization of Bône was imminent due to Bassano's iron works. Built in 1846 within easy walking distance of the gates of Bône, Bassano's blast furnace at l'Allelick utilized iron ore from Bassano's La Meboudja mine. *La Seybouse*, the local Bône newspaper and only the second paper to be published in Algeria, was beside itself. It saluted 1846 as "the era of a new life for Bône," and crowed about

... the immense importance of M. de Bassano's enterprise. In a few months we will see its advantages in the progressive growth of the population, by the public activity, by the visits to our region, which has been too neglected up until now, of influential people whose opinion once converted to our cause will win us sympathy and will encourage the establishment of new industries.[31]

A few short years later, however, the iron works shut down after producing only a few tons of cast iron. Bassano's concession was revoked in 1851 for failure to develop his mine sufficiently. Although it could be argued that the other concessionnaires had done even less, the bottom line is that Bassano's blast furnace failed. Some say the cost of production was too high and the local market too small. Some say it was too costly and inefficient to import two tons of coal from France to produce every ton of iron. But if so, why were the forests surrounding Bône not used? After all, the Berber Kabyles used wood in the Edough to make charcoal; the forests of England were certainly utilized during the Industrial Revolution. In any case, however, the era was not propitious for such a venture – not with the financial crisis of 1847, not with the Revolution of 1848.

Yet Bassano's failure was not the end of l'Allelick; far from it. By

1851 it had interested none other than the Pereires who, with French and German backing, took it over and produced a million tons of cast iron between the end of 1853 and the beginning of 1855. But this venture failed ultimately too, primarily because the Meboudja mine was simply not rich enough to supply sufficient quantities of iron ore to the l'Allelick blast furnace. Nonetheless, it was "the only attempt at implanting a metallurgical industry on a large scale in Algeria" in the nineteenth century.[32] In fact, no other serious attempt was made to produce iron in Algeria until independence. It was not until 1955 during the Algerian Revolution that the French, in a last-ditch effort to woo the Algerians from the FLN, drew up the so-called Plan de Constantine, which included plans to build a steel mill outside Bône. Nothing came of it, but after independence in 1962 the Algerians hired the British and Russians to build the steel mill at Duzerville, renamed El Hadjar. Today this mill, run by the state steel company, is the single largest steel mill complex in the whole of North Africa.[33]

This leads us to consider the Talabots and their mines.

> *It was a French organization which built from 1859 to 1863 a carriage route from Beirut to Damascus. The* Compagnie des Chemins de Fer de Paris à Orléans *and the* Chemins de Fer Paris-Lyon-Méditerranée, *controlled by the investor Paulin Talabot, held shares in it. These two companies transported travelers and merchandise from Paris to Damascus by rail, sea, and road.*[34]

Paulin Talabot, the head of the family, was unquestionably one of the most important businessmen of the Second Empire; at the same time he was a Saint-Simonian and close associate of Père Enfantin himself. Paulin was involved in railroad building: he built the Alès-Beaucaire (with his brother Leon) and Paris-Saint-Germain lines, which were important in perfecting railroad construction techniques; and the Lyon-Marseille line, which became part of the giant Paris-Lyon-Méditerranée (PLM) network. Paulin was involved in mining: he exploited mines in Provence and Languedoc, and coal mines at Grand Combe. He was involved in banking: while the Pereires founded the Crédit Mobilier, he launched the Société Générale as well as the Société Générale Algérienne. He was involved in the rebuilding of Paris: while the Perieres built the rue de Rivoli, he opened up the boulevard de Magenta and the rue Turbigo. Paulin was involved in shipping: he controlled the majority of French shipping in the Mediterranean with the Compagnie des Messageries maritimes. He was involved in port construction: his Docks de Marseilles constructed and exploited the basins of Joliette. He was involved in the Ottoman Empire and Italy and Egypt as well as France: his Société d'Etudes pour le percement de l'isthme de Suez would have been chosen to build the Suez Canal had it not been for the intrigues of the Empress's cousin, although with his close ties to Napoleon, Talabot came out ahead more often than not.[35]

Significantly, Paulin's Mediterranean and Levantine outlook corresponded more closely to Enfantin's vision than did the Periere's north Atlantic orientation. Also, Paulin understood better than the Perieres what we would call today the vertical integration of industry, which he derived of course from the doctrines of Saint-Simon. This is where Algeria played an important role in the Talabot empire. For Talabot's "Mediterranean dream" consisted in "the exploitation of the mines of the Bône region, which would feed his coal mines in the Grand-Combe by means of rapid transport in his ships of the Compagnie générale transatlantique, relayed by his Algerian railroad cars and those of the PLM."[36] At the center of this grandiose plan was the Mokta el Hadid mine near Bône, the single richest iron mine in all of Algeria.

So even before Fournel had finished his surveys, three of the four iron mines in the Bône region were conceded in 1845 to the Talabots or their close associates; the fourth mine went to Bassano. Thus, the production of iron ore in North Africa became a virtual Talabot monopoly. In fact, "the Talabot's had the firm intention of constructing an ironworks in Algeria."[37] This was in 1848; combined with Bassano's blast furnace, this is the situation which led the leading Saint-Simonian journal to foresee Bône becoming the "Saint Etienne of Algeria." The prophecy was not exactly fulfilled, however. In the first place, the areas around the mines were hardly safe from attacks by the Algerians. Second, Talabot's plans for constructing a steelworks "ran up against the inflexible opposition of the masters of Le Creusot [the Schneiders]," who "threatened to exclude Algerian iron ore from the French market, and Paulin Talabot was forced to give in to this veto."[38] Third, the richest veins were located sometimes just outside the boundaries of the concession, and the government refused to redraw them. Lastly, the richest vein at Ain Mokra was not even discovered until later. For these and other reasons, including lack of capital and shortage of labor, all three Talabot concessions were revoked by the government in 1849 and not restored until 1852 by which time Louis Napoleòn had carried out his successful coup d'état and launched the Second Empire.[39]

With Napoleon III in power, things began to look up for the Talabots. They now had the Emperor's ear thanks to his cousin, prince Napoleon. But the turning point came in 1857 when the Mokta el Hadid mine was discovered and the concession went to the Talabots. The mine consisted of a vein 2,500 meters long which varied between ten and fifty meters in width; it was magnetite, a particularly rich variety of ore which yielded up to seventy percent pure iron. Next, the three Talabot mines were combined to form a single company to exploit all the holdings with a capital of more than eighteen million francs. And the head of the board of directors? Paulin Talabot.[40]

It is at this point that Talabot dreams his Mediterranean dream to vertically integrate his coal from northern France with his iron ore from Algeria; no longer is he thinking about building a steelworks in Algeria. This is also the historical moment when the Mokta el Hadid mine plays a key role in the development of the French and European steel industry. By the early 1860s the Bessemer process of producing steel had become practicable. The only problem was that it required nonphosphorous ore which England had in abundance, but which continental Europe generally lacked. Yet it so happened that ore from the Mokta el Hadid was low in phosphorous. Therefore, the Makta el Hadid filled a niche for a decade as the only French supply (along with that of Elba) of nonphosphorous iron ore necessary for the Bessemer process. "The spread of the Bessemer process was henceforth tied – if large-scale production was desired – to Algerian supplies. Owner of mines, directing the means of transport, tied to powerful banks [the Rothschild's], the Talabot's had the possibility of making a fortune from the Algerian soil."[41]

Thus, we have the "paradox of men identified with a socialist creed" inspiring the industrial spurt of the Second Empire.[42] Talabot achieved, moreover, the vertical integration he desired by allying with the Société des Acieries de Firminy so that between them they controlled Algerian iron ore mines, coal mines in the Gard, and factories in the Tarn. In short, the 1860s and especially 1870s were the heyday of the development of a European steel industry; as demand rose the price of iron ore rose even faster, especially after the early 1870s. From ten francs per ton at the port of Bône, the price for Mokta el Hadid ore climbed to twenty-five francs per ton.

But what technology giveth, technology taketh away. By 1880 the Thomas-Gilchrist process had been invented, and the technological window that had made the fortune of the Mokta el Hadid and Talabot closed. Where nonphosphorous ore was necessary for the Bessemer process, phosphorous-rich ore was required for Thomas-Gilchrist; where Algerian ore from the Talabot's Mokta was low in phosphorous, the Schneider's Lorraine ore was high in phosphorous. The Schneiders bought the Thomas-Gilchrist patents, and where Britain with its nonphosphorous ore relied on Bessemer, continental Europe with its phosphrous-rich ore adopted the Thomas-Gilchrist process. In any case, Talabot had long since made his personal fortune. The "Mokta had thus profited from two important facts. The first was the discovery of the Bessemer process, which could only be utilized insofar as Algerian ore was obtained. The second was the industrial growth which followed the crisis of 1872."[43]

Two other aspects of Talabot's development of the Mokta el Hadid mine demonstrate how it impinged directly on the growth of Bône. The richest vein of the Mokta el Hadid was discovered in 1857, and mining began in 1860. At this point a problem arose: how to transport the iron ore to Bône for shipment to Europe? Talabot was willing to build a 20-mile-long railroad from Ain Mokra to the Seybouse river, which empties into the Mediterranean at Bône, but the cost of importing construction materials and buying property along the right-of-way was prohibitive. It took Talabot four years before Emperor Napoleon declared the line in the public interest, and then only thanks to the maneuvers of prince Napoleon. The railroad may have been short and slow (it was dubbed the "Tortillard," a local train which makes innumerable stops), but when it was finished in 1861 it was the only railroad in Algeria other than the one between Algiers and Oran.[44]

Production at the Mokta el Hadid began in earnest in 1865, but Talabot ran up against another obstacle two years later. Talabot wanted to extend the rail line from the Seybouse River directly to the docks of Bône so he could avoid having to transship the iron ore. Fine; the government declared this extension in the public interest in 1867, but when Talabot proceeded to build warehouses at dockside, the government cried foul: Talabot was building on government land. Adroit politician that he was, Talabot threatened to lay off all his workers; the newspaper *La Seybouse* declared that the government's action meant the ruin of Bône; and in France Talabot paid a visit to the Minister of War. The Minister of War caved in to Talabot, and throughout the nineteenth century the Mokta el-Hadid company was the single largest presence at the port of Bône.[45]

That was the way things got done during the Second Empire, from Haussmann's rebuilding of Paris to Talabot's building of Bône's infrastructure. An even better example was Talabot's crowning Algerian venture: the Société Générale Algérienne (SGA). The SGA was formed in 1865 when Napoleon agreed to exchange 100,000 ha. in Algeria on extremely generous terms – one franc per hectare per year for fifty years – in return for a 100 million franc loan to spend on public works projects in Algeria. In the competition to form a limited liability company to raise the money first, the two leading groups were headed by none other than Paulin Talabot and Isaac Pereire. This time Talabot bested Pereire by raising the capital first and formed the SGA. Headed by Paulin Talabot, the board of directors consisted of his friends.[46]

Talabot's SGA victory was also Enfantin's victory, for along with the construction of the Suez Canal and the *mise en valeur* of Egypt, the colonization of Algeria was the chief item on the latter's Saint-Simonian agenda. And the form Enfantin wanted Algerian colonization to take was precisely that of the SGA, that is, a large-scale state undertaking which would supercede the military. Thus, Enfantin's Saint-Simonian dream for Algeria was realized by Paulin Talabot's SGA. But there was more: the preferred field of activity of both Enfantin and Talabot was the province of Constantine in general and the region of Bone in particular. This is where Enfantin had wanted to locate his *école normale de la colonisation*; this is where Talabot's mines were located. Thus, it should come as no surprise that nearly ninety percent of the SGA's 100,000 ha. from the state were located in Constantine province, while Algiers and Oran together split there maining ten percent. The SGA founded five villages to spur colonization in Algeria, and two of these were located in the Bône region: Randon and Ain Mokra. It was no coincidence that Ain Mokra was also the site of Talabot's Mokta el Hadid mine.

As if this were not enough, Talabot used SGA funds to pay for initial construction of the port of Bône, all the better to ship his iron ore overseas and achieve thereby the vertical integration of his commercial operations. Perhaps it took a Talabot or a Talabot's money to galvanize construction of the port. Certainly it was realized from the beginning of the French conquest that a viable port was necessary, that a viable port meant a deep-water port, and that such a port would have to be built virtually from scratch. Before the 1830 invasion there had been no port, but simply an anchorage sheltered from the prevailing winds by the Edough Mountain chain. This proved insufficient in storms such as the one in 1835 which grounded twelve ships against the shore. Yet after the takeover of Constantine city in 1837, headquarters of the province were moved from Bône to Constantine and interest in construction of a port went with it, since port construction began at Philippeville, another town located closer to Constantine rather than at Bône. When a group of coral fishers who had arrived from Tunisia four years previously left Bône in 1838 to settle near the Tunisian border, things did not look good for a port.[47]

While port activity vegetated, discussions over construction dragged on. No fewer than three plans were proposed before one was officially adopted in 1845; it took another ten years to receive final approval from Paris. Finally, construction of an outer harbor plus breakwater was carried out desultorily between 1856 and 1869. This is where the SGA, and through it the Makta el-Hadid mine, played a part. Loading ore onto ships in the Seybouse estuary was hampered since the tendency of the river to silt up with mud prevented larger ships from being used.

Talabot's interest in resolving the Mokta's problem through the SGA was expressed in cold cash: of the total 7,156,000 francs it cost to build the port, as much as 5,200,000 francs may have been provided by the SGA. "'If the Saint-Simonians were unable to make Bône an 'Algerian Saint-Etienne' as they had hoped, it is no less true that it was due to the iron of the Mokta that one must attribute the creation of the modern port.'"[48] And what was good for the port was good for the Mokta. "The creation of this port has had as an immediate effect the reduction of the price of the iron ore of the Mokta el Hadid by two francs per ton to the profit of the metallurgical industry of the *métropole*.[49]

Despite this and its other activities, the SGA foundered at the end of the Second Empire. A grave economic crisis affected Algeria and especially Constantine province in the late 1860s. An epidemic of locusts destroyed crops in 1866, a severe earthquake occurred in southern Constantine, a cholera epidemic broke out, and, following a dry summer and cold winter, a major famine decimated the Algerians in 1867. Concentrated in Constantine, the SGA was hard hit; land earmarked for European colonization was rented back to the Algerians. In addition, there was Talabot's fixation with Egypt. After the opening of the Suez Canal in 1869, the khedive Ismail of Egypt embarked on a new round of development schemes ranging from railroads in the Nile delta to the rebuilding of Cairo, and took out new loans from French and English banks, including the SGA. Already by the mid-1870s it was clear that Ismail was insolvent and Egyptian finances were placed in the hands of the English and French; in 1879 Ismail was deposed; in 1882 the British took over Egypt. But well before the final denouement, Talabot's bad Egyptian loans coupled with the economic crisis in Constantine province had led very nearly to the collapse of the SGA, and in 1877 it was lucky to reorganize as the Compagnie Algérienne. Thus it happened that the Saint-Simonian SGA founded during the Second Empire was transformed into the capitalistic Compagnie Algérienne under the Third Republic. The ideals of Père Enfantin jettisoned; it became one of the most powerful financial institutions in Algeria and the largest enterprise for colonization in North Africa.

The People of Bône

First, the French occupied the buildings of Bône. Second, they grabbed the land on the plain outside Bône. Third, they took over the cork oak forests. Fourth, they mined the area for minerals. Fifth, they displaced the Algerians and peopled Bône with Europeans.

The French invasion of 1830 ruptured entirely the centuries-long history of Annaba. Where there had been an estimated two or three thou-

number of persons

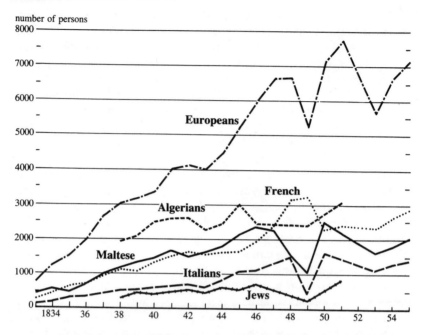

Figure 3.1 Bône population, 1833–55. *Source:* TEFA, 1833–51, 1853–5.

sand Algerians before, they had all fled at the time of the French take-over, and only drifted back desultorily. In fact, we have no record of any Algerians living in Annaba-become-Bône before 1838, when we find two thousand. For the French and other Europeans, the situation was the exact reverse. From a literal handful of traders and others before 1830, there appeared first a military population, and in its wake followed a civilian population. From slightly more than 750 in 1833, the number of European settlers grew to approximately 3,000 five years later in 1838, to 5,000 in 1845, 7,000 in 1850, and nearly 10,000 in 1861 (Figure 3.1).

What we see happening in Bône after 1830, therefore, is the peopling of a colonial city totally different from the population of protocolonial Annaba before 1830. Literally from scratch, from a demographic *tabula rasa*, we see a people forming itself. And one of, if not the most striking, characteristics of the people of Bône – and one with profound implications for the shape that this colonial society would take later – is the fact that from the very beginning of the colonial period there were more Europeans than Algerians in this city on the North African littoral. and Outnumbered three to two in 1838, already by the mid-1840s there was only one Algerian for every two Europeans, a proportion that was to remain constant through much of the colonial period, in fact until the

86

late 1920s and early 1930s when rural migrants driven from the land swelled the Algerian population of Bône.

Moreover – and this is the second main characteristic of the Bône population – the Europeans differed demographically in quite striking ways from the native Algerians and Jews. Whereas both the Algerians and especially the Jews exhibited demographic features characteristic of settled populations in this early period, the Europeans resembled nothing so much as a temporary, migrant population which settled down and took root only gradually over time.

The third main feature of this colonial population is that while the French may have been the masters of Bône – lording it over the other Europeans as well as the Algerians – they were a minority even among the Europeans, and a small minority at that (Figure 3.1). In the early years of colonial rule the French numbered slightly more than one-third of all Europeans. The other Europeans were predominantly Maltese and Italians. The Maltese migrated in large numbers especially in the early years of French rule from the island of Malta in the Mediterranean between Sicily and Tunisia, a short sailing distance from Bône. So many migrated in fact that there were as many Maltese as French in Bône during the first fifteen years of French rule. The Italians, also numerous, migrated mostly seasonally, and renewed their Bône colony continuously through migration.

The number of Europeans grew steadily overall, but there were particular years when the population dropped, for example, in 1849 and 1853.[50] Gaining a demographic foothold in North Africa proved a precarious matter, and periodic population declines only underscore the difficulties. Nondemographic events could also affect population trends adversely. In 1845 financial crisis, in 1846 an Algerian revolt, in 1848 the revolution in France, not to mention discovery of gold in California – all these had negative effects on the number of Europeans who came and stayed in Bône.[51]

More important still were the universal constants of birth and death. The people of Bône procreated at nearly the maximum biological rate possible, but they died off even more rapidly (Figure 3.2). In fact, the fourth key to understanding this population is that it simply could not reproduce itself, at least until the 1860s. "In the first period of the occupation the sanitary situation of this city and its environs was extremely poor; few inhabitants either military or civilian escaped the miasmatic influence of the locality; infections take generally a serious form; the numerous intermittent fevers become pernicious very rapidly and result in considerable mortality."[52] In the first decade of European settlement in Bône, the 1830s, the death rate surpassed 80 per 1,000 five times in seven years! After this the rate at which the Bônois died

87

births or deaths per thousand

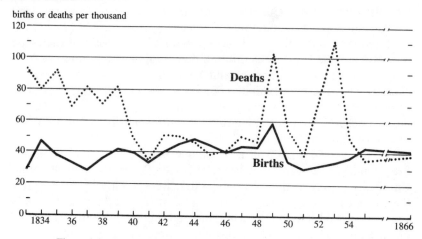

Figure 3.2 European crude birth and death rates, 1833–66. *Source:* TEFA, 1833–51, 1853–5, 1866.

declined generally, only to skyrocket periodically. In 1849, in 1852, in 1853, and in 1868 more than ten percent of the population died off each year. Cholera was the main killer; there were epidemics in 1832, 1835, 1836, 1837, 1849, 1850, 1851, and 1867.[53] Now, cholera is a body delimiting disease, that is, a person is weakened rapidly and drastically through dehydration, but it is not necessarily fatal. Yet among people who are not strong physically due, for example, to poor diets, or when the process of dehydration cannot be countered rapidly enough, cholera can kill a person within hours and decimate a community within days.

There was typhus, too. An epidemic in 1868 followed the 1867 cholera outbreak, and together they exacerbated a famine which had appeared already in 1865–6 to make the late 1860s the most murderous years of French rule, especially for the Algerians in eastern Algeria.

Finally, malaria was endemic in the Bône region. There were deadly epidemics in 1832, 1833, and 1834. But in early 1834 Dr. François Maillot arrived in Bône and began to work in the military hospital.

> *In 1805 Mungo Park journeyed to the upper Niger and all the Europeans died of malaria. In 1816–17 Capt. James Tuckey explored the Congo River and nineteen out of fifty-four Europeans died of malaria. In 1832 Macgregor Laird reconnoitered the Niger and 39 of 48 Europeans succumbed to malaria. Cinchona bark was known to cure malaria long before it was known why. Native to the Andes, cinchona was disseminated primarily through Spanish Catholics; Protestant Oliver Cromwell is alleged to have refused the "popish" remedy when he was dying of malaria. The British Royal Botanic Gardens at Kew were instrumental in first stealing cinchona from Latin America and then cultivating it on plantations in India*

and Indonesia. In 1820 two French chemists extracted the alkaloid of quinine from cinchona bark. By 1830 quinine was being produced commercially.

But quinine was not necessarily being consumed, and this is where Maillot fits in. Instead of large amounts, small doses were prescribed; instead of immediately taking quinine, it was used only after the onset of fever. Moreover, contemporary medical wisdom prescribed purgatives and bleedings, which only further weakened people already sick. From 1834 on Maillot changed all this in Bône; he was one of the first anywhere to use quinine in significant amounts as a prophylactic. Where only two of every seven soldiers admitted to the Bône military hospital in 1833 left there alive, nineteen of every twenty were discharged healthy between 1834 and 1836. "Consequently, sick soldiers began fleeing other hospitals to come to Maillot's."[54] Maillot achieved conspicuous results, but he was one doctor among many, malaria was one disease among many, and the total Bône death rate declined only gradually. Twenty years later in 1852 and 1853 Maillot had to deal with epidemics as severe as those of 1833 and 1834.

In 1835 Maillot described his methods to the medical establishment in Paris. In the following years he published his results in treatises such as My Last Word on the Fevers of Bône. *In 1854 Macgregor Laird stayed on the Niger and Benue rivers a total of 112 days, and as a result of quinine prophylaxis none of the European crew died. In 1880 the protozoan that causes malaria was discovered. In 1897 the Anopheles mosquito was identified as the vector of malaria. By 1881, near the end of his life, Maillot was lionized as a hero of French science: "It is thanks to Maillot that Algeria has become a French land; it is he who closed and sealed forever this tomb of Christians."[55]*

Periodic outbreaks of epidemic disease notwithstanding, the relation between births and deaths, between living and dying, gradually improved in Bône, and by the 1860s the number of those born increasingly outnumbered those dying. The first year births exceeded deaths in colonial Bône was 1845; in the last four years of Napoleon's Second Empire births regularly outnumbered deaths except for the great dying of 1868 caused by famine, cholera, and typhus.

Different Europeans died at different rates; the French died much more frequently than the Maltese and Italians. In the first twenty years of colonial Bône the non-French Europeans far outnumbered the French, but more French died than all the other Europeans combined. More than fifteen percent of all the Bône French died in the single year 1853; it is the highest death rate recorded among the Europeans.[56]

Since the Europeans of Bône could not reproduce themselves as rapidly as they were cut down, the population grew only through inmigra-

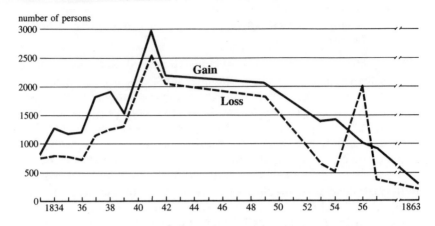

Figure 3.3   European transiency, 1833–63. *Sources:* APCA, Mouvement de la population européenne pendant 1849, 1854–7, 1863; TEFA, 1837–9, 1841–6, 1852–8.

tion. However, the number of people leaving was so high that it required an even greater number of arrivals for the population to increase at all. Those who arrived combined with those who departed made for an extremely volatile, transient population (Figure 3.3). In fact, the very high rate of population turnover is the final major characteristic which distinguishes the people of colonial Bône. In the first year of European settlement, the number of those who arrived and departed was twice the city's total population – the population turned over twice in its first year! Throughout the first decade, the Bône population turned over in less than a year on average. After this, the relative number of those who arrived and departed decreased somewhat, but in the early and middle 1850s the European population still renewed itself completely once every three-and-a-half years. Not only was this extremely high rate of population turnover higher than that of most nineteenth-century cities elsewhere in Europe and America; it also indicates how unsettled rather than settled the European population of Bône was in the first several decades after the French conquest.[57]

Two additional indices, the ratio of men to women and place of birth, only confirm further the demographic portrait of this European population created from scratch and which settled down only gradually over time. In terms of the proportion of men to women, it is a truism that men tend to migrate more than women, single men more than single women, particularly single men in the productive age range of fifteen to forty-nine years. This certainly happened in Bône (Figure 3.4). At the beginning of French rule in 1833 there were fully seven times as

number of males to one female

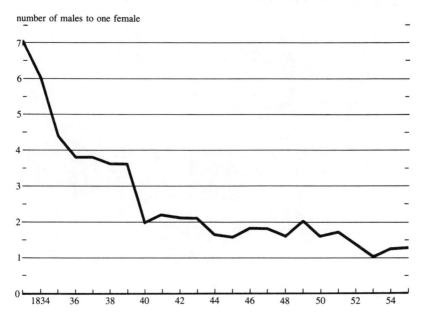

Figure 3.4 European male/female ratios, 1833–55. *Source:* TEFA, 1833–51, 1853–5.

many men as women. In the next decade there was a large decline in the proportion of men, but in 1843 they still outnumbered women two to one. Following this big early drop, there occurred a slower, more gradual one until by the end of the Second Empire in 1870 European men outnumbered women by only five to four.[58] Considering the various European groups, proportionately more French women migrated to Bône than other European women (data not included here).

Where these European residents of Bône were born indicates again the extent to which they constituted a migrant population (Figure 3.5). The earliest data on birthplace, which is from 1848, indicate that less than one in every six Europeans were born in Algeria, and the rest had migrated from Europe. Nearly twenty years later in 1866, more Europeans were born in Algeria but the proportion was still only one of every three. By this date, however, there were slightly more Maltese and Italians than French born in Bône, which indicates that the other Europeans were settling down more rapidly than the French.

Conclusion

We can conclude this discussion of early French colonialism in Bône, especially economic colonialism, with some general reflections. As a

91

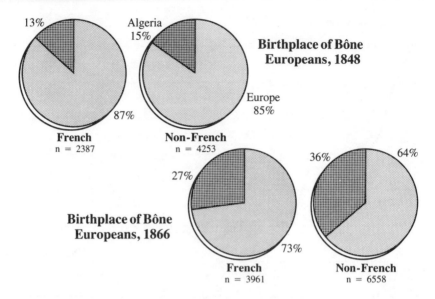

13%

Algeria 15%

Birthplace of Bône Europeans, 1848

Europe 85%

87%

French
n = 2387

Non-French
n = 4253

27%

Birthplace of Bône Europeans, 1866

36%

64%

73%

French
n = 3961

Non-French
n = 6558

Figure 3.5 Birthplace of Bône Europeans, 1848 and 1866. *Source:* APCA, *Listes nominatives*, 1848, 1866.

typical colonial city, what went on inside Bône between 1830 and 1870 was determined primarily by what went on outside Bône. Rather than a patient, intensive sort of *mise en valeur*, we witness the crude activities characteristic of booty capitalism intent on extracting the forest and mineral resources quickly, efficiently, and completely. Moreover, it is a situation in which big businessmen predominate over individuals acting in isolation. Fournel may have surveyed the mines, but it was Talabot who exploited them – and reaped the profits. As such, colonial Bône constitutes a textbook case of a dependent economy oriented towards export. After abortive attempts by Bassano and Talabot to produce iron in Algeria, Talabot had to be content to export iron ore to France and elsewhere to be smelted. Moreover, it can be shown that the rhythm of exports shipped from Bône corresponds closely to the rhythm of production in Constantine province: virtually all that was produced in Bône was exported out of Bône.[59]

The consequences of these mostly economic developments determined the shape of colonial Bône at least between 1830 and 1870. Thus, the first railroad in the area was built to haul iron ore, not passengers. The impetus for construction of a port came from the desire to export minerals more than the need to transport people. A road to the Edough Mountains was built to reach the cork oak forest, not to settle the area

Illustration 3.3   Napoleon III visits Makta el Hadid Mine, 1865
(Bibliothèque Nationale Cabinet d'Estampes).

with Europeans. What occurred outside Bône, therefore, reverberated throughout the city.

In short, the fulcrum of the local economy was located not in Bône, but somewhere between Bône and the Mokta el-Hadid mine twenty miles away at Ain Mokra. The Mokta alone employed two out of every three miners working in Algeria during the 1870s. This labor force at Ain Mokra contributed very substantially to the local Bône economy. Every Saturday night the narrow-gage "Tortillard" transported the miners to Bône. No wonder there were nearly 150 bars in Bône, one for every 40 Europeans. Moreover, the canteens at the mines which supplied food and other goods to the workers bought their goods almost entirely from shopkeepers in Bône. Truly it could be said that "the local petty commerce lived almost entirely on the close proximity – providential for them – of the exploitations of the Mokta el-Hadid company."[60] No wonder that when Napoléon III visited Algeria in 1865 he paid a visit to the Mokta mine as well as to the city of Bône; no wonder that the main iconographic artifact from his trip to Bône is a photograph of the Emperor and his entourage outside Ain Mokra at the mine site enjoying a *diffa*, a traditional Algerian feast under a tent.

PART II

Bône: The formation of a
settler colonial city, 1870–1920

4

The urban economy and the
regional setting

> *Algeria buys nearly all the manufactured goods that it uses. . . . The most
> ordinary piece of sheet metal, the smallest pair of tongs, the most ordinary
> ball of thread, the smallest nail, the thinnest candle all come from abroad,
> as well as nearly all of the cloth and dyes, all metal and machine made
> goods: all railroad equipment, automobiles, arms and munitions; but also
> a large proportion of the chemical products and all medicines, ice cream,
> glass, ceramic tiles – with a few exceptions – cement, lime, tiles, up to and
> including the bronze statues which celebrate colonial glory and which are
> cast in France. . . . Lead pipe – and there is lead in Algeria –, zinc gutters
> and containers – and there is zinc in Algeria –, paper and pasteboard boxes
> – and there is esparto grass in Algeria –, mineral water – and Algeria is
> rich in mineral springs –, the bulk of the marble – and there is marble in
> Algeria –, comes from abroad.*
>
> *Algerian exports are characterized by the overwhelming preponderance
> of raw materials which constitute 96 percent of its exports in value. The
> only manufactured goods which Algeria exports besides some chemical
> products, are cigars, handworked furs and fabrics.* – Gilbert Meynier[1]

The same could be said of colonial Bône. The economy of Bône –
and Annaba before it – can be likened to a funnel through which products
from the Mediterranean and beyond arrive and are exchanged for goods
that are literally scraped out of its interior and exported. By and large
this trade consists of raw materials exported and manufactured goods
imported. The structure of this trade is colonial; the colonial city, especially the colonial port city, acts as the primary mechanism which
channels this trade into and out of the colony; and a settler colonial
port city is one in which the demand of a significant settler population
is reflected in the total volume and nature of trade.

The regional economy

To get at the heart of the Bône economy we have to look at it from a
distance. And when we do, it is not I, but other authors who characterize

97

the structure of this trade, and the local economy engaged in it, as a dependent economy. Listen to what they have to say.

Dependent from the point of view of commerce, dependent from the point of view of capital, Algeria's situation is a typically colonial one.[2]

It is quite evident that the essential thing about [the iron and phosphates extracted] was that it responded to the needs of European industry . . . by engaging only in those operations in Algeria strictly necessary for transport to Europe. In this regard the *département* of Bône offers a perfect image of a dependent economy. . . .[3]

The relatively important mineral resources of the Bône region constitute one of its most characteristic riches. But only an infinitesimal fraction of these riches goes to the profit of the department. On the one hand, nearly all of what is produced is exported as raw material, without being transformed in Algeria; on the other hand, the bulk of the profits generated thereby do not remain in the region, but are transferred abroad, which is also where the investment capital comes from. . . . Mining production seems to be attached to another economy besides that of the department. It does not make its own definite imprint, does not seek to develop the local economy.[4]

There is no better way to understand the dependent nature of the Bône regional economy, the historical development of underdevelopment, than by examining the phosphates of Tebessa and the iron ore of the Ouenza.

Mining and minerals

In November of 1975 King Hassan of Morocco called for a "green march" to the Spanish Sahara on the southern border of Morocco, and 350,000 unarmed volunteers undertook a peaceful invasion of the Spanish Sahara where they claimed it for their king. The Spanish Sahara was the last Spanish colony in North Africa except for the tiny outpost of Ceuta on the Mediterranean not far east of Tangiers. In 1975 Hassan thought that he could take advantage of Franco's recent death to present Spain with a fait accompli, and at the same time boost his sagging stock with the Moroccan people. The plan was to divide up the Spanish Sahara between Morocco to the north and Mali and Mauretania to the south. The area was large – 266,000 square kilometers – but the population was mostly desert nomads and miniscule – 75,000 in all; the only significant town was El-Ayoun with 40,000 people. Morocco, already one of the world's biggest phosphates producers, was interested primarily in the Spanish phosphates. The idea was to build a gigantic open air conveyor belt in the desert at Bou-Craa along which the phosphates would ride to the port of El-Ayoun, built especially for the purpose, and from there shipped around the world.

Hassan thought no one would object besides Spain except maybe Algeria. He was right about Spain – the Spanish were preoccupied with restoring democracy after forty years of Franco – but wrong about Algeria. Algeria became the main backer of the Saharawis, the inhabitants of the Spanish Sahara, who promptly declared independence in reaction to Hassan's green march, and launched a guerrilla movement against the occupiers of their began desert land. Finding the Saharawi resistance not worth the mineral treasure, Mali and Mauretania bowed out early on, which left Morocco to battle the Saharawis and their Algerian backers. After nearly ten years, a war scare between Morocco and Algeria, and deep divisions within the Organization of African Unity over the issue, the conflict has still not been resolved. It is hard to imagine such a struggle continuing for such a long period of time, that is, if it had not been for the phosphates....[5]

Two hundred and twenty five kilometers south of Bône are the largest phosphate and iron ore deposits in Algeria. One such area is the mountains of Tebessa, where phosphates formed during the Eocene period occur in alternating layers with limestone.[6] By the nineteenth century in western Europe there was a great demand for phosphates for use as fertilizer to literally fuel Europe's agricultural revolution of new crops and new techniques. In the case of Tebessa, it was an Algerian who originally discovered phosphates there in 1885. How Salah ben Khelil cut in the secretary of the local commune, and together they sold the concession to Dominique Bertagna who transferred it to his brother Jérome, who sold it in turn to an English businessman in Bône acting on behalf of the Scottish firm Crookston Brothers; how the government was interpellated in Paris about the matter and the Minister of the Interior revoked the departmental prefect, and had Mayor Jérome Bertagna of Bône suspended from office and investigated for suspected influence peddling – all this is a later part of the story (see Chapter 6). For now, suffice it to say that it was two Scottish companies and not French ones that initially exploited this French "national treasure" that was the Tebessa phosphates.

Production began at several sites in the Tebessa Mountains between 1893 and 1895, but narrowed to one after the turn of the twentieth century, that of Djebel Kouif (*jabal*, Frenchified as *djebel*, is Arabic for mountain or hill). Kouif alone supplied the bulk of Algerian phosphates until the early 1960s when it finally petered out. In seventy years Djebel Kouif yielded thirty million tons of phosphates; in 1955, a not atypical year, it accounted for eighty-eight percent of all the phosphates produced in Algeria (Figure 4.1). All but twelve percent of the phosphates produced were exported, more than a quarter to France – where the company exploiting the Kouif deposits was headquartered – and nearly a third elsewhere in Europe. All this is in keeping with what we would expect of a dependent economy. "In 1954 every mining company was headquartered in Paris: we have already seen, moreover, that the

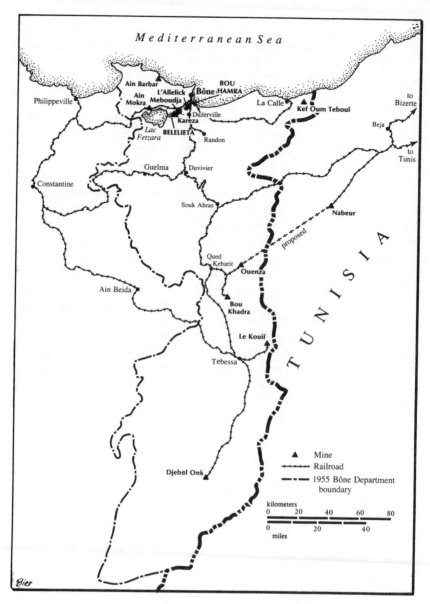

Figure 4.1   Map of mines and railroads in colonial Bône region. *Source:*
After Tomas, *Annaba*, p. 197.

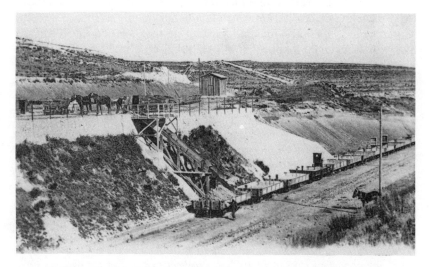

Illustration 4.1   Djebel Kouif phosphates mine, 1918 (collection of the author).

market for the minerals produced depended as much on the economic conjuncture in Europe as the technical capabilities of extraction."[7]

The explosive used to quarry the phosphates was liquid oxygen, but since the mineral was only sixty-five to seventy percent pure, the phosphates were dried as well as crushed and sorted to increase their phosphate content so that they were competitive on the world market. The large size of the Kouif mines plus the processing necessary before shipment by rail to Bône required a large-scale labor force. At its peak Kouif employed 1800 workers; in 1923 of more than 1500 workers, over sixty percent were Algerians, twenty percent convicts, nine percent Italian, and eight percent French. Even so, it was hard to find Algerians willing "to accept such difficult, dangerous work and for which they were paid a derisory salary."[8] Moreover, the region of Tebessa was little developed, and in fact had been the home of seminomadic Algerian sheepherders until very recently. Therefore, it was necessary to provide housing for the mine workers, and the company town of El Kouif was built in one of "the most underprivileged" areas of Algeria, and became a "genuine small city."[9]

By the time the Kouif deposits had been mined out, phosphates from an even larger exploitation were coming on line. Djebel Onk, located 92 kilometers south of Tebessa and 319 kilometers from Bône, had reserves conservatively estimated at 200 million tons. Geologically similar to Kouif, Djebel Onk phosphates were even lower in phosphate

101

content, and elaborate techniques were necessary to make it marketable. All this delayed exploitation which finally began only in 1966. The same Compagnie des Phosphates de Constantine that worked the Kouif deposits had received a concession for Djebel Onk in 1925. But in 1966 the company was nationalized, and today some of the phosphates produced are utilized in the superphosphates factory in Annaba and others are exported as far as China.[10]

> *The Société Nationale de~la Sidérurgie (SNS), or Algerian national steel company, dominates the Annaba economy today. Utilizing imported coke and iron ore from the Ouenza, the SNS steel mill at El Hadjar is the largest in North Africa.*
>
> *It is a long way from the village of Duzerville founded by former General Monck d'Uzer in the 1830s, after he had been kicked politely out of the army, to El Hadjar today – which is what the Algerians call Duzerville these days. El Hadjar is nine kilometers from downtown Annaba, but most of the upper echelon workers live in Annaba and commute, certainly all of the foreigners do. Stop and talk to an Annabi on the street and chances are good he works at El Hadjar, excellent that one of his relatives does, for certain that a friend or friend of a friend does.*

The Ouenza saga all began when a prospector by the name of Wetterlé discovered copper and iron in the Ouenza region, 190 kilometers south of Bône and not far from Tebessa.[11] Originally from Alsace-Lorraine, Wetterlé, along with many others, formed one of the largest waves of immigrants in Algerian history which occurred when the province was lost to Germany in the 1870 Franco-Prussian war. Wetterlé settled in Souk Ahras, the birthplace of St. Augustine and located between Bône and Ouenza, and began excavations in the old Roman mines around Ouenza. The Romans had been searching for copper, a precious metal, and had ignored the iron ore, which was too bulky to transport economically, and Wetterlé was following in their footsteps.

Looking for copper, Wetterlé found iron ore, a mountain of it. Today the hill of the Ouenza actually looks like a huge dark garnet-red protuberance rising up in the middle of a large flat expanse. Limestone had been transformed into iron carbonate through metasomatosis, which in turn had oxidized to form iron hematites. The iron ore formed thereby occurred in layers within the limestone along with some smaller veins of copper. Iron ore from the Ouenza is 53–58 percent pure, compared to only 40 percent for French ore from Lorraine, and more than 60 percent for the best Swedish ore used in making special steels. Reserves are conservatively estimated at 100–150 million tons. Given its geographical location, moreover, the Ouenza can be worked relatively cheaply as a vast open-pit mine.

Wetterlé was interested mainly in the copper, however, since it was worth twenty-five times more than iron at the time. In fact, before the Ouenza no one in Algeria had considered it economically profitable to transport iron long distances to market because it was worth so much less than copper – or lead or zinc for that matter. It is no coincidence that the Mokta el Hadid iron ore mine was close to the port of Bône as we have seen, and that by the time it gave out the same Mokta el Hadid company had already located another rich iron mine in western Algeria also close to the sea, that of Beni Saf, and in fact had built the port of Beni Saf so that "the mine is practically on the beach."[12]

In nineteenth-century Algeria iron was mined and transported to the nearest port where it was sold to an intermediary who shipped it to steel mills in Europe. "Algeria does not work its own ore, since it does not have coking coal; moreover, it does not sell the ore on the European market itself, because it does not have the ships to transport it."[13] Iron ore which sold for twenty francs/ton at an European mill sold for half that at the port of Bône. Add on another five francs for hauling the ore from the Ouenza to Bône, and you have iron ore worth twenty francs at a steel mill in Europe worth about five francs at the Ouenza. No wonder Wetterlé concentrated on the copper and did not bother with the iron ore. No wonder it took a financial visionary, a Talabot, for example, to realize that despite the low cost per ton the extremely large reserves of the Ouenza meant huge potential profits.

What happened was that Wetterlé's discovery spurred others to investigate, and in 1901 another prospector by the name of Pascal obtained a concession for the Ouenza copper plus the iron, which he had included just to be on the safe side. But while "it is geologists like H. Fournel [discoverer of the Mokta el Hadid mine] . . . or prospectors like G. Wetterlé and F. R. Pascal who discovered the mines . . . it was only possible for them to begin production with capital supplied by banks and European steel companies, especially French ones."[14] And the chief French steelmaker involved in the Ouenza affair was none other than the Schneiders of Le Creusot fame. With the Mokta el Hadid mine nearly exhausted, the Schneiders were casting about for new sources of ore, and so too was the Mokta el Hadid. This time Schneider beat the Mokta to new iron ore supplies by obtaining Pascal's Ouenza concession through an intermediary in 1901.

Normally, this would have been considered the end of the matter. But the Ouenza was no ordinary mine, and the Ouenza no ordinary affair. Figuring 100 million tons at twenty francs/ton – a conservative estimate – adds up to two billion French francs at pre-1914 rates. Not surprisingly, therefore, others were interested; they were not all French, and there was the rub. The Schneiders main competitor was the Dutch firm of Muller based in Rotterdam. Muller himself was no stranger to

Algeria where he already ran a mine. But Muller's main activity was
shipping, and his main clients were German. It was no coincidence that
Muller's headquarters were located in Rotterdam at the mouth of the
Rhine, for his main clients were the German steel barons upriver in the
Ruhr valley, namely, Krupp and Thyssen. In fact Krupp was one of
Muller's best clients.

Muller's plan was to obtain Pascal's concession to the Ouenza mine.
And that is what he did, for in 1902 the intermediary had Pascal revoke
the agreement with Schneider and instead cede the concession to Muller,
who formed in turn the Société concessionnaire des Mines de l'Ouenza
in 1903. In Muller's firm Krupp, Thyssen and other foreign, especially
German, interests figured prominently. Outflanked but not yet outdone,
Schneider applied for a lease to the *minière*, or above-ground exploitation, in 1902 and when he received it in 1903, he formed the Société
d'Etudes de l'Ouenza. Two-thirds of the shares were held by French
steelmakers – one-fourth of those were in Schneider's hands – and the
rest were divided between British, Belgian, and German steelmakers.
Among the Germans figured Krupp, apparently hedging his bets should
Muller lose out.[15]

Two companies and one mine – but how is that possible? It is possible
because outdated French mining legislation, first formulated in 1810,
distinguished between a *mine*, or underground mine – Pascal's original
concession now held by Muller – and a *minière*, or aboveground mineral
outcropping – Schneider's lease. Unchanged substantially since the early
nineteenth century, this legislation applied to Algeria, since Algeria was
considered an integral part of France. In France, this antiquated legislation made little difference since few new mines were still being discovered in the late nineteenth century; in Algeria it made the Ouenza
affair possible.

At the end of 1903, therefore, the Ouenza affair began in earnest as
a battle between Schneider-Le Creusot and Muller-Krupp; to economics
had now been added politics in the form of nationalism. Although the
Algerian colonial administration clearly favored Schneider, competition
between the two lasted until 1908 when the Société d'Etudes paid off
Muller's Société concessionnaire handsomely and in exchange won control of both the underground and aboveground exploitation. At this
point, it looked as though the Ouenza affair was over, and Le Creu-
sot/Schneider had bested Muller. In fact, it was just getting rolling. This
was because mining the iron was connected inextricably to its transport
by rail to Bône, for as we have seen, it was virtually worthless to Le
Creusot or Krupp or anyone else in the ground at the Ouenza. "The
mine and the railroad were inseparable."[16]

Who then was going to build the railroad, the Schneider's Société d'Études, the private Bône-Guelma railroad which already operated a narrow-gage line between Bône and Tebessa, or the Algerian colonial government? It is only at this point that the Ouenza affair becomes really interesting, because any railroad built on French territory had to be authorized by Parliament, and Algeria was again considered an integral part of France rather than a colony like Tunisia, for example. In other words, the economic issue of building a railroad in Algeria now became a political issue fought out in Paris. The Ouenza now became a cause célèbre, and "for a long time a Parisian preoccupation."[17]

What Schneider and the Société d'Etudes wanted was for the Chamber of Deputies to authorize them to build their own railroad. The advantage of this plan was that it avoided utilizing the slow, narrow-gage Bône-Tebessa line, which was scarcely able to transport all the phosphates of Kouif from the Tebessa region just down the line from Ouenza let alone iron ore from Ouenza (Figure 4.1). But in proposing the construction of an entirely new railroad, the Schneiders opened up another whole can of worms. For if another railroad was to be built, and if it was to be the cheapest and shortest one over the easiest terrain, then it would have to run from Ouenza not to Bône but to theTunisian town of Nabeur linked already by rail to the Tunisian port of Bizerte. Bône and Algeria would have been bypassed altogether in favor of Bizerte and Tunisia.

The climax of the Ouenza affair, therefore, was the pitched battle fought between the Bônois and the Bizertians for the right of handling the Ouenza ore. The arguments pro and con – Bône versus Bizerte – were straightforward, but the denouement was a long time coming. In its favor Bône could argue that it was closer to Ouenza than Bizerte by sixty kilometers, and that it already had a port with a greater capacity than was necessary to handle the ore. But its trump card was that, after all, the Ouenza was in Algeria not Tunisia, and thus "Bône was by all indications the port of embarcation."[18] In its favor, Bizerte could argue that a railroad needed to be built a shorter distance to hook up with a line already connected to Bizerte, and moreover, that construction would cost much less per kilometer because the Tunisian terrain was flatter and more gently sloping. Finally, iron ore would make an excellent return cargo for ships already supplying the French naval base at Bizerte with coal. In short, Bizerte's strong suit was geography, but Bône held the trump in the form of politics which, after all, could override geographical considerations.

Sure enough, it was not economic realities so much as political interests which determined in the end the outcome of the Ouenza affair. Georges Clemenceau, head of the government, favored a railroad to Bône, and so did cabinet member Alexandre Millerand and Jonnart, the governor general of Algeria who had authorized the 1903 lease to

Schneider and had favored the Société d'Etudes all along. So, too, did the deputies who had received *parts de fondateur*, or founder's shares, in the proposed railroad, as well as "in Algeria itself, all the supporters of expansion, all the local potentates, all the press and even the *petite peuple* of Bône."[19] And then the fact that Clemenceau's brother Paul worked for Le Creusot as a consulting engineer, and that Jonnart had business connections with Le Creusot through his father-in-law could not have hurt.[20]

On the other side, however, were arrayed an odd but powerful assortment of bedfellows: the navy which favored Bizerte because of the naval base located there, nationalists who cried treason (Krupp in a French mining scheme!), individuals including Clemenceau's other brother, Albert, who was a lawyer for one of Muller's partners in the Société concessionnaire, plus French socialists and syndicalists. Merrheim, leader of the Confédération Générale du Travail, the French labor confederation, denounced the project in the syndicalist newspaper, *La Voix du Peuple*, and the socialists led by Jean Jaurès – and who included the nationalisation of mines in their party platform but ignored it in practice – decried the scheme in *L'Humanité* and opposed it in Parliament. Both syndicalists and socialists argued that the workers were mistreated in the proposed agreement, since the miners were not even mentioned, and that neither a minimum salary nor an eight-hour day were stipulated.

Finally, in March 1909, the government withdrew under pressure its proposed law to allow the Schneiders to build a railroad to Bône. Instead, it looked as though a second railroad was going to be built in Tunisia and at least part of the Ouenza ore would be shipped from Bizerte. Apparently, Bône and Algeria had lost as well as Schneider and the Société d'Etudes.

In Bône people took to the streets by the thousands to demonstrate against this latest turn of events.[21] The day after the government withdrew its proposed law a crowd estimated at 10,000 to 15,000 staged a mass demonstration on the Cours Bertagna, the main street of town. The mayor harangued the crowd. The crowd paraded with placards which read "À bas les voleurs! À bas les vendus! À bas Tunis! À bas Jonnart! À bas Thomson!"[22] The municipal council voted to resign in protest, then reversed itself and adopted the more prudent course of threatening to resign if Paris did not fall into line behind Bône. The representatives of Bône in Parliament were likewise called upon to resign. The chamber of commerce voted to withhold funds owed the state for port construction until Bône had prevailed over Bizerte. That evening a delegation of local dignitaries, seven French and one Algerian, departed for Paris to plead Bône's case in person – the first of no fewer than six such delegations despatched to Paris before the Ouenza affair was finally settled.

While Paris tergiversated, Bône continued to demonstrate. A week later a "Committee of Bône youth" organized a rally that drew 10,000. In addition to the now familiar speeches and placards, the crowd sang a tune, "Pioupious d'Auvergne" ("The Private from Auvergne"), the refrain of which recalled the anti-Jewish song sung at the time of the Dreyfus Affair a decade earlier. At other demonstrations, other songs: a funeral march to evoke the burial of the Ouenza, the "International," the "Marche Bônoise," and "l'Ouenza," "a local song currently popular."[23] Demonstrations the following month were smaller but violent. All municipal officials except one stayed away from a rally organized by the "Committee of Bône youth" and the printers' union, but when police moved to break it up the crowd of 2,000 responded by throwing rocks and chairs from the nearest cafe. A dozen were arrested.

From March 1909 until the Ouenza affair was resolved, therefore, sporadic demonstrations occurred in Bône. Yet this Bône crowd was no Thompsonian crowd resurrecting a threatened moral economy; this was a crowd acting in what it perceived to be the economic interest of all Bônois, united in sending a message to France on the other side of the Mediterranean. The number of demonstrators may be inflated, since 10,000 and 15,000 are very large turnouts for a town of 40,000, but photographs of the time show the Cours Bertagna jammed. The demonstrations were massive and noisy for colonial Bône, but "in sum, much noise, nothing very serious," as one police report put it.[24]

Yet nothing had been settled in 1909 when the government withdrew the railroad project; everything had only been put off, with the result that the entire Ouenza affair continued to drag on for another four years. During this period, alliances were made and unmade in an attempt to arrive at a solution: Le Creusot made overtures to Tunisian phosphate and steel interests implicitly backing Bizerte thereby; the Bône-Guelma railroad company was revealed as a front acting in the interests of Le Creusot; and Bône economic interests allied with Tebessa phosphate producers – who were themselves Scottish and not French!

Yet these shifting coalitions were unable to produce an agreement. Then in 1913, the 1908 truce between Schneider and Muller expired without an agreement having been made between Schneider and the government concerning the railroad. This could have meant starting again from square one, but instead it set the stage at long last for the denouement of the affair. For the colonial administration in Algeria seized the opportunity to reconstitute the Ouenza company and to renegotiate the terms of exploitation. First, the Algerian administration separated the issue of the railroad from the issue of the concession.

Rather than having Parliament deal with the railroad, the government in Algeria assumed responsibility, and when the Bône-Guelma company refused to reform its rate structure, the Algerian administration simply bought back the railroad and ran it itself. Next the colonial administration began negotiating a new lease with Schneider. However, Algiers was forced by Paris – itself worried about political fallout – to throw open the entire process and accept bids. And in the open bidding which ensued, Muller and the Société concessionnaire simply offered terms that Schneider and the Société d'Etudes could not match and which the Algerian administration could not refuse.

The lease with Muller was signed finally in 1913, and the Société concessionnaire became the Société de l'Ouenza. At the time it was formed, the Ouenza immediately became the second largest mining company in Algeria after the Mokta el Hadid, and it became the largest in 1927. Moreover, "the new agreement [of 1913] was infinitely more advantageous to the colony than the old one [of 1903]," both in terms of the large royalties per ton and the colony's total share in the profits. "Muller has poured money into Algeria's hands [*a fait à l'Algérie un pont d'or*]."[25] And it was not a French firm (Schneider) using local French interests (Jonnart) to wangle the best deal it could, but a German-Dutch consortium that actually offered much more attractive terms to exploit this French national treasure. Thus it came about that the Ouenza affair finally came to a close, although the First World War delayed until 1921 the arrival of the first load of iron ore at the port of Bône for shipment to Europe.

The Ouenza affair and the peripheral role Bône played in it illustrates in a striking manner the economic dependency of Bône to France, the political dependency of the French settlers upon France, and the degree to which the mass of Bône's European settlers identified their interests with those of the better-off French settlers in taking to the streets in 1909 and again in 1910. For the overriding feature of the entire Ouenza affair was that Bône did not control its own destiny, that the interests of Bône – and Bizerte too for that matter – were almost always the last to be taken into account, that a whole skein of tangled interests, private and public, fought it out in France and not in Algeria, and that the final decision was made not in Bône but in Paris.[26]

Creating an infrastructure

When people said not to take trains in Algeria, I figured they were comparing them to trains in Europe, whereas by Third World standards they probably were not so bad. I was wrong. If you think the train trip, say, across the south of France from Bordeaux to Marseilles is interminable, try making the nine-hour, less-than-450-kilometer trip from Algiers to Constantine some time. Distances in the Third World tend to become longer; time has an Einsteinian way of lengthening out. If Algeria has that effect on the visitor today, think what it must have been like before the advent of the automobile in the early twentieth century, before the coming of the railroad in the late nineteenth century.

The Bône-Guelma railroad may have been slow, but it formed literally the backbone of the transport system which hauled iron, phosphates, and agricultural goods from the interior to the port of Bône for export. In fact, the shape of the railroad network of the Bône region has been likened to a dorsal fin (Figure 4.1). Headquartered in Bône, the Bône-Guelma played a key role not only in the Ouenza affair, and the *mise en valeur* of the Tebessa phosphates, but also in the commercial rivalry between Bône and Bizerte to the east and Philippeville to the west. Call it the weight of historical geography, political economy, or whatever, but a geographical determinist could make a strong argument that the geographical features of the Bône region determined its political contours. Significantly, Bône called sporadically for the creation of a Bône department to be carved out of the *département* of Constantine ever since the administrative headquarters had been transferred from Bône to Constantine back in 1849. All this could be simply written off as the posturings of an upstart, except for one thing: the department of Bône was formed in 1955. And what is significant here is the geographical shape of the new department: extending deeply and narrowly into the interior from Bône on the coast, it fleshed out the bony skeleton traced by the Bône-Guelma railroad.[27]

We have already discussed the short rail line running from the Mokta el Hadid's mine at Ain Mokra to the docks of Bône, only the second railroad built in Algeria (see Chapter 3). The manager of the Mokta el Hadid in Bône, Philippe de Cerner, persuaded the government to extend the line westward from Ain Mokra to where it connected up with the main line to Philippeville, then convinced the government to take over the line and run it in the public interest, and finally directed it personally between 1908 and 1917. Today, this same railroad forms a link in the line which spans the entire Maghrib from Casablanca to Tunis.[28]

But it was the Bône-Guelma railroad which gave the future department of Bône its dorsal fin shape. The Bône-Guelma was opened in 1874 after what later became the Bône-Guelma company enlisted the support of the Bône and Guelma municipal councils, which agreed to guarantee the interest on the necessary loans. Three years later in 1877, Guelma was linked in turn with Constantine. The idea was that this fait accompli would force the proponents of a direct Constantine-Philippeville line to fall in line and build a Philippeville-Guelma link, which would connect in turn to Constantine. All this was an effort by Bône to thwart the competition posed by a direct Constantine-Philippeville line. Philippeville wanted to compete with Bône as a port, and business leaders in Constantine favored Philippeville as a way to cut a growing Bône down to size. Here is where it becomes interesting, for what happened was that the proponents of a direct Constantine-Philippeville line won the government over to their position even though such a line was to a certain extent a duplication and – more important – even though the cost of constructing a line through the rugged terrain south of Philippeville cost significantly more per kilometer.[29]

This was by no means the only occasion on which politics influenced railroad construction in Constantine department, nor the only instance of competition between Bône and Constantine and Philippeville. It was only after much further wrangling that a "laborious compromise" was hammered out in Paris – not Algeria – between the representatives of the various chambers of commerce involved according to which Constantine and Philippeville were granted a railroad from Ain Beida to Constantine and from there to Philippeville, and Bône received permission for a normal-gage line to Souk Ahras and a narrow-gage from there to Tebessa. This happened in 1885. Hardly had these lines been completed when the magnitude of the Tebessa phosphate deposits became known. The Constantinois felt they had been taken for a ride. Using as an excuse the narrow-gage Souk Ahras-Tebessa line, and with the support of the president of the departmental commission, they demanded the construction of a new line linking Ain Beida to Tebessa. The Bône chamber of commerce saw this as the grab for the Kouif phosphates that it indeed was, denounced this ploy "the obvious aim of which is to divert the phosphates traffic to the profit of the port of Philippeville," and after recalling "the engagements agreed to in 1885" attempted to obstruct construction.[30] Bône failed to prevent the line from being built, but it did succeed in delaying it and keeping the phosphates on the Souk Ahras line to Bône.

This is where the Ouenza affair fits in, because the narrow-gage line south from Souk Ahras, which could hardly cope with the Kouif phosphates, could not hope to handle the Ouenza iron ore. As we have seen, the government took over the Bône-Guelma in the end, and widened the line from Souk Ahras to the Ouenza and also to Tebessa further south; meanwhile, the Société de l'Ouenza had built a spur from the mines to Oued Kebarit in order to meet it.[31] With this extension, the dorsal fin shape of the future *département* of Bône was complete. Bône had successfully staved off commercial threats from both Philippeville to the west and Bizerte to the east to extend its economic and political influence southward deep into Constantine department.

*   *   *

The development of the port of Bône and the mise en valeur *of the mineral riches of eastern Constantine province are two connected facts.*[32]

The above was written by the leading urban historian of Algeria during the interwar period, René Lespès. He went on to characterize Bône as a "mining port."[33] Port construction in the nineteenth century was among the largest scale building projects undertaken, and Bône was no exception. The stakes were high, and the larger and more complex the port works, the higher the cost and the greater the potential for private profit. Due to the nature of construction, the building industry has always had a reputation for graft and corruption, kickbacks and bribery. In what is usually considered purely a matter of economics, politics is everywhere evident.[34]

In Bône the initial impetus for port construction was the exploitation of the Mokta el Hadid's iron ore mine at Ain Mokra, and extensive construction was carried out between 1856 and 1869 (see Chapter 3). At the end of this time the port consisted of eighty hectares of sheltered area in which to handle the Mokta's iron ore, but there were two unresolved problems. First, mud and silt from the Bou Djima river, which emptied directly into the breakwater, clogged up the harbor; and second, the outer harbor was open to the east and thus exposed to storms. The first problem was rectified in 1875–76 by diverting the Bou Djima away from the harbor and into the Seybouse river upstream (Figure 4.2). Now the railroad from Ain Mokra instead of stopping at the Seybouse could cross it and link up directly with the port, thus reducing significantly the cost of transporting the iron ore. Now the Bône-Guelma railway station and repair yard could be expanded, which was done in 1879. Most important of all, diverting the Bou Djima meant eliminating its marshy banks, which improved the salubrity of the new city significantly. The former bed of the Bou Djima was covered over and converted into one of the main streets when the new French city was laid out (see Chapter 5).

Even after the Bou Djima had been diverted, however, everyone realized that this amounted to a mere holding action, that if Bône was to compete seriously as one of Algeria's major port cities along with Algiers and Oran, major construction was necessary. Therefore, the French business leaders of Bône, which in practice meant the chamber

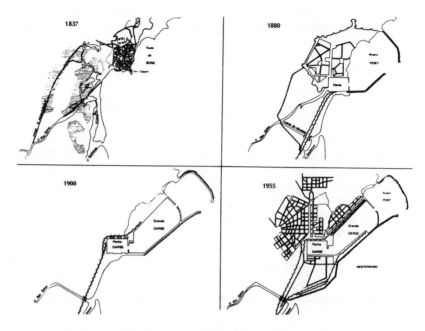

Figure 4.2   Map of port of colonial Bône, 1837–1955. *Source:* Tomas, *Annaba*, p. 203.

of commerce led by Mayor Jérome Bertagna, decided to build a port not simply for the present but for the future as well. It was clear, however, that the requisite funds were not going to come entirely from the state. By 1879 a program of the work necessary was prepared, which included creation of a new outer harbor and breakwater, dredging both to a depth sufficient to accommodate deep-water vessels, and construction of extensive docks. The cost? Mayor Bertagna told the government 10 million francs, an absurdly low figure. Later it was alleged that Bertagna had connived with state engineers in Bône to deceive the state by deliberately underestimating the costs. Of the total cost the Bône chamber of commerce proposed to furnish 1.4 million francs to be repaid by the government at a later date, and the city pledged to buy up land worth 1.6 million francs which was necessary to supply building materials for the project. To cover its loan, the chamber of commerce received authorization from the state to impose a duty on incoming ships and to spend the profits on port construction.

What Bertagna was proposing in fact was a grandiose scheme designed more to meet future port needs than present ones. Production of the chief commodity exported from the port, iron ore from the Mokta mine, had already begun to decline by the late 1870s. And it was not until the turn of the twentieth century that port traffic increased substantially thanks to the Kouif phosphates. After intensive lobbying by Bertagna, the state agreed to the 1879 plan, declared the project in the public interest, and work began in 1886. Soon, however, actual costs began to exceed estimated costs substantially. By 1894, after eight years of effort, all the money appropriated had been spent, approximately 10.5 million francs, and the works simply ground to a halt.

By then, however, it was not simply a local matter. A "general outcry" was raised against Bertagna, and the government was interpellated on the floor of the National Assembly in Paris.[35] All to no avail, however, for Bertagna weathered criticism in Paris over his handling of work at the port. Meanwhile, in Bône, he had a series of supplementary works drawn up to complete the original project at a cost of an additional six million francs. This time, however, the terms were considerably stiffer, and the chamber of commerce anted up virtually the entire amount. With the chamber of commerce solidly behind Bertagna, work started up again in 1899 after a five-year hiatus.

By 1904 the volume of Kouif phosphates already arriving at the port, combined with the Ouenza iron ore expected to start arriving soon, led to the proposal of a final series of port improvements – construction of additional quais along the breakwater and a vast thirty-five-hectare land-fill along the Seybouse River. These works were simply tacked on to those already in progress and carried out between 1905 and 1911. Thus, the second major round of port works were completed in two separate stages between 1886–94 and 1899–1911.

The total cost from 1886 to 1911 amounted to approximately nineteen million francs, nearly double what was initially projected. Although "it was never known whether the underestimates were the results of errors in calculations, or if they had been consciously organized," as one local historian sympathetic to Bertagna writes, "it is difficult to believe that the enormous difference between the projected costs and the actual costs were the result of a simple error of judgment."[36] This extremely large cost overrun was made up for largely by the local chamber of commerce. Luckily, the Bône chamber was able to make enough money in tolls from increased exports of Kouif phosphates and later Ouenza iron ore to provide the funds necessary. In fact, it was so bullish on Bône that the chamber of commerce passed a motion in 1899 protesting "against maintaining Tebessa in the subdivision of Constantine and re-news the resolution of attaching this region to Bône in conformity with the request of the people concerned, and with *geographical and com-mercial exigencies.*"[37] But what if there had been no phosphates and additional iron ore deposits discovered? For without sufficient funds from the chamber of commerce, Bertagna would have had to approach the state, and it is highly unlikely that the government would have provided money to build on the scale Bertagna envisioned. In the end the port construction succeeded and Bertagna's backers lauded him as a visionary who planned big and looked far into the future, but the port could easily have become Bertagna's biggest boondoggle – considerably more serious than an interpellation on the floor of parliament.

By 1911 in any case, Bône had its port, the outlines of which did not change significantly before the beginning of the Algerian revolution in 1954. And "since the nature of the traffic was the same, it was still the typical mining port described by R. Lespès."[38]

The urban economy

> The Annaba economy today is Algerian. It is run by Algerians except for the steel mill outside of town. The goods provided are tailored to its mostly Algerian customers (jallabas, harissa, *henna*), plus selected Western goods made in Algeria or imported from Europe (plastic buckets and gas bottles, Peugeot sedans for those with the money and connections, sitcoms for the few with TVs, commercial films for everyone). Goods are dispensed primarily in a modern suq, or bazaar, although the government runs a supermarket and department store also. French and other Europeans are physically absent from Annaba today for the most part, but Western economic influences persist, like only partly covered over layers of historical sediment laid down originally in the colonial period.
>
> Thus if you go shopping for food, you may head first for the market. The French-style supermarket, a former Monoprix, is located downtown, but the street outside is busier than the store inside. The shelves are virtually empty, and the tinned goods are unappetizing – the canned pâte looks, smells, and tastes like cat food. Comparatively few people do their shopping here; they are all in the marché a few blocks away, a modern, two-story concrete structure built in the 1930s which houses a traditional Middle Eastern suq. Downstairs fresh fish is sold daily, but you have to get there early because it is all sold and the market is closed by midmorning. Upstairs you can buy fruits and vegetables in season, oranges from Morocco all the time or so it seems, brown eggs which cost more than white ones because they taste "better," dates grown in the Sahara and still sold on their branches, a slab of raw butter sold by weight rather than by size, and meat which is not usually covered with too many flies. The beef is tough and stringy although the camel meat is tender, yet behind you an Algerian housewife waits to buy a pair of sheep hooves for the family couscous which will cost her ten dollars a pound.

The regional economy of Bône typified by the extraction of mineral resources, plus the creation of a rail and port infrastructure for the export of these same goods can be described best in terms of dependency – dependent on companies and corporations based in Paris more often

114

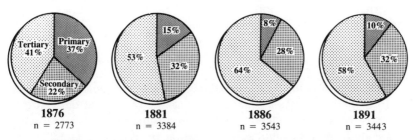

Figure 4.3   Colonial Bône employers by economic sector, 1876–91. *Source*: APCA, *Listes nominatives*, 1876, 1881, 1886, and 1891.

than in Bône, dependent on the prices of goods set in Europe not in Algeria. If we now move from the regional economy to the urban economy, what we see is that the Bône urban economy constitutes the mirror image, the other side of the coin, of the Bône regional economy. In the *mairie*, or city hall, on the main street in town, documents found in the municipal archives categorize all employers in the last quarter of the nineteenth century who owned or managed farms or businesses by economic sector (Figure 4.3). Clearly, commerce in colonial Bône predominated over industry; the tertiary, or service, sector overshadowed the secondary, or manufacturing, sector. This links directly to the preeminent role of Bône's port as a funnel through which mostly raw materials are exported and mostly manufactured goods are imported, and the related lack of processing and industry.

If we scrutinize individual industrial firms, the nature of Bône's industry is even more clear-cut. In 1902, for example, an official report listed as the city's leading industries a number of bottle cork factories, a tile factory, five brick factories, a Muslim pottery works, a number of tobacco factories, two new vegetable fiber works, a recently created superphosphates factory to produce fertilizer, and a match factory employing fifty workers a day.[39] Not a bad beginning. But thirty years later, in 1932, industrialization had advanced little if any. The main businesses were a bottle cork factory, a pasta factory, oil mills, the Algerian pottery works, the superphosphates factory, a factory producing unspecified chemical products, a charcoal works, a tobacco factory, brick works, a cigarette factory, and a factory producing gutters and cement pipes. The vegetable fiber works had folded by 1904.[40] If this constitutes the leading edge of "industrialization" in Bône, then it is not surprising that heavy manufacturing in the form of a state-run steel mill complex did not arrive until after the Algerian Revolution. At the beginning of the twentieth century when the leading economies of Europe and the United States were starting what David Landes and others have referred to as the second industrial revolution based on automobiles, chemicals, and

115

electricity, Bône had only a handful of plants and factories engaged primarily in processing raw goods and materials.[41]

* * *

How do we account for the imbalance between commerce and industry in Bône and the rest of Algeria? One school of thought derived from Marx is mode of production analysis, according to which a theoretical explication of the economic organization of a society, including the forces of production, means of production, and social relations of production, leads to an understanding of the concrete form a given social formation takes. Although the bulk of mode of production analysis which deals with the Third World focuses on precapitalist modes, such an approach offers certain advantages when applied to colonial Annaba.[42]

Since Algeria and France were at different stages of socioeconomic development when France invaded Algeria, and since colonial Bône consisted of French colonizers, or settlers, and Algerian colonized, it seems logical to identify European Bône with a capitalist mode of production, and Algerian Bône with a precapitalist mode of production.[43] The capitalism of the colonizers formed the dominant mode of production, and the precapitalist mode of the colonized was subordinate, but the two were articulated together in a way determined by the form colonialism took in Algeria, namely, settler colonialism. Thus, the dominant capitalist mode pulled Algerian migrants from rural areas, and in the process converted Algerian villages into pools of reserve labor.[44] Therefore, the advantages to a mode of production analysis of colonial Bône are twofold: (1) differences between colonizers and colonized are explained by the economic organization of colonial society, and (2) the way modes of production articulate together mirrors the dominant-subordinate colonial relationship.

The disadvantage of such an analysis is that it implicitly assumes that capitalism in colonial Algeria – the capitalism of the capitalist mode – is the same as capitalism in Europe. But as we saw above, it clearly is not, since commerce predominates over industry, and because early efforts to develop a steel industry were stymied. Colonialism in Algeria differed, moreover, due to the disproportionate number of permanent European settlers relative to Algerians. To argue, therefore, that capitalism in Algeria simply lagged behind capitalism in France as capitalism outside England lagged behind capitalism inside England preserves the logic of the theoretical analysis but runs the risk of violating historical reality. Rather than developing more slowly, it could be argued that capitalism in colonial Algeria developed differently.

This in fact is precisely what theorists of both dependency and world systems argue.[45] The incorporation of Algeria into the capitalist world economy occurred under the aegis of French colonialism after 1830. It was at this time that Algeria assumed its position in the periphery of the world economy, a position it has held ever since. The role of Algeria in the periphery vis-à-vis France in the core is to export primarily raw materials and import mostly manufactured goods. Thus is explained the predominance of commerce over industry in Bône: raw materials were not transformed in Bône but only processed through Bône. Instead of capitalist development, there occurred the development of underdevelopment in Algeria.

The advantage of such a world systems analysis is that the division of the world into core, semiperiphery, and periphery accounts for the different course capitalism takes in Algeria compared to France. The disadvantage is that the theory itself cannot distinguish adequately between different historical situations in the periphery, which in the case of Algeria means settler colonialism and the different economic formations of colonizers and colonized. Where world systems analysis provides insight, therefore, into the form capitalism takes in Bône by situating it in the periphery of the world system, mode of production analysis has the advantage of distinguishing between the economic formations of colonizer and colonized.

*   *   *

Another set of documents from the former Bône municipal archives lists all the commercial establishments in the city in 1883, which provides telling evidence of economic dualism (Table 4.1).

Clearly, Algerian tradesmen are more likely to be engaged in hotels, restaurants, and cafes (subgroup 1); trades related to food (subgroup 2); and dry goods and clothing (subgroup 3). European businessmen, on the other hand, were more active in wood and metal trades (subgroup 4), miscellaneous goods and services (subgroup 5), the liberal professions (subgroup 6), and diverse other businesses (subgroup 7). To be sure, these differences could simply reflect the tendency for certain people to specialize in certain trades more than others, rather than the existence of Algerian businesses catering to the needs of the Muslim community and European businesses serving by and large the European community. But look closer at the individual trades within these broad subgroups. Subgroup 1: hotels, restaurants, and cafes, for example. All the hotels in town are owned by Europeans; all the *funduq-s* (Muslim inns for Muslim travelers) are owned by Algerians. Almost all of the restaurants are owned by Europeans; all of the *gargotes* – cheap Algerian

117

Table 4.1. *Number of European and Algerian businessmen in Bône by trade (per 15,000 population), 1883*

Trade	Europeans	Algerians	Total
Subgroup 1: Hotels, restaurants, cafes			
Restaurants	15	2	17
Cheap restaurants (*Gargotes*)	—	86	86
Cafes	64	—	64
Turkish cafes	—	152	152
Barkeepers, wine merchants	29	—	29
Breweries, distilleries	4	—	4
Hotels	6	—	6
Muslim inns (*fondouks*)	—	29	29
Apartments, furnished rooms	36	—	36
French baths	1	—	1
Turkish baths	—	12	12
Subtotal	155	281	436
	(36%)	(64%)	
Subgroup 2: Food and related goods			
Groceries	59	45	104
Vegetable sellers	55	14	69
Fruit sellers	4	55	59
Butchers	10	21	31
Delicatessens (*charcuteries*)	4	—	4
Poultry sellers	4	10	14
Bakeries	25	—	25
Pastry shops	5	—	5
Fritter (*beignet*) sellers	1	10	11
Pasta makers	3	—	3
Grain merchants	4	26	30
Salt, soap, oil, and coffee merchants	4	7	11
Tobacco sellers	10	33	43
Subtotal	180	221	409
	(46%)	(54%)	

	Europeans	Muslims	Total
Subgroup 3: Dry goods and clothing			
Haberdashers	7	—	7
Dry goods dealers	8	—	8
Secondhand dealers (*brocanteurs*)	8	21	29
Cloth merchants	3	79	82
Burnoose merchants	—	12	12
Dyers	1	—	1
Tailors	6	2	8
Shoemakers	22	10	32
Barbers, wigmakers	11	7	18
Subtotal	66	131	197
	(34%)	(66%)	
Subgroup 4: Wood and metal crafts			
Carpenters, joiners	22	—	22
Carpet makers	5	—	5
Founders, tinsmiths, glaziers, housepainters	15	—	15

Table 4.1. *(cont.)*

Trade	Europeans	Algerians	Total
Coopers, coppersmiths	5	—	5
Locksmiths	6	—	6
Harness makers, saddlers	5	—	5
Pack makers (*batiers*)	—	19	19
Wheelwrights, farriers	15	—	15
Blacksmiths	3	12	15
Subtotal	76	31	107
	(71%)	(29%)	
Subgroup 5: Miscellaneous goods and services			
Pottery merchants	1	10	11
Charcoal sellers	8	—	8
Coachmen, carriage rentals	4	7	11
Sewing machine dealers	2	—	2
Agricultural implements dealers	1	—	1
Gunsmiths	7	—	7
Watchmakers	11	—	11
Photographers	2	—	2
Steamship company representatives	2	—	2
Subtotal	38	17	55
	(69%)	(31%)	
Subgroup 6: Liberal professions			
Pharmacists, doctors, notary, architect, surveyor	13	—	13
Subtotal	13	0	13
	(100%)		
Subgroup 7: Diverse other trades			
Diverse other trades	55	10	65
Subtotal	55	10	65
	(85%)	(15%)	
Grand Total	591	691	1,282
	(46%)	(54%)	

Source: APCA, *Situation Industrielle*, 1883.

eating places where you can buy a bowl of *chorba* (lentil soup) or a plate of *couscous* for a pittance – are owned by Algerians. All of the cafes here belong to Europeans, all the *cafes maures* (Turkish cafes serving mint tea) are owned by Algerians. There are French public baths like you find in Paris and other French cities, again owned by Europeans, and there are Turkish baths (*bains maures* in French; *hammams* in Arabic) like you find throughout the Arab world from Afghanistan to Morocco, owned by Algerians. This is not an economy like that of France where some of the restaurants are owned by Auvergnats, others by Franc-Comtois, and still others by Provençaux. Specialization to that extent is common everywhere. This is specialization, however, carried to an extreme, an extreme which adds up to economic dualism. This is an economy where quantitative differences result in a qualitative difference, namely, the existence of a dual European-Algerian economy, one alongside yet distinct from the other.

And subgroup by subgroup, the case is the same.

Subgroup 2: Food and Related Goods. There are European grocers and there are Algerian grocers, but the Europeans, often designated *epiceries suisses*, specialize in *denrées coloniale*, that is, goods imported from France, while the Muslims specialize in commodities basic to the Algerian cuisine such as tea, cooking oil, and *harissa*, chili and tomato concentrate. The majority of vegetable sellers are Maltese who have bought their goods as middlemen from Maltese truck gardeners who live and farm on the outskirts of town, whereas the overwhelming majority of fruit sellers are Muslims who raise fruit trees just as their forebears grew citrus fruits in 1830. All the French-style pastry and sweet shops, *confiseries* and *pâtisseries*, are owned by Europeans, and all the Algerian-style sweet shops, which specialize in *beignets* (doughnut-shaped deep-fat fried pastries), are owned by Muslims. All those who make pasta, *pâtes alimentaires*, are either Italian or Maltese. The Algerians supply the bulk food products to Europeans and Muslims alike: wheat, barley, oats, rye, and other grains; salt, soap, cooking oil. The Algerians eat yogurt and drink whey, but it is the Maltese who supply goat's milk from the goats they herd, and it is the French who make cheese and butter. Tobacco is one of the few commodities dominated by the Algerians from the Beni Urgine tribe, who grow it in the plain of Bône and sell some to the French state tobacco monopoly and some to Algerians who cure it and roll it into cigarettes, to the petty retail merchants who sell it in French-style kiosks on the Cours Bertagna and elsewhere throughout town.

Subgroup 3: Dry Goods and Clothing. All the dry goods stores, knick-knack venders, and haberdashery shops are European-owned, and sell goods imported mostly from France. Nearly all the cloth stores are owned by Mozabites, long-distance traders from the Sahara who virtually monopolized the cloth trade in Bône. Few if any shops sold ready-made clothing. What you did was select cloth from bolts and take it to a Jewish tailor who sewed it on a sewing machine bought from a French merchant who had imported it. The *burnoose* merchants were Algerians who sold the loose-fitting Muslim outer garment to their Algerian clientele. The secondhand dealers were mostly Muslims who set up shop in a booth in the Arab market, or who peddled their wares in pushcarts from neighborhood to neighborhood.

Subgroup 4: Wood and Metal Crafts. Every one of the shops that specialized in cabinetmaking, carpentry, carpet making, casting, tin-

120

smithing, glazing, coppersmithing, barrel making, and lock making was owned by a European. All the harness and saddle makers were European, whereas all the shops which made the packs the Algerians used for their pack animals were owned by Muslims. All the wheelwrights and farriers worked in shops owned by Europeans; all the blacksmiths worked in smithies owned by Algerians.

Subgroup 5: Miscellaneous Goods and Services. Of the miscellaneous goods and services provided, Europeans monopolized those specializing in imported goods, metal goods, and precision instruments, such as agricultural implements used by the farmers in the region, sewing machines, guns and gunpowder, watchmakers, who were predominantly Jews, and charcoal merchants who contracted with the forest concessionaires in the Edough to supply the city. The steamship companies which linked Bône to France, Italy, Malta, and Tunisia were all run by the French, and the bulk of coachmen who rented horse-drawn carriages to the Europeans were Algerian. The Algerian pottery merchants marketed the pots thrown on Muslim wheels, and Tunisians arrived every summer in *chebecs*, Mediterranean sailing ships, from Djerba with pots patterned after vases made for 2,000 years which "breathed" when wet and served effectively as refrigerators before the advent of electricity.

Subgroup 6: Liberal Professions. Every one of the people who practiced a liberal profession was European. If you bought a patent medicine, risked going to a dentist, had a notary prepare the document required by the government because you were illiterate, or saw a lawyer because the city had expropriated a chunk of your choice urban property by right of eminent domain in order to lay out a new street in the Colonne, you went to a European in every case, and most likely to a Frenchman besides.

Subgroup 7: Diverse Other Trades. This subgroup is a heterogeneous grab bag of diverse occupations ranging from a longtime French bookseller and stationery store owner to the Jewish secondhand clothes dealer to a Muslim *kif* merchant, from the town's midwives and tripe sellers to a lute maker and a sculptor who fashioned objects from the local coral.

*   *   *

> It is a matter of simple observation that the economies of a great many
> developing countries are organized in two parts, structurally and behav-
> iorally so different that they deal with one another largely on the basis
> of trade – almost as though they formed two different societies and
> economies.[47]

Almost, but not quite – and there is the rub. In colonial Bône we see different people playing different roles, exercising different functions, working at different tasks, and earning different wages. Thus, the problem lies not in observing such economic dualism, but in adequately analyzing, interpreting, and accounting for it. Although a multitude of theoretical models exist, they differ substantially on how to explain it.

First, there is the so-called dual economy, which consists of a traditional bazaar sector and a modern firm-oriented one. Such a model was developed initially as a corollary of the plural society notion, and is also related to modernization theory insofar as it is based implicitly on a growth model of economic development and modernization (see Chapter 1). In the case of the dual economy, the two halves of the dual economy are essentially unrelated and isolated from one another, and only merge during the process of economic development when the traditional sector modernizes as a result of backward linkages with the modern one. Critics of the dual economy notion also tend to be critics of modernization theory, which they fault on the grounds that instead of two unrelated sectors of the urban economy, the development of the "modern" sector entails the underdevelopment of the "traditional" sector. While the "objective" observation of significant differences within the same urban economy is useful, the "subjective" implications usually associated with the dual economy regarding relations between the sectors and how economic growth proceeds renders its use problematic at best.[48]

A second approach is that of segmented or dual labor markets.[49] Such a theory is based on the observation that people have differential access to jobs, which cannot be accounted for by the theoretical existence of a single labor market. For example, different labor markets exist for blacks versus whites, and by extension for colonizers versus colonized. Generally speaking, different labor markets are linked to the different stages of capitalism represented in the economy studied. More work has been done on industrial economies than colonial ones, and much less attention has been paid to how different labor markets are identified generally with different ethnic and racial groups than with how segmented labor markets correspond to stages of capitalist development. Thus, there is disagreement on whether such segmented labor markets are due to sociocultural attitudes, as Piore contends, or to structural economic characteristics as Gordon, Reich, and Edwards argue.

The "informal" economy offers a third way to approach the Bône urban economy.[50] The informal sector exists alongside and in relation to a formal economic sector. It consists of peddlers, street traders, hawkers, and others who engage in casual or disguised wage labor, or who are self-employed in petty production and trade. Such an approach recognizes explicitly the sizeable number of underemployed people in contemporary Third World cities who eke out an existence in the interstices of the formal economy; by extension, it is characteristic of the colonial city as well. But instead of forming an economy apart as with the dual economy, the informal sector consists of individuals who pass back and forth between the two sectors during their working lives. Moreover, it has been shown that people in the informal sector utilize kinship ties and patron/client networks to find work and provide services. Rather than passively accepting their economic marginality, it has been "discovered" that people actively seek ways to earn money and maximize profits. "Contrary to the usual image, the response of the exploited to conditions created for them by the capitalist system is seldom passive acquiescence."[51] Although the idea of the informal economy does not describe entirely the workings of an economy like that of colonial Bône in all its facets, it will be utilized below as another indication of the role played by the Algerians compared to the Europeans.

A final theory based implicitly on economic dualism is that of an export enclave economy in which an outsized export-oriented sector dominates economic activity.[52] Certainly colonial Bône can be characterized as an export enclave economy in which the extraction and transport of goods for export played a preponderant role. Moreover, it can be shown that much of the emphasis on commerce compared to industry was geared to this export trade, that the French owned and controlled such commerce to a disproportionate extent, and that Algerians supplied the bulk of the labor required, especially as dockers. However, in purely economic terms the idea of an export enclave economy fails to adequately account for the relationship between such an economic enclave and the rest of the local economy, as well as the larger question of how such enclaves fit into the larger world economy. Perhaps even more important, it lacks an analysis in terms of race and ethnicity which would explain why different groups play different roles in such economies.

All of these models share certain similarities and dissimilarities. They are all based on postcolonial rather than colonial situations. They all posit a radical bifurcation of the economy into segments or sectors. They are all better at suggesting how local economies function than on how these local economies fit into larger economic units. And they all are stronger on economic analysis than on economic observation which would show how people do and do not actually fit into the economic sectors and segments.[53]

In short, the chief distinguishing characteristic of the colonial Bône economy was economic dualism. Taking the economy as a whole, commerce predominated over industry, the service sector overshadowed manufacturing. The main economic fault line ran, however, along ethnic lines, splitting the Europeans from the Algerians. Both had their industrial as well as commercial sectors, but the main point is that the European economy can be likened by and large to a firm-centered, capitalist economy, while the Algerian economy can be compared to a bazaar-oriented, precapitalist economy.

*   *   *

Economic dualism does not tell the whole story, however. Significant differences existed within the European and Algerian sectors. For example, many more Algerians were unskilled than Europeans, but many more Berbers were unskilled than Arabs. Moreover, Jews constituted "strangers," socially and culturally different from Europeans and Algerians, yet they supplied economic goods and services to both. Finally, the naturalized French and other Europeans – the Italians, Spanish and Maltese – together constituted what I call "European colonies within the French colony," by which I underscore their subordinate position compared to the native French.[54] Such European intermediate groups were certainly closer to the French than the Algerians, yet included the bulk of the *petits blancs*. After all, the Algerians were not the only ones whom the French colonialized.

Let us look closer at these colonies-within-the-colony, because their existence was often covered up. In the Annaba archives on the top floor of the city hall, annual *Statistique Industrielle* data from 1883 onwards divides business owners into Europeans and Algerians. But for three years between 1904 and 1907 Europeans are further broken down into native French and other Europeans. Table 4.2 shows that the Italians and Maltese were less likely to own businesses than the native French, but more likely than the Algerians. These non-French Europeans stand out mainly in two subgroups, construction and leather. The high number of Italian building contractors is not surprising considering the number of Italians who labored as building trades workers. All of the Italian and Maltese who own businesses having to do with leather and hides make shoes. Bône's shoe shops are not factories; they employ on an average three workers.

The native French clearly dominate, therefore, the industries of colonial Bône. They are more likely to own and manage business enterprises than either the other Europeans or the Algerians. Even more significant, the French tend to dominate the more "modern," the more technically advanced industries. Handicrafts are in the hands by and large of the Algerians; the French monopolize the metalworking trades. Every one of Bône's printing shops is French-owned. It is here that the newspapers were printed, and French control of politics in the city was

Table 4.2. *French, other European, and Algerian business owners in Bône by trade (per 15,000 population), 1904–7*

Businesses	French	Other Europeans	Algerians	Total
Food	55	19	9	83
Chemicals	6	1	16	23
Construction	18	15	2	35
Wood	26	9	2	37
Bodywork	9	1	4	14
Ceramics	6	1	4	11
Leather, hides	9	16	8	33
Printing	9	—	—	9
Extractive industries	6	1	—	7
Metal, metalworking	20	2	—	22
Clothing	3	2	—	5
Transportation	44	15	7	66
Others	1	4	3	8
Total	212	86	55	353
	(60%)	(24%)	(16%)	

Source: APCA, *Statistique Industrielle*, 1904, 1905, 1907.

cemented by French printers who often doubled as editors and as politicians, *hommes politiques*. Almost all of the metal and metalworking trades were owned or operated by the French. The biggest single establishment, the Bône-Guelma railway maintenance yard, employed more than 100 workers in 1904–7. Every one of the extractive industries was owned by the French, from the rock and chalk quarries to the Bou Hamra iron ore mine located in the outskirts of colonial Annaba.

Food, wood, transportation – the story of French domination is everywhere the same. In the food industry, the beer breweries, pasta factories, oil presses, mineral water factories, and flour mills all belong to the French. The non-French and Algerians own a few butcher shops and bakeries. In wood and related trades, the carpentry and cabinetmaking workshops, and the sawmills are French-owned. All the bottle cork factories utilizing cork oak from the Edough are French-run and operated. When it comes to transportation, all those who contract to load and unload ships at the port of Bône are French, whereas those who operate stagecoaches and rent carriages are mostly French but also include other Europeans and a few Algerians.

Whereas Algerian businesses tended to be more "traditional" in the goods produced and the services provided, more akin to the bazaar economy, the Europeans were firmly entrenched in the more "modern" firm-centered sectors of the economy. Every large firm from the gas works to the superphosphates factory and from Alban's cigar and cigarette factory to the Bône-Guelma workyards was dominated by the Europeans – and the French at that.

*   *   *

Economic dualism existed over time in colonial Bône. Most likely, so too did differences within the European and Algerian sectors, but we cannot be sure, *faute des sources*. It is difficult enough to document economic dualism, because no information exists which compares all Algerian and European businesses over time. However, there are data which compare French and Algerian *patrons* in certain trades, namely, the owners and managers who were members of the Conseil des Prud'hommes, a labor conciliation board. There is no need to go into detail here concerning the operation of this body. It is necessary simply to know that four major groups of trades and occupations were covered, the building, metal, and leather and clothing trades, plus a diverse category ranging from brewers and distillers to pasta makers and dyers, from cigar and cigarette makers to municipal gas workers. Between 1884 and 1911, we know the relative number of French and Algerian owners of enterprises in these selected trades. Even after adjusting to take into account the relative number of French and Algerians in the population as a whole, it is clear that the gap between Algerians and French, which is already visible in 1884, widens substantially over time. Trade by trade the data documents the growth of economic dualism. In the leather and clothing trades the Algerian *patrons* are shoemakers, tailors, and harness and saddle makers. The second category, construction, is overwhelmingly dominated by the French, primarily building contractors. After a Muslim cabinetmaker leaves Bône for Constantine, there follow several years in which not a single Algerian *patron* is working in the building trades. The majority of Algerian business owners in the third category are the pottery shop owners we have met before; the French owners and managers are predominantly metalworkers and watchmakers. In the fourth category, all the Algerian *patrons* are drawn from the cigar and cigarette workshops, whereas the French are brewers, mineral water bottlers, ice makers, plus the gas works manager. The data cover only a selected number of trades, but show clearly that the number of Muslim businessmen, low to begin with, declines further still in comparison to the French in the 15 years on either side of the year 1900. Are we not back to the development of underdevelopment?

A shopping trip

> Today the local neighborhood market in the Orangerie neighborhood of
> Annaba beyond the Colonne Randon consists of congeries of makeshift
> wooden stalls covered mostly with canvas which dumps water from its
> pockets in the rainy season, and which sags in all seasons. During the day
> the mountains of tangerines are rivaled only by the heaps of chilis and
> cumin, the stacks of tinned harissa, hot sauce. At night the market is bare,
> the goods removed, except for the ubiquitous mounds of tangerines,
> guarded by young Algerians sprawled on top and warming themselves by
> fires built in discarded oil barrels.

Economic dualism existed in space as well as over time. In the late
nineteenth century the existence of the European covered market and
Algerian *funduq* virtually side by side in downtown Annaba symbolized
the city's economic divisions (Table 4.3).[55] The covered market was
divided into booths in 1883 such as you see in local markets in France
today. The Arab *funduq-s* were located right across the street.

Not only were a paltry six of the fifty *funduq* merchants European,
but three of them were Jews naturalized French, that is, "strangers"
catering to the needs of the Algerian population.

* * *

The data on commerce and industry which I have discussed so extensively in Table 4.1 distort the economic situation in one important
respect. The number of Algerian and European businessmen relative
to their population is one thing, but the absolute figures tell another
story. The relative percentage of commercial establishments in 1883 was
45 percent European and 55 percent Algerian, but in absolute terms a
full 71 percent were European and only 29 percent Muslim. The relative
percentage of firms in 1904–7 was 84 percent European and 16 percent
Algerian, but the absolute percentage was 89 percent European to only
11 percent Muslim. Did not this quantitative imbalance make for qualitative difference?

* * *

The informal economy of Bône was largely invisible, literally beyond
the ken of most European settlers. It was an economy of poverty. In
Algerian society, it included such groups as *as-sifla*, riffraff, and *al-
barraniyin*, recent rural inmigrants. It ranged from water carriers, bar-

127

Table 4.3a. *Covered market retailers, 1883*

Markets	European	Algerian
Butchers	8	4
Delicatessens (*charcutiers*)	3	—
Tripe sellers	1	—
Dry goods	6	—
Haberdashers	2	—
Vegetable sellers	72	6
Fruit sellers	4	1
Fowl merchants	5	4
Pastry sellers	2	—
Milk retailers	3	—
Florists	1	—
Cheese retailers	1	—
Butter retailers	1	—
Total	109	15

Table 4.3b. *Algerian* funduq *Retailers, 1883*

Funduq-s	Algerian	European
Moorish cafes	1	—
Tobacco dealers	1	—
Dry goods sellers	1	—
Fruit sellers	22	1
Shoemakers	1	—
Cloth sellers	4	2
Secondhand dealers	7	3
Sweet sellers	2	—
Milk retailers	2	—
Butter sellers	1	—
Tailors	1	—
Pottery dealers	1	—
Total	44	6

Source: APCA, *Statistique Industrielle*, 1883.

bers, and masseurs to jugglers, sorcerers, and hucksters. One local historian glimpses this informal economy outside the *funduq* in the space along the sidewalk next to a palm tree. "This place which was thus added to the *fondouk* was constantly occupied by a very dense crowd, drawn by all the tellers of adventure tales, the prestigitators, come there to make their coreligionists marvel and draw the substantive core [*substantifique moelle*] of their existence."[56] He recalls as a young boy joining the crowd of gawking natives and sharing their astonishment at the snake charmers and those with a porcupine, a gazelle, or a lion on a rope.

Illustration 4.2   Algerian market, 1880s (Bibliothèque Nationale Cabinet d'Estampes).

This economy of poverty, this informal economy, exists, of course, the world over. Outside of and marginal to the regular economy, it worms its way into the interstices; it lives off the fat of the "normal" economy. It is the Djakarta street vender who must watch for the cops and keep her cart moving.[57] It is the Mexican shoeshine boys Luis Buñuel got on film in *Los Olvidados*. It is the kind of traveling vaudeville troupes with which Molière got his start, and Federico Fellini too. It is Picasso's saltimbanques, Watteau's *Pierrot le Fou* hanging in the Louvre, and Anthony Quinn, the carnival strongman in *La Strada*. It numbers many inhabitants of squatter slums from the *chowks* of Bombay to the *bidonvilles* of North Africa. It is, of course, the beggars, the professionals as well as the genuine beggars.

Statistics miss this informal economy by and large. Economists can reckon employment and unemployment; they are less good at gauging underemployment. And the fact of the economic matter is that those who comprise this informal economy are not noticed. Marginally productive, if at all, they can be shunted aside and the difference will not

129

show up on the bottom line. The 1891 French census, for example, lumps them into a catchall category of prostitutes and vagabonds, saltimbanques and bohemians, and stigmatizes them all with the label "no profession."[58] Qualitative descriptions, eyewitness evocations, miss them just as often. The picture postcard genre of "scenes and types" (*scènes et types*) renders individuals as types.

For these and other reasons, therefore, it is next to impossible to define, dissect, and delineate the informal economy as rigorously as I would like. But it is there nonetheless; random shards of evidence testify to that.

> *Item*: Mayor Jérome Bertagna complains to the subprefect about allowing Berber Kabyle peddlers in Bône, "who only come to our region to practice usury to the detriment of the natives and under the cover of commercial operations. Numerous acts of vengeance, sometimes resulting in death, have been the consequence of these reprehensible practices."[59]

> *Item*: An Algerian writer describes the musicians who wander the streets of Bône's old city at dusk "looking for bread to maintain their existence – this existence which is so costly, even full of disappointments, to the most unfortunate among the unfortunate." Going from alleyway to alleyway, they sing about "our vanished glories and the exinguished light which lit up the Arab nation for several centuries," and receive money from the Algerians listening at the windows above.[60]

> *Item*: The same writer also portrays Zineb the sorceress, idolized by the young girls. She meets her client at night at the foot of a tree, because the client is afraid of looking ridiculous if she shows up during the day. Her method of calming a person's worries is to take the girl's hand and look into her eyes. She starts talking, trying out some phrases. If the girl's eyes brighten, she continues in the same vein. "Zineb is inoffensive, powerless to do good, incapable of doing evil."[61]

> *Item*: Beni Ramassés is a village in the city, a cluster of shacks overlooking the European cemetery on the outskirts of town. Here the villagers-become-urbanites grow figs, apricots, peaches, almonds, and the "carrot of mendicancy"; the vegetable gardens are protected by fences of prickly pear. Every morning the shoeshine boys troop downtown with their brushes and tambourines, which they use for a shoeshine box, soliciting business from the passersby, "*çiri, moussou*."[62]

Item: A local chronicler recounts "a charming promenade," a Sunday carriage ride, "especially diverting for us children due to the small *yaouleds* [Algerian kids, gamins] who lined the road." Thirty, forty or more would be there, none more than seven years old, calling out, "Aia, moussou, donnar oun sou; donne un sou, attine sourdi." When finally someone threw them some money, "that was then a fun sight, the chief attraction," as they all dived for it in the dirt, "arms and legs flying." Then the refrain began over again, "Donne un sou. . . ."[63]

Pasting together these bits and pieces, certain themes recur again and again. Beggars, especially women with children, calculated to elicit sympathy; shoeshine boys, the younger and brasher the better; jugglers, acrobats, snake charmers, bear baiters, and fortune tellers – the purveyors of popular culture. Transiency is their mode, prying a little money loose today, moving on tomorrow; this is the "floating population" which the French authorities worried about and tried to keep tabs on by issuing travel passes. The scams down pat, the territory staked out, made the competition for scarce material resources no less fierce. There was violence, and the crime was not only petty crime. If the working classes of Paris shaded off imperceptibly into the dangerous classes in the mind of the middle class, as Louis Chevalier has argued, what must the French image of the Algerians have been like?[64] But what I am struck by most is how pervasive, how thoroughgoing and all-encompassing the poverty was, the sheer amount of circumscribed human potential. Severe malnutrition in the infant damages permanently the brain in the adult. Did not the economy of poverty extend to and encompass also the poverty of mind?

*   *   *

Expressed in figures as in Table 4.3 – 109 European retailers and 15 Algerian in the covered market, 44 Algerian and 6 European sellers in the *funduq* – it is easy to forget the people the numbers represent. The Maltese truck gardeners, for example, got up in the dark to get their produce to the covered market before dawn, sold their vegetables to the Maltese middlemen (*revendeurs*) on the sidewalk because the market gates were still not open, and consummated their transactions in one of the five Maltese cafes surrounding the market, perhaps in Louis Xerri's Cafe du Théâtre, or Camillieri's Cafe Ste. Helène named after his daughter, or Grech's Cafe des Quatre Saisons, the Cafe des Deux Halles, or Jean Gauci's Bar d'Apollon.[65]

Or step inside the *funduq* for a minute. Those Algerians who can

Illustration 4.3   Mozabite quarter (Bibliothèque Nationale Cabinet d'Estampes).

afford it have arrived by stagecoach or train from the surrounding region. The others walk with their donkeys packed with grain, fruit, poultry, charcoal, and wool to sell. The shopkeepers have set up in narrow stalls: a fruit seller here, a dry goods seller there, and farther away a Muslim shoemaker. Next to a Mozabite amidst his cloth sits a Jew in a stall overflowing with knickknacks. A few steps away a weaver finishes a burnoose by embroidering the edge of the woolen cloth. In the middle of the market, in a rectangular court, a group of Algerians sits on the floor selling oil cakes and roasted beans. Farther away, blacks, covered head to foot in blue robes striped with white, hawk their cakes, dried raisins, and white aniseeds.[66]

It was just a moment's walk to the all-European Cours Bertagna. This was the administrative, financial, and elite commercial center of colonial Annaba. At the top of the Cours, the Catholic church; to the right, as you face the port, was the post office located in the Salfati mansion. The justice of the peace was installed in the Rossi mansion. Next to it was the Banque de l'Algérie, itself overshadowed by the Compagnie Algérienne building, successor to the Société Générale Algérienne. Also in the Compagnie Algérienne building was the Tribunal de Commerce.

The offices of the Mokta el Hadid, the company which exploited the richest iron ore mine in Algeria, located a scant twenty kilometers outside Bône, were on a side street just off the Cours. The two largest and most important cafes in Bône were the Cafe St. Martin, where the Opportunist Republicans congregated, and on the opposite side of the Cours the Café Couronne, frequented by the Radical Republicans. Next to the Café St. Martin was the Municipal theater. The leading hotel and restaurant, the Hotel de l'Orient, was farther down the Cours. The Chamber of Commerce was headquartered along the quai near the customs office. On either side of the lower end of the Cours were the Bronde mansion, built by the first president of the Chamber of Commerce, the Lecoq mansion, owned by the holder of the single largest cork oak concession in the nearby Edough Mountains, and the Calvin mansion. Farther up the opposite side of the Cours was the grandiose *mairie*, or city hall, new in 1884, the biggest and most handsome building in the city. Luxury shops and boutiques dotted the Cours, occupying the choice locations under the areades of the private buildings: Marie Grosso's pastry and candy shop at no. 6; Ferdinaud Aufiero, a marble cutter at no. 28; Mathieu Mariani, the leading publisher of colonial Bône, at no. 23; Mme. Spiteri, who supplied funeral wreaths for use in the European cemetery; the office of Narbonne, a lawyer; the jewelry stores of Jean Vassalo, Giraud & Tanti, and Cosandier; and the tailor shops of Marius Menagro at no. 3, Garcie at no. 4, Madona at no. 15, and Pio Mizzoni at no. 23. In the center of the Cours the Bônois promenaded under the shade of the plane trees and ate ice cream out of doors in the summer months. At kiosks you could buy newspapers and magazines, cigars and cigarettes. A few of these were run by Muslims, including that of Hadj Omar Bengui; they were the only Algerian presence on the Cours. What could make for a more striking contrast to the Annaba economy today?[67]

Conclusion

Taken as a whole, the Bône regional economy is characterized by dependency; viewed from afar, it resembles nothing so much as a funnel. Dependency is clearest in the twin cases of Tebessa phosphates and Ouenza iron ore. Economic dualism marks the Bône urban economy proper. As a settler colonial city, Bône developed a variegated urban economy which reflected its European and Algerian population. Thus, the de facto division into European and Algerian economic sectors mirrored the colonial situation just as much as the preponderance of commerce over industry typified the dependent position of Bône within the world economy. Although different economic sectors provided different

133

Illustration 4.4   Hadj Omar Bengui's kiosk (right) on Cours Bertagna, 1904
(Bibliothèque Nationale Cabinet d'Estampes).

goods, the largely separate European and Algerian economies were by
no means equal, as the existence of a predominantly Algerian informal
economy attests. Thus, the bifurcated colonial situation carried over
into the colonial economy, and the economic dominance of the settlers
was apparent to all the Bônois as they shopped in the covered market
and the *funduq*, in the stores along the Cours Bertagna.

5

The people of Bône

A colonial society is not like other societies, a settler colonial society is not like other colonial societies. And by 1870 Bône was well on its way to becoming a settler colonial society. Four decades had passed since the French invasion, four decades in which enough French and Italians and Maltese had come to Bône first to reconnoiter and then had stayed to try their hand at making a go of it that the Europeans outnumbered decisively the Algerians (Figure 5.1). Admittedly, the number who departed rivaled the number who arrived, and thus, it looked for years, even decades, as though the Europeans would never take root. Before 1870 the transiency of the Bône population makes the men in motion of the nineteenth-century American city look stationary.[1]

Even more serious, the place was just too damned unhealthy. Bône may have had a Mediterranean climate, but the early settlers seemed to die off as fast as they did in Conrad's Congo and along Gordon's Nile, certainly as rapidly as Braudel's sixteenth-century Mediterraneans draining the marshes of the Po. Yes, the Bônois drained Lake Fetzara; yes, they diverted the Bou Djima out of town and into the Seybouse River, but even today a good torrential storm can put much of Annaba under three or four feet of water in minutes flat. It took forty years before this people could stand on its own reproductive feet, and not have to fall back on inmigrant infusions to sustain itself.

If the story of the French in Bône before 1870 is about hanging on, the story after 1870 is about settling down; yet the proportion of settlers to Algerians did not change after that year from what it had been before. Well before 1870 the Europeans had established their demographic hegemony in Bône; well before 1870 they preponderated over the Algerians they were colonializing so assiduously. Thus, we have the first anomaly in this settler-colonial situation, itself anomalous: the Algerians outnumbered the Europeans by some six to one in Algeria as a whole, but the Europeans outnumbered the Algerians two to one in Bône

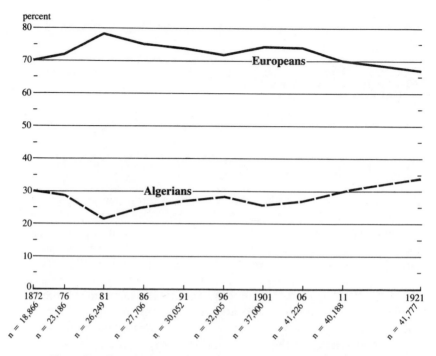

Figure 5.1   Europeans and Algerians in colonial Bône, 1872–1921 (Jews excluded from European totals except for 1921). *Source* APCA, *Listes nominatives*, 1872–1921.

(Figure 5.1). It would be hard to overemphasize the consequences which result from this demographic fact of Bône colonial life.

Settler demographics

What sealed the settlers' demographic success in Bône and elsewhere in Algeria was what occurred in Paris in 1870. For it was then for the first time that France ratified the settlers' demographic fait accompli, that France, the *métropole* around which all revolved, the center of civilization, acknowledged the settlers' existence by not only replacing military with civilian rule, but also by making the three coastal provinces of Algeria – Algiers, Oran, and Constantine – full-fledged *départements* of mainland France. Now, the peasants of Cantal, Ariège, and Périgord that Paris was so busy colonizing, the periphery that a centralizing state was incorporating assiduously into *la grande nation* were one thing, but adding to *la patrie* Italians and Maltese resident in Algeria, not to mention the Arabs and Berbers, was quite another.[2] Of course, the Auvergnats and the Ariégeois and the Vosgiens could vote in France, even

136

Illustration 5.1   View of Bône, 1880. The main church (right) is at the end of the tree-lined Cours, which divides the old city (lower left) and new city (center) (Bibliothèque National Cabinet d'Estampes).

if they followed their local notables too docilely to the polls, whereas in Algeria only French citizens could vote in local and national elections and noncitizens could vote only in local elections and only for a fixed number of representatives. And there precisely was the rub: a *département* of metropolitan France in which noncitizens outnumbered citizens but in which citizens counted for more at the polls, that is, some people were more equal than others. Thus, Algeria was a French colony – the colonizers maintained hegemony over the colonized, and at the same time Algeria was not a French colony – it was an integral part of France. In short, Algeria had been incorporated but not integrated into France in 1870, ingested but not digested.

To be sure, this was a political reward bestowed by a grateful Léon Gambetta and his Government of National Defense in recognition of *colon* republican loyalty, payment for services rendered in the past (1848, 1870) and a downpayment for the future (*seize mai* 1877). Nevertheless, what transpired in 1870 did constitute de facto recognition that the French and other European settlers of Algeria already were numerous enough in relation to the Algerians that Algeria was not like other French colonies, and that if Algeria was not unique it was certainly exceptional. Thus, political lobbying and backroom politicking in Paris

137

and Bordeaux may have been the immediate cause for the institution of civilian rule in Algeria after 1870, but it was founded at base on the demographics of sheer numbers, and on tens of thousands of them – French and Spanish and Italian and Maltese. No wonder the replacement of the illiberal Second Empire by the liberal Third Republic resulted in increased settler power in Algeria. And does it come as any surprise that such settler power was turned mainly against the Algerians to create an increasingly illiberal regime in Algeria only nominally controlled by a liberal regime in France? Therefore, 1870 did not result in an even stronger European implantation relative to the Algerians, but 1870 did mean a tilt in the colonial equation of power in favor of the settlers.[3]

At the same time as the French replaced military with civilian rule in 1870, they also naturalized en masse the Jews of Algeria (Figure 5.6). In doing so, the French triggered unwittingly a time bomb which was to detonate three decades later at the time of the Dreyfus affair. For the veneer of French citizenship could not hide the fact that the Jews resembled the Muslims more than the Christians. How could it not be so given their past history?[4]

Although the Jews had lived in Annaba for centuries prior to the French invasion in 1830, the Algerians viewed them as outsiders living in the midst of Muslim society. On the one hand, they were despised as infidels, a repugnance tempered only by the admission that they were monotheists, "people of the Book." They lived in their own ghetto, called *mellah*, near the center of Turkish Annaba. During the festival of Achoura Muslims dressed as Jews in order to act out what at other times would have been socially unacceptable behavior in a ritual of status reversal à la Victor Turner. On the other hand, Jews were suffered by the Algerians and Turks as valuable brokers and go-betweens. Turks often gave money to Jews to be lent at interest, since usury was forbidden by the Koran, and then shared in the profits – when they did not try and renege on the deal. Moreover, there was a subterranean view according to which the Jews possessed certain secret knowledge of ritual potency. Thus, "as hated and despised as they were, the Jews possessed, however, a magical power and their old rabbis were held to possess arcane knowledge and to be among the most learned wizards."[5]

What seems clear is that despite their segregation from the larger Muslim society – a segregation at once residential, social, and religious – Jews and Muslims nonetheless rubbed shoulders often enough that communal mores rubbed off and interpenetrated; mutual contempt did not preclude social intercourse and interchange.[6] The Jews and Muslims worshiped each others' saints, for example. In Bône the *ghariba*, or Jewish synagogue, was venerated by Muslims and Jews alike because of the myth of the sacred scrolls housed there, and pilgrims of both faiths came from far and near. Certain marriage customs were similar. Polygamy among Jews was not altogether unknown. The Jews took their shoes off before entering the synagogue, as did the Muslims before entering the mosque. Their manner of prayer, and the *yous-yous* uttered at funerals were very similar to Muslim practices. Moreover, the Jews dyed their hands and feet with henna. They feared the evil eye, and used sorcerers and amulets to ward it off, as well as killing a black cock. Both Jews and Muslims ate *couscous* and *chorba*, soup.[7]

In short, the Jews of North Africa struck the Jews of France as so unlike them and so like the Muslims in whose midst they lived, that parallel to the French colonialization of Algeria, the French Jews undertook what has been called the colonialization of the Algerian Jews.[8] At the same time, the French takeover in 1830 opened the same sort of doors of opportunity for the Jews that it had for others, perhaps more so. The Jews "were primarily artisans, peddlers, struggling shopkeepers, and petty brokers." They were tailors and jewelers, who sat "for long hours in their small, narrow booths"; they engaged in petty commerce, few if any were agriculturalists.[9] In some respects, the Jews were better situated to act as brokers and intermediaries, interpreters and traders than, for example, the Italians and Maltese. After all, they were already longtime residents of Annaba-become-Bône. They were already established in commerce and had developed a network of commercial contacts. They had ties with the Algerians and could speak their language. They knew how to do business with them. They also had connections with Europe, not so much with France and Christian Europe as with Jewish communities elsewhere in the Mediterranean – Alexandria, Tunis, and especially Leghorn.[10]

Given this background, it should come as no surprise that the real turning point in the Jews' fortunes was the decision to grant French citizenship to Algerian Jews in 1870 – something which would never happen for the Algerians. From this moment forward the Jews began to detach themselves increasingly from the Muslim world and gravitate towards the Christian one – not however without running into trouble. For the Jews were never fully accepted by the European settlers, and as we shall see, when a recognizably *pied-noir* society and culture were formed around the turn of the twentieth century, the Jews were excluded.[11]

In 1870 France ratified the demographic fait accompli the settlers had presented to the *métropole*. In return, the settlers settled not all of Algeria but selected parts of it, namely, the cities – especially those along the coast – and much less so the rural areas located in the interior. Now, the Algerian settlers are often referred to as *colons*, French for rural settlers, whereas in fact already by 1900 more than sixty percent of these so-called *colons* had colonized the cities rather than the country, had plowed their money into business rather than the soil, had opened stores downtown rather than cultivate farms outside town.

Bône and the surrounding region was one of the best examples of the manner in which the French and other settlers spread out across the Algerian landscape. Arriving first in Bône – and Oran and Algiers – some turned right around and left again back the way they had come, some stayed and hunkered down in the city, some passed through Bône and into the countryside, where in turn they either stayed on or drifted back to Bône. Thus, the settlers bunched up in the Mediterranean ports; the closer you got to the Sahara, the more thinly spread out across the land they were. In the desert itself, there were only isolated pockets of them huddled around the water holes that were the oases of Laghouat and El Oued, Timimoun and Ouargla. Even there they were shopkeepers and military hangers-on rather than settlers, plus a smattering of world travelers before their time, such as André Gide, aristocratic visitors like the Luxembourg duchess whose passage through Timimoun is memorialized in the wooden plaque over the door to the room she stayed in, and those other seekers after transcendental truth such as Père Foucauld in his Tamanrasset redoubt in the heart of the heart of the Sahara.

Back in Bône, a replica of Third Republic France was abuilding. After all, so many Europeans had come to the *arrondissement*, or region, of Bône and stayed on that it was the area most densely populated by settlers after Algiers and Oran.[12] While the Spanish migrated to Oran in the west, the Italians and Maltese gravitated to Bône in the east. But whereas the Europeans outnumbered the Algerians within the walls of Bône, the Algerians clearly predominated over the Europeans outside in the Bône region both in the *communes de pleine exercice*, fully fledged French communes, and the *communes mixtes*, predominantly Muslim settlements administered by a French official (Figure 5.2). Thus for example, Italian miners and forest workers formed thickets of settlement inland, and Italian fishermen formed clusters of encampments along the coast.

It is no coincidence, therefore, that in the coastal port city of Bône Europeans outnumbered the Algerians; it is no coincidence that it was the land along the Mediterranean that was formed into overseas départements of mainland France. And yet it is worth stressing that it could have been otherwise, that Bône could have been peopled differently. After all, Algeria was the only settler colony at the time in the Mediterranean, only the second in the continent of Africa, only one of a handful in the world. Unlike South Africa, for instance, the root cause of European population growth was geographical propinquity: the Spanish and the Italians and the Maltese rivaled the French in numbers not

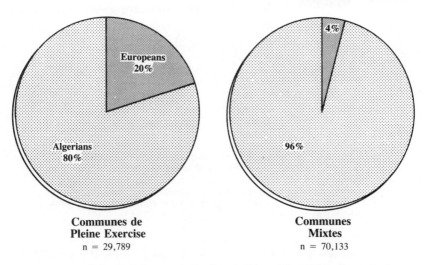

Communes de   Communes
Pleine Exercise   Mixtes
n = 29,789   n = 70,133

Figure 5.2 Europeans and Algerians in Bône region, 1907. Corresponds to
arrondissement of Bône, less Bône itself, plus La Calle, the only other port
city in the region and with a population structure similar to that of Bône.
Communes de pleine exercice include Ain Mokra, Barral, Bugeaud, Duvivier,
Duzerville, Herbillon, La Calle, Mondovi, Morris, Nechmaya, Penthièvre,
and Randon. *Communes mixtes* include Beni Salah, Edough, and La Calle.
Source: Gouvernement Général de l'Algérie, *Tableau Général des
Communes* (1907), pp. 132–9.

because the French welcomed them with open arms, but because Spain
and Italy and Malta were so close, as close or closer to Algeria than
France itself. It should also be remembered that France and Europe
had long been interested in the southern shore of the Mediterranean,
but without forming any settler colonies, without forming any colonies
to speak of before the takeover of Algeria. While Europeans had been
interested in Egypt earlier than Algeria, and Napoléon's 1798 invasion
of Egypt served as a model for the 1830 invasion of Algeria, it is nonetheless worth recalling that the European population of Cairo, for example, never amounted to more than five percent of the total population
under either the French or the British. For the opening of the Suez
Canal in 1869, Khedive Ismail invited the other Napoléon's Empress
Eugenie, commissioned Verdi to compose *Aida*, and refurbished Cairo
à la française, but the city resisted on the whole what was in fact a
superficial Europeanization which extended only as deep as the building
facades Ismail had painted over, was only as spotty as the French formal
gardens which dotted the city.[13] But Algeria first and foremost, Tunisia
and Morocco later and less so, these were colonies in the Mediterranean
that were bastions of European settlers.

To reproduce itself in Algeria, France had to sink roots in the land,

141

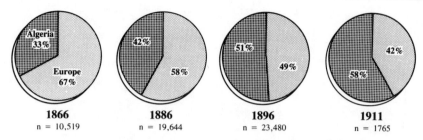

Figure 5.3   Birthplace of Bône Europeans, 1866–1911. In 1886 data, "Europe" includes Algeria outside Bône as well as Europe. However, only three percent native French and one percent other Europeans were born outside the Bône region in 1896, for example, and, therefore, this category combines Europe and other Algeria together in 1886. *Source:* APCA, *Listes nominatives*, 1866–96; 1911 census sample data.

it had to settle the countryside, or so the myth went. But instead the Europeans flocked to the cities and reproduced France there – as well as themselves. Speaking demographically, what did not change in Bône before and after 1870 was steady although not spectacular population growth, and a two-to-one proportion of Europeans to Algerians; what did change was that the settlers settled down. First, they were born more and more in Algeria and less and less in Europe (Figure 5.3). It was in the 1890s that for the first time the European people of Bône were born more frequently in Bône and Algeria than in France, Italy and Malta. In 1866 whereas only one out of three Europeans was born in Bône, by the 1890s those born in Bône outnumbered those born elsewhere, and by 1911 three out of every five Europeans were born in Bône.

Second, the age and sex structure of the population altered as the people of Bône settled down increasingly and reproduced themselves in Algeria rather than relying on inmigrants. Thus, the ratio of men to women continued to decrease after 1870, although the big decline had occurred before 1870 (Table 5.1). Moreover, there was no particular tendency for productive age European males (aged 15–49), to predominate over productive age European females. Notice, however, that the situation was exactly the reverse for the Algerians. Between 1876 and 1911 male/female ratios increased among all Algerians, and the ratios among productive age Algerians was even higher. What was happening was that Algerian males between the ages of 15 and 49 were migrating increasingly to Bône which had the effect of raising the male/female ratios for all Algerians.

Third, European birth and death rates declined gradually after 1870, and especially between the late 1880s and the first decade of the twentieth century. This indicates that a demographic transition was occurring

Table 5.1. *European and Algerian male/female ratios, 1876–1911*

Year	Overall male/female ratio		Productive age (15–49) male/female ratio		Number
	Europeans	Algerians	Europeans	Algerians	
1876	1.33	1.39	1.39	1.55	1,806
1891	1.17	1.36	1.18	1.49	2,188
1911	0.97	1.50	0.96	1.67	2,810

Source: Calculated from census sample data, 1876–1911.

in Algeria among the Europeans just as in Europe (Figure 5.4). Birth and death rates from 1870 until at least the end of the 1880s were more or less in equilibrium, but in the twentieth century a gap opened up to produce an excess of births over deaths as the birthrate fell but the death rate fell even more. Among the Algerians, however, no such demographic transition occurred (Figure 5.5). In every year between 1870

rate per thousand persons

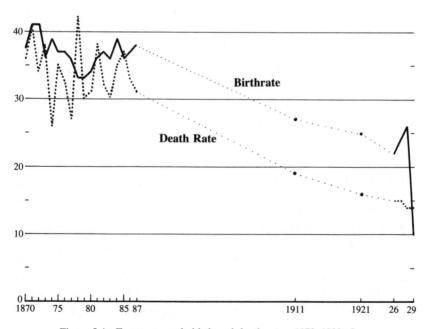

Figure 5.4   European crude birth and death rates, 1870–1929. *Source:* APCA, Actes de naissance, 1866–1931; Actes de décès, 1866–1931; *Listes nominatives*, 1866–1926; SGA, 1867–87.

rate per thousand persons

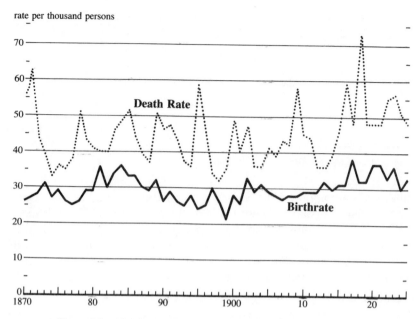

Figure 5.5   Algerian crude birth and death rates, 1870–1925. *Source:* APCA, *Actes de naissances musulmanes,* 1870–1925; *Actes de décès musulmans,* 1870–1925; *Listes nominatives,* 1866–1926.

and 1925 more Algerians died in Bône than were born there. Only through inmigration did the Algerian population grow. The Algerian birthrate in the 1870s and 1880s was actually slightly lower than that of the Europeans, but it remained more or less stationary while European fertility decreased. Worse still, mortality remained extremely high. Twelve years between 1870 and 1925 more than 50 per 1,000 Algerians died, between 1915 and 1925 the death rate never dropped below 46, and in 1918 the highest death rate since 1870 was recorded – 73 per 1,000! The French may have come to Algeria bearing civilization, but they were unable to keep the Algerians from dying off in record numbers. The settlers viewed such bulletins from the demographic front with calculated self-interest clothed in pseudoscientific disinterest. After all, aboriginal peoples elsewhere – Indians in North America, pygmies in Australia – were dying out. Surely this was what the brave new world of science and civilization had in store for the Algerians as well? As in so many other spheres of life, therefore, there was an increasing not decreasing gap between Algerians and Europeans in terms of birth and death rates between 1870 and 1920.

As we might expect, Jewish birth and death rates occupy an inter-mediate position between those of the Europeans and the Algerians.

144

Table 5.2. *European and Algerian household structure (percent),*
1876–1911[a]

1876 (n = 558)	Solitaries and coresidents	Single families	Extended families	Multiple families	Indeterminate
Native French	38.3	50.3	7.7	0.4	3.3
Other Europeans	30.7	59.0	4.9	2.2	1.2
Algerians 1891					
(n = 813)	33.1	53.1	8.6	1.3	4.0
Native French	57.2	36.9	5.0	0.5	0.4
Other Europeans	44.3	50.8	4.2	0.5	0.1
Algerians 1911					
(n = 828)	44.5	44.1	7.9	2.2	1.3
Native French	41.0	51.5	6.6	0.8	—
Other Europeans	36.3	56.5	6.5	0.7	—
Algerians	43.4	45.1	8.7	2.4	0

[a]Naturalized French excluded. See text for discussion.
Source: Computerized census sample, 1876–1911.

On the one hand, Jewish fecundity remains higher than that of the Europeans throughout the period, higher than that of any other population group in colonial Bône. On the other hand, Jewish mortality is lower than that of the Europeans at the beginning of the period in question, and although it does not decline as much as the European death rate, it remains well below that of the Algerians. Thus, a high death rate combined with an even higher birthrate to produce a healthy excess of births over deaths in every year between 1870 and 1887 except one.[14]

Fourth, household structure altered by and large to reflect a more permanent and less transient European population (Table 5.2). On the one hand, fewer single and unmarried individuals, and on the other hand, proportionally more nuclear families indicate people were settling down and raising families. That there were fewer extended and especially multiple families among the Europeans compared to the Algerians was evidence of the widespread cultural differences in general and childrearing practices in particular which separated the two cultures.

Within the European community, moreover, it was the native French who were more likely to live alone and with coresidents – indicative of a high proportion of single inmigrants – and less likely to form single family households than other Europeans. The sizeable number of tem-

thousands of persons

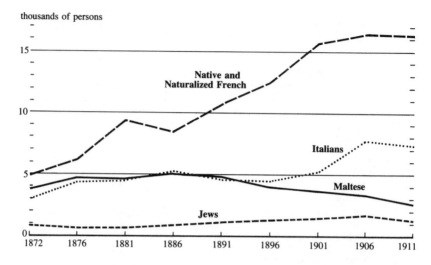

Figure 5.6   European subgroups in colonial Bône, 1872–1911. Native and naturalized French includes Jews. Figures for Italians and Maltese in 1901 are extrapolations. *Source:* APCA, *Listes nominatives*, 1872–1911.

porary French immigrants, particularly colonial administrators, officials, and businessmen, explains why so many of the native French lived alone or with coresidents when compared both to the non-French Europeans and the Algerians. Otherwise, however, there was no significant difference between French and other Europeans in their propensity to form extended and multiple family households.[15]

If the single most significant demographic fact about colonial Bône was the high proportion of Europeans to Algerians, then the second most important feature was that the non-French outnumbered the French, at least before the naturalization law of 1889 (Figure 5.6). Whoever heard tell of a French colony peopled primarily by Italians and Spanish and Maltese? And yet that was precisely what was going on in colonial Algeria, where the Italians plus the Maltese outnumbered the French in the east and the Spanish outnumbered the French in the west. Parallel to the European colonialization of the Algerians, therefore, we have a secondary colonialization by the French of the other Europeans, of European colonies within the French colony. And the other Europeans differed from the native French in more than one way.

For one thing, the non-French Europeans were born more often in Algeria than the native French between 1866 and 1911 (Figure 5.7).[16] In this settler colony, therefore, the Italians and Maltese settled down more rapidly than the French. And even the French of France who

146

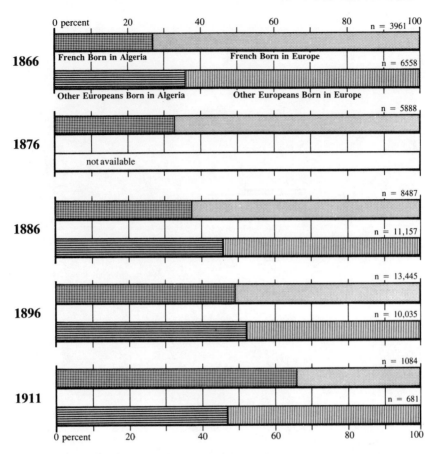

Figure 5.7 Birthplace of French and other Europeans, 1866–1911. In 1886 data, "Europe" includes Algeria outside Bône as well as Europe. However, only three percent native French and one percent other Europeans were born outside the Bône region in 1896, for example, and, therefore, this category combines Europe and other Algeria together in 1886. *Source:* APCA, *Listes nominatives*, 1866–96; 1911 census sample data.

emigrated to Algeria were born more often in the south along the Mediterranean, in any case below the line Marc Bloch drew across France from west to east and which for him represented the dividing line between two Frances, different in agricultural practices, language, household structure, and settlement patterns, not to mention cultural outlook (Figure 5.8).

The native French and other Europeans also differed in the rate at which they procreated (Table 5.3).[17] The fertility rate among all Europeans is actually higher in 1876 than that for the Algerians, but from

147

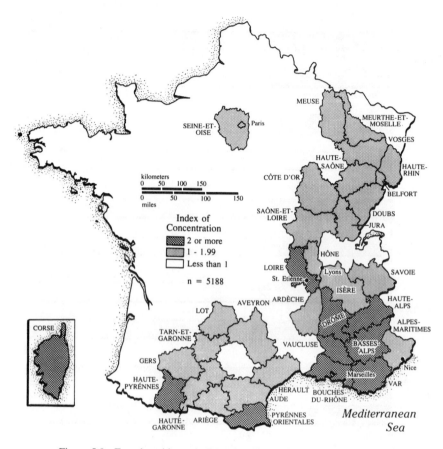

Figure 5.8 French residency in Bône by department of birth, 1896. The index of concentration is interpreted as follows. A value of one means that the number born in a given department is represented in the native French population of Bône in the same proportion as the population of the department in the population of France. The greater the value over one, the more a department is overrepresented; and the smaller the value under one, the more a department is underrepresented. *Source:* Calculated from APCA, *Liste nominative*, 1896; France, *Dénombrement de 1896*, pp. 66–8.

then on it decreases whereas the Algerian fertility rate actually increases. Jewish fertility also decreases during the period but it still remains higher in 1891 and 1911 than that of all Europeans.[18] But notice that both the native French and the other Europeans exhibit a steady decline in fertility from 1876 to 1911. Here again is evidence that the Europeans are passing through their own demographic transition as we saw in Figure 5.4. Yet the Italian and Maltese fertility rates lag a step or two behind those of the French. The French fertility rates are the lowest of any

Table 5.3. *European and Algerian fertility ratios, 1876–1911*[a]

Year	Native French	Other Europeans	Total Europeans	Total Jews	Total Algerians	Total Bône	Number[b]
1876	386	561	472	733	455	478	654
1891	244	486	362	381	458	389	804
1911	275	372	346	387	500	391	1,003

[a]Defined as the ratio of children aged 0–5 to women in childbearing ages 15–49 × 1,000.
[b]Women and children combined.
Source: Calculated from census sample data, 1876–1911.

group in colonial Bône, but it takes the Italians and Maltese until 1911 to match the French fertility rate of 1876. What we see occurring among the settler community, therefore, is a demographic transition, but one in which the other Europeans follow the lead of the French.

Different places of birth and different fertility rates between the native French and other Europeans are telling indicators that the life experiences of the Italians and Maltese differed radically from those of the French. To examine who and where the Italians and Maltese came from is to understand something of the manner in which settler society formed in colonial Algeria.

Consider the Maltese, for example. Long before they arrived in Algeria, the Maltese had made themselves known in the Mediterranean. In 870 the Arabs conquered Malta. In 1090 it was the turn of the Normans. In 1523 the island was given over to the crusading Knights of St. John by Charles V. Throughout the resurgence of Muslim power during Fernand Braudel's "long sixteenth century," Malta played a key role. It was only in 1798 that the Knights of St. John were ousted by Napoleon on his way to invade Egypt. Two years later, in 1800, Malta changed from French to British hands and remained a British possession until the twentieth century.[19]

The British used Malta primarily as one of their main Mediterranean naval bases. During the nineteenth century Malta experienced the vicissitudes of a Mediterranean economy based primarily on the sea: technological changes in shipbuilding (from wind to steam and wood to iron), the opening of the Suez Canal in 1869 and the resulting increase in shipping, and the cotton boomlet made possible by the American Civil War and the impossibility of continued production after 1865 due to renewed American competition. In 1837 a faltering economy led to a mass demonstration of Maltese peasants clamoring for "work or bread."

But more than economic, the problem was demographic. In spite of the naval base at La Vallette with its greatly expanded arsenal plus

149

extensive refueling and repair facilities, there were simply too few jobs for too many Maltese. The islands which comprise Malta – Malta and Gozo – were simply too tiny – 315 square kilometers – and the number of Maltese simply too many: 100,000 when Napoleon invaded in 1798, 140,000 in 1871. Already in 1823 there were 350 people per square kilometer. As a result, peasants left the land in search of work primarily at the port of La Vallette. Not finding any they embarked for the United States and Australia first and foremost, as well as Greece, Italy, Tunisia, Egypt, and after 1830 Algeria.

Algeria was a logical choice. Malta was relatively close, only 320 kilometers from Tunis, and not much further from Bône: Moreover, Maltese is a dialect of Arabic; both are Semitic languages. Thus, the French takeover of Algeria, which created a demand for intermediaries to act as interpreters, soldiers and suppliers of all sorts of goods, opened a door of opportunity for the Maltese. These factors account for why the Maltese concentrated in eastern Algeria in general and the Bône region in particular (Figure 5.6). Nor is it surprising that the Maltese in Bône rivaled the French in numbers early on, and outnumbered the Italians until the 1880s.

Or what about the Italians? They were no more strangers to Bône before the coming of the French than were the Maltese. The Pisans attacked Bône in 1034 as part of the European reconquest of the Mediterranean from the Muslims. The Genoese fortified their trading station just outside Bône in the fifteenth century, Fort Génois. In the seventeenth century the Duke of Toscany made a pirate attack on Bône to counter, of course, the Barbary corsairs in their lair. And although based more often in Tunis, the Jews of Leghorn were also no strangers to the Bône region.[20]

The Italians who emigrated came primarily from the north (Piedmont) and the south (Sicily, Sardinia, Calabria, Naples), but not central Italy. From Lucca, Sardinia and the island of Elba came agricultural workers and truck gardeners to Bône; from the valley of the Po in the north came masons, shoemakers, and miners.[21] Of all the Italians who left Italy between 1891 and 1897, nearly one-half were agricultural workers, another one-quarter were ditch diggers and day laborers, and one in every seven were masons and stonecutters. Most agricultural workers migrated to colonies where they were offered free land, such as Argentina, but not Algeria, where free concessions were reserved for the French. Thus, the occupations of Italians emigrating to Algeria differed from those emigrating elsewhere: they tended to be masons and shoemakers, miners and unskilled workers, fishermen and forest workers, and included very few agriculturalists.[22]

"Fleeing starvation wages . . . these emigrants certainly did not constitute a social elite.... "[23] Having decided to emigrate, the Italians generally took one of two routes to Algeria. Some made it to Naples, where they booked passage on the only boat which sailed regularly between Italy and Bône, the *Principe-di-Napoli*, on its monthly trip "filled with a crowd of poor people fleeing the misery of the big city."[24] The majority, however, first went to France looking for work, and from there booked passage to Algeria on a ship leaving from Marseilles. "Heaped up like cargo on the decks or in the holds, they made the Mediterranean crossing in the worst possible conditions."[25]

Some migrated temporarily, some permanently. We have two descriptions of Italian immigrants to Bône, the first from 1870.

Each year as winter approached, an entire floating population of workers without jobs journeyed from Italy to Bône where they spread out looking for work, some working on construction gangs building railroads, roads, bridges and irrigation canals, the others clearing waste land, draining swamps, working as miners in the iron, lead and zinc mines. With the coming of summer, the harvest scarcely ended, and work in the mines halted due to the excessive heat, all these workers headed back to their native land, without any desire to return to Algeria where they were "paid too little." But soon they were replaced by new recruits, "so sad is the lot of the workers of Italy."[26]

Ten years later not much had changed.

For the last twenty years in Bône every time a mail ship arrived one could see a crowd of Italian immigrants rushing to the offices of the [Italian] consulate to obtain information and advice on work to undertake, on the areas where labor was scarce, and what to do to find a job more easily. "Very rare," said the Italian representative in a report to the *Consulta*, "were those who arrived with the promise of a job. Still, these favored immigrants were only the friends or relatives of other immigrants already established in the region, and these other immigrants had taken work *a cottimo*, preferring then to stupidly invite the new arrivals to join them so they could work together rather than utilize the large number of Italians already established and who lacked work, whom they could have hired under much better conditions."[27]

Italian emigrants to Algeria clustered in the eastern province of Constantine just as the Spanish concentrated in the western province of Oran – geography tells the story. Considering the Italian population in Bône as well as the total Italian population in Algeria, three main phases can be discerned: first, steady but not spectacular growth before 1872; second, a much greater increase between 1872 and 1886; and third, a decrease in the absolute number of Italians 1886–96 due to increasingly restrictive laws in 1886 and 1888 concerning fishing, plus the 1889 naturalization law which affected all Europeans. These same general trends can be seen both in the Italian population of Bône and all of Algeria.[28]

151

However, the département of Constantine was more heavily populated with Italians than any other. Moving across Algeria from west to east, that is, increasingly further away from Italy, we find in 1900, 20,000 Italians in Constantine département, 14,000 in Algiers, and fewer than 4,000 in Oran. Moreover, two-thirds of all Italians in Constantine province were living in colonial port cities on the Mediterranean: 6,000 in Bône, 3,500 in Philippeville, and 1,000 in La Calle. Even more telling is that the ratio of Italians to French increased as you moved west to east across Constantine province. Whereas French outnumbered Italians four to one in Bougie, at Philippeville the proportion was only two to one, and in Bône the number of Italians equaled the number of French. Elsewhere in the interior of Constantine province, there were only small pockets of Italians – "scattered islands in the vast expanse of this *département*" – at Tebessa and Morsott in the center of the phosphates region, at Batna and in the Aurès where the copper mines were located, at Souk Ahras where forests of cork oak were found, and at Ain Mokra, famous for its rich iron ore mine.[29] Truly, "The region of Bône has always been the one most populated with Italians."[30]

What we have then is a French colony in which the French were outnumbered by the Italians, Maltese, and Spanish together – not to mention the Algerians. It was bad enough that too few French were too little interested to emigrate to Algeria. Granted, not many French emigrated many places relative to other Europeans in the nineteenth century given the low French birthrate in France. But the problem then became: How do you make Algeria a French colony, and a colony administered as an integral part of the *métropole* at that? The initial French response was to offer prospective French settlers the inducement of free land. But relatively few accepted the offer, and of those who did, more would-be *colons*, or rural settlers, preferred to congregate in the cities than settle on the land, as we have seen.

Meanwhile, the Italians and Maltese were demonstrating relatively more success in settling Algeria than the French. Born more often in Bône than the native French, they also reproduced at a greater rate than the French. After failing to attract sufficient numbers of French to Algeria with the enticement of free land, therefore, the French adopted a second strategy, namely, to offer the other Europeans French citizenship on an individual basis. But few Italians and Maltese took the bait. It seemed that so long as their livelihood was not threatened in Algeria, the non-French Europeans saw no particular advantage to obtaining their own key to the *cité française*.

In short, the French faced a dilemma. On the one hand, they were loath to grant French citizenship to Europeans whom they considered often culturally inferior and politically backward. On the other hand, to shore up their demographic defenses against the other Europeans and even more against the Algerians, and because so few among the growing non-French population opted for French nationality, the government was forced at last to liberalize its naturalization procedures. This it did with the naturalization law of 1889, which went so far as to naturalize automatically the children of European immigrants at age twenty-one unless they specifically refused it. This was an important step in the creation of the *pied noir* community because it had the effect of nearly doubling the nominally French population and reducing by an equal amount the number of Italians and Maltese (Figure 5.6). Yet it would be years before these naturalized French were absorbed fully into the French community. Until then, the naturalized French and non-French Europeans continued to constitute colonies within the larger French colony.

Social stratification in colonial society

A settler colonial society in which the European colonizers outnumber the Algerian colonized two to one. A French colony in which the Italians, Spanish, and Maltese are as numerous as the French, and form colonies within the colony. A French colonial society created largely by naturalizing Jews and Europeans. A colonial society stratified along lines of ethnicity and class, the one reinforcing the other.

The fundamental basis of social stratification in colonial Bône was ethnicity. In the sort of ethnic ladder image prevalent among people at the time, the native French occupied the top rung of the social hierarchy followed in descending order by the naturalized French, the Italians and Maltese, and, several rungs down, the Jews, Arabs and Berbers.[31]

Yet ethnic or "vertical" divisions did not coincide completely with class or "horizontal" divisions. For what the French had done by naturalizing first the Jews in 1870, and second the Europeans in 1889, was to construct a colonial society in which ethnicity and class corresponded most of the time but not always. The French were as surely at the top of this society as the Algerians were at the bottom. Yet there were tension-producing overlaps when class ran up against the "color line," which occurred, for example, among lower class Europeans who were nonetheless colonizers, and among upper class Algerians who were nonetheless the colonized. Such status anxiety was especially clear in the case of the Jews. Unlike the Algerians, the Jews were nominally French citizens; unlike the French socially and culturally, the Europeans considered the Jews more like the Algerians. The Jews occupied, therefore, a liminal social position: detached

153

from the Muslim community, they had not been welcomed into the European community.[32]

A more analytical but straightforward model of colonial social structure which incorporates both class and ethnic criteria is the one proposed by Abu-Lughod for Rabat in Morocco but equally applicable to Bône in Algeria.

By the 1920s, Rabat had begun to develop a four-tiered class system with a caste line dividing the highest two from the bottom two. At the apex of the system were the predominantly French . . . entrepreneurs and civil servants. . . . In the second tier were the more proletarian European workers, many of them from southern Europe. . . . A caste-like gap separated these two groups from the Moroccans who were, in turn, subdivided between the group that was urbanized before the colonial period . . . and the newcomers from the hinterlands. . . .[33]

Abu-Lughod's last two tiers correspond by and large to the division in Bône between Arabs and Berbers, although the sort of massive rural-urban migration that she is referring to occurred in Bône beginning only in the decade 1926–36.[34] On the other hand, Abu-Lughod's first two tiers correspond to what I have called the European colonies within the French colony. In fact, she is only the latest of a long line of observers to argue that the mass of poorer-off Italians and Spanish and Maltese, sometimes referred to as *petits blancs* (poor whites), or *va-nu-pieds*, differed clearly from the native French. These southern Europeans

aspired to a life not at the level to which they had been accustomed, but at the level to which they wished to become accustomed. For, as was the case with Englishmen who went to India, most of the immigrants who flocked to Morocco were working-class or petit-bourgeois at best. They migrated chiefly to improve their positions, and the standards they wished to establish for themselves in Morocco were definitely at a level far above their life styles at home; they were commensurate with their new position as part of the ruling caste.[35]

No wonder these people, known later as *pieds-noirs*, have gotten a bad press. No wonder they have been looked down upon by their alleged social betters who could or did stay home, criticized as colonial parvenus by mainstream writers; faulted for exploiting the Algerians rather than joining with them to form a broad-based popular movement by left commentators; and despised by the Algerians themselves for lording it over them on the basis of neither wealth nor education but only race and ethnicity.

The way in which ethnic or racial plus class criteria combine to produce a distinctively colonial social structure was seen clearly in the case of Algeria by Frantz Fanon.

When you examine at close quarters the colonial context, it is evident that what parcels out the world is to begin with the fact of belonging to or not belonging to a given race, a given species. In the colonies the economic substructure is also a superstructure. The cause is the consequence; you are rich because you are white, you are white because you are rich. This is why Marxist analysis should always be slightly stretched every time we have to do with the colonial problem.[36]

Marxist or class analysis needs to be slightly stretched to take into account race and ethnicity. Not only do Abu-Lughod and Fanon agree on how race or ethnicity and class together determine social stratification in a colonial situation, but Fanon argues, furthermore, that race and class do not simply overlay each other but actually reinforce one another in ways which create a more unequal and racist social order than one based on either race or class alone. "You are rich because you are white, you are white because you are rich": this is a classic double bind situation. And it is precisely such a double bind which the colonial encounter in Algeria engendered, as Pierre Bourdieu, the foremost anthropological observer of Algerian society, has noted.[37]

How different such a self-reinforcing and self-perpetuating view of colonial society is from the optimistic prognostications of turn-of-the-century colonial apologists! For during most of the nineteenth century the goal of official French colonial policy in Algeria was assimilation. To be sure, this was as much a colonial ideology as a colonial policy, enunciated in Paris rather than implemented in Algeria. Instead, the gap between Algerian colonized and European colonizers was widening rather than narrowing in virtually every sphere of colonial life.[38]

In the case of colonial Bône, therefore, we have a settler colonial society in which the main division was the one which separated colonizers and colonized, Algerians from Europeans, and the Jews from both. Within the Muslim community there were distinctions primarily between Arab and Berber. Within the European community, class differences separated less well-off Italians and Maltese from the better-off native French. These latter differences were not so great, however, as to preclude the formation of a recognizably settler society and a distinctively colonial culture. In short, the Algerian melting pot did not dissolve individual European ethnic differences, but instead created a heady new Mediterranean stew – what later came to be known as the *pied-noir* community.[39]

In what follows these social cleavages will be examined by looking in

155

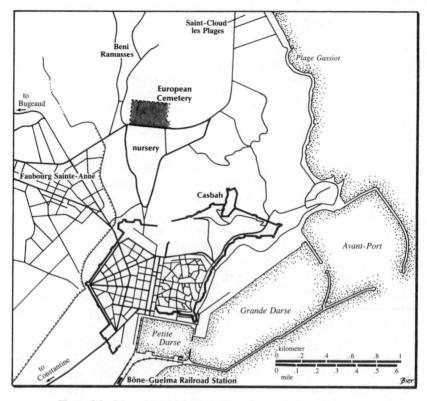

Figure 5.9   Map of colonial Bône, 1909. *Source:* After AOM, Port de Bône (1909).

turn at residential segregation, the cultural division of labor, vertical occupational specialization, functional occupational specialization, position in job, and finally, unequal pay for equal work.

Residential segregation

Residential segregation is one of the essential features of the colonial city from southern Africa, where apartheid laws prohibit blacks from residing in urban areas, to colonial New Delhi where the British formulated an extremely fine-grained hierarchical housing schema, and from colonial Morocco, where Marshal Lyautey enforced a separation of the races in distinct districts, to Chinese treaty ports where foreigners were confined to their own housing and trading compounds.[40] Clearly, segregation is connected to social distance, assimilation, and race relations in general. For Frantz Fanon, the radical division of the colonial

156

city into segregated halves epitomizes the radical bifurcation of colonial society as a whole.[41]

The data on segregation in Bône may be analyzed in two stages. First, we will pinpoint the city areas where various population groups concentrated; second, we will measure the degree of segregation between these groups (Fig. 5.9). Let us compare first the housing patterns of the Algerians and Europeans taken as a whole. Table 5.4 indicates the relative proportion of people in various city areas in the form of what I will call an index of relative concentration.[42] The index is interpreted as follows. A value of 1 means that the population group is represented in the city area in the same proportion as it is in the total Bône population, whereas the greater the value over 1, the more a group is overrepresented; and the smaller the value under 1, the more a group is underrepresented. Thus, the reader can easily determine whether the concentration of an ethnic group in any given city area is more or less than for the city as a whole.

The single most important conclusion which can be drawn from Table 5.4 is that the Europeans and Algerians each had their own distinctive housing pattern in colonial Bône. The Europeans were most overrepresented in the new city in relation to their total population in Bône, and they were most underrepresented in the outskirts (*banlieue*). Contrast this to the Muslim pattern: the Algerians were most overrepresented in the outskirts compared to their citywide population, and they were most underrepresented in the new city. In other words, the relative concentrations of Europeans and Algerians in the new city and outskirts are mirror images of one another.

The population mix of the old city matched more nearly that of Bône as a whole than any other single quarter. Yet a significant population shift occurred between 1881 and 1901, which is connected with the expansion of the new city and especially the Colonne Randon. During this twenty-year time span the total population of the old city remained virtually stationary, but nearly 3,000 Europeans left and some 2,000 Algerians moved in. During this same period the new city and Colonne Randon added about 4,000 Europeans apiece. As the Europeans moved out of the poorer, overcrowded old city and into the newer and wealthier sections of the new city and Colonne Randon, therefore, they were replaced by Algerians (data not presented here). This was a process repeated often in colonial cities in North Africa and elsewhere.

Compared to the ethnic heterogeneity of the old city, the new city was virtually homogeneous. The new city may have been where Algerian businesses were concentrated, but in terms of residence it was overwhelmingly European. In 1872, at the time when the new city was beginning to expand rapidly, a full ninety-one percent of all those who

157

158

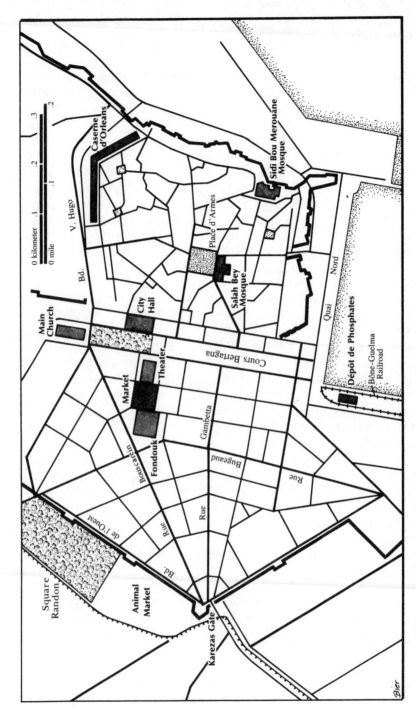

Figure 5.10   Map of central Bône, 1909. *Source:* After AOM, Port of Bône (1909).

Table 5.4. *Europeans and Algerians in major city areas, 1872–1906*

Year	Old City	New City	Colonne Randon[a]	Outskirts[b]
Index of relative concentration of Europeans				
1872	0.95	1.40	—	0.85
1876	0.96	1.26	—	0.85
1881	0.96	1.20	1.12	0.59
1901	0.73	1.29	1.36	0.50
1906	0.72	1.26	1.36	0.52
1911	0.72	1.34	1.32	0.46
Index of relative concentration of Algerians				
1872	1.03	.27	—	1.50
1876	1.03	.45	—	1.45
1881	1.13	.38	.63	2.29
1901	1.58	.27	.19	2.50
1906	1.56	.37	.22	2.37
1911	1.47	.31	.41	2.23

Note: See text for method of calculation and interpretation of the index.
[a]The Colonne Randon does not exist as a separate census quarter in 1872 and 1876. The 1881 census defines as outskirts (*banlieue*) an area that includes, but is larger than, what will later be known as the Colonne Randon.
[b]The 1881 census uses the term rural population (*population rurale*) instead of outskirts (*banlieue*). See text for discussion.
Source: Calculated from APCA, *Listes nominatives*, 1872, 1876, 1881, 1901, 1906, 1911.

lived there were Europeans. In contrast, Algerian indexes of relative concentration in the new city are consistently the lowest in Bône. Moreover, the new city retained its European flavor throughout the colonial period, for as late as 1954 it was still nearly three-quarters European.[43]

The Colonne Randon was also a European bastion. In 1881 as new city expansion tapered off and Colonne Randon growth accelerated, the Colonne was 85 percent European and only 15 percent Algerian. Twenty years later in 1901 at the peak of its growth, Europeans accounted for a full 95 percent of the Colonne's population and the Algerians a mere 5 percent. Moreover, it can be shown that Europeans in the new city enjoyed a higher socioeconomic status than their counterparts in the more working-class Colonne.[44] In the twentieth century and especially during the interwar years, Muslims moved into the Colonne in such numbers that they outnumbered the Europeans there by 1954.[45]

The high number of Algerians living in the outskirts is perhaps the single most significant aspect of residential segregation in colonial Bône. Throughout the 1872–1911 period and on into the twentieth century approximately 30 percent of all Algerians lived outside the city's central districts. In contrast, the Europeans were least likely to live in the outskirts of all areas of Bône.

159

What is particularly striking about these findings is that the main residential patterns are clearly discernible throughout the 40 years between 1872 and 1911, for which data exist. Although the indexes of concentration vary over time, the Europeans and Algerians are underrepresented or overrepresented in the same districts toward the end of the period as they are at the beginning.

Although the biggest contrasts in residence patterns occur between Europeans and Muslims, differences also exist within the European community, in the European colonies within the larger French colony (Table 5.5). First, however, consider the Jews. The Jews exhibit an utterly unique residential pattern which differentiates them not only from the Europeans but from the Muslims as well. Despite French citizenship, the Jews are not part of the nascent *pied-noir* community at least in terms of residence.

The Jews clustered to a greater extent and for a longer period of time in a single city area – the old city – than any other group in colonial Bône. No doubt this was due to their small number and the fact that the synagogue was located in the old city. In 1872, for example, 96 percent of Bône's Jews resided in the old city, and 40 years later fully three-quarters still lived there. Moreover, 75 percent of all old city Jews in 1872 clustered in the census district which included the synagogue (the old city was divided into three census districts at the time). In the years 1901, 1906, and 1911, 61 percent, 59 percent, and 74 percent, respectively, of all Jews in the old city lived in only two of the area's six census districts. If there was a ghetto in colonial Bône in the sense of a high concentration of people of the same race or ethnic group, then surely it was the Jewish neighborhood around the synagogue.[46]

Despite the fact that the Jews continued to live first and foremost in the poorer old city, a relative shift to the wealthier new city took place in the thirty-five years between 1872 and 1911 (Table 5.5).[47] Does this movement indicate upward Jewish social mobility? It has often been argued that when the Jews were naturalized French in 1870 they were at the same low socioeconomic level as the Algerians. But between 1870 and 1954, the argument runs, the Jews basically caught up with the French socially and economically, and finished by identifying themselves as more French psychologically and culturally than the French themselves.[48] To argue that the Jewish shift from the old to the new city is evidence of Jewish social mobility is admittedly crude. Scarcely more sophisticated is to contend that the growing differences between Algerian and Jewish indexes of relative concentration in the wealthier new city between 1872 and 1911 indicate a bifurcation between an upwardly mobile Jewish community and a stagnant Muslim one (Tables 5.4 and 5.5). However, the different geographical distributions of Jews natu-

Table 5.5. *European subgroups and Jews in major city areas, 1872–1911*

Year	Old City	New City	Colonne Randon[a]	Outskirts[b]
Index of relative concentration of native French				
1872	N.A.	N.A.	N.A.	N.A.
1876	0.92	1.64	—	0.72
1901	N.A.	N.A.	N.A.	N.A.
1906	0.62	1.62	1.19	0.57
1911	0.56	1.84	0.88	0.40
Index of relative concentration of naturalized French				
1872	N.A.	N.A.	N.A.	N.A.
1876	1.00	1.00	—	0
1901	N.A.	N.A.	N.A.	N.A.
1906	0.79	1.32	1.26	0.37
1911	0.88	1.06	1.75	0
Index of relative concentration of Italians				
1872	1.00	1.31	—	0.63
1876	0.95	1.26	—	0.84
1901	N.A.	N.A.	N.A.	N.A.
1906	0.84	0.95	1.68	0.37
1911	0.89	0.94	1.56	0.50
Index of relative concentration of Maltese				
1872	1.05	0.90	—	0.95
1876	1.10	0.85	—	1.00
1901	N.A.	N.A.	N.A.	N.A.
1906	0.63	1.13	1.50	1.13
1911	0.57	1.00	1.14	1.29
Index of concentration of Jews[c]				
1872	1.40	0.20	—	0
1876	1.67	0.33	—	0
1901	2.00	0.75	0	0
1906	2.00	0.75	0	0
1911	2.33	0.67	0	0

Note: See text for method of calculation and interpretation of the index.
[a]The Colonne Randon does not exist as a separate census quarter in 1872 and 1876. The 1881 census defines as outskirts (*banlieue*) an area that includes, but is larger than, what will later be known as the Colonne Randon.
[b]The 1881 census uses the term rural population (*population rurale*) instead of outskirts (*banlieue*). See text for discussion.
[c]Jews in 1872 include those naturalized French (652) plus those not yet naturalized (229). In subsequent years, they are all naturalized French.
Source: APCA, *Listes nominatives*, 1872, 1876, 1901, 1906, 1911.

ralized in 1870 and of their children is much more compelling. As Table 5.6 shows, fewer second-generation naturalized Jews than first-generation naturalized Jews lived in the old city, and a correspondingly higher percentage of second-generation versus first-generation Jews

Table 5.6. *Jews of two generations in major city areas (percent)*

1906	Old City	New City	Colonne Randon	Outskirts	Number
Jews naturalized French in 1870	77	19	3	1	1,071
Children of Jews naturalized French in 1870	66	32	2	—	591

1911	Old City	New City	Colonne Randon	Outskirts	Number
Jews naturalized French in 1870	88	10	1	1	707
Children of Jews naturalized French in 1870	64	35	1	—	547

Source: Computed from APCA, *Listes nominatives*, 1906, 1911.

lived in the new city. In other words, the younger generation increasingly moved out of the *mellah* and into the predominantly French new city.[49] The case for upward Jewish social mobility is still by no means proven, but the data in Table 5.6 certainly points towards this conclusion.[50] Moreover, the same pattern was found elsewhere in colonial Algeria, for example, in Tlemcen. "The old Jewish quarter . . . remained almost exclusively Jewish until the end of the colonial period. . . . However, as the Jewish population increased in number and as the Jews became more Europeanized and more closely linked with the privileged European minority, some wealthy Jewish families moved out to the predominantly European residential quarters outside the city walls."[51]

Let us now return to the European colonies within the French colony. Table 5.5 demonstrates that the native French, naturalized French, and other Europeans exhibit residential differences which are considerably less than those which separate Algerians, Europeans, and Jews, but which indicate nevertheless residential segregation among the European subgroups. The historical literature on colonial Algeria often assumes implicitly that there were marked socioeconomic differences between the various Europeans but that these differences decreased over time as a distinguishable *pied noir* community formed.[52] Although place of residence is certainly not an altogether accurate index of socioeconomic standing, it is certainly suggestive. The question to ask is whether the native French lived more often in the wealthier new city and whether the Italians and Maltese resided more often in the old city, working-class Colonne Randon, and rural outskirts.[53] While the data in Table 5.5 cannot be considered conclusive, it suggests that there were indeed significant differences between the native and naturalized French, but not between the naturalized French and other Europeans, at least up to 1911. The native French are consistently more overrepresented in the new city than the naturalized French and vice versa for the old city and Colonne Randon. On the other hand, the naturalized French are overrepresented in the new city and Colonne Randon, the Italians are overrepresented in the Colonne, and the Maltese are overrepresented in the new city, Colonne Randon, and the outskirts.

We have one further piece of evidence regarding socioeconomic differences between the European settlers, namely, the proportion of Europeans who lived in one of the city's two swankiest neighborhoods, Saint-Cloud-les Plages. In 1906, 41 percent of native French in the outskirts resided in Saint-Cloud as opposed to 33 percent of naturalized French, and only 17 percent of non-French Europeans. In 1911, the respective percentages were 57 percent native French, 57 percent naturalized French, and 18 percent other Europeans.[54] In 1906 and 1911 then the native French were significantly overrepresented in Saint-Cloud in proportion to their total numbers in Bône, the non-French Europeans were underrepresented, and the naturalized French fell somewhere in between.

Now that the areas of Bône where the various ethnic groups clustered have been pinpointed, let us measure next the actual degree of residential segregation between these groups using the so-called index of dissimilarity.[55] The index of dissimilarity is defined as the percentage of a given population group which would have to change residence in order to achieve perfect integration. The formula for the index of dissimilarity, D, is

$$D = \left(\text{Sum of positive differences of } \frac{A_i}{A} - \frac{B_i}{B}\right)$$

where A is the total number of households in the city of population group A; B is the total number of households of population group B; A_i is the number of households of population group A in census district i; and B_i is the number of households of population group B in census district i. The resulting index can range from 0 to 100. The higher the score, the more residential segregation since the greater the proportion of a given population group which would have to move to eliminate integration.

What light do the indexes of dissimilarity shed on residential segregation in colonial Bône? In the first place, Table 5.7 demonstrates that segregation increased greatest between the French and Algerians, and French and Jews between 1872 and 1911. In every case, a very much higher percentage of French, Algerians, or Jews would have had to

Table 5.7. *Segregation indexes between native French and other population groups, 1872–1911*

Year	Naturalized French	Italians	Maltese	Algerians	Jews
1872[a]	N.A.	13	19	28	46
1876	40	9	24	34	42
1906	14	24	28	60	52
1911	34	27	27	62	58

[a]In 1872 native French (4,833 total) includes 36 naturalized French.
Source: APCA, *Listes nominatives*, 1872, 1876, 1906, and 1911.

change residence at the end of the period than at the beginning to achieve integration. Not only was colonial Bône a divided society, but the lines which divided community from community became more rigid over time.

Increasing segregation was most pronounced between the native French and Algerians. The percentage of Algerians or French who would have had to move rose from a low of 28 percent in 1872 to over 60 percent by the first decade of the twentieth century. Whereas in 1872 the French-Algerian segregation index was actually lower than that between the French and Jews, by the twentieth century it was the highest. Or to put it another way, in 1872 the French were more segregated from the Jews than from the Algerians, but by the twentieth century the opposite was the case. Moreover, it can be shown that the situation failed to improve during the twentieth century, that the French and Algerians were at least as segregated from each other at the time of the last French census in 1954, before the Algerian war, as in 1911.[56] However viewed, the Algerian position was the worst.

Furthermore, the Jews fared scarcely better vis-à-vis the French than the Algerians. They were more segregated from the French in 1872 than the Algerians were, and their position deteriorated over time at least through 1911. Data shows that in four out of five census dates between 1872 and 1911 the Jews were more segregated from the Europeans than they were from the Muslims. After thirty-five years as French citizens, therefore, the Jews were as segregated from the French and other Europeans more than ever.[57]

Table 5.7 also shows that segregation increased noticeably among all European subgroups between 1872 and 1911. This is additional evidence which points to the existence of European colonies within the French colony. Still, segregation indexes for the naturalized French, Italians and Maltese are appreciably lower than for either Algerians or Jews. Furthermore, native French/naturalized French and native French/other

European indexes do not differ significantly, whereas they would if the naturalized French were more assimilated to the native French than the non-French Europeans.

Two major conclusions emerge from this examination of residential segregation. First of all, the major differences in housing patterns occurred between Algerians, Europeans, and Jews. The Europeans lived primarily in the new city and the Colonne Randon, the Jews congregated in the old city, and the Algerians predominated in the outskirts. By and large, people tended to reside in 1911 where they had in 1872. The boundaries differentiating Europeans from Algerians and both from the Jews rigidified rather than relaxed over time. Most serious was the deteriorating Algerian position; Algerian/French segregation worsened appreciably in the late nineteenth and early twentieth century. Moreover, the position of the Jews improved much less than we might expect. What is striking is not the small Jewish gains but the gap that remained between the Jews and the French community.

The second main conclusion is that the Europeans also were segregated in their own colonies within the larger French colony. The native French lived more often in the new city, and the other Europeans resided in the working-class Colonne Randon. Although relatively low, segregation between the native French and other Europeans certainly did not decrease over time. And more important, the recently naturalized French were apparently more similar to their Italian and Maltese confrères than to the native French in terms of residential patterns. Thus, tensions existed at the very center of the French community. We should not lose sight of the primary fact, however, which is that the non-French were significantly less segregated from the French than from either the Algerians or the Jews. Perhaps there were separate European colonies within the larger French colony, but the Europeans were never so isolated as to preclude assimilation and acculturation.

Occupational specialization

The work a person performs, his or her occupation, is arguably the single best indicator of a person's place in society. Colonial society is typified both by a high degree of vertical occupational stratification and by a large measure of functional occupational specialization. To assume that Italian fishermen, Jewish jewelers, Maltese milkmen, Berber dockers, Arab peddlers, and French colonial officials inhabited one and the same job universe is to assume they had more in common than they actually did, but to make in-depth comparisons between ethnic groups offers nonetheless telling insights into the social structure of colonial Bône.

165

The world of work can be viewed, of course, from any number of angles. You can slot occupations according to economic sector – primary (extractive), secondary (manufacturing), tertiary (service). You can classify occupations by industry, that is, by the product produced. You can arrange occupations by function, by what a person does. You can rank occupations "vertically," that is, by a combination of status, wealth, and skill. You can sort occupations by stage in the job cycle, that is, master, journeyman, or apprentice. Or you can group types of work according to worksite, where the job is performed.[58]

In order to compare systematically ethnic groups by occupation, I have organized here data on work in three occupational schemas: industrial, vertical, and functional. An industry code surveys the entire breadth of a given economy at a given time from those people engaged in small-scale hand production to mechanized mass production, from those working in agriculture to handicrafts to manufacturing. It is a "horizontal" code insofar as it combines workers in broadly similar lines of work, irrespective of job position, irrespective of whether they are foreman or laborer, owner or artisan. Where I described in Chapter Four the economic dualism characteristic of colonial Bône by discussing business firms and employers, the use of an industry code elaborates further the shape of such an economy by examining all workers' occupations. A "vertical" code attempts to rank occupations by socioeconomic position in a hierarchy, from "high" nonmanual work to "low" manual labor. Finally, a functional occupational code groups jobs by the actual task performed. Thus, it incorporates features of both vertical and horizontal codes, and thereby serves to elucidate both, but from a different perspective.

Here I analyze data on the labor force comparing ethnicity and occupation using successively industrial, vertical, and functional occupational schemas. For each occupational code, I first compare Europeans and Algerians, and then among the Europeans I sort out the Jews, non-French Europeans, naturalized French, and native French.

First, consider what a comparison of ethnic and racial groups by industry reveals. In this schema the world of work is divided into fifteen major industries. Most categories are self-explanatory.[59]

A comparison of Algerians and Europeans by industry reiterates the economic dualism discussed above in Chapter 4, but this time in occupational terms (Table 5.8). Generally, the Europeans are more likely than the Algerians to work in the same sectors of the economy that they own and operate. In other words, Europeans are more likely than Algerians to work in all areas except agriculture, food preparation, tobacco, textiles, public services, and unclassifiable jobs, plus a few industries with insufficient data on which to base conclusions (skins, dry

Table 5.8. *Algerians and Europeans by industry (percent), 1876–1911*

Occupations	Algerians (N = 789)	Europeans (N = 1,842)	Total
Agriculture	21.1	11.9	14.6
Food	3.7	7.7	6.5
Food preparation	3.8	2.9	3.1
Tobacco	0.8	0.4	0.5
Liquor	0	0.9	0.6
Hotels, boarding houses	0	0.4	0.3
Skins, apparel, textiles, dry goods	5.5	6.2	6.0
Metals, precious metals, wood, home furnishings, building and construction, transportation	8.8	26.0	20.9
Fuel	0.7	1.3	1.2
General manufacturing, chemicals, printing	0.1	1.0	.7
General commercial	9.2	12.1	11.2
Arts, liberal professions, clergy, education, government, military, leisured	2.4	10.6	8.2
Private services	0.6	2.7	2.0
Public services	15.3	2.3	6.2
Unspecified unskilled	27.9	13.5	17.9

Source: Computerized manuscript census sample drawn from APCA, *Listes nominatives*, 1876, 1891, 1911.

goods, home furnishings). As the reader can see, those areas where Algerians concentrate are the same as we found when the Bône economy was discussed earlier. For example, a larger proportion of Algerians derive their income from working the land than Europeans. Tobacco grown by the Beni Urgine and other groups on the Bône plain is cured, processed, and converted into cigarettes in Algerian and Jewish workshops where the labor is performed by Algerians and Jews. The relative concentration of Muslims in food preparation reflects the large number of *gargotes*, cheap eating places. In a different way, the relative propensity of Algerians to work at unspecified unskilled tasks and in public service jobs is symptomatic of their low socioeconomic status vis-à-vis the Europeans, which will emerge even more clearly when we discuss vertical occupational ranking.

Look next at the major ethnic and racial groups of colonial Bône compared by industry (Table 5.9). The major contrasts occur between Algerians and Europeans, but the differences within these large umbrella groupings serve to nuance the occupational situation. In the first place, note the often striking differences between the Berber Kabyles and the Arabs. In contrast to the Arabs, the Berbers are confined to a much narrower range of the economic spectrum. In many occupational groupings Arab concentration is low, but the proportion of Berbers is even lower, such as those working in tobacco, skins, dry goods, metals, wood, and home furnishings. The more often sedentary Arabs are much more likely to farm land in the outskirts of Bône than the migratory Berbers. Likewise, the Arabs supply the tiny handful of liberal professionals and religious leaders of the Muslim community, not the Berbers. It is significant that the only industries where there are proportionately more Berbers than Arabs are food preparation, which reflects the high number of Kabyle *gargotiers*, and construction, where it can be shown that almost all the Berbers were unskilled construction laborers.[60] In fact, the key here is unskilled labor. The Algerians as a whole accounted for far and away the greatest number of unskilled workers in Bône who did not designate a specific job and those who worked at mostly menial public service jobs, but among the Algerians Berbers were half again as likely to work at public service tasks than Arabs.

Next consider the striking position of the Jews in colonial Bône. Like the Algerians, the Jews occupy a relatively narrow range of the occupational spectrum. Typically, they are less likely to work the land than any other population group. They are also underrepresented, relative to their population, in many craft industries, including food preparation, skins, dry goods, wood, home furnishings, building and construction, fuel, chemicals, and general manufacturing. Instead, they concentrate in the same industries and trades pinpointed earlier, such as apparel (tailors), textiles (cloth merchants), and precious metals (jewelers). But what is most striking is the propensity of the Jews to engage in commerce and trades related to commerce. Unlike American censuses, French censuses unfortunately contain no data regarding wealth or property, so that it is impossible to compare, for example, Jewish and European merchants except on the basis of occupation. As we pointed out above, however, people at the time ranked Jewish retailors and wholesalers lower than their European counterparts in terms of per capita wealth.

Finally, distinctions between native French, naturalized French and other Europeans point again to the existence of European colonies within the larger French colony. Highly significant is the fact that the native French virtually monopolize government and military positions plus the liberal professions (doctors and lawyers), the perquisites of colonial rulers. Moreover, the native French are more likely to engage in commerce than either the naturalized French or other Europeans, and less likely to work at menial public service jobs or unspecifed unskilled labor. As we have seen already, the Europeans who are not native French carved out their own niches within the overall economy (Chapter 4). The naturalized French, especially Italian-born, concentrate in the construction and building industry, and the non-French Europeans, especially the Maltese, practice farming. Different Euro-

Table 5.9. *Algerian and European subgroups by industry (percent), 1876–1911*

Occupations	Berbers (N = 138)	Arabs (N = 622)	Jews (N = 64)	Europeans (N = 758)	Naturalized French (N = 211)	Native French (N = 809)	Total
Agriculture	7.4	25.0	2.8	14.9	4.4	11.6	14.8
Food	2.7	3.5	2.6	10.7	12.3	4.1	6.4
Food preparation	7.7	3.1	1.0	2.8	1.1	3.5	3.2
Tobacco	0	0.7	5.7	0.1	0	0.4	0.5
Liquor	0	0	1.1	0.7	1.2	0.4	0.7
Hotels, boarding houses	0	0	3.8	0.1	1.3	0.1	0.3
Skins, apparel, textiles, dry goods	1.2	5.2	27.4	4.6	4.0	6.7	5.7
Metals, precious metals, wood, home furnishings, building and construction, transportation	9.8	8.7	7.1	26.7	54.5	19.4	21.0
Fuel	0	0.8	0	2.9	0	0.3	1.2
General manufacturing, chemicals, printing	0	0.1	1.0	0.7	0.7	1.5	0.8
General commercial	4.2	10.0	30.1	4.7	10.9	17.9	11.2
Arts, liberal professions, clergy, education, government, military, leisured	0	2.8	11.1	2.5	0.8	20.8	8.2
Private services	0	0.7	0.8	2.1	0.3	3.9	2.1
Public srvices	26.9	13.0	0.7	3.8	1.4	1.3	6.2
Unspecified, unskilled	40.2	26.3	4.9	22.6	6.9	7.5	18.0

Source: Computerized manuscript census sample drawn from APCA, *Lists nominatives*, 1876, 1891, 1911.

peans predominated in different jobs: there was what could be termed a "cultural division of labor" in colonial Bône.[61] The socioeconomic gradations which such pronounced job clustering entailed will be discussed below.

Consider next a comparison of ethnic groups using a vertical occupational schema.[62] Most of the categories are self-explanatory. Although more refined than many, the vertical code employed here is by no means perfect. Variations exist within each category. The French, other Europeans, and especially the Algerians, earned substantially different wages for the same work. Variations exist also between categories: are five, four, or two divisions most representative of late nineteenth- and early twentieth-century social reality?[63] Not even the dividing line between the world of white collar and blue collar work, or between employers and employees, can be considered as definitive in the nineteenth century as it has become in the twentieth century. Because the skills required were often less for low white collar work than for skilled blue collar work, and because the capital required to go into business was considerably less than now, some scholars have argued that movement from skilled work to low white collar sometimes represents not upward but downward social mobility.[64] It is clear in the case of Bône, for example, that peddlers and food sellers who ran stalls in the local markets (*revendeurs*), whether they were Maltese, Berbers, or Jews, did not occupy a higher socioeconomic position as judged by their contemporaries – although they were technically the owners of the means of production – than European skilled workers, who were wage workers, however relatively well off they were.[65]

Figure 5.11 compares Algerians and Europeans according to this vertical occupational schema. Generally speaking, there are no surprises here: the Europeans are more likely to hold both high and low white collar positions and skilled blue collar jobs than Algerians, and Algerians hold relatively more unskilled jobs than Europeans.

If we now distinguish Arabs and Berbers among the Algerians, and the European colonies within the French colony, these gross distinctions can be nuanced considerably (Figure 5.12). First of all, neither Arabs nor Berbers hold many white collar positions relative to their population in Bône, although the Arabs are more likely to hold white collar jobs than non-French Europeans. But what is striking about the Arabs and Berbers is the contrast between blue collar workers. Where the Arabs are skilled workers nearly as often as the Europeans, only a miniscule number of Berbers are skilled workers; of all Berbers in the labor force a whopping eighty-nine percent were unskilled, a much higher proportion than for any other single group. In short, the Algerians were at the bottom of the occupational heap in colonial Bône, and the Berber Kabyles were at the

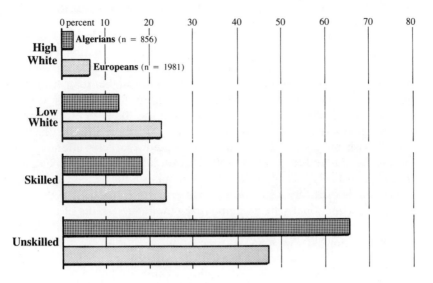

Figure 5.11   Algerians and Europeans by vertical ranking (percent), 1876–1911. *Source:* 1876–1911 census sample data.

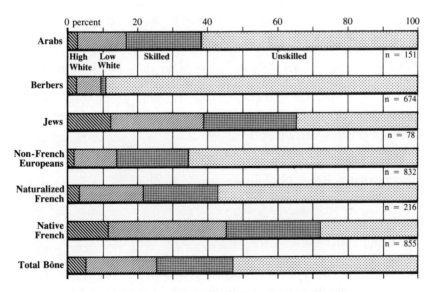

Figure 5.12   Algerian and European subgroups by vertical ranking (percent), 1876–1911. *Source:* 1876–1911 census sample data.

171

bottom of the Muslim heap. Whereas the Arabs were comparable in some ways to Europeans not naturalized French in skill levels, the Berbers occupied clearly the lowest rung of the vertical occupational ladder.

In the second place, note the high overall socioeconomic standing of the Jews when based on occupational title alone – higher than any other group according to this measure. They are more likely to work at high white collar and skilled blue collar jobs, and less likely to be employed as unskilled laborers than any other group. The main problem here is that Jewish merchants, for example, occupied a largely different economic world than French merchants. Census data enables us to compare French and Jewish occupations, but not to nuance the actual wealth and social status of those occupations. Furthermore, to the extent that the vertical occupational schema emphasizes the higher status of all white collar positions as opposed to skilled craftsmen, I would argue that it distorts somewhat the Jews' socioeconomic position. For example, I would contend that Jews who engaged in petty trade were not "higher" than skilled workers as the classification schema used here suggests – if anything they were "lower." The fact remains, however, that the Jews have not only detached themselves definitively from the Algerian community socioeconomically, but that they are now competing with the Europeans on their own ground. Different from both, the Jews constitute clearly a "stranger" economic group thriving as commercial intermediaries between the Algerians and Europeans.

Thirdly, the native French are much more likely to hold both high and low white collar positions compared to the naturalized French and the other Europeans, and considerably less likely to work as unskilled laborers. On the other hand, the proportion of skilled workers among all Europeans is nearly the same. Here again, then, is striking testimony to the existence of European colonies within the larger French colony, of classes within the settler community. In both white collar jobs and unskilled work, the naturalized French and other Europeans are much more similar to each other than either of them are to the native French. This is further evidence that the Europeans naturalized primarily by the 1889 law did not differ substantially from the Europeans who retained their original Italian or Maltese citizenship. Moreover, these other Europeans who differed so markedly from the French were very similar to the Arabs in socioeconomic terms. Where the non-French Europeans ranked slightly below the Arabs in the relative number of white collar and blue collar workers, the naturalized French ranked slightly above. Here is the socioeconomic basis for the status anxiety expressed by the *petits blancs*, the lower class settlers, vis-à-vis the better-off Muslims and Jews. Status anxiety results when elevated social status does not correspond with equally elevated occupational status; it is a theme to which I will return later in this chapter.

Finally, let us compare the ethnic and racial groups of Bône using a functional occupational schema. Whereas an industry code classifies occupations by product, by what a person makes or produces, a functional schema classifies by function, by the task a person performs. Based on functional and linguistic criteria, a functional code refines and elaborates, therefore, findings based on an industry or vertical code. Again, most of the categories are self-explanatory. "Unskilled functions" are specified unskilled tasks; "work" is unspecified unskilled jobs, and "miscellaneous work" is a residual category consisting of children and helpers.

A comparison of Algerians and Europeans according to occupational function reveals the same broad distinctions we have noted earlier between these groups (Table 5.10). Europeans are more likely than Algerians to perform work pertaining to the professions, manufacturing, government, and the military, even when skill level is not taken into account. More Europeans than Muslims work at traditional artisanal crafts and even more at "new" crafts such as machinist, mechanic, engineer, and lithographer. Whereas slightly more Europeans work at specified unskilled functions than Algerians, far more Algerians labor at unspecified unskilled tasks ("work") than do Europeans. But the most significant finding here results when commercial functions are distinguished from proprietary ones. Commercial occupations range from bookkeepers and commercial agents to clerks and salesmen. Proprietors include all those who sell to the public – from bakers, butchers, and grocers to peddlers and hucksters to owners, keepers, and dealers. Whereas the Europeans are clearly more likely to perform commercial functions than Muslims, the Algerians are slightly more likely to work at proprietary functions than Europeans. This interesting finding reflects no doubt the number of small-scale Arab and Berber peddlers and petty traders, on the one hand, and the propensity of Europeans to work in relatively larger business firms where commercial tasks were more often defined, on the other hand.

Table 5.11 compares the six main population groups of Bône according to occupational function. First of all, contrasts between Arabs and Berbers show again that the Arabs were clearly better off than the Berbers. Whether you consider professional, government, military or supervisory posts filled by Algerians, they all were held by Arabs and none by Berbers. Moreover, substantially more Berbers labored at specified unskilled jobs and especially unspecified unskilled ones compared to Arabs. Thus, the striking contrasts we saw earlier between blue collar Arabs and Berbers are evident here as well.

Table 5.10. *Algerians and Europeans by functional ranking (percent),*
1876–1911

Occupational functions	Algerians	Europeans
	(N = 857)	(N = 1,990)
Professional	0.8	4.0
Commercial	4.9	10.8
Proprietary	13.8	9.3
Manufacturing	0	0.5
Crafts	17.9	22.6
"New" Crafts	0.1	1.6
Private services	0.5	2.5
Waiter-porter	11.9	1.5
Longshoreman	1.1	0.3
Sea-related	0.1	5.9
Military, government, and supervisory	0.9	3.8
Transportation	1.0	1.7
Unskilled functions	13.3	13.8
Work	23.9	11.0
Miscellaneous work	0.1	0.3
Miscellaneous (leisured, housekeeping)	9.7	10.6

Source: Computerized manuscript census sample drawn from APCA, *Listes nominatives*,
1876, 1891, 1911.

In the second place, the functions the Jews performed deepens our understanding of Jewish occupational structure in Bône. The Jews practice skilled crafts more often than other groups, and they work at unskilled functions less often than others. This reiterates our earlier findings. But again the distinction between commercial and proprietary functions proves to be a useful one. For what is most striking about the Jews is that they are far more likely to be proprietors than any other group in Bône, whereas significantly, a higher proportion of native French perform commercial functions than the Jews. In other words, the Jews may have been oriented towards commerce, but it was more toward petty trade than commercial work as clerks and employees. Therefore, the distinction here between commercial and proprietary functions clarifies the tendency of Jews to concentrate especially in low white collar occupations.

Finally, a comparison of the functions of native French, naturalized French, and other Europeans points again to the existence of European colonies within the larger French one. More native French than naturalized French, and more naturalized French than non-French Europeans worked at professional, commercial, manufacturing, "new" crafts, and supervisory functions. Similarly, fewer native French than naturalized French, and fewer naturalized French than non-French Europeans performed unskilled functions. Furthermore, in most of these cases the

Table 5.11. Algerian and European subgroups by functional ranking (percent), 1876–1911

Occupational functions	Berbers (N = 146)	Arabs (N = 681)	Jews (N = 78)	Europeans (N = 833)	Naturalized French (N = 216)	Native Total French (N = 863)
Professional	0	1.0	6.3	1.5	0.1	7.2
Commercial	3.2	5.3	14.4	3.2	8.9	18.2
Proprietary	11.6	13.1	22.9	10.0	13.0	6.3
Manufacturing	0	0	0	0.1	0.6	0.9
Crafts	1.4	20.9	25.3	21.8	22.3	23.1
"New" Crafts	0	0.1	0	0.1	1.1	3.2
Private services	0	0.7	0.6	1.9	0.3	3.7
Waiter-porter	22.5	10.1	0	3.1	0.3	0.1
Longshoreman	1.6	1.1	0	0.5	0.1	0.1
Sea-related	0.8	0	0	6.1	27.7	0.9
Military, government, and supervisory	0	1.2	1.2	0.3	1.0	8.1
Transportation	0	1.2	0	1.8	2.5	1.5
Unskilled functions	16.7	12.7	6.0	19.7	13.0	9.0
Work	32.5	23.0	2.8	19.3	5.7	5.0
Miscellaneous work	0.4	0	0	0.4	0.7	0.2
Miscellaneous (leisured, housekeeping)	9.3	9.8	20.4	10.2	2.5	12.2

Source: Computerized manuscript census sample drawn from APCA, Listes nominatives, 1876, 1891, 1911.

percentage of naturalized French is closer to the other Europeans than to the native French when it comes to their propensity to work at a given job. Again, therefore, the naturalized French resemble the other Europeans more than the native French. Moreover, it is interesting to note the differences between commercial and proprietary functions. Whereas the native French are more likely to work at commercial pursuits than any other European group – more than any other group in Bône, for that matter – they are less likely to be proprietors than the other Europeans – in fact, less than any other group in Bône. Clearly, distinctions existed within business and commerce, within the world of white collar work; equally clearly, these were distinctions rooted in the cultural division of labor.

The cultural division of labor

The tendency for the European colonies within the larger French colony to cluster in certain jobs, to form a cultural division of labor, certainly ran counter to the countervailing tendencies towards assimilation, chief among which was mass naturalization. Such assimilationist measures could have knitted the European communities together over time despite pronounced job clustering. Instead, however, occupational specialization by ethnic group was reinforced in two important ways: through unequal pay for equal work, and through a job hierarchy in which the native French were firmly ensconced in positions of authority.

Unequal pay for equal work: as late as the first years of the twentieth century, the Italians and Maltese were earning significantly less than the native French, although substantially more than the Algerians. Clearly, the Algerians were the worst off, and the wage spread separating Algerians from non-French Europeans is greater than that between French and other Europeans. Yet the continued existence of unequal pay for equal work between the French and other Europeans is strong evidence for the continued existence of European colonies within the larger French colony. The data in Table 5.12 covers trades in the secondary, or manufacturing, sector. How wage levels changed over time is unknown, because earlier wage data lumps all ethnic groups together. But even if wage differentials are decreasing – which is highly unlikely given the increasing gap in other areas of this colonial society – what is most significant is the still very substantial disparities which exist in the first decade of the twentieth century.[66]

French businessmen preponderated over both non-French Europeans and especially Algerians in their propensity to own business firms in colonial Bône, and the French position in the economic hierarchy carried over as well into the wage-earning labor force dependent on French

176

Table 5.12. *French, European, and Algerian wages by position in job (average* francs *per day), 1904–7*

Position in job	French	Europeans	Algerians	Total workers
Foremen				
1904	5.38	5.20	4.25	94
1905	5.33	5.04	—	90
1907	5.56	4.36	—	67
Skilled Workers				
1904	4.54	4.13	3.39	1,187
1905	4.59	4.23	3.51	1,187
1907	4.66	4.13	3.34	1,160
Unskilled Workers				
1904	3.54	3.60	3.57	1,344
1905	3.52	3.30	3.55	1,510
1907	3.72	3.66	3.25	1,652

Source: APCA *Statistique Industrielle*, 1904, 1905, 1907.

capital (Figure 5.13). The proportion of the French labor force that were either owners, foremen, or skilled workers was consistently greater than both the other Europeans and especially the Algerians; and a greater proportion of Algerians were unskilled workers than either the French or other Europeans. Moreover, the labor force data represented in Figure 5.13 has been adjusted to reflect the relative size of each population group, whereas the absolute numbers of Algerian owners and foremen, for example, was actually much less since the Algerians were outnumbered in Bône by the Europeans.[67]

A settler colonial society in which the European colonizers outnumber

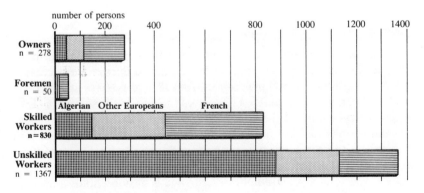

Figure 5.13   French, other European, and Algerian job positions (per 10,000 population), 1904–7. *Source:* APCA, Statistique industrielle, 1904–5, 1907.

Illustration 5.2   Cours Bertagna, early twentieth century (Bibliothèque Nationale Cabinet d'Estampes).

the Algerian colonized two to one. A French colony in which the Italians, Spanish, and Maltese are as numerous as the French, and form colonies within the colony. A French colonial society created largely by naturalizing Jews and Europeans. A colonial society stratified along lines of race and class, and typified by residential segregation, vertical occupational stratification, functional occupational specialization, plus unequal pay for equal work. It all fits together.

Appendix A: The Census Sample

The manuscript censuses (*listes nominatives*) of colonial Bône form the statistical backbone of this study. I have enjoyed unrestricted access to a virtually continuous run of censuses from 1848 to 1960 (see the Sources and Bibliography for details). I have used the data in the summary tables (*états récapitulatifs*) of the censuses, especially for the analysis of residential segregation, but far and away the major use I have made of the censuses is to draw a ten percent household sample from each of those for 1876, 1891, and 1911, which I then analyzed with the aid of a computer. The total sample numbers 2,283 heads of households and 6,803 total individuals.

This makes the census sample one of the largest data bases drawn from Maghribi sources extant, and the largest – perhaps the only – census sample based on sources for the colonial period. Certainly there is no comparable study on Algeria of which I am aware. René Lespès clearly looked at the manuscript censuses for his studies of Algiers and Oran published in the 1930s, but the necessary statistical procedures had not been developed at the time, and he presented no quantitative results.[68] The two closest comparable works to mine are both on Morocco, and both are based on postcolonial censuses. Janet Abu-Lughod applied the sophisticated statistical techniques of factorial ecology to a ten percent household sample of the 1971 census of Rabat, which amounted to a sample population of 53,767.[69] Hildred Geertz provided a computer analysis of the entire population of Sefrou (20,961 people) based on the 1960 census.[70] Neither of these works analyze, however, the population of a colonial city during the colonial period.

To classify and analyze the sample data I had coded, especially regarding occupation, I turned first to French historiography. However, the closest comparable study to my own for either France or Algeria is not based on census data, and is not based on a sufficiently detailed occupational classification scheme to be of use.[71] I turned, therefore, to the so-called new urban history: from the pioneering early work of Stephen Thernstrom to the more recent sophisticated analyses of Olivier Zunz, but first, last and always to the work of Michael Katz. For family data, I used the work of Peter Laslett and his associates on household structure, but especially helpful was the advice on coding provided by John Modell.[72] For occupational classification, I relied primarily on Michael Katz, the Philadelphia Social History Project, and the others involved in the so-called Five Cities project.[73]

The sample as drawn in Annaba was skewed, however, due to an attempt to draw a truly random rather than simply a representative sample. By systematically comparing the sample with the population, it has been possible to correct the skewness, although the results for large households remains more reliable than that for small ones. The computer analysis was performed at the University of California, Berkeley, and the University of Illinois utilizing primarily SPSS. I thank Prof. Kyuhan Bae for assisting me with the data analysis.

179

6

Patronage, corruption, and the "Boss" of Bône: Jérome Bertagna

To fully comprehend the Bône political scene, it must be viewed from the angle of settler colonialism. However, the Algerian case differs from other settler colonial situations in the manner in which the struggles for power over Algerian affairs were fought out in terms of rival bureaucratic and patronage claims. The important point here is that the official bureaucracy was controlled by metropolitan French representatives whereas the unofficial patronage network was dominated by the European settlers. Again, the situation differed from period to period in colonial Algerian history, since patronage politics in Algeria, including Bône, functioned – as patronage politics elsewhere – in relation to formally constituted authority. Thus, in the initial 1830–70 period, the French military established the basic bureaucratic institutions and the settlers played a distinctly inferior role. But the watershed came in 1870: Second Empire military rule before, Third Republic civilian rule after.

The real significance of this change in regime occurred, however, at a deeper level – in the political structure itself. Whereas the military had kept a relatively tight institutional rein on the *pieds noirs*, the civilian government inadvertently allowed the settlers to create local pockets of power in the interstices of the "looser" republican administration. More important still, this room for greater political maneuver was gained at the expense of the Algerians, who saw themselves pushed back further from their already drastically reduced positions of power in the same way as they were pushed off their land. Put briefly, the military had acted earlier as a buffer, to a certain extent, between the settlers and the Algerians, while, paradoxically, the introduction later of a more liberal regime in name resulted in a more illiberal rule in practice. In Bône and elsewhere in colonial Algeria, therefore, the potential for conflict inherent between a formal political system of bureaucracy and an informal political network of patronage – a structural relationship at once symbiotic and antagonistic – was exacerbated by the fact that the bureaucracy and the patronage system corresponded largely to two of

180

the three main forces contending for hegemony in Algerian affairs, namely, metropolitan France and the European settlers.

To unravel the skein of politics in Bône, where a political system was based partly on bureaucracy and partly on patronage, is the task of the present chapter. After outlining briefly the political structure of the 1830–70 period, I shall detail changes which occurred after 1870, namely, communal organization, elections, and machine politics. Then, after considering the connections between poverty and patronage, I shall discuss the Bône municipal administration under Mayor Jérome Bertagna, the political "boss" of Bône par excellence, and conclude by examining the crisis of 1896.

The political situation before 1870 and after

In late nineteenth century Bône the Muslim Algerians were still politically quiescent and were to remain so well into the twentieth century. However, tensions between settlers and metropolitan France, represented by the colonial administration, were becoming increasingly difficult to ignore. But in the period prior to 1870 differences between the government and the settlers were largely nonexistent, primarily because the military government in pursuing its policy at the same time pursued the interests of the settlers. The point is clear in the Bône careers of General Monck d'Uzer and General (later Marshal) Randon. As we have seen, d'Uzer, the military commander of Bône and the surrounding region between 1832 and 1836, managed to have an 1832 law, which forbade Algerians to sell land to Europeans, revoked for Bône, bought some two thousand acres of land himself, and furthermore had it worked by soldiers under his command. But d'Uzer's particular brand of military colonization was too much even for his military superiors who recalled him to Paris where he was revoked. Shortly thereafter, d'Uzer returned to Bône as a private citizen, where he lived and worked his land until his death.[1]

The congruence of settler and military interests can be seen less blatantly but no less clearly in one of the pet projects carried out by General Randon, commander of the Bône region from 1841 to 1847, and who later served Napoleon III as Governor General of Algeria and Minister of War. Desirous of making Bône safe from the attacks of nearby Berber hill tribes, Randon had one thousand soldiers build a road twenty kilometers long in the hills immediately outside Bône in 1841. The effect of this venture was to make Bône safe for the colonists by driving the Berbers further into the interior, and led directly to the creation of a new quarter of town called, appropriately enough, the Colonne Randon. Moreover, the road foreshadowed the commercial exploitation of the

181

abundant corkwood forests which later upset completely the political economy of the Berber peasant agriculturalists. No wonder that when Randon left in 1847 he was hailed by the settlers as the "father of Bône."[2]

This dovetailing of settler and military interests did not last long, particularly because the paternalistic policy of the *Bureaux Arabes* (Arab bureaus) vis-à-vis the Arabs incensed the settlers. By the time Napoleon III visited Algeria in 1863 and shortly thereafter enunciated his pro-Muslim *royaume arabe* (Arab kingdom) doctrine, the Europeans were openly hostile. It was military antipathy not Republican sympathy, therefore, that drove the settlers to Republicanism. Here again the turning point came in 1870. The settlers were well situated to embrace the advent of the Third Republic. Both Gaston Thomson, who represented eastern Algeria, and Eugène Etienne, who represented western Algeria, for example, were proteges of Léon Gambetta. The settlers' elected representatives provided unflagging support when every Republican vote was needed during the difficult second founding of the Third Republic (1875 Wallon amendment, *seize mai* 1877).[3] In exchange for their support, the Republican government gave the settlers what amounted to a free hand in Algeria.

By instituting electoral politics, moreover, the Republican government created the potential for political party patronage. To understand how the settlers took advantage of local electoral politics under the Third Republic to further their own political ends, we must describe the changes in communal organization which underlay the new political system.

After 1870 Algeria was divided into three administrative areas. In the south the military held sway. In the central highlands, where Muslims preponderated over Europeans, *communes mixtes* were formed each with a French administrator. In the northern littoral, which had been divided into three French départements in 1870 and administered since then as integral parts of metropolitan France, French-style *communes de pleine exercice* fittingly prevailed. But these latter communes, which included the port city of Bône, resembled those in France in name only. For one thing, they were considerably larger. In France, *communes de pleine exercice* averaged 1,643 hectares at the beginning of the 1880s, in Algeria 8,839 ha. Paris, for example, comprised 7,645 ha., Bône 10,431 ha.[4]

But the main differences stemmed from the presence of the Algerians. In terms of political organization, colonial Algerian communes like Bône were French. Communes were established, and Algerian *douars*, or groups of tents, were submerged in them. In terms of political representation, however, colonial Algerian communes were part French and part Algerian. Universal suffrage was extended to French citizens, but for the Algerians suffrage was limited to property owners and civil servants, and restricted to municipal elections. The French electoral law of 1884 was applied to Algeria, but for the Algerians it was an "incontestable regression."[5]

In addition, the Muslim *djemâ'a-s*, or political assemblies of *douars*, were suppressed. In place of the *djemâ'a* selected by the Algerians themselves, the *adjoint indigène*, or native representative, emerged as the most important Muslim political figure. As the intermediary between the Europeans and Algerians it was inevitable that the *adjoint indigène*, whose main function was to enforce French measures in the Muslim community, would be called later a collaborator.[6]

When it came to taxation, the French also established a dual system. On the one hand, they retained the Turkish taxes which were collected only from the Algerians. On the other hand, they assessed the Europeans some but not all of the same taxes as in France, the most important of which were the *patente* and the *octroi de mer*. The former was a business license tax assessed most businesses, while the latter was a tax on imports which was divided among the communes. The point here is that although the French paid more taxes in absolute terms, they very likely did not pay as much in proportion to their population as the Algerians did, and they certainly did not pay as much as they would have in France. Even more important, the proportion of tax monies spent in the Algerian community was undoubtedly smaller than the share that the Algerians paid out in taxes.[7]

The results of transplanting French communal organization from metropolitan France to colonial Algeria could be seen in Bône and everywhere else. The size of the municipal administration was padded. In Bône in 1878 (1876 population: 23,186) there were forty-three employees working in the city hall alone (others paid by the city – police, teachers, religious officials – not included); in 1910–11 (1911 population: 40,188), there were eighty-three.[8] Municipal salaries were bloated. Operating expenses, which consisted primarily of salaries, accounted for twenty-nine percent of all communal expenses in Bône at the beginning of the 1890s.[9] Municipal buildings were grandiose and costly. The Bône city hall was built in 1884 and compares favorably in size and splendor to those found in metropolitan French communes many times as large.

No wonder that Jules Ferry said, "The *commune de pleine exercice* is the exploitation of the native in broad daylight *à ciel ouvert*," or that it was said in Algeria that the French communes lived "by eating the native."[10] The point is important, because the communal organization of Algeria during the Third Republic was imposed in the name of the Republicans' universalistic doctrine of assimilation. A progressive, liberal policy when applied in France, assimilation was a retrogressive,

183

Illustration 6.1 Bône city hall, early twentieth century (collection of the author).

illiberal policy when applied selectively in Algeria. For in the name of assimilation the settlers carved out their own power base in the civil regime which they used to gain hegemony over the Algerians. "Algeria 'assimilated to France' was in reality in the hands of colonization."[11]

These were not the only results of transplanting French communal organization from France to Algeria. Republican-style communal organization presupposed Republican-style local politics and elections. Metropolitan French communal organization gave birth to colonial Algeria local politics. Thus the primary historical significance of the establishment of French-style communes, especially *communes de pleine exercice*, from our point of view, is that they constituted a series of political vacuums within the larger colonial administrative structure, a series of political vacuums which the settlers were only too eager to fill. How they filled them can best be seen by examining local municipal elections in Bône.

Municipal elections and machine politics

What follows is a historical reconstruction of a typical Bône election campaign. As such, it is not an exact or "true" account of any one election, but rather a composite of many, which in its veri-similitude represents and re-creates the historical reality of electoral contests during at least the last two decades of the nineteenth and the first decade of the twentieth century.[12]

There were two main political parties in late nineteenth century Bône: the Opportunist (moderate) Republicans, who were continuously in power throughout the period, and the Radical Republicans. It should be recalled that Algeria was not simply a French colony, and Bône – though mostly European – was not primarily a French city. As we have seen, roughly one-third of the forty thousand people in 1911 were Muslim Algerians, and of the remainder there were as many Italians and nearly as many Maltese as French, plus a smattering of North African Jews. Voting rights were essentially the same as in France, since the Algerian littoral was administered as an integral part of France after 1870. But who was "French" for voting purposes was another matter. According to the 1884 French electoral law, which was applied to Algeria, the Bône Conseil Municipal, or city council, was composed of twenty-seven French and six Algerian members. However, the right to vote for Muslims was limited to property owners and civil servants. Whereas one of every six Europeans voted, only one of every thirty-one Algerians did.[13] Even more important was the 1889 naturalization law which radically simplified naturalization procedures. The French voter ranks swelled thereby with a flood of newly naturalized Italians and Maltese.

The quadrennial municipal elections were "so heated," according to one native son, that they "often transcended the city and reverberated throughout the four corners of [Constantine] département and even beyond, so that elections in Bône were said to be a local industry."[14] Electoral activity centered around two cafes frequented, respectively, by Opportunists and Radicals and which were located, of course, directly opposite one another on the tree-lined and arcaded main boulevard. As the spring weather heated up so did the election campaign, and from the terraces of the opposing cafes could be heard "howls and cheers, insults, cries, gibes, guffaws, and those guttural and farting-like onomatopetic words [*ces onomatopées grasseyantes et pétaradante*], which are, it is said, a genuine Bône specialty."[15]

Concurrently, several new newpapers appeared. More election broadsides than newspapers *d'information*, as the French say, these four-page papers were generally born and died in the course of an election campaign. *La Démocratie Algérienne*, a long-lived and substantial paper by colonial Bône standards, was founded expressly to back Gaston Thomson for his first bid to Parliament in 1877. Thomson, the longest-sitting deputy of the Third Republic (1877–1932), represented Bône's interests in the Assemblée Nationale. The vast majority of the more than fifty other papers begun in the 1880s and 1890s were less than successful.[16]

In Bône the election campaign got underway with the revision of the *listes electorales*, the voter registration lists. An election commission appointed by the municipal administration updated the list of eligible voters; their decisions could be – and were – contested before the *juge de paix* (equivalent to municipal court judge). The aim, of course, was to inscribe as many supporters and eliminate as many opponents as possible. The key was to not inform the voters affected in time to be reinstated. One election year the *sous-préfet*, or subprefect, based in Bône, and the secretary of the commune persuaded the *juge* to eliminate more than six hundred voters, and the *Cour de cassation*, or appellate court, did not overrule the *juge* until two days after the election.[17] More ingenious still was a ploy the Radical Republican Algerians came up with. The six Radical candidates running together on a slate bought a one-eighth share in a cheap house and put it in the names of fifty-seven supporters, thus qualifying them automatically to vote as property owners. Through a series of similarly suspect transactions the number of Muslim voters ballooned two-and-one-half times over the previous year "with a multitude of false landowners or farmers ordinarily living hand to mouth (*au jour le jour*) or receiving subsidies from the Bureau de Bienfaisance (city welfare agency)."[18]

At the same time as the voter registration lists were being updated, election campaigning began in earnest. When it came to campaigning the rule of thumb seems to have been anything goes if you could get away with it. *Courtiers électoraux* (equivalent to precinct workers) began to line up voters licitly if possible, illicitly if not. A rabbi exhorted Jews in no uncertain terms to vote for Mayor Bertagna. A local *marabout*, Muslim holy person, had the faithful swear on the Koran not to vote for an opposing slate or else God would curse them. More extreme was the "pernicious maneuver" whereby the mayor who succeeded Bertagna had lists of his opponents printed up with the logo, "candidates of the Freemason lodge," and mailed them to the rabidly Catholic Maltese voters.[19]

Some *cartes d'électeurs*, or voter cards, which were supposed to be obtained at the city hall and which served to identify bona fide voters when they voted, were distributed elsewhere, for example, at the Consistoire Israélite, at Bertagna's residence, with a *courtier électoral*, or at a supporter's conveniently located shop. Such an arrangement created numerous possibilities for fraud: cards withheld from some and given to others, cards transferred to those ineligible, cards used more than once. It is not surprising, then, to hear protests that the voters included people who were out of town, bankrupt, convicted criminals, serving in the military – or even dead.[20]

But the surest way to obtain votes was to simply buy them. Vote-buying was endemic to elections in Bône; only the number who sold their votes varied. In particularly hard-fought elections, of five thousand voters perhaps two thousand could be bought. "Voters were openly solicited on the public thoroughfare," claimed a protestor, and twelve hundred votes reportedly had been purchased in the last three days alone of one campaign. Every racial and ethnic group in town participated in this electoral trafficking. Leaders of the Jewish community "publicly bought Jewish votes" in the store of a Jewish merchant, while "it was a fact universally known," according to their opponents, that the incumbent Algerian council members had established "a campaign chest to buy votes."[21]

Voters were plied with food and drink on a truly grand scale. Electoral gatherings – called significantly *punchs* and *apéritifs* – were held which were attended by up to hundreds of voters, especially if the main feature – in addition to the "numerous libations" – was someone such as Deputy Thomson. The Bônois developed the free distribution of food and drink into a minor art. Chits were handed out good in any of several designated bars, at each one of which a young man kept a record of the amount consumed – absinthe was the preferred beverage – and the barkeeper paid later. Little wonder that "The number of free drinks served on Sunday (the day of the election) in the different bars in town is incalculable." In addition, "monster banquets" were held, the menu varying according to the group. Italian fishermen celebrated at a favorite beach outside town with a traditional *macaronnade*, French railway workers feasted on *bouillabaisse*, and Algerians were regaled with "immense plates" of *couscous*.[22]

Other blandishments included temporary jobs and welfare subsidies. Forty thousand francs saved for street repairs allegedly was spent in the six weeks prior to one election. As for the three hundred workers hired, "if you weren't a voter, you didn't get work!" Or, again, it was claimed that eighty-four street cleaners were fired the day after an election.[23] It was also repeatedly claimed that the Opportunists used the Bureau de Bienfaisance as a campaign slush fund. Each of the administrators supposedly had *bons*, or coupons, worth one, two, and three francs to use at their discretion, and which they handed out the day after the election at the home of the mayor's brother.[24]

These various inducements were part of a comprehensive electoral package; generally it was one and the same voter who sold his vote, received free food and drink, and perhaps some additional personal favor. Thus, one candidate installed in his office a booth "exactly like in a bank" to buy votes, and had to put up a wooden barrier in the street outside to control the "invading flood" of voters who came to pick up their voter cards, get paid for their vote, and then go vote "in a landau escorted by two guards."[25] Similarly, a group of Algerian voters handed in their cards, were fed prodigious amounts of *couscous* in a

187

cheap restaurant, and then taken to a Turkish bath where they were "kept from view the entire night" by courtiers. The following morning they were shepherded to a house where they received their promised twenty-five francs plus voting card and ballot, and then were accompanied "sometimes alone and sometimes in groups" to the polls.[26]

The day of the election was understandably "very animated. There were scuffles and brawls all over, and it was not rare that gunshots were fired,"[27] not to mention allegations concerning stuffed ballot boxes, the use of transparent ballots, and campaigning inside the polling place.

The ritual aftermath of the election was the filing of protests with the prefectoral administration contesting the outcome. Between 1870 and 1910 literally hundreds of protests were filed by dozens of people. And during these first forty years of the Third Republic the elections of thirty-five municipal council members were annulled, including all those elected in the second round of voting in 1870, all of the Algerian candidates in 1904, and all those elected in the second round in 1908. Furthermore, Gaston Thomson's elections of 1877, 1885, 1893, and 1898 all were contested.[28]

What this election description reveals – intensely competitive elections, a large number of voters easily enticed by short-term gains, voters voting *en bloc* – all are characteristic of a political machine, of a nonideological organization interested less in political principle than in securing and retaining political office for its leaders, and distributing material rewards to the voters who maintain it in power.[29] In other words, Bône elections are a case of political party patronage, of machine politics, consisting of exchanges between a political "boss" and voters.

In the first place, it should be noted that the basis of political parties in colonial Bône was personalities and not principles. Politicians in Algeria spoke not of French-style parties but of *çuff-s* (Frenchified as *çoff-s*, Muslim factions), not of the Opportunist Republican or Radical Republican Party but – and the fact is significant – of the "Etienne-Mauguin-Bertagna-Thomson party."[30] In Bône it was the same. Elections were waged not between the "Parti Français" (used sometimes to designate the Radicals) and everyone else, but between the "Bertagnistes" and the "anti-Bertagnistes." Moreover, Opportunism in Bône was opportunism with a small "o."

The *Bônois* are reputed to have always been Opportunists. Their opportunism, however, was not the same as that of the great *Parti Opportuniste.* . . . No, it is an opportunism simpler and more egotistic, which consisted in doing all that was necessary to be always on the side of the government, whatever it was, Radical or otherwise, in order to obtain always the greatest profits possible.[31]

Just as the parties were not parties of principle but based on people, so the voters – and this is the second point about machine politics in Bône – were less interested in the broad policy issues characteristic of an "issue-oriented electorate"[32] than in "the greatest profits possible": money, food, drink, work. For those at the bottom of the social pyramid, the machine represents a patron.[33] In exchange for patronage favors, the voters manifest their support at the polls.

Consistent electoral support meant uninterrupted Opportunist power in Bône between 1870 and 1910. Noteworthy also is the fact of smooth political succession. The second mayor during the Third Republic was the close collaborator of the first, Bertagna had been deputy mayor to the second, and Bertagna's successor had been *his* deputy. At once the cause and the effect of strong patronage bonds, continuity in power such as the Opportunists enjoyed is another hallmark of a political machine.

Bloc voting is a fourth distinctive trait of Bône machine politics. Now "Algeria has always known voting by group [*le vote par ordre*] which is perhaps the essential given of its *vie politique*,"[34] and numerous indications in the description above point to the fact that members of the same racial or ethnic group in Bône voted for the same candidates. Voting *en bloc* is typical of a machine electorate for whom vertical ties of family and ethnic group are more important than horizontal ones of class and occupation.[35] However, the electorate of Bône was in all probability composed of several electorates, each at a different level of socioeconomic and political development. But unfortunately *faute des sources*, we cannot know in any precise way what proportion of those in a given ethnic group or socioeconomic category voted for a particular political grouping.[36] It is only speculation, therefore, but I would guess that Bertagna's Opportunists derived the bulk of their support from the naturalized Italians, Maltese, Jews, and to a lesser extent from the French and Muslim Algerians, whereas the Radicals drew mainly on the native French. Although the Radicals probably counted a larger proportion of French in their ranks than the Opportunists did, I would argue that the gap in Opportunist election victories surely meant that more French voted Opportunist than Radical, and certainly the city's economic and political elite were solidly Opportunist.

The last feature of machine politics in colonial Bône is that it extends beyond Bône in the sense that politicians there formed patronage chains with politicians elsewhere. The most important – because most efficacious – chain was the one connecting Mayor Bertagna in Bône to Deputy Thomson in Paris. Bertagna disbursed patronage in Bône (some of which came through Thomson) in exchange for electoral support, and Thomson represented Bône's interests in Parliament in exchange for which Bertagna delivered the vote.

Throughout Algeria local settler power was linked to and cemented by an influential settler lobby in Paris, comprised largely of the *élus algériens*, the French representatives of Algeria who sat in the Assemblée Nationale. In turn, these *élus algériens* played a major role in the *parti colonial*, the foremost interest group lobbying for colonial expansion during the Third Republic. The *parti colonial* and its parliamentary component, the *groupe colonial*, have received a good deal of historiographical attention recently.[37] Broadly speaking, the *parti colonial* is interpreted as a highly successful pressure group which was responsible for late nineteenth- and early twentieth-century French expansion rather than any widespread, mass-based enthusiasm from ordinary Frenchmen. Key here is that European settlers from Algeria and their representatives comprised the major faction within the *parti colonial*. Eugène Etienne, deputy from Oran, was the unquestioned titular head; he was seconded by Gaston Thomson, representative of Bône. The *parti colonial* has been studied mostly from "above" rather than "below," from Paris rather than Algeria. Yet interest groups such as the *parti colonial* could not have functioned, indeed, would have had no raison d'être, had it not been for the sort of grassroots support provided by settlers in local Algerian cities like Bône.

Patronage and politics

Why were municipal elections in Bône so hotly contested? Why was politics so important? The answer, I would argue, is to be found in the nature of patronage and patronage politics. People in the Mediterranean use different words to express different facets of patronage. The Algerians talk about *service fait*, *service rendu*; the French, *rendre service* and, above all, *piston*; the Italians, *clientelismo* and *clientela*. Social scientists in turn have devised their own grammar of patronage. "Patrons" dispense patronage to "clients," and such individual patronage relationships rapidly form complex patronage "chains" and patronage "networks," since a patron (or client) can be involved as either patron or client in several relationships simultaneously. Thus, individual patron/client threads knit together to form patronage chains and patronage networks until an entire society is stitched together in a fine mesh of social networks.

Ultimately, it is poverty, or more precisely, limited access to scarce material resources that underlies patronage. In an agrarian-based society this means primarily access to land (whether owned, sharecropped, rented, or a variation thereof); in a more "modern" industrial society this means access to state resources (either bureaucratically or electorally controlled).[38]

Access to resources may be constricted for any number of socio-structural reasons, ranging from a closed system of social stratification to low or limited social mobility to a high degree of social distance as, for example, in the case of pronounced ethnic cleavage. Or, access to resources may be pinched off for political reasons, for who gets what is the quintessential problem of politics, of power. The powerlessness engendered by poverty is aptly expressed by Jeremy Boissevain writing about a Sicilian town:

Every Leonesi feels himself to be beset by problems and to a certain extent isolated in a hostile world. The more one descends the socio-economic ladder the more noticeable this attitude becomes, for the farther removed people are from those who wield power and thus control the forces shaping one's life.[39]

This is where patronage comes in, for it links the powerless with the powerful, and thereby to resources in the control of the latter or available through them. Thus, patronage is "a kind of 'intervening mechanism'" between the local community and the nation" in which "the patron provides connections . . . with the institutional order" which together link "entire villages to the structure of government."[40] Just as an Indian peasant, hedging his bets, will sow not simply wheat but wheat and oats and barley and rye all in the same field, so people forge bonds with others as a kind of primitive social insurance. Patronage is another mode of access to material resources.

The form patronage takes may vary over time. For example, the patronage relationship between lord and peasant typical of a traditional, agrarian society in which vertical ties are predominant, obviously differs fundamentally from that between the "boss" of a political machine and the voters characteristic of a more modern mass society in which horizontal ties are increasingly important. Yet what changes is not so much patronage per se, as the relationship of patronage to the formal structure of constituted authority – government and bureaucracy. Patronage is not parallel to bureaucracy in the sense of being independent to it; instead, the former is supplementary to and inversely correlated with the latter. Why? Because patronage functions against the backdrop of organized authority, or to use our earlier phraseology, patronage thrives where access to resources through formal political institutions is restricted. In fact, "the functional deficiencies of the official structure generate an alternative (unofficial) structure to fulfill existing needs somewhat more effectively."[41] At the same time there must exist "gaps," "holes," interstices in the formal political structure where patronage can take root. The political machine variety of patronage, for example, is most likely to occur "where there is enough concentration of resources to prevent the creation of independent feudal domains but not so much as to allow the central authority to dictate terms to the petty leaders with whom it must deal."[42]

The key here, I would contend, is that the patron and the official are often one and the same person. The patron thus derives his influence in good measure precisely from his official position. This is where corruption comes in, for political corruption stems from the tension between these two roles.[43] The bureaucrat who dispenses patronage favors to aggrandize his own personal position is constantly faced with the conflicting patronage/particularistic and bureaucratic/collective demands of his two-in-one position.

The relevance of this discussion for the Bône case is readily apparent. First of all, the French bureaucracy established in Algeria after 1870 permitted the creation of political party patronage in cities such as Bône. Second, the patronage network thus established acted as a mechanism which channeled state resources from Algiers and Paris to Bône and other local communities. As a result, control of the Bône municipal administration – determined in quadrennial municipal elections – became a highly sought-after political "spoil." Third and finally, the potential for corruption inherent in a political system in which patrons and officials were frequently the same people was exacerbated when local communities used state resources to build up effective grass roots political lobbies which then competed through the *parti colonial* with the French state to determine colonial policy in Algeria.

In short, the primary feature of what I would term the political culture of colonial Bône is patronage. Patronage relationships characterize both the municipal elections in which officials are elected, and the municipal administration to which officials are appointed. Patronage typified settler political power not only in Bône but elsewhere in Algeria. The formal political structure consisted of the colonial administration which represented the interests of metropolitan France. The informal political structure consisted of an extensive patronage network centered in the local Algerian communes and the group of Algerian representatives in Parliament, the *élus algériens*, which looked after the interests of the European settlers.

Patronage politics in Bône

How patronage politics was practiced in Bône can be illustrated graphically in the career of Mayor Jérome Bertagna (1888–1903), beginning with his management of the municipal administration. For within the city limits – and beyond as we shall see – Bertagna was boss; whether such-and-such a measure was legal, or of only dubious legality, there was no effective countervailing power to countermand him.

Illustration 6.2   Inauguration of monument to Jérome Bertagna, 1907
(collection of the author).

In 1888, for example, Bône contracted with a local entrepreneur to
build a sewer. When it was finished inhabitants of the neighborhood
requested that it be extended further, but there was no more city money
to pay for it. Bertagna ordered that the work be done anyway and a
state engineer, M. Burger, agreed to have false invoices drawn up in
order to pay the contractor with departmental funds (which were later
reimbursed).[44] Even before he became mayor, Bertagna indulged in
shady deals involving public works. In 1884 he lent another contractor,
M. Soual, 100,000 francs in exchange for one-third of his profits for the
following three years. During this period Bertagna was deputy mayor
and responsible for overseeing public works projects carried out by the
city. This classic case of conflict of interest only came to light years
later.[45]

The most colossal misuse of funds in a public works project, however,
concerned the port of Bône. Estimated to cost 10,000,000 francs, the
final price was 19,000,000. Begun in 1885, work on the port had to be
stopped in 1894 for lack of funds. The government was interpellated
about the project. Even a generally pro-Bertagna local historian conceded that "it is difficult to believe that the enormous difference" between the projected cost and the final cost was "the result of a simple
error of judgment."[46]

More outrageous still was Bertagna's high-handed treatment of Bône
brothels, because it was so clearly an abuse of his power as mayor. In

193

1891 he had an illegal municipal ordinance passed requiring madams to pay five francs per month per prostitute, plus he charged the most notorious madam in town, Mme. Borelli, various amounts to reopen her two brothels whenever they were closed for disturbing the peace – which was often. He further stipulated that this money be paid to the city welfare agency as "voluntary gifts." Borelli alone paid 4,540 francs in this manner between 1891 and 1896. In addition, Bertagna charged Borelli 100 francs per month starting in 1893 to station a cop outside one brothel to maintain the peace. This money was credited to the police budget. To the state prosecutor investigating the case, Bertagna's abuse of power was "incontestable." The "voluntary gifts" were no such thing. The city ordinance had been passed without prefectoral approval, which would never have been granted because it was blatantly illegal to tax a single group of taxpayers.[47]

This litany of Bertagna's misdeeds could be prolonged ad nauseum since twenty-eight *instructions judiciaires* (roughly equivalent to grand jury investigations) were launched against him.[48] But the point here is that Bertagna was able to get away with his corrupt practices because they were part and parcel of the personal influence he wielded over individuals and institutions. In turn those further down the pecking order of power owed allegiance to those higher up.

At the pinnacle of power in Bône sat Bertagna, and his influence – pervasive in Bône – extended well beyond. Concerning engineer Burger, state prosecutor Broussard remarked, "This engineer's chief preoccupation was to oblige M. Jérome Bertagna. . . . " Likewise, the judicial arm of the local chamber of commerce "comes under the influence of M. Bertagna." The "zeal and perspicacity" of the Bône judges "cannot be counted upon," lamented Broussard, when "they have to exercise their functions against the administration of which M. Jérome Bertagna is the head." In another scandal he remarked that Bertagna was able to literally "hold in check [*tenir en échec*]" the prefect, that the prefect's "willingness to oblige M. Jérome Bertagna is incomprehensible." The prefect was later revoked.[49]

Bertagna's power, moreover, was such that he had a corrupting influence on employees in the municipal administration. When questioned about the false invoices he had prepared for the sewer work, Burger said, "I dared not refuse M. the mayor this favor [*ce service*] because he was President of the *Conseil Général* [departmental council]." At the same time, another employee had been caught using roadmen to work his land at state expense. The employee said he had learned this dodge from his boss – M. Burger.[50]

The point is clear: engaging in corrupt practices in the performance of one's duties was in no way limited to Bertagna alone. He may have encouraged it by the example he set, but it existed before him and it continued after him. In fact, there is ample evidence that the Bône administration was riddled with corrupt officials. The head of the accounting section, M. Barriol, appropriated to himself the power to simultaneously draw up invoices, to pay out money for them, and to keep records on them. "A more convenient scheme for fictitious charges, including embezzlement, cannot be imagined." A similar arrangement in Algiers had led to the embezzlement of 130,000 francs.[51]

Burger engaged in several underhanded practices. He sold a house to a contractor who had just won a city contract worth 160,000 francs which Burger was responsible for overseeing. He had a state rest house refurbished and then used it to entertain his mistress. In 1887 he borrowed 60,000 francs from the two contractors who were in charge of work on the port, and increased their monthly expenses by a like amount (Burger claimed that the money was reimbursed later). And concerning Burger's bookkeeping practices, a state inspector observed that his "forging of fictitious invoices had become a habit."[52]

Burger's immediate superior, M. Dormoy, "knew, tolerated, and tacitly approved" Burger's bookkeeping procedures according to the same state inspector. In the opinion of Procureur Général Broussard, "The willingness of Dormoy and Burger to oblige M. Bertagna knows hardly any limits."[53]

The corruption practiced by officials from Bertagna on down spread until it became endemic to municipal administration in Bône. Three examples should serve to make the point. First of all, Bertagna and Burger admitted only that paying for the sewer from departmental funds was "an irregularity, perhaps a prohibited transfer." If so, it was a regular irregularity. We have seen the sort of bookkeeping methods practiced by Barriol and Burger. We also have the admission of another employee involved that other public works were paid for in the same manner.[54]

Second, public works contracts were let privately (*marché de gre à gre*), whereas "the system of competitive bidding for contracts, which ought to be the rule, had been almost abandoned." In theory this was possible for projects costing less than 3,000 francs, and then only with prefectoral approval, but in practice it was supposed to be done only in exceptional cases.[55] The consequences of not opening up public works projects to competitive bidding, especially in a city where enormous sums were spent on such projects, can only be imagined.

Lastly, after the death of Bertagna in 1903 the new mayor felt constrained to issue a memorandum to all municipal employees reiterating that "no remuneration is due them by the public for carrying out the duties of their jobs" (sic), and warning them that they would be pen-

195

alized if they acted as intermediaries and collected taxes from taxpayers instead of the duly authorized tax officials.[56] That the mayor felt that such a circular was necessary reflects the state of the Bône municipal administration.

It may seem that the preceding has been more a discussion of political corruption than of political patronage. It must be remembered, however, that corruption arises from the tension between simultaneous patronage and bureaucratic demands placed on the same person. Burger knew full well that the bureaucratic demand of his position required that he not disburse state funds for a city sewer. But the patronage demand (to render a *service* to Bertagna) to which he acceded, meant that he corrupted himself. So corruption is not intrinsic to patronage, but often associated with it.

Patronage was both the cause and result of power and influence. The more patronage relationships with numerous and important people, the greater a person's power and influence. At the same time, the more a person's power and influence, the greater the scope for patronage. The circle was thus closed. One of Bertagna's critics pictured him sitting at the apex of the "mechanism of an infernal machine"; his power was such that "nothing in Constantine *département* could resist" his influence.[57] Similarly, Gaston Thomson's power – "The power of political personages like Thomson . . . surpasses the imagination" – was such that deputies as influential as he or Eugène Etienne of Oran "became under a mediocre governor like Tirman (1881–91) the true masters of Algeria."[58] Neither Bertagna nor Thomson are representative in the sense that they were typical. But they are illuminating precisely because they realized the possibilities, they actualized the potential more than most of their contemporaries of patronage in colonial Algeria.

The following was written of the Algerian representatives in Parliament like Thomson, but it applies equally to the leaders of local communes like Bertagna.

. . . the representatives of the first rank used their authority for the benefit of their loyal supporters. It depended on them, for example, that a road connected up the farm of a friend, and above all, they had in fact the final say [*la haute main*] in administrative appointments, because the governors knew that they had to reckon with their power based at once in Paris and in their electoral fiefs.[59]

Apropos of one category of appointments, namely those to the Constantine judiciary, Procureur Général Broussard said:

It is not in effect without a profound feeling of sadness that one is forced to observe that the majority of judges which comprise the courts of this *département* have been appointed to the positions they occupy as a result of the influence of politicians who are concerned less with the professional merit of the candidates than with the favors [*services*] that they hope from them. These judges are honest men, but the majority lack character and civic courage.[60]

"The circle was thus closed again," writes Baroli. "The favors and patronage given generously extended their [that of the parliamentary representatives] electoral influence and assured stability, which in themselves were the conditions of a para- or supra-administrative power which allowed them to 'oblige' the voters to a very large degree."[61]

The fabric of patronage in Bône has now been unraveled, and the threads scrutinized to reveal how each is tied to the other. The main purpose in all this has been to demonstrate that politics in Bône can be explicated largely in terms of a thick patronage web of who-you-know. It is now time to weave the disparate strands together again by presenting the following case study which embodies much of the preceding. Neither "representative" nor "typical," nonetheless it exemplifies how patronage worked in Bône.

In 1888 the *Conseil Général* of Constantine approved a contract whereby the state agreed to pay the Compagnie de Bône-Guelma, the state railway company based in Bône, to build a line from Combes to Randon, two settlements outside Bône. As part of the construction of the railbed, a branch line was built to transport necessary material. Now it so happened that this branch line ended three kilometers from the wine cellers belonging to two brothers named Julien, who owned a "very important" vineyard. Seeing the possibility of a direct rail link from their cellars to the port of Bône for the export of their wine, the Juliens asked Dominique Bertagna, the brother of Jérome and a *Conseiller Général* of the canton in which the Juliens lived, if it could be arranged for the Compagnie de Bône-Guelma to extend the railroad to their cellars and to maintain the entire branch line (which was of no use to the Compagnie after construction of the main line). In a "purely electoral interest" Dominique spoke to his brother, who spoke in turn to M. Duportal, the chief engineer of the Bône-Guelma. The Bône-Guelma agreed to build the extension and to maintain the branch line provided that someone else build the railbed. Thus, the Bône-Guelma agreed to build a branch railway without carrying out a preliminary survey, without having the line declared to be in the public interest, and without prefectoral approval – all of which were prescribed by law. (The prefect later claimed he was "completely ignorant" of the project, as if a préfet could fail to know about the construction of a railway in his département.)

Meanwhile, the Bertagnas arranged for a "willing contractor" named Malassis to construct the roadbed. Next the Bertagnas and the Juliens put Malassis in touch with none other than Burger, whom they "told

197

to come up with a scheme which would satisfy their diverse but convergent interests." Ever-obliging Burger arranged to pay Malassis out of departmental funds earmarked for two bridges to be built as part of the larger railroad project. (He also diverted departmental maintenance funds to pay for upkeep of the branch line.) However, Malassis was forced to wait for payment since no money had been made available yet by the state for the Bône-Guelma's work. Malassis agreed to do the work anyway at his own expense and to be reimbursed later. This he did at a cost of more than 28,000 francs, and afterwards the Compagnie de Bône-Guelma laid the track.[62]

As an electoral favor, therefore, the Bertagnas conspired with state officials to build a branch railroad at state expense solely for the Juliens' private profit. It is all here: an electoral *service* done in exchange for electoral support; the linkage between this electoral favor and the municipal and state administration (to carry out the electoral favor required the collusion of the administration); a patronage chain (the Juliens – Dominique Bertagna – Jérome Bertagna – Duportal and Burger) consisting of a series of patronage relationships (Julien brothers–Dominique Bertagna, Jérome Bertagna–Duportal, Jérome Bertagna–Burger, Jérome Bertagna–Malassis); the use of political power (". . . another example of the omnipotence that the two Bertagna brothers had been able to acquire in the arrondissement of Bône. . . .") for private, electoral purposes, and which entailed the corruption of state officials (". . . and of the docility with which the railroad company and the government officials obeyed them."[63]).

The crisis of 1896

As long as settler interests coincided with those of metropolitan France, the colonial French bureaucracy cracked down only on the most outrageous excesses of local patronage politics. Beginning in the 1890s, however, the situation began to change. It was then that a series of reports issued in quick succession alerted Parliament in Paris to the practice in Algeria of the French theory of assimilation. But when the showdown came, metropolitan France learned to its dismay how powerful the settlers had become politically with their patronage-based political network extending from the local municipalities of Algeria to the settler lobby in Paris. The city of Bône and its mayor, Jérome Bertagna, were key to this settler political network and at the center of the ensuing conflict.

As a result of the parliamentary reports issued in the 1890s, Jules Ferry among others demanded that metropolitan France act as arbiter between the European settlers and the native Algerians. Growing government dissatisfaction led to the appointment of reform-minded Jules Cambon as Governor General in 1891. No stranger to Algeria – he had served briefly as prefect of Constantine in 1877–79 – one of Cambon's primary undertakings was a wide-ranging purge of Algerian mayors. In less than a year beginning in November, 1895 Cambon suspended or revoked no fewer than nine mayors.[64] It is no coincidence that within the context of his purge, Bertagna was clearly Cambon's biggest and most important prey.

It so happened that at the same time as other activities of Bertagna in Bône were being investigated – the illegal taxation of brothels, municipal administration procedures, the Combes-Randon railroad – another scandal involving him was revealed in Parliament: the affair of the phosphates of Tebessa.[65] It was alleged that Bertagna had engaged in influence peddling in order to have a concession for phosphates awarded to an English company. Rich phosphates deposits had been recently discovered by an Algerian outside Tebessa located 125 miles south of Bône. Unable to capitalize on his find by acting on his own, Salah ben Khélil agreed to cut in M. Perette, the secretary of the local commune. Perette used his influence to obtain the concession, and then the two began looking for a buyer. Dominique Bertagna heard about it, and talked to his brother Jérome, who contacted an English businessman in Bône by the name of Henry Jacobsen. Mayor Bertagna and Jacobsen negotiated a contract whereby Bertagna agreed to use his influence to obtain the necessary prefectoral authorization in exchange for a flat 30,000 francs plus one to three francs per ton of phosphates extracted. Once the authorization was obtained, the concession was brought from Perette and in rapid succession transferred from Salah ben Khélil to Dominique Bertagna to Jérome Bertagna to Jacobsen.[66]

The potential profits were huge. Termed a "national treasure" by one engineer, production continued throughout the 1950s; in 1955, 661,000 tons were extracted which amounted to eighty-eight percent of the Algerian total. However, late in 1895 the government in Paris was interpellated about the matter, and Minister of the Interior Georges Leygues appointed a commission to investigate. On the basis of the report submitted to Leygues, the prefect was revoked, the prefectoral authorizations were rescinded, and *instructions judiciaires* were launched against the Bertagnas and Perette for suspected influence peddling. On the basis of the investigation Cambon first suspended Mayor Bertagna in December, 1895, and later revoked him in March, 1896, pending the outcome of the judicial inquiry.[67]

Furthermore, Deputy Thomson had been implicated. In December, 1895, Viviani, a socialist deputy born in Algeria but who represented Paris, accused Thomson of interceding with officials in behalf of Jacob-

199

sen. More serious, in a confidential memo Senator Pauliat, a left-wing senator from the Cher, said that " . . . it appears Bertagna has ceded one-third of his profits to one of the most influential members of the Algerian band." The reference could only be to Thomson, but no evidence was ever produced to substantiate Thomson's involvement.[68]

As for the involvement of the Bertagnas, they clearly appeared guilty. On the basis of the Bertagna-Jacobsen contract alone Procureur Général Broussard argued that Jérome Bertagna was guilty. Even more damaging was a series of letters which charted Bertagna's progress in influencing state officials. Writing to an intermediary, Jacobsen said:

I hope M. Bertagna will not complain if I don't walk at a rapid enough pace. To which you will probably offer your favorite motto: "You cannot dance faster than the music." I say to you: But there are ways to make the musicians play faster. Find them! Once the ground is broken, we will deploy the same activity and with the precious aid of the Messieurs Bertagna, I hope that we will outdistance our rivals [September 14, 1893].

The same date Jacobsen telegraphed the following message.

Remind Bertagna to obtain permission to place portable railroad border new departmental road Tebessa-Kef. Let us hope all formalities finished for transfer concession in two week period when will be in Bône.

Five days later, Bertagna telegraphed the following from Tebessa to the intermediary: "You will probably be able to announce to your mandator [*mandant*] solution day after tomorrow." Finally, September 22 Jacobsen telegraphed: "Very good. Sincere compliments Messieurs Bertagna. Now, forward!"[69]

Dominique Bertagna's guilt was no less clearly established. Writing to Perette he said:

Before going to Tebessa, I will go to Constantine day after tomorrow to destroy the impression the *préfet* has as a result of talking to your detractors, and will do all in my power to obtain the approval of the meeting in Salah's favor.

Four days later he wrote:

I went to see the *préfet* with whom I had a very long discussion . . . after a detailed examination of the case, it appeared indispensable to us to launch an inquest which will be done by a *Conseiller de Préfecture* [prefectoral advisor]. . . . It is superfluous to tell you that I will go to Tebessa to be present at the inquest, which will only be done when I judge the time opportune. . . . The *préfet* waits for me to advise him when to begin the inquest.[70]

When the *instruction* was finished in June, 1896, Broussard concluded that "MM. Jérome and Dominique Bertagna have sold to M. Jacobsen, who wanted to obtain a favor or a profit resulting from an agreement concluded with the public authorities, the influence which their electoral mandates gave them." Furthermore, he recommended that the case be tried in France because Bertagna's power precluded a fair trial in Algeria.[71]

But it was already too late. Despite Bertagna's suspension and then revocation, he was overwhelmingly reelected mayor by loyal Bônois in a bitterly contested, "life or death" election in May, 1896. At the time of his investiture he went on the offensive lambasting the administration and in particular the judicial system.

The judiciary, unable to prove my guilt after six months of tortures which it has inflicted on me, has invented for me a penalty unknown in our legal codes: "perpetual investigation" [*l'instruction perpetuelle*]. This justice system has prostituted itself and has submitted to political demands. I await proudly all the persecutions which can still afflict me strengthened by my past of rectitude and honesty, for without blemish and without fear I have the legitimate conviction of being invincible.[72]

And so he was, for the Bône *juge* who conducted the phosphates investigation concluded – as did every other *juge* who ever investigated him – that there was insufficient evidence to bring Bertagna to trial.[73]

The judicial inquiry had indeed become embroiled in politics, but not in the way Bertagna claimed. The Opportunist press usually portrayed such investigations as political maneuvers on Cambon's part to favor the Radicals, and such charges undoubtedly had an effect on the government of Jules Meline. In 1896, for example, the Radical prefect was revoked for intervening in the Constantine municipal elections won by the Radical anti-semites.[74]

With his failure to unseat Bertagna, Cambon's mayoral purge sputtered out. His own end came the following year when Cambon's opponents – Thomson was "his most decided adversary" – succeeded in having him ousted as Governor General.[75] As Cambon himself accurately expressed it:

I am Governor, and I do not govern. I command, and I am not obeyed. I want to do right, and I am powerless to prevent wrong. I have received the mission to have the administration of France liked and respected: I do not have the power to wrest it from the jaws of sharks [*aux griffes des aigrefins*].[76]

The confrontation in Bône in 1896 which pitted the settlers against the government, and the bureaucracy against the patronage system had clearly been won by the settlers and their representatives. Elsewhere in Algeria the settlers also beat back the metropolitan French challenge, but in a manner which requires some discussion.

The attempt by metropolitan France to reform Algeria, to act again as an intermediary between Europeans and Algerians, spawned a settler reaction which is usually discussed in terms of an anti-semitic crisis between 1898 and 1901, but which amounted in reality to a revolution *manquée*. This larger crisis comprised several components in addition to anti-semitism: *colon* insecurity vis-à-vis the Algerians, French settler fears of non-French settlers ("foreign peril"), an economic crisis over colonization, plus a movement for autonomy. Crisis in Algeria added to the *crise de conscience* felt in France over the course the settlers were steering, and led to a political confrontation, the opening round of which cast Cambon against Bertagna in 1896. But if Cambon's defeat at the hands of Bertagna resolved in large measure the Bône situation, Cambon's removal failed to still emotions elsewhere in Algeria. "With Cambon gone," Ageron writes, "the political crisis only worsened until the revolutionary attempt of the years 1898–1901, misunderstood as the anti-Jewish crisis, and by which the Algeria of the Europeans meant to obtain its autonomy."[77]

At the peak of the Dreyfus affair in France, Algeria experienced its own outbreak of anti-semitism. Scholars concur that Algerian anti-semitism was primarily an electoral phenomenon born as a result of the 1870 Cremieux decree which enfranchised en masse the Jews of Algeria. Because of the close competition between the Opportunist and Radical Republicans for political power, the Jewish vote frequently swung elections in the Opportunists' favor, especially since the Jews had a reputation for voting *en bloc*. Jews comprised a full twenty percent of the electorate in Oran in 1871 compared to only three percent in Bône in 1870. In 1899 Jews constituted nine percent of all electors in Algeria, but fifteen percent in Oran department. Key, however, was the Jews' identification with the Opportunists. For voting Opportunist only confirmed Radical anticapitalist rhetoric which portrayed Jews as unscrupulous moneylenders and the like – rhetoric to which the Spanish, Maltese, and Italian *petits blancs* were particularly susceptible. Well before the turn of the century, therefore, the Radicals had discovered the efficacy of using anti-semitism as a political stick with which to beat the Opportunists. "Anti-Jewishness had become the common denominator of the Algerian Left."[78]

Anti-semitism at the turn of the century went well beyond electoral contests, however. Periodic anti-semitic outbursts had occurred earlier, but they hardly rivaled May, 1897, when rampaging crowds sacked Jewish shops in Oran and pillaged the Jewish quarter of Mostaganem for three days in agitation which spread throughout Oran department; or January, 1898, in Algiers when for five days after Zola published his *J'accuse*, Jewish shops and residences were attacked, two people were killed, and one hundred wounded. Anti-semites scored, moreover, a stunning string of electoral victories beginning with the takeover of the municipal councils of Constantine (1896) and Oran (1897), and culminating in the parliamentary elections of 1898 when four of the six deputies elected from Algeria were declared anti-semites, including Edouard Drumont himself representing Algiers. Only Gaston Thomson in Bône and Eugène Etienne in Oran held onto their seats.[79]

The strongholds of Algerian anti-semitism were Algiers, Oran, and Constantine where more than fifty percent of the Jews lived. The Jews of Bône – numbering only three to five percent of the population – never became the lightning rod for *colon* resentments they did elsewhere. Moreover, the opposite side of the coin of anti-semitic weakness is Bône's Opportunist strength. "During the Third Republic, Bône is the departmental capital and the impregnable fortress of the moderate Republicans. . . . Never will the radical *antijuifs* succeed in challenging the opportunists in their fief."[80]

Notable for its relative lack of anti-semitic agitation, Bône was not immune however. Here as elsewhere, anti-semitism manifested itself primarily in a plethora of virulent newspapers, vociferous leagues, and noisy demonstrations. Five anti-semitic papers appeared in Bône which poisoned public discourse, but the main ones were based elsewhere.[81] The same was true of the anti-semitic leagues. For one thing, membership fluctuated widely. An anti-semitic meeting in 1899 which drew only thirty people was put off a week "because of the small audience."[82] As the crisis aggravated, the anti-semitic crowd developed a ritual of collective action which engendered its own reaction. An 1898 meeting attended by three hundred and fifty people heard a speaker whose theme "was first anti-semitism, then taking the battle to Jewish sympathizers, and above all to MM. Bertagna and Thomson." When the crowd exited, it was met by a two hundred-strong, Opportunist counterdemonstration. "Some clashes occurred . . . , some rocks were thrown . . . , some damage done," but it was nothing like Algiers or Oran.[83]

Anti-semitism was not as grave in Bône, but it seriously worried Bertagna and the Opportunists. In 1898 on the advice of Bertagna, Thomson ran for election from Bône instead of Constantine, which he had represented since 1876. He won, but his election was again contested, and a confidential report to the *préfet* warned that "The Bertagna's . . . greatly fear that M. Thomson may be invalidated. Opinion . . . has it that M. Thomson was elected thanks to a *tour de force* that cannot be repeated a second time. . . . Thus, the friends of M. Thomson, notably the Bertagna brothers, are making every effort to prevent the invalidation which is considered here nearly certain."[84] Not until the 1900 municipal elections did the Opportunists breathe easier when Bertagna & Co. crushed the Radicals. "The results have surpasssed my hopes," the subprefect reported to the prefect. "The *Parti Nationaliste*

Antisemite no longer exists, properly speaking."[85] In Oran the crisis subsided between 1898 and 1900, although the anti-semites held onto city hall until 1905. In the 1902 parliamentary elections for Algeria, all four anti-semites elected in 1898 were defeated.

Clearly, anti-semitism became more than simply an electoral phenomenon in *fin-de-siècle* Algeria. "Racial anti-semitism can be considered one of the givens of colonial Algerian psychology."[86] It functioned as a lightning rod which collected and deflected, as much as it focused, a whole range of collective resentments. The better-off native French settlers were well aware that the métropole viewed them as inferior, and Algeria as a "dumping ground" (*l'Algérie-dépôtoir*). These same French settlers feared being overwhelmed both by the Algerians, and the Spanish, Italian, and Maltese *petits blancs*, whom they considered a "foreign peril." The non-French settlers themselves came down with a classic case of status anxiety. Ethnically, they were colonizers; economically, they were often little better off than the colonized Algerians. "In the colonial Algerian psyche we witness a transference of racial hostility from the Muslim to the Jew," one scholar writes. "Shared by the ensemble of Europeans, it seems it was strongest among the *petits blancs*."[87] All settler strata exhibited anti-semitism, but in different degrees. "We are all *antijuifs* in Algeria, we who have combatted the anti-semites, we are as much as they," a leading journalist wrote. "We differ from them only insofar as we want to neither pillage shops nor massacre our adversaries."[88]

This is the situation into which Cambon stepped. Rapidly his reform effort became embroiled in Algerian politics. Given Opportunist opponents like Thomson and Bertagna, he was inevitably identified with the Radicals, and accused of anti-semitism besides. Scholars debate whether Cambon was anti-semitic – certainly the zealousness he displayed in the 1895 revision of Jewish electoral rolls is a strike against him – but the point is that he was perceived by contemporaries to favor the Radicals and anti-semites.[89] Settler leaders like Thomson and Bertagna successfully used this to undercut his position in Paris. Yet Cambon's departure in 1897 failed to resolve the Algerian crisis, because it was more than a crisis over anti-semitism.[90] To anti-semitism was added calls for autonomy, and even outright separation from France. As Ageron explains, the ties between France and Algeria consisted in "a sort of contract" whereby the task of France was to defend the settlers and to maintain their social supremacy over the Muslims; should it fail to do so, the settlers had the right to claim their independance. By 1898 large numbers of settlers felt France had broken this contract.[91]

At the height of the Dreyfus affair, therefore, a besieged Republic needed all the support it could get, and in the end caved in to the settlers' more moderate demands in exchange for their support against the anti-Dreyfusards. In a series of decrees issued in August, 1898, and completed by a 1900 law, the settlers failed to obtain outright political autonomy, but they did gain financial autonomy, the creation of a colonial assembly (*Délégations Financières*), and perhaps most important, the "unwritten promise that metropolitan interference would cease."[92] These concessions satisfied all but the hard core anti-semites, tensions attenuated from the end of 1898, and by the parliamentary elections of 1902 Algeria returned to the Opportunist fold.

But at what a cost. Algerian reform had been shelved. And measures for autonomy only strengthened the hand of the settlers at the expense of the metropole. Just as Bertagna had bested Cambon in 1896, therefore, so did the European settlers emerge victorious in their confrontation with metropolitan France at the turn of the century. By capitalizing on among other things the possibilities of patronage politics in a settler colonial situation, they had taken a giant stride forward in securing their de facto control over colonial Algeria.

7

The creation of a colonial culture

The formation of a colonial society recognizably Algerian occurred between 1890 and 1914. It included all the Europeans – French, Italian, Spanish, Maltese – and excluded Jews as well as Muslim Algerians. Contemporary observers perceived a melting pot effect, a fusion of the European ethnic groups which resulted in a new race. "A new race" is precisely how André Gide, who was in North Africa at the time, described what he saw.[1] Others discerned the same phenomenon. A jurist and future deputy: "There is formed in Algeria a new race"; a colonial publicist: "a new people, a race superior by intelligence and energy [to the French race]."[2]

Later historians have borne out the early observers. Charles-Robert Ageron, the foremost student of the 1870–1919 period, argues that "These European communities did not simply cohabit in Algeria, they began to mix very soon. . . . In brief, the amalgamation was itself effected by the school, by the street, by the barracks."[3] Emmanuel Sivan, author of a first, exploratory assay of popular culture in colonial Algeria, concludes that "the turn of the century saw there [in Algeria] the fusion of the numerous immigrant European ethnicities into one *pied noir* community."[4] Finally, Marc Baroli, one of a handful who have studied this community directly, states: "The beginning of the [twentieth] century marks the moment when the fusion between the diverse European elements is almost accomplished, thanks to the mixed marriages, the assimilation of ethnic groups to each other, and the common adaptation to conditions of life in Algeria within a French setting." He continues:

Thus in 1914 whereas the Arabs remain or are held apart and the Jews, assimilated practically speaking, have not fused and lead a life very similar to that of the Europeans but alongside them, the great mass of the latter have formed a unified community in spite of the social differences and those which separate the cities and the countryside. It is neither a question of a race, nor of a nation, but of a society which has its own values and common tastes and that suffices to individualize it.[5]

As evidence of this new society, both contemporaries and later observers have pointed to factors such as the relatively large size of the European community viz-à-vis the Algerians, the relatively large number of non-French Europeans in this French colony, the fact that the Europeans in Algeria were born more often in Algeria than in Europe starting in the 1890s, that the male/female ratio dropped from one characteristic of an immigrant population to one typical of a settled population, that while the number of mixed marriages among Europeans was one in four the number of marriages between Europeans and Algerians or Jews was negligible. Moreover, compulsory education and obligatory military service further fostered assimilation. Some of these factors have received extensive discussion, others merit further elaboration. But what I want to do here is to examine another set of indices, a body of cultural data which evidences the formation of a settler, or *pied-noir*, society in colonial Bône, namely, language and literature, street names, and picture postcards.

*   *   *

Downtown Casablanca, the business and hotel district, could be anywhere in the European Mediterranean. There is a little bit of Marseilles, a little bit of Nice, a little bit of Algiers, but other than the tomb of Sidi Belyout, in a little park at the entrance of the port area, there is little that is Moroccan.[6]

The same could be said of colonial Bône. Physically, Bône was a French city, not an Algerian one. The new city and Colonne Randon soon engulfed the old city, the city built by the Muslims. The urban landscape was predominantly French; so were the street names. The Cours Bertagna was entirely French, and the shade trees down the middle were reminiscent of the south of France, Aix-en-Provence, for instance. The *mairie* looked like it had been transplanted from a French provincial city such as Nimes, or Tours for that matter. Men, Frenchmen that is, played *boules* at the beginning of the Colonne Randon right opposite the square where the 1890 Exposition – modeled after the agricultural and industrial expositions of nineteenth-century France – was held. Not to mention the fact that the people of Bône were more often European than Algerian.

Was there not a tendency for the Algerians to be overshadowed in this French city, to become invisible? Perceptions are tricky to seize hold of, yet arguably they are what is most important. For one could argue that it is not the brute physical form of the city, but rather the way the cityscape was interpreted that was significant. Not the city itself but the perception of the city formed the basis of action and reflection.

Taking perceptions seriously, however, requires a new way of seeing. What we need is a grammar of perception.

Such a grammar would have to include the city's physical scale as one element. Annaba today is a sprawling city, but Bône yesterday was relatively small. You could walk from one end of the new city to the opposite end of the old city in ten minutes. You could stroll leisurely down the Cours stopping to buy a newspaper in the same amount of time. The small scale of the city made it more intimate, increased the number of face-to-face encounters. But social distance – another element in our syntax of perception – was a countervailing factor here. Social distance can be broken down into residential segregation and social segregation. Because it is susceptible of measurement, residential segregation can be dissected and examined (see Chapter 5). Social segregation is more slippery, harder to get a handle on. Yet surely the words we use, the gestures we make, and the forms of social relations we follow all define space and segregate "us" from "them" just as effectively as living in different parts of town. The *tutoiement* of Algerian by European, that is, the use of the informal *tu* rather than the formal *vous*, is important here. So is the tendency to address Algerians not by name but by an all-purpose moniker, usually "Ahmed."[7] The human use of physical space also requires elucidation. My city is not your city; the European city is not the Muslim city. In Bône the Europeans strolled on the Cours and took Sunday promenades by the European cemetery. The Algerians had their own circuit of *cafés maures* and Turkish baths.

Or consider the following. In colonial south and southeast Asia the British built hill stations, small settlements in the mountains, the chief attraction of which "lay in the absence of the three major constraints which restricted social life on 'the plains': the unfavorable climate, 'official' authority, and, most important of all, large numbers of the indigenous population."[8] In colonial Algeria there were no hill stations. In India the capital was moved laboriously every summer from New Delhi on the plains to Simla in the Himalaya foothills. In the Bône region the hamlet of Bugeaud at the crest of the Edough Mountains could have developed into a hill station. It did not, although the fatigue-inducing trip from Delhi to Simla takes hours even today, while driving Randon's road from Bône up to Bugeaud, now renamed Seraidi, takes only minutes. Were not the European settlers, the *pieds-noirs*, so firmly ensconced in Bône that there was little need to get away – at least from the Algerians?

Returning to the built environment of Bône itself, there are a number of possible ways to "read" the city. One obvious approach is to explicate the architectural styles and motifs in relation to the ethnic and racial groups which made up the population. Is it only coincidence that the large-scale *funduq*, the Arab market – the most handsome building in the city after the city hall, according to one local historian – was erected as early as 1865 but never rebuilt as planned after it was torn down in 1885?[9] In a slightly different way, is there any significance in the fact that there were no Italian-style buildings in Bône, although the Italians outnumbered the native French and certainly supplied more than their share of the construction workers?[10]

Or take the case of statues. The cityscape of colonial Bône was dotted with statues from the goddess Diana to Adolphe Thiers. Far and away the most grandiose statue, however, was that of Jérome Bertagna, unveiled after his death in 1903 in a ceremony presided over by the Governor General of Algeria. The symbolic significance with which these hunks of stone were imbued certainly rubbed off on the Algerians; they got the point. Frantz Fanon understood; he writes that the colonial world is "a world of statues: the statue of the general who carried out the conquest, the statue of the engineer who built the bridge; a world which is sure of itself, which crushes with its stones the backs flayed by whips. . . . "[11] After Algerian independence the Algerians tore down the monument to Bertagna and every other statue in Bône-become-Annaba as well save one.

Or what about the *monuments aux morts*, the monuments to the war dead? In France most of these date from the First World War. In Algeria such monuments are located around the village square as in France, and are sculpted in the same general style. But in Algeria they commemorate the *mujahidun*, the Muslim freedom fighters who died fighting the French during the Algerian Revolution. Is there a more clear-cut case of a cultural pattern which has been transferred to a different social and historical context and filled with a different but analogous content?[12]

Street names and picture postcards

Granted, such cases are suggestive rather than conclusive. But let us consider another one in some detail, namely, the names the Bônois chose for the streets which they built. Rue Ernesto "Ché" Guevara, rue Patrice Lumumba, rue Colonel Lotfi, rue Zighout Youcef, Cité Larbi Ben M'Hidi, rue Colonel Amirouche, Cité Didouche Mourad – these are some of the revolutionary heroes and martyrs, Algerian and otherwise, after whom the streets and government apartment buildings have been named in Annaba today.

Who did the French name the streets of Bône after? One local historian grouped the streets of the old city into a number of categories.[13] There were streets named after battles or personages of the Napoleonic era, especially concerning Napoleon's invasion of Egypt: rue Kléber, rue Castiglione, rue Josephine, rue d'Heliopolis, rue des Pyramides, rue Jemmapes. There was another group of streets named after the Orleanists of the July Monarchy: rue Louis-Philippe, rue d'Orléans, rue Joinville, rue Nemours, Impasse Montpensier, rue Louise et Marie. Later in the century, Third Republic people and places would supply the bulk of the street names in the new city and suburbs, such as Anatole France, Jean Jaurès, and Léon Gambetta. Two streets took their names from Christian saints, one of whom, Saint Nicholas, was venerated by the Turks. A second set of two streets were Jewish in origin: rue Jerusalem and rue Rabbin Khan (a leader of Bône's Jewish community). Other streets were named after geographical locations: rue de Carthage, rue d'Hippone, rue de Constantine, rue d'Algér. Although our local historian describes one category as names drawn from the history of Africa, it reflected in fact a very narrow reading of African history, namely, the French and their imperial forebears the Romans in Africa: rue de Foy, Place Terence, Impasse Scipion, Place des Numides, rue Bélisaire, rue Saint-Louis, rue Caraman, rue Rovigo, rue Sidi Ferruch. Only two streets had explicitly Muslim names: rue de Croissant, after the Muslim crescent, and rue de Cadi, after the Muslim tribunal located there.

Far and away the largest – and for our purposes the most important – group of street names referred to the French colonization and colonialization of Bône, and in particular to the conquest and early occupation. First, there were the names of warships – frigates, brigantines, barks – which transported the French troops: rue Béarnaise, rue Suffren, rue de Bedouin, rue de la Surprise, rue Bellone. Most numerous, however, were the streets named after those who had taken part:

> rue Damrémont, the general who first occupied Bône in 1830.
>
> rue Huder, the major who was killed in the 1831 occupation.
>
> rue d'Armandy, the general who captured control of the Turkish Casbah in 1832.
>
> rue du Lion, the rock in the harbor where d'Armandy disembarked in 1832.
>
> rue Joseph, the Christian name of Yusuf, the renegade Jew born in Italy, captured by pirates, and raised in Tunis, who took over the Casbah with d'Armandy and later was named Bey of Constantine by the French.
>
> rue Fréart, the commander of the warship Béarnaise.
>
> rue Cornulier-Lucinière, a sailor, later admiral, on the Béarnaise.

rue Charry, a sergeant who took part in the storming of the Casbah.

rue d'Uzer, the general discussed earlier who commanded the French troops in Bône, 1832–6.

rue Trézel, d'Uzer's successor as commander at Bône, 1836–7, and later Minister of War.

rue Randon, the general, later marshal, discussed earlier, who commanded Bône, 1841–6.

rue Bugeaud, the general, later marshal and Governor General of Algeria, who defeated the leader of the Algerian resistance, Abd al-Qadir.

rue Negrier, the colonel, later general, who served at Bône and later took part in the repression of the June Days of 1848 in Paris.

rue Bouscarein, a colonel stationed at Bône in 1845.

rue Perregaux, a colonel, later general, at Bône, who was killed in the assault on Constantine city in 1837.

rue Mesmer, the head of the Arab bureau at Bône, who was killed later by Algerians in the plain of Bône.

This very pronounced military flavor carried over in the names given to the villages the French founded in the region of Bône. First, there were the centers named for Bugeaud, Randon, and d'Uzer (Duzerville). In addition, there were the villages of:

Herbillon, named after the general who led numerous expeditions against the Berber Kabyles in the Edough Mountains.

Barral, after the general who commanded part of Constantine province early in the conquest.

Duvivier, after the general who took part in the first attack on Constantine, wrote several books on the colonization of Algeria, and who died during the June Days of 1848.

Morris, after the colonel stationed in Bône in the early 1830s, who helped conquer the plain of Bône.

The military tinge to the streets of Bône faded somewhat but was visible throughout the French occupation of Algeria. The Place Faidherbe derived its name from General Faidherbe. Best known for colonizing Senegal, he commanded the Bône subdivision in 1867–70. The rue des Volontaires commemorated the Bône volunteers who responded to Gambetta's call to defend France against the Prussians in 1870. Moreover, Bône was the birthplace of Marshal Alphonse Juin, who was Resident General of Morocco immediately prior to Moroccan independence in 1956.

Compared to the plethora of military figures, few civilians and settlers had streets named after them in the old city, even if we include two doctors who served in the army:

> rue Lacombe, one of the first mayors of Bône, 1849–54.

> Passage Casimir Bronde, the first president of the Bône Chamber of Commerce.

> Place Xavier Martin, the founder of a number of philanthropic societies.

> rue Maillot, an army doctor in Bône from 1833 on and one of the first anywhere to prescribe large doses of quinine against malaria.

> rue Moreau, another military doctor who tended a group of lepers.

To round out this survey of old city street names, there were three other streets named for people or events prior to 1830:

> rue Saint-Augustin, bishop of Hippo.

> rue Française, the street on which the *comptoir*, or warehouse, of the French Compagnie d'Afrique was located in the eighteenth century.

> rue Tabarka, named after the Tunisian port to which the Corsican survivors of an Algerian massacre in Bône fled in 1821. The Compagnie d'Afrique bought most of its coral from these Corsicans who had had their own storehouses in Bône prior to this Muslim popular uprising which decimated their community.

What can we make of the names the French gave to the streets of Bône? Certainly nothing definitive given the serious problems of interpretation which exist. Who and under what conditions the names were decided is unknown. Given a ruler's prerogative, how representative can we expect the names to be in any case? However, this does not preclude us from assessing the names entirely. If it is unwise to interpret the names as significant symbols laden with meaning, they can certainly be read as signs, as expressions of French colonialism in Bône. That said, the French street names of Bône reflect an extremely biased, distorted, and unrepresentative reading of the city's history. The Algerians are virtually absent; only two streets have clearly Muslim names. Only two streets are named after Jewish personages or places. No streets at all are named after Europeans who are not French, that is, Italians or Maltese. Rather, the overwhelming number of streets commemorate the presence of France in Bône, especially the early years of colonization and colonialism. Moreover, street names which refer to Bône's past before 1830 skip over the Arab and Turkish periods entirely to highlight instead the Romans and the world historical figure of St. Augustine. There is even the rue des Numides, which links the Berber Kabyles of the present to their ancestors before the Arabs arrived in North Africa. All this mirrors clear-cut French colonial policies in Algeria, namely, to resurrect the Romans as imperial progenitors of the French in Africa, to reassert the now defunct Christian past, and to divide Arabs and Berbers in order to rule them both more effectively.

Granted that the history of Bône as read in the street names of Bône is unrepresentative, is there any way to gauge how unrepresentative it is, the degree to which it misrepresents the city's history? In an interesting epilogue to his catalogue of Bône's street names, the local historian referred to above suggested additional names which would present a more balanced picture of Bône's history.[14] Although the bulk of the names proposed relate to France and French colonialism, there are several which revive Bône's Muslim and European past. In chronological order, then, he suggests the following streets:

> Impasse des Phéniciens, after the Punic founders of Hippo rue Massinissa, the Numidian king who made Hippo his capital.

> Place Boniface, the defender of Hippo from the Vandals during the siege in which Augustine died.

A series of names follows that highlights Bône's Arab and Muslim past:

> Place Sidi Belit, the Muslim saint who built the mosque later known as Sidi Bou Merouane.

> Place Sidi Bou Merouane, the thirteenth-century Muslim saint of Bône after whom the leading mosque was named.

> rue des Romanets, after a mosque of the same name that the French closed down in 1833.

> Impasse Djerada, the Muslim woman of Constantine who donated her privately owned wells in Bône to the community.

213

Next, the Turkish, Spanish, and Italian occupations of Bône are recalled:

> Impasse Kheir-ed-Dine, after Khaireddin Barbarossa, who captured Bône from the Tunisians in 1534–5.
>
> Impasse Don Alvar Gomez el Zagal. In 1535 the Spaniards under Charles V and Andrea Doria recaptured Tunis from the Turks and moved west, conquering Bône the same year. The Spanish, under Charles V's lieutenant, Don Alvar Gomez el Zagal, ruled Bône from 1535 to 1540. Both this street and the previous one recall local events connected to the larger Spanish-Turkish rivalry of the sixteenth century.[15]
>
> Impasse Piccolomini, the Duke of Toscany, who sacked Bône in 1607 in retaliation for the pirate raids launched from the city against Europe.

Lastly, a cluster of streets refer somewhat obliquely to the three-hundred-year period of Turkish rule which ended in 1830:

> Avenue du Fort Cigogne, after the Turkish fort of the same name, demolished in 1909.
>
> Avenue des Casarins, a second Turkish fort and the site where ships anchored half of the year.
>
> Impasse Salah Bey, after the Bey of Constantine, who built the mosque of the same name in 1791.
>
> Impasse du Bataillon Turc, a Turkish regiment organized by Yusuf after 1830 to combat the Arabs and Berber Kabyles.
>
> Impasse Caid Omar, the first Turk of Yusuf's regiment killed.

These additional names, proposed but never put into effect, indicate in some measure the extent to which the French conveniently "forgot" Bône's Arab, Turkish, and non-French European past, the extent to which they suffered a case of historical amnesia, as they went about building the city in general and naming the streets in particular. The colonialist message embedded in the very infrastructure of French colonization was as clear to the Algerians as it was unequivocal: a consistent downgrading of things Muslim and a concomitant glorification of things French. Although it is unwise to read too much into the names the French gave the streets of Bône, to see the hand of colonialism too much in the stone of colonization, one thing is clear: the Muslims received the colonialist message, they got the point. For at the time of Algerian independence from France, they changed every street name in town. The Cours Bertagna of Bône became the Cours de la Révolution of Annaba. Rue Gambetta was changed to rue Ibn Khaldun. Rue Saint Augustine is now the rue des Frères Boucherit, martyrs of the Algerian Revolution. Rue Narbonne, named after a twentieth-century mayor of Bône, is now called the rue de ler Novembre 1954, the day the Revolution was launched. In a particularly striking reversal, rue Bugeaud is now called rue El Emir Abdelkadar for the Algerian leader whom Bugeaud vanquished. So it goes: every street of note in Bône has a different name in Annaba today.[16]

* * *

Street names constitute one set of collective representations of colonial Bône; photographs comprise another. On the one hand, we have Bône and its built environment, and on the other hand, a photographic image of that environment, or rather selected portions of it. For the question here is to what extent is the photographic record a faithful reflection of the built environment?

Photographs of colonial Bône can be divided for our purposes into one of two main categories. "Private" photographs are those taken for private use and delectation – souvenirs, mementos, family portraits. "Public" photographs are marketed and sold to consumers, who purchase them primarily in the form of picture postcards. Eliminated from consideration here are private photographs on the grounds that we cannot know the photographer's intention, that is, why one scene was chosen and not another. Included here are postcards on the assumption that those marketed conformed in a rough and ready fashion to what some seller thought some buyer would purchase. One final consideration is necessary. Picture postcards of colonial Bône can be further divided into those specific to Bône – buildings, streets, monuments, general views of the city – and those which could have been taken in Bône, but also any number of other places in colonial Algeria. In this latter case, I am thinking about the genre of *"scènes et types,"* generic representations of certain kinds of people (Arabs, Berbers, Jews, Mozabites), practicing certain kinds of occupations (barbers, musicians, shoeshine boys), participating in certain kinds of activities (*fantasias*, making *couscous*), and depicted in certain kinds of environments (in front of *gourbis*, "under the tent"). The processes whereby individuals are transformed into collectivities, abstracted from three-dimensional flesh and blood people living down the street into two-dimensional consumer goods suitable for mailing to friends in the *métropole*, is a subject full of fascinating possibilities for future research. Since by definition, however,

215

"scènes et types" postcards are not tied to a particular locale, I shall focus here solely on those postcards specific to Bône.[17]

If we consider the picture postcards of Bône extant, we see rapidly that far and away the largest number are views of the port and Cours Bertagna, Bône's main street. For such a short thoroughfare – it takes only minutes to stroll from where the church stood at the top to the port at the foot – the Cours Bertagna was easily the most photographed street in colonial Bône. For example, there are postcards of the church, which was torn down in 1962 (full view, *sortie de messe*); of the *mairie* halfway down the Cours, a grandiose work of civic architecture for a city the size of Bône; the original municipal theater opposite the city hall with a fine Greek-style fresco atop its two-storied colonnaded front; the Hotel d'Orient, the city's premier hotel, located immediately adjacent to the theater; and at the foot of the Cours the elegant palais Calvin with its arcades and fancy shops. But this is not all. Perhaps the chief allure of the Cours was its combination of statues, gardens, trees, squares, and benches, which made it the focal point for a leisurely promenade, for an outing for ice cream in the hot season, and the location of the most frequented European cafes in all seasons. Numerous postcards celebrate the ambience created thereby, a feeling more reminiscent of Europe than Africa, of towns in southern France such as Arles, Nimes, and Aix-en-Provence.

As we have seen, the expansion of the port was the single largest public works project undertaken in nineteenth-century Bône. Stymied by lengthy delays, tinged with scandal, it was Mayor Jérome Bertagna's most impressive and costliest achievement – literally, since he was interpellated on the floor of the Assembleé Nationale for cost overruns before it was all over. No wonder it is celebrated so profusely in picture postcards. There are views of the port and the new port, views of the entry to the port, the *darse*, and views of the various quais: the quai Warnier which runs perpendicular to the Cours and which includes the Palais Lecoq which housed the local Chamber of Commerce, and the offices of the Transatlantique, the leading navigation company. In addition, there are photographs of the quai des Phosphates on the southern edge of the port where the phosphates of Tebessa were stored prior to shipment, as well as postcards depicting various other goods which passed through Bône's port, from esparto grass to barrels of wine from the plain of Bône.

After the port and Cours Bertagna, it is Hippo, the beaches, and general views which turn up most frequently on picture postcards. The beaches were a logical subject, since they are one of the chief attractions of the Bône environs. Postcards of all of Bône's beaches could be purchased ranging from the plage de la Grenouillère immediately north of

216

Illustration 7.1   The main church of Bône (Bibliothèque Nationale Cabinet d'Estampes).

Illustration 7.2   The Hôtel d'Orient and Municipal Theater of Bône
(Bibliothèque Nationale Cabinet d'Estampes).

Illustration 7.3   Quai des Phosphates, Bône (Bibliothèque Nationale Cabinet
d'Estampes).

town, to the plage Gassiot with its ramshackle beach *cabanons*, to the
ritzy plage St. Cloud, one of the city's exclusive neighborhoods, and
finally to the plage Fabre where seasonal Italian fishermen lived six
months of the year in little more than shacks.

In a number of late nineteenth- and early twentieth-century photo-

218

Illustration 7.4   Saint-Cloud beach, Bône (Bibliothèque Nationale Cabinet d'Estampes).

graphs, European colonials gaze at us from the ruins and sites of earlier civilizations which they are touring – from the British at the Hindu temples of Khajuraho in India and the Great Sphinx in Egypt to the French visiting Timgad and Djemila in Algeria. This symbolic linkage between one society and another, composed of one part touristic fascination and one part desire to legitimize present hegemony by tapping past grandeur, no doubt explains why the ruins of Hippo located immediately outside Bône are depicted so frequently on picture postcards. Tourist visits to ruins are captured in private photographs, but picture postcards record the deserted site from every conceivable angle: clusters of columns still standing, views of the amphitheater, closeups of carved pedastels. Significantly, several postcards artfully juxtapose the Roman ruins in the foreground with the French-built basilica of St. Augustine on the hill in the background.

The many general views of Bône need not detain us here. Simply described, they survey the town from various angles: over the rooftops of the old city, Bône seen from Hippo, the entire plain of Bône with the St. Augustine basilica in the background.

The scenes discussed so far – the Cours and the port, the beaches and Hippo – are represented on many different postcards. But in the Bône scenes depicted on the remaining postcards, we have only one postcard in each case. First there are buildings, less important or less centrally located than those on the Cours, for example, the post office

Illustration 7.5   Ruins of Hippo (foreground) and Basilica of Saint
Augustine (background) (collection of the author).

located on the Cours but farther up than the church; the Collège de
Jeunes Filles located on the outskirts of town; the original *poissonnerie*,
an elegant wrought-iron structure in the Place d'Armes of the old city,
unfortunately torn down when the fish market was transferred to the
new city; the church of Ste. Anne, the main parish church of the Colonne
Randon quarter; the mosque of Salah Bey, the leading mosque of Bône
located also in the Place d'Armes; the *marché arabe*, a distinguished
Moorish-style structure located in the new city and torn down like the
poissonnerie; and the *qūbba*, or tomb, of Sidi Brahim, the chief *qūbba*
in Bône located outside of town on the road to Constantine. In addition,
there are single postcards of two of Bône's five gates, the porte Randon
and porte des Caroubiers, plus images of the ramparts (*vieux remparts,
passarelle des tranchées*). Both the gates and the ramparts were torn
down as the city expanded outward from its original central core. Finally,
two postcards depict streets and quarters: the quartier Mozabite and
the commercial street, rue Gambetta.

What are we to make of these postcards? Let us perform the following
exercise. If we take the various postcard scenes and plot them on a map
of Bône, what would be the result? In the first place, we would see a
very pronounced upside down "T" formed by the intersection of the
Cours Bertagna with the port at its base. For the rest, we would perceive

Illustration 7.6   Tomb of Sidi Brahim, Bône (Bibliothèque Nationale Cabinet d'Estampes).

Illustration 7.7   Rue Gambetta, Bône (Bibliothèque Nationale Cabinet d'Estampes).

a barely visible arc designating Bône's string of beaches (barely visible due to the slight number of postcards), and a dark cluster of dots where the ruins of Hippo are located – every other postcard scene is represented by isolated points scattered more or less at random.

221

To compare such a "map" of postcard scenes with a street map of
the city demonstrates, therefore, that the image of Bône represented on
the postcards simplifies drastically how the city actually looked. Now, is
it merely coincidence that the Cours Bertagna constitutes the core of European Bône? From the Catholic church to the French city hall to the
European businesses under the arcades, virtually the only Algerian presence on the Cours was the merchant Ben Gui's kiosk selling tobacco Illustration 4.4). Likewise, the port was a European venture, planned and
organized by and Europeans, even if Algerian workers labored on it.

What about other city areas? The new city, which includes the Cours
Bertagna, is overrepresented on postcards, but every other area of town
is underrepresented: the old city where the bulk of the Jews and a
majority of the Algerians could be found; the Colonne Randon, the
predominantly European working class suburb for which we have only
postcard images of the *porte* Randon and the Ste. Anne parish church;
and the *banlieue*, populated primarily by Algerian agriculturalists.

Not only are the old city, Colonne Randon, and *banlieue* underrepresented when compared to the new city, but these living areas of
the city are also slighted compared to the dead remains of Hippo. Yet
the numerous postcards of Hippo should not surprise us, for they underscore a theme we encountered in the discussion of Bône's street
names, namely, the tendency of the French to highlight Bône's Roman
past and the figure of St. Augustine at the expense of the city's Muslim
past. This tendency is illustrated graphically in the juxtaposition of Roman ruins and the French-built basilica on the same postcard.

Clearly, the postcard image of Bône reveals first and foremost a primarily European town with very few examples of Islamic architecture
or of the Algerians, who comprised after all one-third of the city's
population. For example, the Berber Kabyles worked at the port as
dockers and lived primarily in the so-called *ville indigène* at the edge of
the Colonne Randon adjacent to the European cemetery, but we have
no postcards which record either. The Arabs turn up on a few postcards
that have been mentioned (mosque Salah Bey, *marabout* Sidi Brahim),
but considering that they comprised such a sizeable fraction of the city's
population, they too are significantly underrepresented on picture postcards. After all, there were other mosques besides that of Salah Bey,
such as the former mosque of Sidi Bou Merouane which the French
converted into the military hospital; and there were other *marabouts*,
including the one located outside town along the plage de la Grenouillère
and still standing today.

And what about Muslim landmarks in the old city? Absent are the
the Fort Cigogne built by the Turks and torn down only in 1909, and
the *mahakma* – not to mention the *cafés maures*. Or what about houses

built by wealthy Algerians, such as the fine seventeenth-century, three-storied, Turkish-style house in the old city; the Muslim villa between the *pépinière* and European cemetery, which was a well-known landmark in the surrounding neighborhood already in 1910 when it figured prominently on a city map; and finally the fancy, Arab-style villa on the exclusive plage St. Cloud, perhaps owned by the Benyacoub family, one of Bône's two leading Algerian families?

In much the same way that Europeans tend to predominate over the Algerians on postcards of Bône, so the French tend to outnumber the Italians, Maltese and other non-French Europeans. In the first place, no postcards of the Jewish quarter have been located, either of the *mellah* in its entirety or of the synagogue. Secondly, the Maltese, who lived mostly in the outskirts where they raised goats and vegetables, do not turn up on any postcards I have been able to discover. As for the Italians who dominated the construction industry in Bône, ironically enough there are no specifically Italian buildings or scenes preserved on picture postcards – not even the handsome villa Sarfati located between the Cours and the market in the new city with its ornately carved arch over the doorway and pleasant inner courtyard.

However Bône on postcards is compared with Bône in concrete, therefore, the result is the same: a radically distorted image which tends to emphasize the Europeans over the Algerians and the French over the non-French Europeans.

Language and literature

The formation of a colonial society recognizably Algerian occurred between 1890 and 1914. And to take the argument one step further, the single most striking feature of this culture is that it was not simply formed around the turn of the twentieth century, but that it formed itself, that it not only came to exist in objective terms, but that it became subjectively aware of its existence. The distinction is analogous to the one often made in labor history between class *an sich*, a class which exists in historically "objective" terms, and class *für sich*, a class which in addition can be said to be class-conscious. It is no coincidence, therefore, that at the very time Governor General Cambon was tangling with Mayor Bertagna, the settlers in Bône and elsewhere in Algeria were beginning to refer to themselves as the "Algerians," the "Algerian people."As for the Muslim Algerians themselves, they were called the *"indigènes."* Thus, at one blow the settlers proclaimed their hegemony in Algeria and at the same time obliterated the native Algerians in the very terms they used to describe themselves. And is not the same process occurring when the settlers named streets and marketed postcards? For the "Algerians" were not Muslims and they were not Jews; rather, they were the native and naturalized French, the Spanish, Italians, and Maltese who had or were in the process of giving up one collective identity and assuming another. When Cagayous is asked, "Are you French?" he answers, "We are Algerians!"[18]

> So who is Cagayous anyway? He "is the biggest voyou [hustler] of Algiers."[19] He is his name.
> "Cagayous" is a portemonteau word consisting of lagagnous plus cagaille. Lagagnous (Languedocian; in Spanish, lagañoso) means rheumy or gummy and is applied to Cagayous "because he had stuff in his eyes." Cagaille (Provençal cagaioun, little turd) is the runs, the shits. Thus, "our chassieux [the one with stuff in his eyes] becomes a chiasseux [one with the runs]."[20]

Not only did the various Europeans refer to themselves as "Algerians," but they created their own language, or rather dialect, as well to express themselves. *Pataouète*, the dialect of French spoken in Algeria, reflects the disparate backgrounds and demographic characteristics of the European settlers, and at the same time expresses the experience of the nascent *pied noir* community. As the colonial society of Algeria formed late in the nineteenth century, so did the dialect its members used increasingly. By 1900 it had established the majority of its characteristics.[21]

Pataouète borrowed some 600 foreign words, 210 from Arabic, 180 from Spanish, 60 from Italian, and 70 from the patois, or dialect, spoken in southern France from Provence to Languedoc. It was a language of the cities rather than the countryside, especially of the coastal cities. Moreover, accents were recognizably different in Algiers, Oran, and Bône. In western Algeria, Spanish influence predominated. In the east Italian was heard most often in the port cities of Stora, Philippeville, and especially Bône. Algiers combined the two: Spanish in the working-class Bab el Oued, Italian in the Marine district. Italian words and phrases were referred to collectively as *bônoises*, that is, related to Bône; parodies of classical literature were sprinkled with Italian phrases known as *hipponismes*, that is, related to Hippo.

From Italian the *pieds noirs* borrowed exclamations and obscenities first, and fishing and nautical terms second. In Bône people exclaimed *Atso!* (derived from *cazzo*, Italian for penis), *Maré dé déo!* (Mother of God), *Sacramento!* (referring to the holy sacrament), *Maladetta!* (literally malediction, curse), *Malapesta! Vergogna!* (Italian for shame), *Manmamie!* (*O mamma mia*), *Basta!* (Italian for enough), *Tchao! Madone! Diomadone! Diocane!* (dog plus God), and *Diomadone!* The inhabitants of Constantine even altered *Diocane!* so they could call the inhabitants of Bône *Diobône*! But the exclamation par excellence used by the Bônois was *Poh*! *Poh*! *Poh*! as in *"Poh*! *Poh*! *Poh*! What progress the little one has made!"[22] The grossest obscenity was probably *va te la pillancoul*! (Italian: *piglia'n culo*), "go get screwed in the ass!" with its close relation *va fangoule*! Throughout the Mediterranean the fig and the tomato are used figuratively for a woman's genitalia. From *pomarola*, Neapolitan for tomato, *la boumarolle* was derived. *Figa*, fig (Italian: *fica*; Catalan and Valencian: *figue*), was used in three ways: *la figa*, vagina; *faire figa*, to blow it, screw up and *faire la figa*, to make the obscene gesture of putting your thumb between the index and middle finger. Moreover, a *katz* (again from *cazzo*) was a penis, a *tafanar* (Italian: *tafanario*) was an ass, and *tchoutche*, a sting ray, was used figuratively to also mean ass.

A second large group of words and expressions heard in Bône had to do with the sea. There were the names of fish (*dintche*, Italian: *dentice*; *matsame*, Italian: *mazzumarro*; *gattarelle*, Italian: *gattarella*; *matsagoune*, Italian: *mazza*), of boats (*outse*, Italian: *uzzo*, a boat for 8–10 fishermen with a motor; *sardinale*, the boat used for sardine fishing), and of winds (*baffoune*). Yet it is not simply a case of using nautical terms, but rather a way of expressing yourself by using phrases related to fishing and the sea figuratively. Instead of *prendre racine*, to take root, you say *prendre mouillage*, to drop anchor. *Jeter le broumitche* is to lure, entice, give the come-on to someone and is derived from the Provençal *broumet* for bait. *Jeter le noir*, literally to squirt black, alluded to the sepia liquid ejected by the squid-related cuttle fish. *(A)vec de l'huile* was to see better; it referred to the practice of sprinkling the surface of the water with a few drops of oil when fishing for sea urchins in order to make the water more translucent. *Salper les palangres* (Italian: *salpare*) was to raise up the fishing nets and by extension to leave, as when Cagayous says *"Salpons*!" "Let's split!"[23]

There were other words and phrases borrowed from Italian in addition to obscenities and those related to the sea. *Pitse* or *pitsa* was the local Bônois term for pizza, *macaronade* for macaroni, *raviolade* for ravioli. Of course, the Italian forms were used also unchanged as in *"Ouvre tes grandes oreilles en raviolis maltais et écoute!*" ("Open your big Maltese ravioli ears and listen!")[24] A *mangiafranque* was a freeloader as in *"Les femmes lançaient des insultes au pauvre Zézé en se le traitant de mangiafranque et de salaouetche"* ("The women hurled insults at poor Zézé abusing him as a freeloader and good-for-nothing").[25] *Faire une gambette* (Italian: *gambetto*) is to trip somebody up. Someone who brings *schkoumoun* (Italian: *scomunicazione*) is a bearer of bad luck; it is related to the evil eye known throughout the Mediterranean. *C'est scouza* (Italian: *scusa*) took on the meaning of something not serious, only a pretext,

225

as when Camus writes, "*Il met la main darrière* (sic) *[a la poche-revolver] mais c'était scousa*" ("He put his hand in his hip pocket but it was nothing, only a pretext").[26] *Tomber la caplate* is to do a belly flop; by extension the Bônois called a poor soccer player *une caplate*. Lastly, *mendja-galette* designates the practical joke of tying the clothes of a bather in knots and wetting them. When the swimmer returns and tries to undo the knots with his teeth, his would-be friends call out, "*Mendja-galette n'ya pas de pain*" ("Eat cake for there is no bread").[27]

Although it is more difficult to track the rise and diffusion of spoken discourse, *la parole* as the French say, than it is to read the literary survivals which remain, *la langue*, there are a number of clues in the case of the patois bônois. For one, there is the local character Luc, a housepainter by vocation, a bard and balladeer by avocation.

> *The Opportunist candidate*
> *Lies night and day with skill. . . .*
> *He says: "I am a Republican,"*
> *But he is only a vile opportunist . . .*
>
> *Algeria is a land of gold*
> *And Bône would be flourishing*
> *If its treasury were not squandered [gaspillait].*
> *So who is to blame for our turmoil and our ruin? . . .*
> *It is* messieurs *the Opportunists.*
>
> – Luc[28]

Luc gained a certain local fame for his poems and songs, all expressed in patois bônois. Another local figure we know something about is Carloutche, humble Italian fisherman and zealous political participant. Carloutche's prototype was carved in stone at the base of Jérome Bertagna's statue on the Cours, the largest and most important statue in Bône before it was torn down by the Algerians in 1962. Sitting at Bertagna's feet, he salutes the mayor with a wave of his cap.[29] Finally, we know that those "howls and cheers, insults, cries, gibes, guffaws, and those guttural and farting-like onomatopoetic words, which are, it is said, a genuine Bône specialty" mentioned earlier and emitted from the cafes on Bône's main street were, of course, the strange sounds of the patois bônois.[30] Thus, Bône political culture, exemplified in Bertagna's political corruption, employed as its favored mode of discourse, the patois bônois.

> Fed up with politicians who have failed to deliver, Cagayous turns to anti-toutisme, *anti-everythingness*. This time, however, he puts his political beliefs, or rather lack of beliefs, into practice and runs for a seat in the National Assembly in Paris to represent Bablouette [Bab el Oued]. The quintessential populist candidate, Cagayous holds a wide-open electoral

Illustration 7.8   Statue of Bertagna with Carloutche (lower right) doffing his cap (collection of the author).

> *meeting. The government is ruining the good fishing spots by dumping dirt*
> *and posting no fishing signs? Cagayous will have the signs removed and*
> *the dirt dumped elsewhere. The wells in Bablouette run dry but not those*
> *in the rich neighborhoods? Cagayous will have water pumped from the*
> *reservoir. A sweeper and his family have no bathroom so that whenever*
> *the family eats bean soup they have to use a field in the middle of the night*
> *where they have to compete with the Maltese goats and Kabyle dogs?*
> *Cagayous asks how many latrines are needed. One with two places, no*
> *more. Cagayous promises to interpellate the government on* les chiottes de
> le peuple, *the shithouses of the people.*[31]

In addition to a language, a *pied noir* literature emerged as well around
the turn of the twentieth century. Albert Camus is far and away the
best known writer produced by colonial Algeria, the only one to have
achieved world recognition. Yet there was a series of practitioners of
what came to be known in Algeria as the *roman colonial*, the colonial
novel. What is particularly interesting about this literature from the
viewpoint of popular culture is that certain works were composed in the
French dialect spoken in Algeria. And it is here that Bône again played
a prominent role. As with the language, this literature was rooted in
the cities rather than the countryside, again predominantly in the port
cities of Algiers, Oran, and Bône. The series of adventures of Cagayous
situated in Bab el Oued, the working-class quarter of Algiers, was the
single most popular example of this genre.[32]

> *Cagayous is firmly anchored in Algiers; he cannot be understood aside*
> *from his particular place. But Cagayous' Algiers is not coterminous with*
> *Algiers the largest city in Algeria, the capital and headquarters of the co-*
> *lonial administration. Cagayous' Algiers is the heavily Spanish Bab el Oued*
> *and the Italian district of the Marine. Cagayous and his friends gravitate*
> *toward the port, the downtown districts, and the central Place du Gou-*
> *vernement. He has little occasion to venture into the districts built up the*
> *hillsides farther away from the city center where the fashionable French*
> *villas and sprawling embassy complexes are located today. Moreover, he*
> *visits only infrequently the Casbah, although it is closer. For Cagayous and*
> *his* copains, *or buddies, the Casbah is a place they make sorties into – to*
> *eat* couscous, *to play a game of cards, to play pranks on the Algerians, to*
> *visit a prostitute – but it is not a place they come from, or spend much time*
> *in.*

The popular literature of Bône rivaled that of Algiers, however. First,
there were newspaper articles written in *pataouète*. The first written
examples of patois bônois I have found consist of a series of columns
in a short-lived Bône newspaper, *Les Clochettes Bônoises*, by one Pepino, which appeared already in the mid-1890s. In 1897 came another
series published in *Les Gaités Bônoises*. In 1898 an entire newspaper in

patois bônois was published, *Le Diocane Bônois*. Satirical in intent, shocking in effect, *Le Diocane Bônois* caused a furor because it featured on its masthead the Italian blasphemy, *le diocane*, loosely "son of a Bônois bitch."[33]

Not only newspapers but also books in patois bônois were published. Although the books generally came later, they usually returned to an earlier period, to the local legends and personalities of the age of Bertagna. There is, for example, *Harmonies Bônoises* by Louis Lafourcade. Jérome Bertagna himself is here, as well as Thaddo, guardian of the European cemetery, and also Carloutche, Italian fisherman and Bertagna devotee. But this local literary genre culminates in the *oeuvre* of Edmund Brua. In *La Parodie du Cid*, Brua recast the classic tale of El Cid in the period of Bône's own classical past, that of Hippo.[34] In *Fables Bônoises*, Edmond Brua retold La Fontaine's fables in Algerian *sabir*, the pidgin French spoken by the Algerians, and satirized the Muslims in the process. The *Fables Bônoises* constitute "one of the summits of *pied-noir* literature."[35] The language of the *Fables Bônoises* is *pataouète*, the literary model the tales of La Fontaine, and the tone ironic, satirical. In these tales transplanted from La Fontaine's France to Brua's Bône, we meet Malakoff the milkman and the Maltese *curé* too, plus Bagur and Salvator and Sauveur. And when the *Fables* were finally collected together and published in 1938, they were reviewed by that other writer from the Bône region, a still young Albert Camus, who wrote that "the singular flavor of these ironic moral tales belongs only to Brua, and through him to those robust people, the Bagurs, the Sauveurs, and the Salvators, who make love and go swimming, who cheat and jeer and bluster in the very places where St. Augustine meditated on the tragedy of the human soul."[36]

There it is. Street names and picture postcards. Pepino and Luc, Lafourcade and Brua. Taken together, what could be a more suggestive indication of the formation of a settler colonial culture in Bône?

Conclusion: Unmaking French Algeria

*Albert Camus was born in 1913 in Mondovi, now called Dréan, which is
located some 20 kilometers outside Bône/Annaba. At the time, Mondovi
was one of the chief wine-producing centers in the Bône plain. One of the
largest and richest estates, known as Guébar, belonged to Jérome Bertagna,
who died in Mondovi in 1903, ten years before Camus was born there.
Bertagna's position as the single most powerful person in the Bône region
at the time of his death was reflected in the grandeur of his estate. Guébar
encompassed 7,500 acres; the three-story chateau he had erected at the end
of a long, tree-lined drive looked not unlike the stately chateaux of the wine
barons of southwestern France. Today in France Jérome Bertagna's descendants reside in Nice and Cannes and Paris, where they live off the
family's former investments in Algeria. But today in Algeria it is not easy
to find Bertagna's estate. The farm has been nationalized, most of the vines
uprooted, the brand name of the wine changed, and when you ask Algerians
directions, no one seems to recognize the name. But then there it is: set
back from the highway, the chateau itself in ruins, the roof caved in, the
stone walls collapsing, it is now uninhabited but on the grounds a number
of Algerian families have thrown up* gourbis, *thatched huts.*

Just down the road a piece from Dréan lies the qūbba, *or tomb, of Sidi
Denden. The* qūbba *itself, a white plastered dome, sits on a low promontory
which juts out over the surrounding plain of Annaba, visible from the
highway long before you reach the cutoff.* Qūbba-s *dot the Annaba plain
today like the now vanished jujube trees which give Annaba its name. Yet
every Algerian you ask has heard of Sidi Denden, and most can provide
surprisingly precise directions, from the scruffy taxi driver in town to the
bemused guys lounging at another* qūbba *outside town. It is unclear when
either the shrine or cult of Sidi Denden was founded, but the tomb was
there certainly before the French invaded in 1830.*

*At the time of the 1876 census, Sadek Denden was seven years old and
lived in the old city of Bône with his parents, plus five brothers and sisters.*[1]
*Perhaps Sadek Denden was a descendant of the original Sidi Denden,
perhaps not.*[2] *The former, a twentieth-century secular, Francophone, proto-
Algerian nationalist, issued from the latter, a family of traditional Muslim
religious adepts – that would make for a nice historical irony. Whether*

230

Illustration C-1 Former parish church at Randon outside Bône, 1976
(photograph by the author).

*descended from Sidi Denden or not, Sadek Denden is the best-known
member of the so-called Jeune Algérien movement, the young Algerians,
to have come out of Bône at the turn of the twentieth century. Together
with his confrère, Khélil Kaid Layoun, Denden edited newspapers, drafted
petitions, and staged mass meetings during the same time Bertagna reigned
as mayor of Bône. While Denden moved on to Algiers and colony-wide
Jeune Algérien activities, Khélil Kaid Layoun remained in Bône to lead
the movement there.*

*Sadek Denden may have died penniless and Jérome Bertagna wealthy,
but Bertagna's familial descendants were later run out of Algeria by the
nationalist descendants of Sadek Denden and Khélil Kaid Layoun. Therefore, we have on the one hand, Jérome Bertagna, who did so much to
make Algeria French, and on the other hand, Sadek Denden, who did so
much to unmake French Algeria. The two men are linked so tightly geographically yet separated by so much in every other way that it is no wonder
Albert Camus was so* complexé.

The creation of settler society and culture in Bône constitutes one
chapter in the formation of settler colonialism in Algeria, one chapter
in the making of Algeria French in the decades prior to the First World
War. And what is striking about the formation of settler colonial society
and culture is that in the process the Algerians tend to drop out of the
picture. Bertagna achieves preeminence in Bône not by taking the Al-

231

gerians into account but by leaving them out – and getting away with it. And yet they were there, if you only bothered to look.

Even the Bônois could not fail to see them in 1909 when they staged a mass meeting, 1,200 strong according to European estimates, three thousand according to the Algerians, which amounted to between ten and twenty-five percent of all Bône's Algerians. They gathered ostensibly to support a recent French law which required French military service of all Algerians, but in actuality they used the occasion to call for reforms. The meeting was organized by none other than Sadek Denden and Khélil Kaid Layoun; they delivered two of the three speeches the crowd heard. Denden urged that Algerians who served in the French military be given the option of becoming French citizens. Kaid Layoun argued that special punitive laws applicable only to Algerians, the *Code de l'Indigénat*, "constitute an insurmountable obstacle to the assimilation dreamed by French and Arabs." The next day accounts of the gathering appeared under banner headlines in the local Algerian newspaper edited by Denden, *L'Islam*.[3]

This mass meeting in Bône constitutes one of the first and most important anywhere in Algeria of the Jeune Algérien movement, that movement of Frenchified Algerians who sought the assimilation of Algeria to France. In theory, assimilation was official French policy; in practice, it was stymied by settler intransigence. The Jeunes Algériens appealed over the heads of the settlers in Algeria to French reformers in France to implement assimilation. In so doing, the Jeune Algérien movement sought closer ties to France, not to cut ties with France; it was a movement of protonationalism, not nationalism.

In 1909 Sàdek Denden was 38 years old; it was an eventful year for him. He had joined the colonial administration after studying in a French *lycée*. In 1909 he quit the administration, cofounded *L'Islam*, and organized the mass meeting at the end of the year. He edited *L'Islam* in Bône until 1912 when he moved to Algiers and took *L'Islam* with him, where it appeared until the First World War. In Algiers Denden became friends with Dr. Benthami, one of the most influential Jeunes Algérien leaders in the capital, and the Emir Khaled, grandson of Abd al-Qadir, the leader of Algerian resistance to the French in the 1830s and 1840s. In 1919 Denden was a candidate for the Algiers city council on a ticket headed by Benthami and defeated by a ticket led by Khaled. A talented journalist, a scathing editorialist, a skillful political organizer, Sadek Denden made *L'Islam* first in Bône, then in Algiers, the single most important Jeune Algérien newspaper. He himself became one of the acknowledged leaders of the Jeune Algérien movement.[4]

While Denden moved to Algiers, Khélil Kaid Layoun remained in Bône.[5] A year older than Denden, Khélil came from a lower middle class Bône family; he worked as a clerk in a French law office. At the time of the French reform effort back in the 1890s, which culminated in Bône with Governor General Cambon's attempted ouster of Mayor Bertagna, he helped publish an Algerian newspaper in Bône called *El Hack*, Arabic for "the truth." Scrupulously apolitical, legalistic, and assimilationist, *El Hack* called on French reformers to prevent settler abuses, it objected to holding Algerians responsible collectively for crimes committed by individuals, and it waxed indignant when all Algerians were lumped together and termed "bandits."

El Hack was printed in French not Arabic; French sympathizers known as *indigènophiles* contributed articles as well as Algerians. *El Hack* was reformist but not nationalist; it criticized the practice of French colonialism but it did not question the theoretical foundations of the colonial regime. What is striking about the reforms advocated by *El Hack* is not how conservative they seem today, but how radical they appeared to the settlers then. Nearly the entire European press in Bône and papers in Algiers and Oran fulminated against *El Hack*'s alleged "anti-French" and "anti-Algerian" tendencies, claiming it was guilty of urging the Algerians to revolt. Freedom of the press notwithstanding, the settlers demanded *El Hack* be suspended, the colonial administration banned its sale in rural areas, and in 1894 it folded after twenty-six weekly issues.[6]

In 1900 Khélil Kaid Layoun was at it again. As part of the metropolitan French reform effort of the 1890s, now winding down, a group of senators on a fact-finding tour passed through Bône. Khélil addressed them on behalf of a group of "young Bône Muslims." He described the situation of these Francophone young Algerian males such as himself, who favored Algerian assimilation to France but could not convert their French education into a job, who were less and less Algerian but prevented from becoming more and more French, who were in short "floundering in civilization." What he wanted was to have the vote extended to young Algerians with a French education and to Algerian businessmen licensed by the French. His deposition was the most far-reaching the senators heard.[7]

Earlier in 1900 Khélil had attempted to form the Djemâ'a El Kheiria El Arabia, or Muslim Benevolent Society. Organized by Kaid Layoun and Mahmoud Hassam, a young tobacco merchant, the society consisted of older, honorary members, and younger, active members. The honorary members included many of Bône's Algerian elite; mostly, they were landowners and businessmen, white collar employees and professionals. The active members were neither as well-established nor as well-off; they ranged from artisans and businessmen to clerks, journalists, and commercial employees. Two occupations in particular were

233

overrepresented, white collar clerks such as Khélil and those who worked with tobacco, either cutting it, selling it, or making cigarettes from it, such as Khélil's cofounder Mahmoud Hassam. These occupations corresponded to the same two groups of Algerian businessmen and French-educated Algerians which Khélil had singled out in his deposition. At an initial meeting of the Muslim Benevolent Society, eighty-four Algerians attended and Khélil was named provisional president. All that needed to be done was to obtain authorization from Mayor Bertagna.[8]

Khélil Kaid Layoun's activities in 1900 are noteworthy for two reasons. First, the leading historian of colonial Algeria, Charles-Robert Ageron, argues that Khélil's deposition can be compared both in form and content to a later and more widely known Jeune Algérien manifesto published in 1912.[9] Thus, Khélil formulated early what became later Jeune Algérien principles. Moreover, the "young Bône Muslims" of 1900 soon became Bône's Jeune Algériens, which demonstrates Bône's precocity within this Algeria-wide movement.[10]

Second, and perhaps more important, Khélil's statement together with the Muslim Benevolent Society reflect significant changes occurring in Algerian society at the turn of the twentieth century. It has been argued before that after the Algerians resisted the French actively from 1830 until roughly 1870, they resisted the French passively, largely by retreating into the Islamic religion and holding onto the Arabic language.[11] In fact, the French confidently predicted during the decades after 1870 that the Algerians, like the "aborigines" of Australia and America, soon would die out. But around the turn of the century a sea change occurred in Muslim society and manifested itself in the Jeune Algérien movement. Although the mass of Algerians continued to live in the countryside and were poverty-stricken, a small number of Algerians in the cities were carving out niches within the French colonial economy. Some, like Sadek Denden and Khélil Kaid Layoun, attended French schools, learned French, and worked in the tertiary or service sector of the urban economy as clerks in French law offices or the colonial administration. Others either grew tobacco on their land and sold it to the French government monopoly each year when it bought in Bône, or sold it to merchants who cut, dried, and rolled it into cigars and cigarettes which were sold in Bône and beyond. Clerking in law offices and raising tobacco may not strike us as particularly promising avenues to economic wealth and social prestige, but in fin-de-siècle Algeria they were. And it is precisely these same Algerians making their way in French Algeria who were now clamoring for a political role concomitant with their economic role, and who were now joining the Jeune Algérien movement. One example is Hadj Omar Bengui, the primary financial backer of *El Hack* in the mid-1890s, who was the only Algerian businessman on Bône's main street, where he sold tobacco from a kiosk. Another example is the Benyacoubs, one of Bône's two leading Algerian families, who had been in eclipse since 1830, and who slowly reconsolidated their wealth and family position due in part to tobacco profits. After the First World War cofounders of a tobacco cooperative with other Europeans, the Tabacoop, and today one of the leading families of Annaba, before the First World War the Benyacoubs were making money from tobacco, investing in Denden's *L'Islam*, and participating in Kaid Layoun's Muslim Benevolent Society.[12]

But Mayor Bertagna viewed the Djemâ'a El Kheiria El Arabia differently. He agreed with his close Algerian collaborator and *chef indigène*, Mohammed Tahar Boumaiza, that Khelil Kaid Layoun and his co-organizer Mahmoud Hassam were "as everyone knows two militant politicians," that the Muslim Benevolent Society had been created with an exclusively political aim, and that the society's slogan ought to have been "political society and not charitable society."[13] As a consequence, Bertagna banned it. Earlier, Khélil Kaid Layoun's *El Hack* had been hounded out of existence by the settler press in the mid-1890s only to return stronger, more independant, and more militant with Sadek Denden's *L'Islam* in 1909. Khélil's 1900 deposition had no immediate consequences, and his Muslim Benevolent Society was aborted by Bertagna before it got off the ground, but a decade later a number of similar but longer-lasting Algerian societies appeared in Bône and elsewhere, and in 1909 Khelil organized with Sadek Denden their mass meeting attended by many more of Bône's Algerians than the 1900 society had ever dreamed of.[14]

It is clear from the above that the Jeunes Algériens were a movement not of the majority of Algerians but of a tiny minority. A new Algerian society was germinating around the turn of the twentieth century, it took root among a number of *évolués* (literally, Algerians who had "evolved" linguistically, culturally and politically towards France), it sprouted with *El Hack* and the Djemâ'a El Kheiria El Arabia, and it blossomed in the Jeune Algérien movement. Second, the Jeunes Algériens were pro-French and protonationalist, not anti-French and nationalist. It could not be otherwise considering the historical soil in which they arose. Initially the intellectual and political reflection of the social and economic transformation of Algerian society, those who were calling themselves Jeunes Algériens were pressing for a more active role, they were reacting against the constraints posed by the rules of the colonial game in Algeria, rules determined primarily but not entirely by the European settlers.

At the same time, the long-term historical significance of the Bône

235

Jeunes Algériens lies in the fact that along with their confrères elsewhere they constituted one of the three main strands of what became Algerian nationalism. To foreshorten a lengthy historical process, we can say that from the beginning of the twentieth century the Jeunes Algériens pushed for a larger Algerian role in an essentially French Algeria. Their biggest hope and first major disappointment was the so-called Jonnart reforms of 1919, which were aimed at enfranchising those Algerians most French, that is, the Jeunes Algériens themselves. But in exchange for French citizenship, the Algerians were required to renounce their Muslim personal status, and in the end only a minuscule number accepted such terms. In 1919 municipal elections were held in their two leading centers of Algiers and Bône, and the Jeunes Algériens split over this very issue.[15] Thus, 1919 marked their first major disillusionment: the Jeunes Algériens had tried to become more like the French, but the French had failed to overcome settler opposition and enact meaningful reform.

The initiative passed next to the Salafiyya, or Islamic Reform movement, associated in Algeria with Abd al-Hamid Ben Badis.

> *This town of Annaba is crushed under the weight of two outrageous forces, one implanted by force and which possesses nearly all the material wealth, and a more reactionary one from Sicily and Malta which occupies our neighborhoods and imposes on us its flotsam and jetsam.* – Bend Badis[16]

Where the Jeunes Algériens had attempted to embrace French society and culture, the Reformists turned away to rediscover the fundamentals of Islam. As such, they waged a battle on two fronts, first, against the secular Jeunes Algériens, and second, against the *tariqa-s*, Sufi brotherhoods, and *mrabtin*, holy men, both of which they argued had strayed from the teachings of Muhammed. Pan-Arab in orientation but advocates of Algerian nationalism, religious at base but implicitly political, the Reformist movement began in the mid-1920s but made significant headway only in the 1930s. Nonetheless, it was already clear by 1939 that Ben Badis and his followers could not transform alone an essentially religious movement of the traditional bourgeoisie into a mass-based nationalist party.[17]

The impetus passed then to Messali Hadj and his successive political organizations, namely, the Etoile Nord Africaine (ENA), the Parti Populaire Algérien (PPA), and the Mouvement pour le Triomphe des Libertés Démographiques (MTLD). To the secular protonationalism of the Jeunes Algériens and the religious nationalism of the Reformists, Messali Hadj opposed his own militant brand of secular nationalism.

At the same time as the Reformists arose to challenge the Jeunes Algériens and the Messalistes challenged in turn the Reformists, the earlier groupings were displaced but not discarded. The most widely

236

remarked-upon example is the Reformists, who succeeded in institution-alizing and thereby legitimizing their program not before but only after independence in 1962. But the same process is clear also in the case of the Jeunes Algériens, who continued to play a significant role at least through the 1930s. The Fédération des Elus Indigènes, the chief organization of elected Algerian officials in the interwar period, was Jeune Algérien in outlook. The Blum-Violette reforms proposed in 1936 were aimed again primarily at those Algerian *évolués* who still called themselves Jeunes Algériens. Ferhat Abbas, perhaps the single best known Algerian leader be-tween the wars, answered to the name "Jeune Algérien."[18]

The apogee of *Algérie française* came in 1930 in that orgy of self-congratulation, the centenary celebrations of the 1830 invasion. But as the Arabist Jacques Berque phrased it in his penetrating study of the Maghreb during the interwar years, "France, in these lands, was una-ware of her own mortality."[19] In 1936 the European mayors of colonial Algeria resigned en masse in opposition to the Blum-Violette proposals; the last best chance to enact meaningful reform since the 1919 Jonnart reforms had failed egregiously.

Now it was the turn of the Arabs and Berbers. The first explosion occurred on the day the Second World War ended in Europe, May 8, 1945. At Setif, located in Constantine department south of Bône, Al-gerians gathered to commemorate their war dead by staging a march to place a wreath on the town's *monument aux morts*. Algerians displayed the green and white flag used by Abd al-Qadir in the 1840s and by independent Algeria after 1962. Police attempted to confiscate the flags and provocative placards, violence broke out, and the crowd retaliated by attacking European settlers. In Sétif and the surrounding region over one hundred Europeans were killed, many mutilated.

Elsewhere similar scenes occurred. Along with Sétif the situation was worst in Guelma, but in Bône it was bad, too. At four o'clock in the afternoon 15,000–20,000 Algerians gathered downtown to place a wreath on the *monument aux morts*, and march the length of the Cours Bertagna. Messali Hadj's PPA, Ferhat Abbas' Amis du Manifeste, Ab-delhamid Ben Badis's Association des Ulemas – all were represented. At the moment the crowd headed towards the central market, flags and banners appeared. As the police waded into the crowd, settlers armed with chains, clubs, and bottles appeared from the neighboring streets, and a riot ensued. The crowd moved to the Cours Bertagna and sacked cafes and tobacco kiosks. Quickly gendarmes and *gardes mobiles* ar-rived, a curfew was declared, and the streets cleared, leaving two Al-gerians dead and fifty wounded, and sixty-six settlers and police hospitalized.[20]

European repression was massive. At Bône, anyone suspected of adhering to any of the organizations represented at the march, or identified from crowd photographs, were arrested and liable to the death penalty or hard labor in perpetuity. Nationalists claim that the majority "perished in the cells of the Casbah as a result of inhuman treatment."[21] It is generally agreed that worse repression occurred in the Bône region at El Hadjar/Duzerville, Dréan/Mondovi, Bouchegouf and Medjez Sfa – where Algerians were summarily executed before firing squads for having gone to Bône to demonstrate – and the worst of all at Guelma. No one will ever know the total number killed in reprisals. The French officially put the figure at between 1,000 and 1,300; the Algerians regularly claim 45,000. Note that the lowest figure represents ten Algerians dead for every European. In short, Sétif constitutes the opening battle in what became the Algerian revolution.[22]

> *My sense of humanity was affronted for the first time by the most atrocious sights [at Sétif]. I was sixteen years old. The shock which I felt at the pitiless butchery that caused the deaths of thousands of Muslims, I have never forgotten. From that moment my nationalism took definite form.*
> – Kateb Yacine

After Sétif blatant vote-rigging only worsened an already bad situation. In 1948 in Bône, for example, the MTLD candidate, El Mehdaoui, received 6,544 votes in the first round but only 96 in the second, whereas the independant candidate went from 3,174 votes to 16,348 in an election scenario repeated throughout Algeria as "electoral fraud became a state institution."[23] Such electoral machinations traduced legitimate Algerian claims; here was the legacy of settler political culture epitomized by Jérome Bertagna, nowhere practiced so skillfully and cynically as in Bône.[24]

Now occurred schisms within schisms, as nationalist groups disagreed on ways to breach the stone wall of *pied noir* intransigeance. One such split led to the formation of the Organisation Secrète, the secret army of the PCA, led by such future revolutionary luminaries as Ahmed Ben Bella, Zighout Youcef, and Benmostefa Benaouda from Bône. Compared to the earlier Jeunes Algériens, the social composition of the OS, like the PPA, was decidedly plebeian. In Bône employees, workers, storekeepers, and artisans predominated; Benzaim was a chauffeur, and Benaouda a gas station attendant.[25]

> *Benmostefa Benaouda. Born in Bône. Joined PPA-MTLD at end of Second World War. Joined OS 1948, put in charge of urban organization. Participated in so-called "Tebessa affair" which led to dismantling of OS, and his arrest 19 March 1950. Tried and convicted in Bône 4 March 1951. Escaped from jail 1952 together with Zighout Youcef, and went underground. One of the "group of 22," organizers of the 1954 uprising. Charged*

with operations in Bône region as far as Guelma on 1 November 1954. Participated in planning August 1955 attacks in Constantinois. After 1956 congress of Soummam, named to Comité National de la Révolution Algérienne (CNRA). Signed Evian accords 1962, ending the war.[26]

In 1950 Organisation Secrète members Didouche Mourad, Mohammed Benzaim from Bône, and Benmostefa Benaouda attempted to kidnap a suspected informer, Khiari, in Tebessa. Termed the "Tebessa affair," the kidnapping attracted the attention of the police, and allowed the French to identify OS militants in the Constantinois, make numerous arrests, and dismantle the organization. The following March 135 OS members were tried and convicted in Bône, and others were tried simultaneously in Oran, Blida, and Bougie.[27] However, several escaped from Bône soon after, including Larbi Ben M'Hidi, Rabah Bitat, Mohammed Boudiaf, Didouche Mourad, and Benmostefa Benaouda. The first four were among the "neufs historiques," the nine leaders of the Comité Revolutionnaire d'Unite et d'Action (CRUA), which now formed. On November 1, 1954, CRUA launched the Algerian Revolution. November 1 was quiet in Bône, but elsewhere in wilaya (zone) 2, which encompassed the northern Constantinois, attacks occurred at Souk Ahras, Conde-Smendou, and Saint-Charles. The attack on Souk Ahras was led by Badji Mokhtar.

Badji Mokhtar. Born in Annaba region 1919. Small property owners, family expropriated during the course of French colonialism, and moved to Souk Ahras where Badji raised. From two of oldest and most learned Bône families, Dar El Badji and Dar Bouzamoundo. In Souk Ahras father exercized functions of bachadel at local mahakma. At beginning of Second World War in 1939, Badji joined PPA. Repression after Sétif in 1945 radicalized him. Elected to Souk Ahras city council in 1947 as MTLD militant, and simultaneously placed in charge of OS in Souk Ahras. For his role in kidnapping Khiari in 1950, Badji arrested, tortured, and condemned to three years in prison. Upon release in 1954, joined "group of 22," and placed in charge of area from Souk Ahras to La Calle. His speciality: derailing iron ore trains that ran from the Ouenza to Annaba. In January 1955 killed in combat near Medjez-Sfa.[28]

But would the uprising catch on or die out? The answer came in August 1955 from the Constantinois in what amounted to a turning point of the revolution. After November 1954 the Front de Libération Nationale (FLN) had taken a beating at the hands of the French. French parachutists launched what were called euphemistically *ratissages*, attacks in which Algerian hamlets were "raked over." Under cover of curfews, the army methodically brutalized the populace. The number of FLN killed and wounded increased, weaponry decreased. The French

refused those captured the rights of combatants. Wilaya 2 was cut off
from other FLN zones. In January, 1955, Didouche Mourad, the leader
of Wilaya 2, was killed in combat by the paras. Zighout Youcef took
over, assisted by Lakhdar Bentobbal and Benmostefa Benaouda.

> *Zighout Youcef. Born 1921 in hamlet of Condé-Smendou, son of peasants.*
> *Opened ironworking and carpentry shop in 1945, and elected to Condé-*
> *Smendou city council. From 1948 hid OS members, and in 1950 jailed.*
> *Escaped from Bône prison 1952, went underground, and became member*
> *of "group of 22." Directed region around Guelma, Constantine, Philippe-*
> *ville, and Condé-Smendou. In August, 1956, elected member of CNRA.*
> *One month later, killed by French troops in combat.*[29]

At the end of June and first part of July Youcef convened a war
council west of Bône in the forest of Collo, "an immense, secret, deserted forest, [with] no roads, few trails."[30] Youcef argued that it was
up to Wilaya 2 to launch "a new November 1," a total war against the
French. "To colonialism's policy of collective repression we must reply
with collective reprisals against the Europeans, military and civil, who
are all united behind the crimes committed upon our people. For them,
no pity, no quarter!"[31] On August 20 Youcef's forces attacked twenty-
five towns in Wilaya 2 simultaneously. At Bugeaud and Sainte-Croix-
de-l'Edough in the Edough mountains "at the beginning of a promising
weekend . . . bursts of machine gun fire tore the air."[32] In Bône *fedayeen*
armed with homemade bombs gutted two police stations, and shot up
bars still frequented by Muslims who were not observing the FLN ban
on alcohol, *kif*, and cigarettes. At Constantine Ferhat Abbas' nephew
was killed for criticizing FLN excesses. At Ain-Abid near Constantine,
the entire Mello family were among the victims of the massacres: the
seventy-three-year-old grandmother, the eleven-year-old daughter, the
father "killed in his bed with his arms and legs hacked off," the mother
"disembowelled, her five-day-old baby slashed to death and replaced in
her opened womb."[33] Repression rivaled Sétif, as armed *pied-noir* vig-
ilantes worked hand in glove with police and army, and Algerians were
shot on sight. The total: 125 Europeans killed, 2,000–12,000 Algerians.

After what became known as the Philippeville massacres, Jacques
Soustelle, an anthropologist of Mexico by training and current Governor-General of Algeria, converted to the *pied-noir* cause. In December
an alarmed Camus arrived from France to float a joint European-
Algerian "civil truce" initiative. But at a public meeting which he addressed jointly with Ferhat Abbas – in one of *his* last appearances as a
moderate nationalist – Camus was booed by the *pieds noirs*, and only
later learned that the two Muslim leaders he had selected had both
secretly become FLN members. Overtaken by spiraling communal vi-

olence, Camus retreated back to France, never to write again about Algeria save once. The victor of August 1955 was violence, but the revolution was back on track.

In Bône, August 1956 was more significant than August 1955, because it was bloodier. On the Muslim holiday *Achoura*, August 19, Aidli Abdelmadjid, a French army veteran of Vietnam, and his partner Bedoui Mohammed, walked up to two French paras on the street, killed one and wounded the other. In retaliation the paras charged en masse into the Place d'Armes in the center of the old city, and "all those on the Place were knocked down, trampled, left for dead." The paras then proceeded to hunt down every Algerian they could lay their hands on in the narrow streets as *pieds noirs* hurled insults, flower pots, and chairs at those fleeing. "Heads were cut off and used as soccer balls" which were kicked from street to street. Five paras entered a Turkish bath and came out with two bathers entirely nude, "beat them with iron bars, then hung them up on the hooks of a veranda, like carcasses in a butcher's shop."[34]

On September 12, 1956 the FLN avenged the August massacre. While bombs went off in the Bône outskirts to attract police and military away from the center city, five Algerians in a car cruised down the Cours Bertagna methodically machine-gunning everything in sight. First hit were soldiers and *colons* sitting on the terrace of the Hotel d'Orient; three other cafes were shot up in succession. As the Algerians drove away, bombs exploded in the Chamber of Commerce and main police station. The FLN was nothing if not symbolic.

> *Bouzered Hocine. Born outside Constantine in 1928. Studied at the renowned Zitouna in Tunis, earned a certificate in Arabic. Moved to Bône where brother directed medersa (school of law and theology) of Association des Ulemas. Unable to obtain work on basis of his diploma, worked successively as waiter, vegetable seller, and in carpentry workshop where lost two fingers in work accident. Joined MTLD 1950. After November 1954 Bouzered, a.k.a. "the man with two fingers and two colts," formed FLN group which specialized in killing cops. In 1956, killed commissaire Brook returning from rendez-vous with his mistress. One year later, Bouzered killed on bicycle, his only means of transportation, when vegetable truck ran him down driven by three cops disguised in chechias and gandouras, who dared not confront him in a shootout.*[35]

On May 13, 1958 *pieds noirs* in Algiers gathered at the massive *monument aux morts* to commemorate the killing of three French prisoners by the Armée de Libération Nationale (ALN), which had been carried out in retaliation for the guillotining of three Algerians by the French in Algiers. The crowd climbed the steps to the Gouvernement Général Building, took it over, overthrew the Fourth Republic, and precipitated

241

de Gaulle's return to power. A general strike begun in Algiers spread to Bône. Two weeks later the ALN fought the French just outside Bône in the battle of Mermera. The ALN withdrew, but not before killing the French commander, Col. Jeanpierre. Four years earlier Jeanpierre had been taken prisoner at Dien Bien Phu.

In October 1958 de Gaulle traveled to Algeria, and in Constantine he announced the Plan de Constantine, an economic development plan which was too little too late. One of the key projects proposed was a steel mill at Annaba using iron ore from the Ouenza. It was the first serious attempt since Bassano and Talabot during the Second Empire, but it was only realized after the revolution when the Algerians adopted the French emphasis on heavy industrialization as their own, and built today's SNS facility at what was Duzerville and is now El Hadjar. In the 1830s General Monck d'Uzer envisioned colonization as development, but not like this.

The movie *Battle of Algiers* ends in an incandescent moment of revolutionary élan, a cinematic evocation of the December 11–13, 1960 demonstrations when Algerians sailed out of the Casbah en masse to confront settlers and troops – three years after the FLN had supposedly been eliminated. The contagious revolutionary enthusiasm infected Bône on December 12. Pouring onto the Cours Bertagna, more than one hundred Algerians were killed. The colonial press lowered the Algerian body count, relegated the dead Algerians to *faits divers*, miscellaneous news items, and featured French victims in lead articles, but for those who could see they saw before their eyes the unmaking of French Algeria. At the beginning of 1960 Albert Camus had died instantly when the car he was riding in from Aix-en-Provence to Paris careened wildly and went out of control on a straight stretch of trafficless road.

The wolves now entered the city in the guise of the Organisation Armée Secrète (OAS). During the last two years of the war Europeans and Algerians divided Bône in half along geographical lines which reproduced the prevailing residential segregation, and only left to plant bombs in the adverse camp. Algerian territory consisted of the old city, outlying housing blocks and Beni M'haffer next to the European cemetery; Europeans staked out the Cours Bertagna and new city, and the wealthy suburbs of St. Cloud and the Menadia. The mixed, working class quarter of the Colonne Randon was caught in the middle as it had been historically, and became a no man's land.[36] The most spectacular hit blew the roof off the city hall and destroyed the ornate cupola, but fortunately Bône did not suffer the damage that Oran or Algiers did.

Finally, a cease fire was agreed to March 1962 at Evian in Switzerland; one of the signers of the accords was Benmostefa Benaouda. The OAS redoubled its scorched earth policy. In Bône between June 20–22, 1962

Illustration C-2   Former European cemetery of Bône, 1976 (photograph by the author)

the OAS abetted by the *colons* destroyed what they could. The most grandiose statue, that of Bertagna on the Cours, was dismantled and shipped to France, where today it sits in the garden of a Bertagna family member somewhere in the Rhône.[37] The statue of Thiers at the bottom of the Cours is now at Saint-Savin in the Vienne, the column commem-

243

orating Randon's 1842 road to the Edough and after which the Colonne Randon took its name stands now in the French Foreign Legion museum in Aubagne, and the bell from the main church named after Saint Augustine and on which is engraved the names of the Bônois who died in the First World War now adorns a church in Antibes which the former bishop of Constantine and Hippo built in 1971.[38] The Bônois then left en masse July 3–5. In a strange premonition dating from 1939 Camus had written, "The whole coast is ready for departure; a shiver of adventure ripples through it. Tomorrow, perhaps, we shall leave together."[39]

On July 5, 1962 the Annabis took over Annaba. They tore down what remained of Bertagna's statue. They converted the Saint Anne church in the Colonne Randon into a mosque. Later they bulldozed down the main church at the top of the Cours. And they changed the Cours Bertagna to the Cour de la Révolution, the Place d'Armes to Place du 19 Août 1956, rue Sadi Carnot to rue Abdelhamid Ben Badis, rue Cardinal Dubois to rue Badji Mokhtar, avenue de la 3e DIA to avenue Zighout Youcef, and boulevard Georges Clemenceau to boulevard Bouzered Hocine.[40]

Today in Annaba there are perhaps 4,000 *pieds noirs* left; if you are quick you can glimpse the old woman hanging out laundry. My landlord and his family came down from their second home in the Edough when the coast was cleared of *colons*, and moved into the 1950s-style French villa where the Bône head of the OAS had lived. They now rent the smaller house on the corner, where they used to live, to Americans working on a land irrigation scheme first proposed in the Plan de Constantine. Upstairs in the living room where the guest is served Turkish-style coffee hangs a large, framed photograph. It looks like just another family photograph, except that it is a blowup of a police mug shot with barbed wire in the background. The family member is dead.

Epilogue: Making *Making Algeria French*

No one traveling overland across the Maghrib can fail to be struck by the differences between Algeria and its two neighbors to the west and east, Morocco and Tunisia. Consider, for example, the contrasts between Tabarka, the westernmost town in Tunisia, and El Kala, the easternmost town in Algeria. A scant twenty-five miles separate them, but beyond similar geography and common physical characteristics these two small coastal ports are worlds apart.

In El Kala at noontime there is little activity; few people are on the streets, and still fewer cars on the roads. The yellowish buildings, their plaster flaking, are heaped up against the hillside which descends all the way to the sea. The ambiance of El Kala can only be described as dreary, drab, somnolent. Algerians sit sipping mint tea in a cafe half-hidden by a brown awning. An open doorway indicates the entrance to a restaurant populaire, a euphemism for a cheap restaurant frequented by Muslims but not usually Europeans, where for the equivalent of a dollar you can buy a piece of mutton in a bowl of broth with all the heavy, doughy Algerian version of a French baguette you want. No wine, of course. Most such restaurants are lit garishly with neon, but electricity scarcely seems to have made it this far the interior is so dark and dingy in the light of a single bare bulb. Seven miles to the west of town are the ruins of the oldest French trading settlement in the Maghrib, built in the sixteenth century to tap the coral along the coast. In the outskirts of El Kala, before the cork oak forests begin in earnest, is a new cellulose factory. At the border an Algerian hitches a ride into town almost as if it were his prerogative. Despite repeated attempts to make conversation, he remains reticent, sullen, proud.

In Tabarka there is more coming and going. The French-style municipal gardens fill a small-sized city block, and the short spring flowers in bloom rise up the gradual incline. The whitewashed buildings contrast with the deep azure sky, although not quite as blindingly intense and shimmering as in Tunis to the east. Here in Tabarka the French word gai aptly describes the ambiance. It seems as if all the buildings have terraces, many of them have bright Matisse-like murals painted on the outside walls, and Tunisians sit in twos and threes at the several open-air cafes drinking hot tea with fresh sprigs of mint. The food here runs to fresh fried fish and greasy fried

245

Illustration E-1   Beni M'haffer settlement (called Beni Ramassés by the
French) near European cemetery, 1976 (photograph by the author).

potatoes, flaky yellow pain tunisien *with poppy and sometimes cumin seeds,
and Tunisian white wine. Even a locally produced fig liqueur is available.
The Genoese were the first Europeans to establish their* comptoir, *or trading
settlement, here for coral fishing centuries ago. A small town, Tabarka
nonetheless hosts annually an internationally known summer festival which
first attracted European jetsetters and now students and world travelers.
The well-tended vineyards outside town remind one of France, and behind
more than one row of cypresses lies a still-secluded chateau. Rumor has it
that one of former President Habib Bourguiba's cronies has been favored
with a concession to run a hotel and hunting lodge where he wines, dines,
and arranges wild boar hunts for wealthy tourists. A Tunisian hitchhiker
chatters incessantly with a constant smile and infectious enthusiasm about
his illiterate father (a gardener), about the French* baccalauréat *he earned,
and about his travels between Sousse, Sfax, St. Malo, and Rotterdam as a
seaman in the Tunisian merchant marine.*

*Just outside Tabarka a highway marker indicates "Bône 125 km." No
markers for Bône exist in Algeria; the few signs there are have all been
changed to Annaba. Likewise, the French transcription, La Calle, has been
changed back to El Kala.*

The contrasts are almost too pat, too stereotypical. El Kala: drab,
inward-looking, with a hint of modern transformation. Tabarka: bright,
cosmopolitan, with a stolid socioeconomic and political structure. One

246

aim of this study has been to render such contemporary impressions historically intelligible. In the case of Annaba, how do we write the history of the present? By rewriting the history of its past presents. For it should be clear by now that the Bône past is not only part of the Annaba present, it is not even past.

Hippo/Bône/Annaba is one of those Mediterranean outposts with a continuous history of 2,500 years and more, one of those port cities people pass through more often than come from, a place which by and large has its history made for it rather than making its own. Contemporaneous with Carthage, its main claim to world historical fame came early with St. Augustine. Sitting in the seat Augustine occupied as bishop in the ruins outside town, it is not easy imagining the author of the *City of God* and the *Confessions* born in the Souk Ahras where Badji Mokhtar was raised south of Annaba. In the St. Augustine basilica, one of the uglier nineteenth-century French remakes of an Italian Byzantine church, sits one of his bones in a reliquary in a dimly lit side chapel. Bône's church bell, now in Antibes, was named after the saint. In 1930 was the 1500th anniversary of Augustine's death during the Vandal siege, as well as the centenary of the French takeover.

After the bishop of Hippo, it was the deluge as far as the Europeans were concerned. First, the Vandals destroyed Augustine's city. Then "fanatical nomads" invaded from the Arabian desert.[1] Thus began *des siècles obscurs*, the centuries of obscurity.[2] For Algerians, however, the era constituted the height of Islam, of successive Berber and Arab dynasties: the Fatimids (909–1171), Zirids (972–1148), Almohades (1130–1269), and Hafsids (1228–1574). Abou Leith El Bouni completed Annaba's main mosque, Sidi Bou Merouane, in 1033.[3] What we know we learn from people who were travelers more often than residents, chroniclers rather than historians. Ibn Hauqal. Al-Bakri. Al-Idrisi. Ibn Battuta. Leo Africanus.[4] In the thirteenth century ancestors of Ibn Khaldun (1332–1406), the great Berber philosopher of history, settled in Annaba, before moving to Tunis a generation later. It can be argued that the history of the Maghrib, from the Arab invasions a millennium ago to the Berber dynasties prior to the sixteenth-century Turks, is the history of successive tribal confederations rising up in the desert and overwhelming the cities. Ibn Khaldun accounted for this cyclical historical movement by showing how the rise to power of tribal society inevitably entailed the transformation of a previously egalitarian society into a hierarchical one. Thus, an internal tension was created which lead inexorably to collapse, and the cycle began again. Where Eurocentric historians disparaged Maghribi history, Ibn Khaldun stressed the grand sweep of social and historical change.

Later, it was the turn of European travelers to Islamic lands. In the

247

eighteenth century, Thomas Shaw, Jean André Peyssonnel, Louis René
Desfontaines, and Abbé Poiret. After the 1830 invasion, Abbé de Pietri,
Grenville Temple, Abbé Suchet, and C.-A. Rozet.[5] These and other
observers were instrumental in inventing the cultural stereotypes
through which Europe viewed North Africa, images of piracy, slavery,
barbarism, Turkish cruelty, renegade Christians, and Moorish exoticism.
What Muslims termed the Maghrib, the land of the sunset, the Europeans called Barbary, the Barbary Coast; from the Vandals we derive
"vandal." Europeans imagined a Maghrib which wove together piracy,
slavery, and the renegade Christians who apostatized to save their lives
at the expense of their souls. Algerians more than reciprocated Europeans' prejudices. When Annabi children saw a Christian in the street
they broke into a song which compared the afterlife of Muslims, who
would live with blue-eyed Muslim beauties on a bed of roses, to that of
Christians who would be stretched over a bed of burning coals.[6]

When Orientalism emerged as a colonial discourse in the nineteenth
century, Annaba-become-Bône acted as a hotel for more than one tourist. In 1846 Alexandre Dumas visited briefly accompanied by his son
and the Orientalist painters Eugène Giraud and Louis Boulanger. "The
city does not contain anything very curious." To get to Hippo, "we
followed the right bank of the Seybouse, along which I killed some snipe
and a wild duck."[7]

Gustave Flaubert passed through Bône in April 1858 on his way to
Carthage, located outside Tunis, to research his historical novel *Salammbo*. The year before *Madame Bovary* had been a *succès de scandale*;
with *Salammbo* he sought artistic success. Unable to create from books
and documents in Paris, he decided to collect impressions on location.
Taken by Tunis, it recalled his first trip to the Orient in 1849–51 when
he traveled to Egypt, Syria, Palestine, and Turkey with Maxime du
Camp. Bône, on the other hand, he found "desert, beastly and dismal."
Across the way stood Hippo, a "green hillock in a valley between two
mountains." He climbed to the Casbah where he found "military prisoners digging the white soil in full sun." Coming back down, "we see
our Neapolitan divers leaving the church of St. Augustine, where they
had gone to pray for an increase in pay."[8]

In 1880 Pierre Loti, a Romantic Orientalist if there ever was one,
visited Bône for a week. Already he had shipped to Tahiti in 1872,
nineteen years before Gauguin. Stationed in Senegal, 1873–4, he rode
into the desert with the nomadic Touaregs, and had a torrid affair with
an unknown member of Dakar's European colony. But two years later
Istanbul changed his life. There he met the love of his life, Hakidje,
the wife of a Turk, and a young man Samuel. Samuel loved Loti, and
Loti loved both of them. Samuel helped arrange rendez-vous with Hak-

248

idje, and a *pied à terre* for Loti. Entering one door in his French sailor's uniform, Loti exited from another dressed as the Albanian Arik Ussim Effendi. In *Aziyade* (1877) he fictionalized Hakidje as Aziyade, and his life in Istanbul; it made his literary name.[9]

Muslim Bône in 1880 reminded Loti of Istanbul, but he was little impressed, to say the least, with the European effort to make Bône French. He was less interested in his European acquaintances than his Algerian friends Salah Moussa and Mohammed Largueche – "already too French for me" with their *lycée* educations – and El Hadj Ahmet, who had pilgrimaged to Mecca and visited Istanbul. Loti frequented Moorish cafes and regaled his Algerian listeners with tales of "Stamboul," but he received sailing orders before he could participate in an Arab *fantasia*.[10]

In 1897 the first point in the Maghrib that Isabelle Eberhardt reached was Bône. Born in Geneva, the illegitimate daughter of a Russian anarchist, she was accompanied by her mother. The two of them rented a house in the Muslim old city, and both converted to Islam before her mother died in December 1897. When Isabelle buried her in Bône's Arab cemetery, she wrote, "On the day fixed by my destiny, I would like my remains to be placed in the red earth of this cemetery of white Annaba."[11] After that, she took off for the desert. She learned Arabic and studied the Koran. She joined a Sufi brotherhood, and was very nearly killed by a member of a rival order. She dressed as a male as well as a Muslim, and adopted the name Si Mahmud al-Sa'di. She married an Algerian, Sliman Ahanni, who served in the French army. Expelled from Algeria, she returned as a French citizen. She met the future Marshal Lyautey, who trusted her as a confidante, as well as Victor Barrucand, an acquaintance of Sadek Denden in Algiers, who heavily edited her posthumously published writings. Her story *Yasmina* appeared in a Bône paper, *Le Progrès de l'Est*, in 1901. The tale of the impossible love of a Bedouin girl and a French army officer, it echoed Eberhardt's own experience.[12] In 1904, at the age of 27, she managed to drown in the desert at Ain Sfra in a flash flood.

In 1900–2 Camille Saint-Saens wintered in Bône, also living in the old city. Already influenced by Middle Eastern music in *Samson et Dalila* (1877) and *Suite algérienne* (1880), Saint-Saens composed an opera in Bône, *Les barbares*, which recounts the Vandal attack on Hippo, and Augustine's death. It opened at the Paris Opéra in 1902 and almost immediately dropped out of the opera repertory.[13]

*   *   *

The first substantial history of Bône appeared in 1892; I first read René Bouyac's *Histoire de Bône* in the Bibliothèque Nationale, Paris.

Born in Bône shortly after the 1830 invasion, Bouyac trained as a military interpreter, and served as a colonial official in Tunisia. Bouyac wrote local history, antiquarian history, a tale of big battles, big events, and big men. He used primary sources, but they are virtually all European: Documents on the Spanish occupation 1535–40; an account of the Duke of Tuscany's expedition against Bône in 1607; documents on the French takeover.[14]

What is most significant is the manner in which he ordered his interpretation of Bône's history. Not surprisingly, he wrote much more on Augustine's Hippo (six percent) and French Bône (sixty-eight percent) than the Berber, Arab, and Turkish epochs (twenty-six percent). Even in the chapters on Muslim Bône, however, he emphasized European people and events: Charles V's expedition to Tunis and the Spanish occupation of Bône (1535–40), the French *comptoir* (warehouse) founded in the sixteenth century, the 1607 Tuscan invasion, the government-chartered Compagnie d'Afrique (1713–94). Throughout Bouyac makes his pro-French, anti-Algerian colonialist prejudices abundantly clear. "Up to the beginning of the eleventh century, the history of Hippo is plunged in darkness." Once firmly established, the Arabs "did not hesitate to spread ruin and desolation to the shores of Europe."[15]

Moreover, Bouyac's *Histoire de Bône* is not a history of Bône, but of European Bône, and not even of all Europeans, but primarily the French and wealthy. We saw in Chapter 3, for example, that General Monck d'Uzer was sacked as commander of Bône in 1836 because he ordered soldiers to work his private estate. Yet Bouyac adopts a distinctly prosettler position and sides with d'Uzer; what is good for colonization is good for Bône. He heads his chapter on d'Uzer, "Unjust attacks of which he [Uzer] is the object," and argues, "we owe him the decency of saying that, if he was mistaken in the means he used, at least his good faith and personal honesty are not suspect."[16] It is precisely the means he used, and his alleged integrity which led Paris to recall him.

Nowhere is Bouyac's pro-French, anti-Algerian attitude clearer than in Colonel Morris's 1833 letter to his mother describing a *razzia* against the Merdès in which Morris played a leading role, and which Bouyac prints in full. As described in Chapter 3, the Merdès had resisted Turkish hegemony, and now they were resisting the French. Two columns of nearly eight hundred men armed with four artillery pieces and led by General d'Uzer were launched against the Algerians. Morris described the ensuing battle with "MM. les Merdès [even the name is not very gallant]" to his mother as "a small matter, a small combat of the advance guard." Morris surprised a half dozen Algerians waiting along a river who fired too hurriedly to hit him. Rather than wait for reinforcements, Morris crossed the river, had his horse shot from beneath him, and then wrestled one of the leading Merdès warriors, Ahmed ben Hassein, in hand-to-hand combat. By this time more troops had crossed the river and began to rout the Merdès. Meanwhile Morris had grasped Hussein's head, held it up – and shot it, "which burned my left eye horribly." With the Merdès now in full retreat, the French decapitated the twenty-five Algerians who had been killed. But Morris did not want to cut off the head of *his* Arab, because "he had fought so well." For Morris, it was "the best day of my life."[17]

Beyond substantial factual detail stands Bouyac's colonialist preju-dices, which deform his work by literally blinding him to the presence of the Algerians in French colonialized Bône. Far from analyzing the effects of French colonialism on Bône, Bouyac echoes the civic boost-erism promulgated by the local chamber of commerce. Of the contem-porary 1890s, for example, he writes of the "immenses works in progress; the abundant vineyards which have invaded the plain and the merchan-dise heaped on the quais," and concludes, "Bône will always be the coquettish city with sumptuous buildings, and wide shady avenues."[18]

Bône militaire. 44 siècles de luttes, by Captain Albert-Charles Maitrot, is not in the Bibliothèque Nationale. The Annaba Secrétaire-Général first lent me a copy. Paperbound and showing its age, it threatened to fall apart while being photocopied. Amateur historian and archeologist, Maitrot arrived in Bône from Saint-Cyr to serve in the army. Active in the local historical society, the Academie d'Hippone, Maitrot wrote two additional books plus several articles on the history of Bône and Hippo.[19] He knew some Arabic, as is clear from his handling of sources. Politically conservative, he viewed the 1870 Algiers Commune – following the lead of the Paris Commune – as "a species of small-scale revolution of which Bône did not want to recognize the illegality."[20]

Published 40 years after Bouyac's history, *Bône militaire* contains more solid information, evidences greater familiarity with the sources, and results from a broader historical vision. Despite the title, Maitrot emphasizes military history no more than Bouyac. He halts the narrative occasionally to present information gleaned, for example, from the 1832 *état-civil*, and to discuss what became of the leading actors in the 1830 takeover. In Part Three, he compares the urban morphology of Hippo, Annaba, and Bône. A colonialist of his time, Maitrot nonetheless dis-tances himself somewhat from the straightforward settler perspective of Bouyac. Both *Bône anecdotique* and his article on "Les rues du vieux Bône" describe Jewish, Arab, and Turkish personages and events, which suggests a somewhat less Eurocentric view of Bône's past.

For all that, *Bône militaire* remains local history of primarily antiquarian interest cast predominantly in a narrative mode. Maitrot still devotes a disproportionate amount of time to the French (seventy percent), and slights the Algerians (thirty percent). Covering substantially the same ground as Bouyac, his history of Berber, Arab, and Turkish Annaba reads as though it too were made largely in Europe. Maitrot draws on the same sources as Bouyac, but also utilizes additional material. He makes better use of Arab chroniclers than Bouyac, and quotes from an Arabic work on the French invasion published in Paris, if only to criticize it.[21]

Maitrot's colonialist prejudices are not as close to the surface as those of Bouyac, but there are no major disagreements between them. He defends d'Uzer staunchly. "The departure of General d'Uzer was the result of maneuvers by his enemies."[22] Maitrot also quotes Morris's letter to his mother in full. In describing events after the 1830 invasion, *Bône militaire* reads like one battle after another, one villainous Arab subdued after another. Take Cheikh Zeghdoud: Originally from the area around Lake Fetzara, he claimed to be a *marabout*, or holy man, whom God had told to wage a holy war against the infidel French. In 1841 a *caid* loyal to the French and a French officer went to the Beni Mohammed in the Edough, where Zeghdoud was staying at the time, to collect taxes. For two days they wrangled over payment, then Zeghdoud walked up to the French officer, "put his hand on his shoulder and blew his brains out with his pistol." From then on, he pillaged the plain, even coming up to the gates of Bône. In December 1841, General Randon attacked the Beni Mohammed in the Edough forest, but Zeghdoud escaped. To break the back of his resistance was one of the chief reasons which led Randon to open up the Edough by building a road. Still Zeghdoud eluded him. Finally in 1843 a large-scale pincers movement was organized against him. Four separate columns coming from Bône, Constantine, Guelma, and Philippeville converged on the Zerdeza tribe in the Edough where Zeghdoud now had sought refuge. Encircled by Algerian troops, he was shot and killed. None of the Algerians were willing to cut his head off, however, so a Turk did it. Zeghdoud's head, "thrust on the end of a bayonet and his left wrist stuck on a gun like a *baguette*," was exposed for three days in Bône "to serve as a lesson to those who might be tempted to imitate his example."[23]

The exception to Maitrot's rule that all Algerians are villains ipso facto is the Boumaiza family, which "has always enjoyed, justly, a large measure of respect in the Bône region." Maitrot traces their ancestry back to the Prophet, uncritically accepting their unlikely genealogical claims. Yet the Boumaizas were Bertagna's leading Algerian collaborators; Mohammed Tahar was Jérome's *adjoint indigène*. Towards the Boumaiza's chief rivals, the Benyacoubs, Maitrot is considerably less charitable. When the Benyacoubs are allied with the French, they are good; when not, they are bad. Thus, Maitrot begins one passage, "Belkassem ben Yacoub, our ally since 1836 and previously our diehard enemy.... "[24] In short, Maitrot is much superior to Bouyac as a historian, but fails to escape prevailing colonialist prejudices.

Bône. Son histoire, ses histoires, by Louis Arnaud, is not in the archives in Paris or Aix-en-Provence, nor in the Bibliothèque Nationale of either Algeria or Tunisia. Although published in 1960 at the height of the Algerian Revolution, the only copy I have ever found belongs to the Archives de la Wilaya de Constantine. There is no xerox machine in the archives, but after lengthy negotiations, a young Algerian accompanied me while I lugged the tome to a xerox shop. Louis Arnaud's grandparents arrived in Bône in 1836, and obtained considerable land in the plain outside town. A lawyer by training, Louis Arnaud married the daughter of a leading Bônois in 1916. Elected to the city council in 1908, he ran on a slate headed by Fernand Marchis, Bertagna's successor as mayor.[25] Clearly, he belonged to the Bône political elite.

Arnaud disavows any attempt to rewrite Bône's history after Bouyac and Maitrot; instead, he aims to record his personal observations. In fact, Arnaud wrote an older sort of social history, a "history with the politics left out," which is valuable precisely because he was a knowledgeable insider. Much is left out – as we shall see – but much can be found nowhere else. Besides the social and political elite, Arnaud devotes attention to the poorer-off Maltese. He devotes short chapters to cafes and music halls. He relates the sad story of Pierre Omessa, an up-and-coming journalist, who discovered his wife with an officer *in flagrante delicto*, shot and killed them both, and fled to Tunis. He details Bône's *petits métiers*, which recall a genre of social description more often identified with Paris: the knife grinder, umbrella repairer, upholsterer, dog shearer. He tells us about Marie l'Absinthe, "whose name said all that was to be said"; our old friend Carloutche, who zigzagged everywhere down the middle of the street repeating constantly, "Eviva Bertagna"; Dio Bône, a blind piano tuner, *accordeur de piano*, who shouted "Vive Marchis! Dio Bône!" when he "had worshipped Bacchus too much"; and Père Bocquet, a Bône version of the Parisian Ferdinand Lop, who perennially ran for office.[26]

But there is a more disturbing side to Arnaud's book, which emerges from what he puts in as well as from what he leaves out. His anti-Algerian prejudice is palpable throughout. A naval officer attacked by three Algerians in the nineteenth century was able to describe his assailants before he died. "Their attitude, in the course of the trial, was cynical and odious, [for] not only did they admit their abominable action, but they glorified it by insulting the memory of their victim and of

France." Although there had been a single victim, "all three of them were guillotined . . . a rare occurrence in the annals of criminal justice."[27] Less blatant but no less racist is the Sunday outing discussed earlier, which describes "the small *yaouleds* who lined the road" asking for money. When someone finally threw them a coin, "that was then a fun sight," as they all dived for it in the dirt.[28] In fact, Arnaud sees even fewer Algerians in Bône than Bouyac and Maitrot; not a single one comes to life in his pages, not even Boumaiza or Benyacoub.

Instead, Arnaud views Bône's history purely from a *pied noir* perspective, more than Maitrot, more consistently than Bouyac. Arnaud also exonerates d'Uzer. He repeats all the standard *pied noir* grievances against metropolitan France: French indifference, the settlers of 1848 stranded by Paris.[29] Over and above everything else, Arnaud trumpets the progress made by the French in Bône after the mess left by the Algerians. "It is not because the 'old city' is dirty" that it should be kept intact, but because "it alone permits the visitor . . . to understand better the grandeur and beauty of the task accomplished by the French in this country after a century in this place previously deserted, barren and virtually without natural resources," this "small, ugly Arab village of scarcely 1,500 people."[30]

Arnaud mentions more visitors more often than Bouyac or Maitrot – Dumas, Flaubert, Loti, Saint-Saens, Eberhardt. Yet Arnaud cannot take seriously these outsiders to the *pied noir* fold. He quotes Eberhardt, but says nothing about her conversion to Islam, about her mother buried in the Arab cemetery. He quotes at length from Loti's journal, yet how far apart the two remain, Arnaud, the native Bônois contemptuous of the Algerians, Loti, the Muslim sympathizer passing through Bône and spending more time with the Algerians than the Europeans.[31]

In short, Arnaud's *Bône. Son histoire, ses histoires* is filled with material unavailable elsewhere. Yet it represents a step backward in our knowledge of the Algerians in Bône. To issue a book singularly blind to the presence of the Algerians at the height of the Revolution, when Arnaud's *confrères* were trying so hard to literally eradicate them, makes too much sense, all of the wrong sort.[32]

*   *   *

I bought Volume One of H'sen Derdour's *Annaba. 25 siècles de vie quotidienne et de luttes* in France. I bought Volume Two in the bookstore at the end of the Cours in Annaba before I had a chance to meet him. Once I zeroed in on the right neighborhood, finding him was easy, a relay of kids leading me to his house in the Colonne. Born in 1911, H'sen Derdour first made a career as a notarial clerk, then worked thirty years for an export company based at the port. President during the interwar years of El Mizhar El Bouni, a performing arts ensemble, he directed the National Theater of Annaba 1964–75. At the time of the First World War, "although only a kid . . . the author of the present work" saw "the ships depart full and return empty. . . . Everyone, mothers, fathers, wives had the profound feeling that France had only declared war in order to exterminate the Algerians."[33]

H'sen Derdour is not a historian by training, and his *Annaba* is not based on archival sources but primarily secondary works. He draws on Maitrot and Arnaud, but especially Arabic works, which he uses to sketch the larger Algerian and Maghrebi background to Berber, Arab, and Turkish Annaba.[34] His history constitutes a valuable insider's account which presents a wealth of information unavailable elsewhere. Since at least the 1930s he has collected oral testimony from his Annabi contemporaries, including El Hadj Abed, whose father fought alongside Zeghdoud in the 1840s.[35] He has also unearthed manuscripts, such as Mme. Ber-rais Fetitem's account of the French invasion.[36]

Reading Derdour is like reading the French historians of Bône turned upside down. As opposed to Bouyac and Maitrot, he devotes half his book to Berber, Arab, and Turkish Bône, ten percent to Hippo, and only forty percent to the colonial period including the Algerian Revolution. Derdour praises Khodja's work on the 1830 French invasion which Maitrot criticizes. For Bouyac and Maitrot, Cheikh Zeghdoud was a dangerous enemy who had to be eliminated. For Derdour, Zeghdoud was a *marabout* of impressive lineage, and deservedly famous freedom fighter against the French. He states his attitude towards General d'Uzer in his chapter title: "The Exploitation of d'Uzer." Rather than civic virtue, Jérome Bertagna personified "*l'affairisme*," the intrusion of business into municipal affairs, "legalized theft for some, misery and humiliation at the hands of the police for others." Derdour titles his section on the Revolution, "Algeria, prisoner in a universal concentration camp, bursts colonialism asunder and obtains its freedom."[37] Another example is Loti. How different are the passages Arnaud and Derdour choose to quote! For Arnaud, Loti's Bône is European Bône; for Derdour, Algerian Bône. Yet Derdour comes much closer to conveying Loti's anti-French and pro-Algerian attitude.

Furthermore, Derdour criticizes Maitrot's colonialist prejudices, and by implication those of Bouyac and Arnaud. "When a chronicler, such as Maitrot, doubles as a captain in the French army, his *Histoire de Bône* takes a special interest in eliminating the names of Arab authors. In effect, . . . he always refers to French historians for the most part unknown. For him . . . to eliminate names confirms the absence of Algerian culture."[38] As one Algerian reviewer correctly put it, Derdour "in effect calls into question the Eurocentric conception of writing history."[39]

Several themes emerge from Derdour's history. Key is the chapter, "In Annaba, Islam retains its grandeur." Besides Loti, he discusses Saint-Saens and French converts to Islam. Derdour makes Saint-Saens sound Algerian: he lived in a "modest Moorish house," and in his music drew on Andalusian musical motifs and Arab instruments.[40] In addition to Eberhardt, Derdour cites several French who converted to Islam and married Algerians. One adopted Arab dress, and his daughter married Mihoub Benyacoub of the Benyacoub clan. The daughter and niece of another both married Annabis. Outside Bône at St. Paul, a blacksmith and carriage maker named Marchiecca celebrated Muslim holidays, frequented Sufi brotherhoods, and employed in his body shop a young Albert Camus.[41] Admittedly, Derdour's cases come mostly from the colonial elite, they are statistically insignificant in number, and he mentions nothing about Franco-Algerian marriages which did not involve conversion. Yet his cases confirm my sense that, while extremely small compared to European mixed marriages, more occurred than either French or Algerians are generally willing to admit.

Especially interesting is the way Derdour handles recent Algerian history, such as Islamic Reformism and the Algerian Revolution. Content with generalities, he pays homage to Abd al-Hamid Ben Badis, the Reformist leader, and the "new revolutionary power of Houari Boumedienne born June 19, 1965," the date when the latter ousted Ahmed Ben Bella, one of the *neufs historiques*, in a military coup.[42] Derdour ignores the period 1962–5, airbrushing Ben Bella out of his account. Derdour's book is presentist; throughout, the Algerian Revolution colors his history of the past. Terms from the Revolution are applied freely to earlier periods. Randon, a *"ratisseur,"* "raked over" the Algerians. French soldiers pursuing Zeghdoude engaged in "massacre." Repression of the Beni Salah in 1852 constitutes "genocide." The implicit argument behind this reading of the present into the past is that early resistance led to later revolution, that there is a straight historical line which runs from the 1840s to 1954–62. Thus, Zeghdoud's revolt constitutes "a glorious page in the history of Algerian resistance." And after 1852 Beni Salah territory "will remain for the French a zone often off limits for their forces up to 1962."[43]

Derdour's only criticism of independant Algeria concerns conservation of the old city, the seat of Annaba's past.[44] This is because Western notions of urbanism adopted by Algeria directly threaten its integrity. Derdour's book also exudes an occasional whiff of anti-semitism.[45] To read Derdour you would never know the Jewish community of Annaba enjoyed a continuous history from at least the fifteenth century until

256

1962. Derdour criticizes French chroniclers who leave out Algerians, yet he omits the Jews.

Where Making Algeria French *began depends on what you mean by beginning. The day I first saw the* Battle of Algiers *on a double bill with* Belle de Jour *in the Fillmore? The day in India when I sat in my compound reading the latest* Newsweek *on how many more Vietnamese – those other Asians – Americans had killed since last week? The visit to Oran when the second or third in archival command, more blunt than his superiors, asked me, "Will your study profit Algeria?" The weekend when I first limned notions of settler colonialism and colonial urbanism in a soon-to-be-burned area of redwoods? Or the weekend at Bloody Run Creek when reading the white heat white lightning of* Dispatches *I got the writing tone right?*

Whatever the circumstances of its making, the project nearly aborted, and more than once. Initially led to believe fulsome French archives would be available for the asking, I should have taken a clue from what was going on outside in the summer of 1973 rather than inside the archives. "Bus Driver Assaulted in Marseilles, 5 Algerians Killed in Reprisals." Applying for a visa at the grungy Algerian consulate in Marseilles – it's easy to find, just look for the crowd of Algerians outside – I was put off, stalled, stymied. No one "visited" Algeria in the summer of 1973 when the 1973 attack on Israel was being planned.

Returning to France a year later, it took only six weeks for the dissertation topic to collapse when I found archival Series A was unclassified, Series B was still in Algeria, Series C contained dossiers on individuals born less than 125 years ago, and Series D was misplaced. Casting about for sources and topics simultaneously, I knew the last thing I wanted to do was formally ask for permission to consult the Algerian archives. After more time spent networking than researching, an incredible stroke of archival good fortune: carte blanche research authorization granted from the level of the Conseil de la Révolution itself. I finally arrived in Algiers after an overnight boat ride with Algerians returning home with cardboard suitcases lashed together. Headed for the Casbah, I found a hotel cheap enough to get sick in, and explored for hours in clammy cold rain. I took a bus to my rendezvous. I go around to the side entrance of the Gouvernement Général Building. How will he know me? You're très reconnaissant.

From Algiers I embarked on a circular tour of Algeria on the hunt for pieces of paper too important to discard, not important enough to publish. In Oran I heard stories of burning archives in the city hall courtyard. In the record room, the metal drawers had all the right labels: Police. Statistique de la population. Sûreté public. Affaires indigènes. When I opened them, they were empty. I took a train to eastern Algeria and Constantine, not having learned yet that the bus was twice as fast. I would like to see the archives. They are heaped up in a corner. Where? Over there. Can we go see them? Tomorrow. Despite my authorization, there was no way I was going to see Constantine city archives, not in the city of Abd al-Hamid

Ben Badis. The whole trip almost ended then and there. Getting on a bus in a crowd of Algerians, I thought this is fun – until I realized my wallet with all my money had been lifted. Damn, these guys are good. Later I learned stealing from Europeans was considered a revolutionary rip-off by some. Borrowing money from acquaintances I had just made, hacking deep down from a cold picked up in a hammam *in Oran – not as memorable as the one in Kandahar – I toted up my archival count: zero and two with one more pitch to come. On the Annaba bus, my first thought driving past the refineries and factories was this is not picturesque like Constantine, it is the oil fields of Long Beach.*

The next day was one of those days. At the entrance to the mairie, *the only foreigner in a mass of Algerians, the guard waved me by. Upstairs I was passed from office to office until I saw the secrétaire-général himself. Everyone scrutinized my authorization, everyone balked – this American, Imperialist Enemy No. 1, he cannot just walk in here – and everyone dared not do as the Conseil de la Révolution ordered. I was passed back down the hierarchy, alternately stalled and entertained, as a key was searched for. A young Algerian gofer finally appeared, I was conducted upstairs to the low-ceilinged third floor, and the door opened on the richest archives in Algeria. In the middle of a large room lined with wooden cupboards filled with packets of archives, stood a metal cabinet. Inside hung the former French archivist's white coat and feather duster; hadn't he stepped out just for a minute? Out came a bronze statuette of Bertagna, a miniature replica of the one previously located downstairs on the Cours. We placed it ceremoniously on the table and laughed. Now, I thought to myself, it is time to start your book.*

Notes

Chapter 1

1 *Le Monde*, February 15, 1961, quoted in Douglas Johnson, "Algeria: Some Problems of Modern History," *Journal of African History* 5 (1964): 221.
2 David C. Gordon, *Self-Determination and History in the Third World* (Princeton: Princeton University Press, 1971), pp. 152–74. For background, see among others, anonymous, *Histoire et historiens de l'Algérie (1830–1930)* (Paris: Alcan, 1931); Mahieddine Djender, *Introduction à l'histoire de l'Algérie. Systèmes historiques. Conception générale de l'histoire nationale* (Algiers: SNED, 1972); Johnson, "Algeria"; Mohamed Cherif Sahli, *Décoloniser l'histoire. Introduction à l'histoire du Maghreb* (Paris: Maspero, 1965); Jean-Claude Vatin *L'Algérie politique: histoire et société* (Paris: Fondation nationale des sciences politiques, 1974); John Wansbrough, "The Decolonization of North African History," *Journal of African History* 9 (1968): 643–50; and Xavier Yacono, "La recherche et les livres sur l'histoire contemporaine de l'Algérie au cours des dernières années (1962–1970)," *Comptes rendus mensuels de l'Académie des sciences d'outre-mer* XXX (séance du 18 decembre 1970): 429–55.
3 S. Bencheneb, "Quelques historiens modernes arabes en Algérie," *Revue africaine* 100 (1956): 475–99; Mustapha Haddab, "Histoire et modernité chez les réformistes algériens," in Jean-Claude Vatin et al., *Connaissances du Maghreb* (Paris: Centre national de la recherche scientifique, 1984), pp. 429–55.
4 More recent historical studies continue to a large extent these themes. Representative examples are Jacques Bouveresse, "Les délégations financqieres (1898–1945)," 3 vols. (unpublished thèse de doctorat, Université de Nancy II, 1979); Mahfoud Kaddache, *Histoire du nationalisme algérien*, 2 vols. (Algiers: SNED, 1980); Gilbert Meynier, *L'Algérie révélée. La guerre de 1914–1918 et le premier quart du XXe siècle* (Geneva: Droz, 1981); Louis P. Montoy, "La presse dans le département de Constantine (1870–1918)," 4 vols. (unpublished thèse de doctorat, Université de Provence, 1982); and Annie Rey-Goldzeiguer, *Le royaume arabe. La politique algérienne de Napoléon III, 1861–1870* (Algiers: SNED, 1977).
5 Johnson, "Algeria"; David Gordon, *The Passing of French Algeria* (New

Notes

York: Oxford University Press, 1966), pp. 183–90; Gordon, *Self-Determination*, pp. 136–73.

6 Julien, *L'Afrique du Nord en marche*, third edition (Paris: Juilliard, 1972); Julien, "Introduction" to Pierre Nora, *Les français d'Algérie* (Paris: Julliard, 1961), esp. p. 23; Charles-Robert Ageron, *Les Algériens musulmans et la France (1871–1919)*, 2 vols. (Paris: Presses Universitaires de France, 1968), esp. p. 1239.

7 Sahli, *Décoloniser*; Mostefa Lacheraf, *L'Algérie: nation et société* (Paris: Maspero, 1965).

8 Gordon, *Passing*, p. 185.

9 "L'Etat intellectuel et moral de l'Algérie en 1830," *Revue d'histoire moderne et contemporaine* (1954): 119–212.

10 Philippe Lucas and Jean-Claude Vatin, *L'Algérie des anthropologues* (Paris: Maspero, 1975); Vatin et. al., *Connaissances du Maghreb* (Paris: Centre national de la recherche scientifique, 1984); *Le mal de voir. Ethnologie et orientalisme: politique et épistémologie, critique et autocritique* (Paris: Collection 10/18, 1976); Edmund Burke, "The Sociology of Islam: The French Tradition," in Malcolm Kerr, ed., *Islamic Studies: A Tradition and Its Problems* (Malibu, CA: Undena Publications, 1980), pp. 73–88; Burke, "Fez, the Setting Sun of Islam: A Study of the Politics of Colonial Ethnography," *Maghreb Review* 2 (1977): 1–7; and Fanny Colonna, "Production scientifique et position dans le champ intellectuel et politique," in *Le mal de voir*, pp. 397–415.

11 Pierre Bourdieu, "Le champ scientifique," *Actes de la recherche en sciences sociales* (Paris: Service des publications de la Maison de l'homme, 1977), pp. 88–104; Colin Gordon, ed., *Power/Knowledge: Selected Interviews and Other Writings by Michel Foucault, 1972–1977* (New York: Random House, 1980); Edward Said, *Orientalism* (New York: Random House, 1979). See also Bourdieu, *Outline of a Theory of Practice* (Cambridge: Cambridge University Press, 1977); and Talal Asad, "Two European Images of Non-European Rule," in Asad, ed., *Anthropology and the Colonial Encounter* (London: Ithaca Press, 1973), pp. 103–18.

12 Ageron, *Les algériens*, pp. 267–92, 873–91. For an application of the same approach to colonial Morocco, see Burke, "The Image of the Moroccan State in French Ethnological Literature," in Ernest Gellner and Charles Micaud, eds., *Arabs and Berbers* (London: Duckworth, 1973), pp. 175–99.

13 The problem turns on the fact – to cite just one example – "that we must take these men and women [French colonial sociologists] and their work as they are: Colonel Daumas was an anti-Arab racist, *and* he was a sometimes shrewd observer of Algerian society" (Burke, "Sociology," p. 87, emphasis in original). How to sort out the one from the other without losing sight of either is the question. What we need is a theory – and a *praxis* – of social description.

14 Yacono's study is *La Colonisation des plaines du Chélif*, 2 vols. (Algiers: Imprimerie Imbert, 1955–6), and Ageron's book is *Les Algériens musulmans*. Their exchange is in *Revue historique* 493 (janvier–mai 1970): 121–34 and 494 (avril–juin 1970): pp. 355–65. I would like to record explicitly my

respect for Ageron's achievement: every student of colonial Algeria is in his debt. His work will remain the *vade mecum* for every researcher of the 1870–1919 period.

15 Ageron in *Revue historique* 494 (avril–juin 1970): 360.

16 Ageron's remark that there are indeed individual liberal settlers but that he along with Tocqueville is interested in classes for "they alone ought to be the subject of history" is entirely to the point. See *ibid.*, pp. 363–4.

17 Nora *Les Français*, p. 98.

18 "Have I minimized the role of the *Français d'Algérie*? Those whom I call ... the *colons* ... have been nevertheless the object of all my attention" (Ageron in *Revue historique* 494 [avril–juin 1970]: 358–9). In his defense, Ageron notes the 80 pages he devotes explicitly to them – in a total of 1244. Likewise, in his splendid synthesis, *Histoire de l'Algérie contemporaine, 1871–1954* (Paris: Presses Universitaires de France, 1979), Ageron devotes two out of thirty-seven chapters to the settlers.

19 Ageron, *Les Algériens musulmans*, p. 1239.

20 Granted, this is entirely in keeping with Ageron's stated aims to determine native policy in Algeria, trace the evolution of this policy in terms of French politics and Algerian circumstances, and to detail the Algerians' social, economic, and political evolution. But I would argue that these topics cannot be fully understood without first comprehending how the role of the settlers bears on them.

21 Vatin, *L'Algérie politique*, pp. 50–1, emphasis in original.

22 Quoted in Ageron, *Histoire de l'Algérie contemporaine (1830–1973)*, fifth edition (Paris: Presses Universitaires de France, 1974), p. 48.

23 Nora, *Les Français*.

24 It is the result of his two-year stint teaching in an Algerian *lycée* between 1958 and 1960. *Normalien* and *agrégé d'histoire*, Nora formerly taught history at the Université de Nice.

25 Nora, *Les Français*, pp. 87, 98, 80, 127, respectively.

26 See Jean Lacouture's review in *Le Monde*, 1961. Douglas Johnson terms Nora's book "polemical" ("Algeria," p. 230, note 4), and Tony Smith characterizes Nora's tone as one of "mocking superiority" (*The French Stake in Algeria, 1945–1962* [Ithaca: Cornell University Press, 1978], p. 102, note 37).

27 *Doctrines of Imperialism* (New York, 1965), p. 60.

28 What I call "settler colonialism" in referring to French colonialism in Algeria, other scholars term "white settler colonialism" when referring to, for example, colonial Kenya, Zimbabwe, and South Africa. To be sure, in most cases of settler colonialism the colonizers have been white and the colonized have been people of color, but not always. For example, Japanese colonialism in Korea, Manchuria, and Taiwan fits the idea of settler colonialism developed here in many respects. See Ramon H. Myers and Mark R. Peattie, eds., *The Japanese Colonial Empire, 1895–1945* (Princeton: Princeton University Press, 1984). I am indebted to Ronald Toby for this reference.

29 Ronald J. Horvath makes this point, for example. See his "A Definition of Colonialism," *Current Anthropology* 13 (1972): 47.

30 See Arghiri Emmanuel, "White Settler Colonialism and the Myth of Investment Imperialism," *New Left Review* 73 (1972): 36; Ibrahim Abu-Lughod and Baha Abu-Laban, eds., *Settler Regimes in Africa: The Illusion of Permanence* (Wilmette, IL: Medina University Press International, 1974); G. Arrighi, *The Political Economy of Rhodesia* (The Hague: Mouton, 1967); E. S. Atieno-Odhiambo, "The Rise and Decline of the Kenya Peasant, 1888–1922," *East Africa Journal* 9 (1972); George Bennett, "British Settlers North of the Zambezi, 1920 to 1960," in Victor Turner, ed., *Colonialism in Africa* (Cambridge: Cambridge University Press, 1969); L. H. Gann and Peter Duignan, "Changing Patterns of a White Elite: Rhodesian and Other Settlers," in Turner, ed., *Colonialism*; Carl Rosberg and John Nottingham, *The Myth of "Mau Mau": Nationalism in Kenya* (Stanford: Hoover Institution Press, 1966); M. P. K. Sorrenson, *Origins of European Settlement in Kenya* (Nairobi: Oxford University Press, 1968); and Harrison M. Wright, *The Burden of the Present: Liberal-Radical Controversy over Southern African History* (Cape Town: David Philip, 1977).

31 The term plural society as used here should not be confused with the notion of pluralism often used in the American context where it refers to the cross-cutting loyalties of relatively autonomous ethnic, racial, religious, or social groups which nonetheless pursue their special interests within the confines of a common polity. See, for example, David Nicholls, *Three Varieties of Pluralism* (New York: St. Martin's Press, 1974), pp. 18–37; and Leo Kuper and M. G. Smith, eds., *Pluralism in Africa* (Berkeley: University of California Press, 1969), p. 3.

32 Clifford Geertz, *The Social History of an Indonesian Town* (Cambridge: The MIT Press, 1965), p. 78. See Leo Kuper, "Structural Discontinuities in African Towns: Some Aspects of Racial Pluralism," in Horace Miner, ed., *The City in Modern Africa* (New York: Praeger, 1967), p. 131.

33 J. S. Furnivall, *Colonial Policy and Practice* (Cambridge: Cambridge University Press, 1948), and Furnivall, *Netherlands India* (Cambridge: Cambridge University Press, 1939).

34 Geertz, *Peddlers and Princes* (Chicago: University of Chicago Press, 1963), p. 28. This concept was not used by Furnivall, but developed instead by J. H. Boeke, a contemporary who worked on Indonesia, and later was modified and expanded first by Geertz and then T. G. McGee and Milton Santos. See J. H. Boeke, *Economics and Economic Policy of Dual Societies* (New York: Institute of Pacific Relations, 1953); Geertz, *Peddlers and Princes*; T. G. McGee, *The Southeast Asian City* (London: G. Bell and Sons, 1967); McGee, *The Urbanization Process in the Third World* (London: G. Bell and Sons, 1971), Chapters Two and Three; McGee, "Rural-Urban Mobility in South and Southeast Asia. Different Formulations . . . Different Answers?" reprinted in Janet Abu-Lughod and Richard Hay, eds., *Third World Urbanization* (Chicago: Maaroufa Press, 1977); McGee, "The Persistence of the Proto-Proletariat: Occupational Structures and Planning of the Future of Third World Cities," reprinted in Abu-Lughod, ed., *Third World Urbanization*; Milton Santos, *Les Villes du tiers monde* (Paris: M.-Th. Genin, 1971); and Smith, *French Stake in Algeria*, p. 86.

35 See his collection of essays, *The Plural Society in the British West Indies* (Berkeley: University of California Press, 1965), esp. "Social and Cultural Pluralism."

36 See Kuper and Smith, eds., *Pluralism*; Kuper, *Race, Class, and Power: Ideology and Revolutionary Change in Plural Societies* (Chicago: Aldine Publishing Company, 1975); Leo Kuper, *The Pity of it All: Polarisation of Racial and Ethnic Relations* (Minneapolis: University of Minnesota Press, 1977); and John Rex, *Race, Colonialism and the City* (London: Routledge & Kegan Paul, 1973).

37 See Kuper and Smith, *Pluralism* for a discussion of these questions. In my opinion the plural society concept should be limited to colonial societies with ethnically and racially mixed populations, especially to settler colonies, and should be distinguished from societies which exhibit plural features such as the United States, Lebanon, Northern Ireland, and Israel.

38 Michael Hechter, *Internal Colonialism: The Celtic Fringe in British National Development, 1536–1966* (Berkeley: University of California Press, 1975), p. 30. See also Pablo Gonzales-Casanova, "Internal Colonialism and national development," *Studies in Comparative International Development* 1 (1965): 27–37; Rodolpho Stavenhagen, "Classes, colonialism, and acculturation: a system of inter-ethnic relations in Mesoamerica," *Studies in Comparative International Development* 1 (1965): 53–77; and R. Blauner, "Internal Colonialism and Ghetto Revolt," *Social Problems* 16 (1969): 393–408.

39 Harold Wolpe, "The theory of internal colonialism: the South African case," in Ivar Oxall, Tony Barnett, and David Booth, eds., *Beyond the Sociology of Development* (London: Routledge & Kegan Paul, 1975), pp. 229–52. Wolpe argues that since there is not a complete coincidence between race and class, at least in South Africa, internal colonialism fails as class analysis although it may succeed as ethnic analysis. While it is certainly true that more attention should be paid to class and class formation within ethnic groups as well as between such groups, this relatively small lack of fit between race and class can be analyzed fruitfully with the notion of status anxiety, and in any case should not be allowed to obfuscate the main point about an internal colony (or a plural society for that matter), which is not that race and class overlap so little but that they overlap so much as to reinforce each other and result in heightened antagonism and conflict.

40 See his "The Colonial Situation" reprinted in Pierre L. van den Berghe, ed., *Africa: Social Problems of Change and Conflict* (San Francisco: Chandler Publishing Company, 1965), and his book, *Sociologie actuelle de l'Afrique Noire* (Paris: Presses Universitaires de France, 1955).

41 Leonard Thompson, "France and Britain in Africa: A Perspective," in Prosser Gifford and William Roger Louis, eds., *France and Britain in Africa: Imperial Rivalry and Colonial Rule* (New Haven: Yale University Press, 1971), pp. 777–8.

42 Pierre Alexandre, "Social Pluralism in French African Colonies and in States Issuing Therefrom: An Impressionistic Approach," in Kuper and Smith, eds., *Pluralism*, p. 195.

43 Balandier, "Colonial Situation," p. 54.

44 Alexandre notes that "There is a surprising scarcity of French materials on plural societies . . . " ("Social Pluralism," p. 195).

45 Philip Curtin presents data ranking former African colonies by percentage of the colonial population which was European. Not surprisingly, the top three countries – South Africa, Algeria, and Rhodesia-Zimbabwe – "are the three places in Africa where European settlers have fought or declared their intention to fight for their local dominance. . . . " See his "Black Experience of Colonialism and Imperialism," *Daedalus* 103 (1974): 23–4.

46 In the case of colonial Algeria, see, for example, John Ruedy, *Land Policy in Colonial Algeria* (Berkeley: University of California Press, 1967); Yacono, *Les bureaux arabes et l'évolution des genres de vie indigènes dans l'ouest du Tell algérois (Dahra, Chélif Ouarsenis, Sersou)* (Paris, 1953); and Sari, *Dépossession*.

47 Thornton, *Doctrines*, p. 43. The model I have in mind here is E. P. Thompson's *The Making of the English Working Class* (London: Gollancz, 1963).

48 Another implication of this view is that it distinguishes between varieties of colonialism on the basis of the intensity of impact on indigenous social structure and culture. Thus, in place of a typology of colonialism based on the various colonizing powers (French "direct" rule, British "indirect" rule), a schema is substituted according to various colonizing agents and the intensity of colonialism ranging from direct and indirect rule to settler colonialism.

49 See Balandier, "Colonial Situation," p. 47; Kuper, "Structural Discontinuities," p. 133; Pierre L. van den Berghe, "Race, Class, and Ethnicity in South Africa," in A. Tuden and L. Plotnicov, eds., *Social Stratification in Africa* (New York: Free Press, 1970), p. 356; Nora, *Les Français*, p. 49; Frantz Fanon, *The Wretched of the Earth* (New York: Grove Press, 1968), p. 40; Emmanuel, "White Settler Colonialism"; A. L. Epstein, *Politics in an Urban African Community* (Manchester: Manchester University Press, 1958); Max Gluckman, "Tribalism, Ruralism and Urbanism in South and Central Africa," in Turner, ed., *Colonialism in Africa*; J. C. Mitchell, "Perceptions of Ethnicity and Ethnic Behavior: An Empirical Exploration," in A. Cohen, ed., *Urban Ethnicity* (London: Tavistock, 1974); Mitchell, "Race, Class, and Status in South Central Africa," in Tuden and Plotnicov, eds., *Social Stratification*; and Immanuel Wallerstein, "The Colonial Era in Africa: Changes in the Social Structure," in Turner, ed., *Colonialism in Africa*.

50 Nicholls, *Three Varieties*, p. 46.

51 *Les Français*, p. 104.

52 "A Tale of Two Cities: The Origins of Modern Cairo," *Comparative Studies in Society and History* 7 (1965): 429.

53 Throughout this study a city is defined broadly to encompass not only what transpires within the city walls or boundaries, but in addition with the political, socioeconomic, and cultural extensions of the city in the surrounding region and beyond. On city-hinterland relationships, see the remarks by C. A. Bayly and Rhoads Murphey in Dilip Basu, ed., *The Colonial Port City in Asia* (Santa Cruz: Institute of Pacific Relations, UC Santa Cruz, 1978), pp. 24, 34, respectively; on local-national political linkages, see Anton Blok,

Notes

The Mafia of a Sicilian Village, 1860–1960 (New York: Harper and Row, 1974); on colonial culture, see King, *Colonial Urban Development*, pp. 58–66; and on regional versus urban analysis generally, see especially, Carol A. Smith, ed., *Regional Analysis*, 2 vols. (New York: Academic Press, 1976).

54 The quotation is from Kingsley Davis quoted in D. J. Dwyer, ed., *The City in the Third World* (New York: Harper and Row, 1974), p. 11. See also, Dwyer, p. 12; McGee, *Urbanization Process*; James L. Cobban, "Uncontrolled Urban Settlement: The Kampong Question in Semarang (1905–1940)," *Bijdragen tot de Taal-, Land- en Volkenkunde van Nederlandsch-Indie* 130 (1974): 403–27; Abu-Lughod, ed., *Third World Urbanization*, p. 105; Bert F. Hoselitz, "The Role of Urbanization in Economic Development: Some International Comparisons," in Dwyer, ed., *City in Third World*, pp. 169–90; and William J. Barber, "Urbanisation and Economic Growth: The Cases of Two White Settler Territories," in Miner, ed., *City in Modern Africa*, pp. 91–125.

55 King, *Colonial Urban Development*, p. 14. Cf. Basu, ed., *Colonial Port City*, p. xiv.

56 See Horvath, "In Search of a Theory of Urbanization: Notes on the Colonial City," *East Lakes Geographer* 5 (1969): 72, and the references cited in King, *Colonial Urban Development*, pp. 22–3. But most of these studies at best simply incorporate colonial cities into their own categories as in Redfield and Singer's orthogenetic-heterogenetic cities, or Hoselitz' generative-parasitic cities. See Robert Redfield and Milton Singer, "The Cultural Role of Cities," *Economic Development and Cultural Change* 3/4 (1954): 53–73; and Hoselitz, *Sociological Aspects of Economic Growth* (Glencoe, IL: Free Press, 1960), chap. 8, "Generative and Parasitic Cities."

57 See King, *Colonial Urban Development*, p. 23. King himself has written virtually the first extended study of the colonial city. Though it can be faulted severely for its lack of conceptual clarity and of a thorough historical grounding, it is the first study to explicitly identify the colonial city as a conceptual category valid in its own right, to offer a case study of colonial New Delhi, and perhaps most important, to offer a number of provocative suggestions on how to "read" a colonial city. See also Horvath, "Notes on the Colonial City"; Richard Fox, *Urban Anthropology* (Englewood Cliffs, NJ: Prentice-Hall, 1977); Basu, ed., *Colonial Port City*; and esp. McGee, *Urbanization Process*, chaps. 1–3, and *The Southeast Asian City*.

58 McGee, *Urbanization Process*, p. 50.

59 *Loc. cit.*; Geertz, *Indonesian Town*, p. 91; Horvath, "Notes on Colonial City," pp. 79–80.

60 It will be seen later that many protocolonial cities become colonial cities and that most colonial cities become postcolonial cities. "Protocolonial" will be used here instead of "precolonial" because, although protocolonial cities exhibit several features of colonial cities in embryonic form, they are by no means transformed automatically into colonial cities as we shall see.

61 A. Das Gupta, quoted in Basu, ed., *Colonial Port City*, p. 39.

62 Is it necessary to point out that the model limned here is an ideal-type, to use Weber's terminology, and thus does not claim to fit all possible cases,

265

or even a single case in all its complexity, but that as with all model-building the ultimate test of its efficacy must be whether it fits enough cases to be analytically useful.

63 McGee, *Southeast Asian City*; Rhoads Murphey, *The Outsiders* (Ann Arbor, MI: University of Michigan Press, 1977); Carlo M. Cipolla, *Guns, Sails and Empires* (Minerva Press, 1965); J. H. Parry, *The Establishment of the European Hegemony: 1415–1715* (New York: Harper and Row, 1961); C. R. Boxer, *Four Centuries of Portuguese Expansion, 1415–1825* (Berkeley: University of California Press, 1972).

64 McGee, *Southeast Asian City*, pp. 43–4.

65 Murphey, *Outsiders*, p. 13; Murphey, "Traditionalism and Colonialism: Changing Urban Roles in Asia," *Journal of Asian Studies* 29 (1969): 67–84.

66 Jim Masselos in Basu, ed., *Colonial Port City*, p. 222.

67 McGee, *Southeast Asian City*, pp. 50–1.

68 *Ibid.*, p. 51. See also Kingsley Davis, "Colonial Expansion and Urban Diffusion in the Americas," reprinted in Dwyer, ed., *City in Third World*, p. 40.

69 To a lesser extent, the form colonialism took in Brazil, namely the Portuguese plantation economy, and in Indonesia, the Dutch culture system, also should be distinguished from European colonialism elsewhere. Cf. McGee, *Southeast Asian City*; Davis, "Colonial Expansion and Urban Diffusion"; and Geertz, *Agricultural Involution* (Berkeley: University of California Press, 1963).

70 Robert R. Reed, "The Foundation and Morphology of Hispanic Manila," in Basu, ed., *Colonial Port City*, p. 170. See also his *Colonial Manila* (Berkeley: University of California Press, 1978).

71 Davis, "Colonial Expansion and Urban Diffusion," p. 37; Reed, "Hispanic Manila," p. 172.

72 Some authors see the introduction of formal political control and the transformation of hinterland areas by steamships and railroads as two distinct stages in the development of the colonial city. See, for example, A. Das Gupta and Thomas Metcalf in Basu, ed., *Colonial Port City*, pp. 247–8. These twin processes are intertwined to such an extent and the number of local variations are great enough that I would argue it is more valid historically to consider them as two aspects of the same general transforming process.

73 McGee, *Southeast Asian City*, p. 74; Josef Gugler and William G. Flanagan, *Urbanization and Social Change in West Africa* (Cambridge, England: Cambridge University Press, 1978), p. 28.

74 McGee, *Urbanization Process*, p. 51. See also Thomas Hodgkin quoted in Gugler and Flanagan, *West Africa*, p. 30; James R. Scobie, *Buenos Aires: Plaza to Suburb, 1870–1910* (New York: Oxford Unitersity Press, 1974); Scobie, "Buenos Aires as a Commercial-Bureaucratic City, 1880–1910," *American Historical Review* 77 (1972): 1035–73.

75 On the tertiary sector, see McGee, *Southeast Asian City*, p. 75; *Urbanization Process*, p. 51 and the references cited at p. 90, note 7.

76 The crucial importance of the plural nature of the colonial city is pointed

out by several commentators. See, for example, Horvath, "Notes on Colonial City," pp. 74–5; McGee, *Southeast Asian City*, p. 74.

77 See Hilda Kuper, " 'Strangers' in Plural Societies: Asians in South Africa and Uganda," in Kuper and Smith, eds., *Pluralism in Africa*; Leo Kuper, "Structural Discontinuities," pp. 141–2; Floyd and Lillian Dotson, "Indians and Coloureds in Rhodesia and Nyasaland," reprinted in van den Berghe, ed., *Africa: Social Problems of Change and Conflict* (San Francisco: Chandler Publishing Co., 1965).

78 M. Bienefeld, "The Informal Sector and Peripheral Capitalism: The Case of Tanzania," *Bulletin of the Institute of Development Studies* 6 (1975): 53–73; Chris Gerry, *Petty Producers and the Urban Economy: A Case Study in Dakar* (Geneva: International Labor Office, 1974); Keith Hart, "Informal Income Opportunities and Urban Employment in Ghana," *Journal of Modern African Studies* 11 (1973): 61–89; Caroline Moser, "Informal Sector or Petty Commodity Production: Dualism or Dependence in Urban Development?" *World Development* 6 (1978): 1048–68; Bryan R. Roberts, "The Provincial Urban System and the Process of Dependency," in Alejandro Portes and H. Browning, eds., *Current Perspectives in Latin American Urban Research* (Austin: University of Texas Press, 1976), pp. 99–132.

79 For a fuller discussion of these points, see McGee, *Southeast Asian City*, chap. 6; and John E. Brush, "Spatial Patterns of Population in Indian Cities," reprinted in Dwyer, ed., *City in Third World*.

80 Brush, "Indian Cities," pp. 113–14; McGee, *Southeast Asian City*, pp. 43–51, 65–6, 103–5; McGee, *Urbanization Process*, pp. 48–51; Gugler and Flanagan, eds., *West Africa*, p. 29; Hodgkin cited in Gugler and Flanagan, p. 30.

81 King, *Colonial Urban Development*, p. 17.

82 Susan Neild in Basu, ed., *Colonial Port City*, p. 237.

83 McGee, *Urbanization Process*, p. 51; McGee, *Southeast Asian City*, pp. 65, 97, 115–22.

84 McGee, *Southeast Asian City*, p. 140.

85 Whereas postcolonial cities used to be viewed as occupying a halfway position between the preindustrial and industrial city, midway between tradition and modernity, they are now seen as mixtures containing preindustrial and industrial elements. In lieu of a "slow movement toward modernization and industrialism," such cities are typified instead by "directionless motion in space." (Fox, *Urban Anthropology*, p. 139). This change in opinion can be seen clearly in the work of Gideon Sjöberg. In *The Pre-Industrial City* (Glencoe, IL: Free Press, 1960), he divided all cities into either preindustrial or industrial ones and presented a detailed study of the former. Five years later Sjöberg added a new category to his schema, namely the "industrializing city," to describe Third World cities in transition from the preindustrial to the industrial mode ("Cities in Developing and in Industrial Societies: A Cross-Cultural Analysis," in Philip Hauser and Leo Schnore, eds., *The Study of Urbanization* [New York: John Wiley, 1965]).

86 McGee, *Southeast Asian City*, p. 99. In my opinion what McGee says about

contemporary Southeast Asian cities applies equally to postcolonial cities elsewhere.

87 *Ibid.*, p. 93.

88 Sten Nilsson, *The New Capitals of India, Pakistan, and Bangladesh* (Stockholm: Scandinavian Institute of South Asian Studies), pp. 158, 204.

89 *The Wretched of the Earth* (New York: Grove Press, 1963), pp. 38–9. On the settler city, see Kuper, "Structural Discontinuties"; Barber, "Urbanisation and Economic Growth"; and Leo Kuper, Hilstan Watts, and Ronald Davies, *Durban: A Study in Racial Ecology* (London: Jonathan Cape, 1958).

90 King, *Colonial Urban Development*, p. 232; Abu-Dughod, *Cairo* (Princeton: Princeton University Press, 1971), p. 98; André Adam, *Casablanca*, 2 vols. (Paris: Centre National de la Recherche Scientifique, 1972), p. 149; René Lespès, *Alger* (Paris: Alcan, 1930), pp. 494, 506, 517; Lespès, *Oran* (Paris: Alcan, 1938), Graphique V; APCA, *Listes nominatives*, 1872–1954.

91 Kuper, "Structural Discontinuites," pp. 135, 137.

92 Smith, *French Stake in Algeria*, p. 86. Smith's distinction between a settler colonial economy (and by extension a settler colonial city) and a "regular" colonial economy (and colonial city) is clear. See also Barber, "Urbanisation and Economic Growth," pp. 109–10.

93 Michael Banton, "Urbanization and the Color Line in Africa," in Turner, ed., *Colonialism in Africa*, pp. 282–3.

94 See King, *Colonial Urban Development*, pp. 156–79 and the references cited on p. 157.

95 Examples in colonial Bône would include the municipal council, where the Algerians were guaranteed no more and no less than six out of twenty-seven seats, the Chamber of Commerce, and the *Conseil de Prud'hommes*, the body which heard labor grievances.

96 Smith, "Institutional and Political Conditions of Pluralism," in Kuper and Smith, eds., *Pluralism in Africa*, p. 56.

97 Ronald Robinson, "Non-European Foundations of European Imperialism: Sketch for a Theory of Collaboration," in R. Owen and B. Sutcliffe, eds., *Studies in the Theory of Imperialism* (London: Longman, 1972), p. 122.

98 See Philip Curtin, "The Black Experience of Colonialism and Imperialism," *Daedalus* 103/2 (Spring, 1974): 25.

99 Marc Baroli, *La vie quotidienne des Français en Algérie 1830–1914* (Paris: Hachette, 1967), pp. 213, 255, 260–1.

100 "En Algérie," *Annales d'histoire économique et sociale* (1938), p. 510.

101 André Nouschi, "North Africa in the Period of Colonization," in P. M. Holt et. al., eds., *The Cambridge History of Islam*, vol. 2A (Cambridge: Cambridge University Press, 1970), p. 306.

102 It is significant that both Ageron (*Les Algériens musulmans*) and Nouschi (*Enquête*) also halt their monumental studies at the same period. There is also the question of sources to consider. It is certainly my impression after working extensively in the Annaba archives that the sources for 1870–1920 are richer, more detailed, and better preserved than those after. (For a description of the Annaba archives, see Sources and Bibliography.) More-

over, the relative decline in the quality of documentation in the Annaba municipal archives after the First World War reflects no doubt the growing size of the town and the concomitant difficulties of record keeping to keep pace – factors by no means limited to Annaba alone. Thus, census categories were reduced and responses tended to be briefer, for example.

103 Jean Duvignaud, *Change at Shebika: Report from a North African Village* (New York: Random House, 1970).

104 Lawrence Stone, "The Revival of Narrative," reprinted in *The Past and the Present* (Boston: Routledge & Kegan Paul, 1981), pp. 74–96.

105 Clifford Geertz, "Blurred Genres: The Refiguration of Social Thought," reprinted in his *Local Knowledge* (New York: Basic Books, 1983).

106 See, for example, Paul Rabinow, *Reflections on Fieldwork in Morocco* (Berkeley: University of California Press, 1978); Renato Rosaldo, *Ilongot Headhunting, 1883–1974* (Stanford: Stanford University Press, 1980); James Clifford, *Person and Myth: Maurice Leenhardt in the Melanesian World* (Berkeley: University of California Press, 1982); Vincent Crapanzano, *Tuhami: Portrait of a Moroccan* (Chicago: University of Chicago Press, 1980); and James Clifford and George Marcus, eds., *Writing Culture: The Poetics and Politics of Ethnography* (Berkeley: University of California Press, 1986).

Chapter 2

1 René Bouyac, *Histoire de Bône* (Paris: Lecene, Oudin et Cie, 1892); Albert-Charles Maitrot, *Bône militaire* (Bône: Mariani, 1934).

2 Precisely the same European travelers I rely on most – Peyssonnel, Desfontaines, Poiret – are the ones Valensi, for example, singles out as being "less ethnocentric" and "imbued with the spirit of the Enlightenment." Lucette Valensi, *Le Maghreb avant la prise d'Alger 1790–1830* (Paris: Flammarion, 1969), p. 17. See Jean André Peyssonnel, *Relation d'un voyage sur les côtes de Barbarie 1724–5*, and Louis René Desfontaines, *Fragments d'un voyage dans les régences de Tunis et d'Alger fait de 1783 à 1786*, both in Dureau de la Malle, ed., *Voyages dans la régence de Tunis et d'Alger* (Paris: Librairie de Gide, 1838); and l'Abbé Poiret, *Voyage en Barbarie, ou lettres écrites de l'ancienne Numidie en 1785 et 1786 sur la religion, les coutumes et les moeurs des Maures et des Arabes Bedouins* (Paris: chez Née de la Rochelle, 1789).

3 The *Exploration scientifique de l'Algérie pendant les années 1840, 1841, 1842* (Paris: Imprimerie Royale, 1844–67) runs to 39 volumes, and the *Tableau de la situation des Etablissements français dans l'Algérie* [hereafter TEFA] (Paris: Imprimerie Royale, 1838–68) to 19 volumes.

4 On the geography of the Annaba region, see Peyssonnel, *Relation d'un voyage*; Poiret, *Voyage en Barbarie*; L'Abbé de Pietri, *Détails sur Bône et ses environs et divers autres sujets* (Algiers: Philippe, 1836); M. Dureau de la Malle, *Province de Constantine. Recueil de renseignements pour l'expédition ou l'établissement des français dans cette partie de l'Afrique septentrionale* (Paris: Gide, 1837); O. Niel, *Algérie. Géographie générale et guide du*

voyageur, 3rd edition, 2 vols. (Paris: chez Challamel, 1883); and Lucette Travers, "Bône. La Formation de la ville et les facteurs de son évolution," *Annales de Géographie* (1958): 498–520.

5 Dureau de la Malle, *Constantine*, p. 67.

6 André Nouschi, *Enquête sur le niveau de vie des populations rurales constantinoises de la conquête jusqu'en 1919* (Paris: Presses Universitaires de France, 1961), p. 45; Yvonne Turin, *Affrontements culturels dans l'Algérie coloniale. Ecoles, médecines, religion, 1830–1880* (Paris: Maspero, 1971), p. 134 and Tableaux des Zaouia. The data on tents and *gourbis* are based on 1845 data. On "reading" such data backwards for 1830, see notes 23 and 25.

7 For descriptions of Annaba in 1830, see Maitrot, *Bône militaire*; Chollet, "Bône, 1830–1880" (unpublished D.E.S., Université d'Alger, 1952); Poiret, *Voyage en Barbarie*; Pietri, *Détails sur Bône*; and Peyssonnel, *Relation d'un voyage*. Cf. also René Lespès, *Alger. Etude de géographie et d'historie urbaines* (Paris: Alcan, 1930).

8 Georges Marçais, "La Mosquée de Sidi Bou Marwan de Bône," in *Mélanges d'Histoire et d'Archéologie de l'Occident musulman*, 2 vols. (Algiers, 1957), p. 234. Marçais's information came from an elderly Muslim who had read it in a manuscript, *Dourra maknouna*, by a local resident, Ahmed al-Bouni. Marçais never saw the manuscript for it had disappeared in 1914 and another copy has never been found.

9 Alexandre Papier, "La Mosquée de Bône," *Revue Africaine* 33/195 (1889): 312; Turin, *Affrontements culturels*, p. 134. But see Maitrot, *Bône militaire*, pp. 486–8.

10 John Ruedy, *Land Policy in Colonial Algeria* (Berkeley: University of California Press, 1967), pp. 70–2.

11 Maitrot, *Bône militaire*, p. 492; Chollet, *Bône*, pt. 3, chap. 2.

12 Maitrot, *Bône militaire*, p. 493. On neighborhoods in particular and social structure in general, see pp. 48–51.

13 Poiret, *Voyage en Barbarie*, pp. 129–30.

14 Peyssonnel, *Relation d'un voyage*, p. 278.

15 See, for example, Thomas Shaw, *Travels or observations relating to several parts of Barbary and the Levant*, 2nd ed., 1757, reprinted in John Pinkerton, *A General Collection of the Best and Most Interesting Voyages and Travels in all Parts of the World* (London, 1814), p. 656; Pietri, *Détails sur Bône*, p. 20. For a discussion of how these and other alleged differences were concretized in later French colonial policy in a variation of "divide and rule," see Chapter 1.

16 Xavier Yacono, "Peut-on évaluer la population de l'Algérie vers 1830?" *Revue Africaine* (1950): 277–307; Nouschi, *Enquête*, pp. 30–1. The figure for the Annaba region is based on the combined 1845 population of the administrative areas, or *cercles*, of Bône and the Edough. Nouschi – and he is the authority on this matter – has estimated the population in 1830 by working backwards from the figures gathered in 1845. The Annaba area was divided into four *cercles* by the French in 1838. While the *cercle* of Bône does not correspond exactly to the plain of Annaba and the *cercle* of the Edough does

not correspond exactly to the Edough Mountains, they are certainly close enough for my purpose here and in the pages to follow which is to convey a sense of the Annaba region as a whole and the contrast between the mountains and the plains in particular.

17 In the North African context, "tribe" is an umbrella term which encompasses a plethora of differing social organizations. For a discussion of the complexities of a seemingly simple concept, see Jacques Berque, "Qu'est-ce qu'une tribu nord africaine?" in *Eventail de l'histoire vivante. Hommage à Lucien Febvre* (Paris, 1953), vol. 1, pp. 261–71.

18 Figures in Table 2.1 are for 1845 and would have to be increased by roughly ten percent to arrive at an estimation of the population in 1830. On the problem of deriving 1830 totals from the 1845 survey, see Nouschi, *Enquête*, pp. 20–30.

19 Nouschi, *Enquête*, pp. 31–2, 34–5; Nouschi, "Notes sur la vie traditionelle des populations forestières algériennes," *Annales de Géographie* 68 (1959): 526.

20 The idealized notion of genealogical descent from a common ancestor is related in turn to lineage segmentation, an all-encompassing theory often invoked to explain the social organization of these Arab and Berber groupings. But "in attempting to describe the nature of 'traditional' Algerian society, foreign observers during the nineteenth century usually accepted these representations [kinship and descent, segment and tribe] at face value, failing to see them as largely ideological..." (David Seddon, "Economic Anthropology or Political Economy?: Approaches to the Analysis of Pre-Capitalist Formation in the Maghreb," in John Clammer, ed., *The New Economic Anthropology* [New York: St. Martin's Press, 1978], p. 87). See this Chapter for a discussion of lineage segmentation. Cf. also Berque, "Qu'est-ce qu'une tribu."

21 A. Sainte-Marie, "Etude des migrations dans la Régence d'Alger," in *Les Migrations dans les pays méditerranéens au XVIIIe et au début du XIXe siècles* (Nice: Centre de la Méditerranée moderne et contemporaine, 1974), pp. 158–73; Valensi, *Le Maghreb*, pp. 31–3.

22 On the Merdès, see AOM, M 71 (283) Sénatus Consulte. Merdès; 21 KK 13 Bureau Arabe de Constantine. Merdès.

23 On the people of Annaba in particular and the Algerians in general, see Grenville T. Temple, *Excursions in the Mediterranean: Algiers and Tunis* (London: Saunders and Otley, 1835); C.-A. Rozet, *Voyage dans la Régence d'Alger* (Paris: Arthus Bernard, 1833), vol. 2, pp. 6–302; Peyssonnel, *Relation d'un voyage*; Pierre Boyer, *La Vie quotidienne à Alger à la veille de l'intervention française* (Paris: Hachette, 1963), pp. 131–77; Poiret, *Voyage en Barbarie*; and M. Eisenbeth, "Les Juifs en Algérie et en Tunisie à l'époque turque (1516–1830)," *Revue africaine*, 96 (1952): 114–87, 344–84.

24 Poiret, *Voyage en Barbarie*, p. 130. Compared at least to Jewish-European relations, Jewish-Arab relations in the Maghrib are generally considered to have been good. But for a revisionist interpretation, see Norman Stillman, "L'expérience judéo-marocaine: Un point de vue révisionniste," in Michel

Abitbol, ed., *Judaïsme d'Afrique du Nord aux XIXe-XXe siècles* (Jerusalem: Institut Ben-Zvi, 1980), pp. 5–24. Cf. also *Les relations entre juifs et musulmans en Afrique du Nord* (Paris: Editions du Centre National de la Recherche Scientifique, 1980).

25 On the Jews of Livorno, see J. P. Filippini, "Livourne et l'Afrique du Nord au 18e siècle," *Revue d'Histoire Maghrébine* 7–8 (1977): 125–49.

26 Dureau de la Malle, *Constantine*, pp. 142–3; Travers, "Bône," p. 499. On crop failures, see Valensi, *Le Maghreb*, pp. 23–4; on illness and disease, see Nouschi, *Enquête*, pp. 37–9.

27 On the plague in Annaba, see Adrien Berbrugger, "Mémoire sur la peste en Algérie depuis 1522 jusqu'en 1819," in *Exploration scientifique, Series II: Sciences médicales*, vol. 2, pp. 214–5, 217, 219, 222–3, 232–3. Cf. Lucette Valensi, "Calamités démographiques en Tunisie et en Méditerranée orientale aux XVIIIe et XIXe siècles," *Annales E.S.C.* 24 (1969): 1540–61; and Nancy Gallagher, *Medicine and Power in Tunisia, 1780–1900* (New York: Cambridge University Press, 1983).

28 Poiret, *Voyage en Barbarie*, p. 107.

29 Quoted in Valensi, *Le Maghreb*, p. 22.

30 On material culture, see Nouschi, *Enquête*, pp. 39–52.

31 Quoted in Nouschi, *Enquête*, p. 42.

32 On the rural economy of the Annaba area, see in particular TEFA 1844–5, pp. 400, 403, 422–3, 426; Nouschi, *Enquête*, pp. 54–75; Nouschi, "Populations forestières"; Desfontaines, *Fragments d'un voyage* in Dureau de la Malle, ed., *Voyages*, pp. 199, 223.

33 As with Table 2.1, data for 1845 should be increased by a factor of approximately ten percent to arrive at the number of animals in 1830 since 1845 was a bad year climatically and because French military raids had reduced the size of the herds.

34 Richard W. Bulliet, "Le chameau et la roue au Moyen-Orient," *Annales ESC* 24/5 (1969): 1092–1103; Bulliet, *The Camel and the Wheel* (Cambridge: Harvard University Press).

35 On land in Algeria, see Ruedy, *Land*, pp. 4–12; Nouschi, *Enquête*, pp. 78–94. On land in the Annaba region, see AOM, M 71 (283) Sénatus Consulte. Merdès; 21 KK 13 Bureau Arabe de Constantine. Merdès; Turin, *Affrontements culturels*, p. 134.

36 AOM, M 71 (283) Sénatus Consulte. Merdès.

37 Nouschi, *Enquête*, pp. 96–102; Claude Bontems, *Manuel des institutions algériennes de la domination turque à l'indépendance, Vol. 1: La Domination turque et la régime militaire 1518–1870* (Paris: Editions Cujas, 1975), pp. 66–9. There were two Koranic taxes, the *achour*, which was widespread throughout Algeria, and the *zakat*, which was not collected in Constantine province. Actually, the *achour* was instituted in Constantine province only after the French had arrived in 1830–2 but before Constantine city fell to the French in 1837. The last Bey of Constantine, Ahmed Bey, substituted the *achour* for the *djabri*, a tax instituted by Salah Bey at the end of the eighteenth century, in an effort to streamline tax collection.

38 The taxes collected also fluctuated enormously from the amounts which

actually ended up in the Bey's coffers, because tax collection was farmed out to private individuals in the absence of a Turkish fiscal apparatus. We can only imagine the amount of corruption the process entailed, the amount of baksheesh which passed hands. It has been estimated that one-third of the taxes assessed found their way to the Bey – and still there was two million francs in the Bey's treasury at the time of the French invasion. See Nouschi, *Enquête*, p. 116.

39 AOM, M 84 (75) Sénatus Consulte. Senhadja; M 78 (275) Sénatus Consulte. Beni Salah; M 71 (283) Sénatus Consulte. Merdès; 21 KK 13 Bureau Arabe de Constantine. Merdès. It was in such a *razzia* against the Merdès that the *azel* Oued Besbes was confiscated.

40 Quoted in Nouschi, *Enquête*, p. 130. For a discussion of the incidence of taxation and the overall standard of living in Constantine province, see Nouschi, *Enquête*, pp. 102–16, 130–55.

41 Charles-André Julien, *Histoire de l'Afrique du Nord*, Vol. 2, second edition, trans. by John Petrie (Paris: Payot, 1968), p. 321. See also Desfontaines, *Fragments d'un voyage*, p. 226; Peyssonnel, *Relation d'un voyage*, pp. 269–70; Valensi, *Le Maghreb*, p. 68; Barbour, "Northwest Africa," pp. 99–101, 125; André Raymond, "North Africa in the Pre-Colonial Period," in P. M. Holt et al., *The Cambridge History of Islam, Vol. 2: The Farther Islamic Lands, Islamic Society and Civilization* (Cambridge: Cambridge University Press, 1970), pp. 282–4; Lespès, *Alger*, p. 139.

42 Raphael Danziger, *Abd al-Qadir and the Algerians* (New York: Holmes & Meier, 1977), p. 25.

43 They included the Les Sâada, Beni Mohammed, Arbouem, Oulhassa, Beni Mouna, Garbes, Chabia, Zaouiah, Ouichaoua, Ain Abdallah, El Guerrerah, Kabyles-Seybouse, Kabyles-Guelma, Beni Ourseddin, Ouled Sidi Aissa, El Marounach, Ouled Salem, Ouled Sidi Afif, Guerarfa, Merdès, Beni Salah, Ouled Bou Aziz, Ouled Senan, Beni Urgine, Sebaa du Kef, Sebaa de Tunis, Hannencha, Biskera, Khareza, Arabes du Sahra, Beni Ouzenat, Zamoura, Beni Fougal, Ouled Diam, Chorfa, Ouled Kebeb, and Saouda. TEFA 1842, p. 95; TEFA 1843, p. 84; Poiret, *Voyage*, pp. 20–1. On rural-urban relations, see Kenneth Brown, *People of Salé* (Cambridge: Harvard University Press, 1976), p. 55.

44 The number of Moors practicing these trades in 1833–4 after the French invasion differed undoubtedly from the number in 1830 before the invasion. Nevertheless, the proportion of Moors working at various trades should give an accurate indication of the range of commercial activity in Annaba. On urban economic life, see also Valensi, *Le Maghreb*, pp. 54–57; Lespès, *Alger*, pp. 141–64; and Nouschi, "Constantine à la veille de la conquête française," *Les Cahiers de Tunisie* 3/11 (1955): 371–87.

45 On guilds, see note 67.

46 Nouschi, "Constantine," p. 381.

47 Peyssonnel, *Relation d'un voyage*, pp. 316, 326–7, 338. Such a caravan constitutes a procession of the sort analyzed by Clifford Geertz in "Centers, Kings, and Charisma: Reflections on the Symbolics of Power," reprinted in his *Local Knowledge* (New York: Basic Books, 1983).

Notes

48 On Annaba's external trade, see Maitrot, *Bône militaire*, pp. 101–69; Bouyac, *Bône*, pp. 85–118; Paul Masson, *Histoire des etablissements et du commerce français dans l'Afrique barbaresque (1560–1793)* (Paris: Hachette, 1903); Eisenbeth, "Les Juifs en Algérie"; Valensi, *Le Maghreb*, pp. 70–83. Cf. also Marcel Emerit, "Les liaisons terrestres entre le Soudan et l'Afrique du Nord au XVIIIe et au début du XIXe siècle," *Travaux de l'Institut des Recherches Sahariennes* 11 (1954): pp. 29–47.

49 Poiret, *Voyage en Barbarie*, p. 20.

50 Quoted in Nouschi, *Enquête*, p. 124.

51 For a recent attempt to synthesize the vast bulk of this work, see Eric Wolf, *Europe and the People Without History* (Berkeley: University of California Press, 1982). On the topic of trade and the nascent world economy, see Philip Curtin, *Cross-Cultural Trade in World History* (New York: Cambridge University Press, 1984). Mode of production analyses shade off into discussions of dependency on the one hand, and world systems theory on the other hand. The literature on these subjects is too vast to be broached here but a useful starting point for world systems is Immanuel Wallerstein, "The Rise and Future Demise of the World Capitalist System," *Comparative Studies in Society and History* 16 (1974): 387–415; and for dependency, see Ivar Oxall, Tony Barnett and David Booth, eds., *Beyond the Sociology of Development* (London: Routledge & Kegan Paul, 1975).

52 René Gallissot et. al., *Sur le féodalisme*, Cahiers du Centre d'Etudes et de Recherches Marxistes (Paris: Editions Sociales, 1971), pp. 147–79. See also Seddon, "Pre-Capitalist Formations in the Maghreb." In Eric Wolf's global view, a worldwide tributary mode of production encompasses European feudalism at one extreme and the so-called Asiatic mode of production at the other. Wolf draws on Gallissot to slot precolonial Algeria on this continuum. Cf. Wolf, *Europe*, pp. 79–88, 403–4. French historians of the *Annales* school contest the French Marxist approach to precolonial North Africa. The two sides of the debate are presented in Gallissot, "L'Algérie précoloniale," and Valensi, "Archaisme de la société maghrébine," pp. 147–79 and 223–32, respectively, in Gallissot, *Sur le féodalisme*. See also Edmund Burke, "Towards a History of the Maghrib," *Middle Eastern Studies* 11 (1975): 312–3.

53 Even as theoretical speculation, however, Gallissot's model fails to account for certain crucial elements. Perhaps the most serious flaw is the fact that "command feudalism" describes the mode of production at work inside precolonial Algeria with no reference to relations outside. Yet as we have seen, precolonial Algeria was not a closed society – it was involved to a certain extent with the Ottoman Empire, Europe, and sub-Saharan Africa – and, therefore, this interconnection must be accounted for. Yet the question of delineating the links between Algeria and the world outside opens up another whole can of worms for mode of production theorists, namely, how do different modes of production articulate with one another? Since this leads even further away from a consideration of precolonial Annaba *wie es eigentlich gewesen*, however, it has not been pursued here.

54 Nouschi, *Enquête*, p. 154.

55 Valensi, *Le Maghreb*, p. 44; Nouschi, *Enquête*, pp. 147–55. The point is often made that one-fifth of the rural population may have been sharecroppers, but at least they had access to the land, and therefore did not constitute a genuine rural proletariat of agricultural day laborers.

56 F. Stambouli and A. Zghal, "Urban life in pre-colonial North Africa," *British Journal of Sociology* 27/1 (March 1976): 1–20; Ira M. Lapidus, "The Evolution of Muslim Urban Society," *Comparative Studies in Society and History* 15/1 (1973): 21–50; Lapidus, "Muslim Urban Society in Mamluk Syria," in A. H. Hourani and S. M. Stern, eds., *The Islamic City* (New York: Oxford University Press, 1970), pp. 195–205; André Raymond, *The Great Arab Cities in the 16th–18th Centuries* (New York: New York University Press, 1984). It should be stressed that such a schema is an idealized view of social reality and reflects the self-conception of those who delineated it, preeminently the *ulama*. Cf. Andrew C. Hess, "Consensus or Conflict: The Dilemma of Islamic Historians," *American Historical Review* (October 1976): 788–99.

57 Nouschi, "Constantine," pp. 383–5. The officials in the Bey's entourage purchased their offices for a total of 290,000 francs.

58 Ernest Gellner, *Saints of the Atlas* (Chicago: University of Chicago Press, 1969). Cf. also his *Muslim Society* (Cambridge: Cambridge University Press, 1981).

59 Two filiations of segmentation theory can be traced, one leading from Robertson Smith (1885) to Evans-Pritchard (1940) and Gellner (1969), and one from Hanoteau and Letourneux (1872–3) and Masqueray (1886) to Durkheim (1893). Cf. Dale Eickelman, *The Middle East* (Englewood Cliffs, NJ: Prentice-Hall, 1981), pp. 33–8, 98–100; and Lucette Valensi, "Le Maghreb vu du Centre: sa place dans l'école sociologique française," in Jean-Claude Vatin et al., *Connaissances du Maghreb* (Paris: Editions du CNRS, 1984), pp. 227–47.

60 Geertz, "In Search of North Africa," *New York Review of Books*, April 22, 1971, pp. 20–4; and "Suq: the bazaar economy in Sefrou," in Geertz, Hildred Geertz, and Lawrence Rosen, *Meaning and Order in Moroccan Society* (New York: Cambridge University Press, 1979), pp. 123–313.

61 Pierre Bourdieu, *Outline of a Theory of Practice* (Cambridge: Cambridge University Press, 1977), pp. 30–71; J. Davis, *People of the Mediterranean* (London: Routledge & Kegan Paul, 1977), pp. 206–18; Ernest Gellner and John Waterbury, eds., *Patrons and Clients in Mediterranean Societies* (London: Duckworth, 1977). For an interpretation of the ties between Moroccans and *marabouts*, or holy men, which contends they are similar to the ties between patrons and clients, see Dale F. Eickelman, "Ideological Change and Regional Cults: Maraboutism and Ties of 'Closeness' in Western Morocco," in R. P. Werbner, ed., *Regional Cults* (London: Academic Press, 1977), pp. 3–28.

62 AOM, 6 H 33: Chefs et personnalitées indigènes. Bône, 1847–1918.

63 Andrew C. Hess, "The Forgotten Frontier: The Ottoman North African Provinces During the Eighteenth Century," in Thomas Naff and Roger Owen, eds., *Studies in Eighteenth-Century Islamic History* (Carbondale, IL: Southern Illinois University Press, 1977), p. 74; Raymond, "North Africa in the Pre-Colonial Period," p. 281; Jamil M. Abun-Nasr, *A History of the*

Maghrib (Cambridge: Cambridge University Press, 1975), p. 175; and Vatin, *L'Algérie politique. Histoire et société* (Paris: Fondation Nationale des Sciences Politiques, 1974), p. 89.

64 Vatin, *L'Algérie politique*, p. 93.

65 Julien, *North Africa*, p. 325 citing Louis Rinn. See also Desfontaines, *Fragments d'un voyage*, p. 217; Poiret, *Voyage en Barbarie*, pp. 153–4; Maitrot, *Bône militaire*, p. 473; Raymond, "North Africa," p. 283; Valensi, *Le Maghreb*, pp. 87–8; Barbour, "Northwest Africa," p. 123. In Morocco the question of the extent of effective rule has been expressed in the dichotomy between *bled l-makhzan*, the area under government control, and *bled s-siba*, the area of dissidence. Cf. Brown, *Salé*, p. 226; Edmund Burke, III, *Prelude to Protectorate in Morocco* (Chicago: University of Chicago Press, 1976), p. 12.

66 See the references cited in notes 41 and 42.

67 See, for example, Danziger, *Abd al-Qadir*, pp. 8–12, esp. p. 8, and the authors he cites there. See Chapter 1 for a discussion of the French myth that the Berbers were more assimilable than the Arabs.

68 Gellner, *Muslim Society*, pp. 1–85.

69 Michael Gilsenan, *Recognizing Islam* (New York: Random House, 1982), p. 34. In Morocco, Edmund Burke notes "that members of the *ulama* were often also strong supporters of particular religious brotherhoods." See his "The Moroccan Ulama, 1860–1912: An Introduction," in Nikki R. Keddie, ed., *Scholars, Saints, and Sufis* (Berkeley: University of California Press, 1972), p. 99. Cf. Fanny Colonna, "Cultural Resistance and Religious Legitimacy in Colonial Algeria," *Economy and Society* 3 (1974): 233–52; Colonna, "Saints furieux et saints studieux ou, dans l'Aurès, comment la religion vient aux tribus," *Annales E.S.C.* 35 (1980): 642–62; and John O. Voll, *Islam: Continuity and Change in the Modern World* (Boulder, CO: Westview Press, 1982).

70 Pietri, *Détails sur Bône*, 8–10; Rachid Boujedra, *La vie quotidienne en Algérie* (Paris: Hachette, 1971), pp. 110–22.

71 Nouschi, "Constantine," pp. 385–6; Brown, *Salé*, pp. 75, 77.

72 TEFA 1844–45, p. 400. See also E. Pellissier de Reynaud, *Annales algériennes*, Vol. 3, second edition (Paris: Dumaine, 1854), p. 489; Valensi, *Le Maghreb*, pp. 36–7.

73 E. E. Evans-Pritchard, *The Sanusi of Cyrenaica* (Oxford: Oxford University Press, 1949); and B. G. Martin, *Muslim Brotherhoods in Nineteenth-Century Africa* (Cambridge: Cambridge University Press, 1976), pp. 99–124.

74 Turin, *Affrontements culturels*, p. 134 and Tableaux des Zaouia.

75 Nouschi, *Enquête*, pp. 66–7; Nouschi, "Populations forestières," p. 534; Valensi, *Le Maghreb*, p. 49.

Chapter 3

1 The most reliable discussion remains Charles-André Julien, *Histoire de l'Algérie contemporaine (1827–1871)* (Paris: Presses Universitaires de France,

1964). On the 1830 revolution in France, see David Pinkney, *The French Revolution of 1830* (Princeton: Princeton University Press, 1972); and John Merriman, ed., *1830 in France* (New York: Franklin Watts, 1975).

2 The quotation is from Marshal Soult speaking before the Chamber of Deputies and quoted in René Bouyac, *Histoire de Bône* (Paris: Lecene, Oudin, 1892), p. 188. On the French invasion of Annaba, see in addition to Bouyac, Albert-Charles Maitrot, *Bône militaire* (Bône: Mariani, 1934); and Comte de Cornulier-Lucinière, *La prise de Bône et de Bougie, d'après des documents inédits* (Paris: Lethielleux, 1895). On Yusuf, whom the French installed in Constantine as their puppet and successor to Ahmed Bey, see Marcel Emerit, "Le mystère Yusuf," *Revue Africaine* 96 (1952): 385–98.

3 TEFA (1840), pp. 94–5; Baron Baude, *l'Algérie*, 2 vols. (Paris: Bertrand, 1841), vol. 1, p. 270.

4 John Ruedy, *Land Policy in Colonial Algeria* (Berkeley: University of California Press, 1967), p. 42.

5 Bouyac, *Bône*, p. 246. On d'Uzer, see TEFA (1837), p. 262; Bouyac, *Bône*, pp. 246–9; Maitrot, *Bône*, pp. 285–7; Louis Arnaud, *Bône. Son histoire, ses histoires* (Constantine, Algeria: Damrémont, 1960), p. 60.

6 Maitrot, *Bône*, p. 321.

7 Julien, *Histoire de l'Algérie*, p. 122.

8 Quoted in Maitrot, *Bône militaire*, p. 319.

9 On the Lavie's, see Louis P. Montoy, "La presse dans le département de Constantine (1870–1918)," 4 vols., doctorat d'état (Aix-en-Provence: Université de Provence, 1982), pp. 50–1, 173, 210, 319, 382, 489, and 724.

10 See Chapter 6.

11 Fernand Rude, "Les fouriéristes lyonnais et la colonisation de l'Algérie," *Cahiers d'Histoire* 1 (1956): 41–63; and David Prochaska, "Fourier and the Colonization of Algeria: *L'Union agricole d'Afrique*, 1846–1853," *Proceedings of the Western Society for French History* 1 (1974): 283–302.

12 François Tomas, *Annaba et sa région* (Saint-Etienne: Guichard, 1977), p. 202. See also Emerit, *Les Saint-Simonians en Algérie* (Paris: Belles Lettres, 1941), p. 184. This latter study is the standard work on the Saint-Simonians in Algeria.

13 Adrien Berbrugger, "M. Marion," *Revue Africaine* 12 (1868): 139–43.

14 Emerit, *Les Saint-Simonians*, p. 101.

15 Julien, *Histoire*, p. 257. Among others, Enfantin's book, *Colonisation de l'Algérie*, influenced the future Napoleon III, who read it while imprisoned in the fortress of Ham for one of his abortive coup attempts.

16 Maxime Rasteil, *Le calvaire des colons de 48* (Paris: Figuière, 1930).

17 TEFA (1837), p. 262; Tomas, *Annaba*, pp. 212–13; Annie Rey-Goldzeiguer, *Le royaume arabe. La politique algérienne de Napoléon III, 1861–1870* (Algiers: SNED, 1977), p. 776.

18 Ruedy, *Land Policy*, pp. 100–1.

19 TEFA (1843–4), p. 237.

20 Tomas, *Annaba*, p. 216.

21 TEFA (1856–8), pp. 406–7.

22 Lucette Travers, "Bône. La formation de la ville et les facteurs de son évolution," *Annales de Géographie* 67 (1958): p. 514. See also Tomas, *Annaba*, p. 214.

23 TEFA (1842–3), p. 5, 114; TEFA (1843–4), pp. 118–9, 145; TEFA (1844–5), p. 152; Arnaud, *Bône*, p. 46; Bouyac, *Bône*, pp. 320–1; Maitrot, *Bône*, pp. 367–70; Eugène Battistini, *Les forêts de chêne-liège de l'Algérie* (Algiers: Heintz, 1937), p. 15; and David Prochaska, "Fire on the Mountain: Resisting Colonialism in Algeria," in Donald Crummey, ed., *Banditry, Rebellion and Social Protest in Africa* (Portsmouth, NH: Heinemann, 1986).

24 Report of concessionaire Cès-Caupenne to Governor-General, extracted in TEFA (1862), pp. 320–1; PP 1893–4, Vol. XCIII, Commercial Reports, Vol. 44, pp. 17–19; PP 1895, Vol. XCVII, Commercial Reports, Vol. 37, p. 57; AOM, 9 X 121, Rapport de la Commission d'Enquête, *Incendies de forêts en 1902 dans la région de Bône* (Algiers: Franceschi, 1903), p. 103.

25 PP 1867–8, Vol. LXVIII, Commercial Reports, Vol. 29, p. 203.

26 Information on forest concessionaires is found in AOM, F 80 1783–7; and Battistini, *Les forêts*.

27 Charles-Robert Ageron, *Les algériens musulmans et la France (1870–1919)*, 2 vols. (Paris: Presses Universitaires de France, 1968), p. 108; André Nouschi, *Enquête sur le niveau de vie des populations rurales constantinoises de la conquête jusqu'en 1919* (Paris: Presses Universitaires de France, 1961), pp. 326–7.

28 While the archival documents regarding Napoleon's concessions are very precise about the size of each concession, they are virtually silent when it comes to determining how much land was taken from which group of Algerians. To find the latter information, we must turn to another set of documents, which, however, were generated for a different reason. This data was produced from the application of the so-called *sénatus-consulte*, which classified and delimited the land of each group of Algerians. At the same time as the French took the measure of the Algerians, however, they used the knowledge obtained to exercise their colonial hegemony, for example, by converting communal *'arsh* to individual *milk* land to break up and sell landholdings more easily, to designate and set aside as yet unconceded forests as state forests, to divide Algerian groups into segments in order to rule them more effectively, or to attach them to *communes de pleine exercice*, full-fledged French communes run by local settlers. A second problem is that the *sénatus-consulte* was applied to some groups in the late 1860s but to others only in the 1890s (including many in the Edough). Yet another problem is that in the course of carrying out the *sénatus-consulte* the French frequently reorganized and renamed the Algerians. Despite these problems, they contain much rich information.

28 Nouschi, *Enquête*, p. 333.

29 *Ibid.*, pp. 333, 336.

30 *La richesse minérale de l'Algérie* (Paris: Imprimerie nationale, 1849), quoted in Emerit, *Les Saint-Simoniens*, p. 183.

31 *La Seybouse*, 24 janvier 1846. On Bassano, see Bertrand Gille, "Minérais

algériens et sidérurgie métropolitaine: Espoirs et réalités (1845–1880)," *Revue d'histoire de la Sidérurgie* 1 (1960): 37–55.

32 Gille, "Minérais algériens," p. 44. Gille says one million tons of cast iron were produced, but Dussert says by the end of 1854 only 3000 tons of ore had been extracted and 600 tons of cast iron produced. See Désiré Dussert, *Les mines et les carrières en Algérie* (Paris: Larose, 1931), pp. 127–8. The enterprise continued to interest steelmakers as late as 1890, for the French firm of Firminy obtained a concession to the Meboudja mine at that date.

33 APCA, Wilaya de Annaba, "Monographie économique de la Wilaya de Annaba" (May 1976, mimeographed). See Chapter 4.

34 Chevallier, in William Polk and Richard Chambers, eds., *Beginnings of Modernization in the Middle East* (Chicago: University of Chicago Press, 1968), p. 215.

35 On Talabot, see A. Ernouf, *Paulin Talabot: sa vie et son oeuvre, 1799–1885* (Paris, 1886); P. Cousteix, "Les financiers sous le Second Empire," *1848: Revue des révolutions contemporaines* 43 (1950): 105–35; Gille, "Minérais algériens"; Gille, *Histoire de la maison Rothschild*, Vol. 2 (1848–1870) (Geneva: Droz, 1967), pp. 188–9, 310–1.

36 Rey-Goldzeiguer, *Le royaume arabe*, p. 672.

37 Gille, "Minérais algériens," pp. 44–5. The Ain Mokra was conceded to Jules Talabot, the Karezas to Charles Girard, who soon ceded it to Léon Talabot, and the Bou Hamra to Louis Peron, who also ceded it to Léon Talabot. Emerit, *Les Saint-Simoniens*, p. 184; Gille, *Minérais algériens*, pp. 38–9.

38 Rey-Goldzeiguer, *Le royaume arabe*, p. 104.

39 TEFA (1846–9), p. 394.

40 Emerit, *Les Saint-Simoniens*, pp. 185–6; Dussert, *Les mines*, pp. 127–31.

41 Gille, "Minérais algériens", p. 46. See also David Landes, *The Unbound Prometheus* (Cambridge: Cambridge University Press, 1969), pp. 255–62.

42 Tom Kemp, *Economic Forces in French History* (London: Dobson, 1971), pp. 157–8; and Alexander Gerschenkron, *Economic Backwardness in Historical Perspective* (Cambridge: Harvard University Press, 1962), pp. 23–4, 191.

43 Gille, "Minérais algériens," p. 52.

44 Tomas, *Annaba*, p. 198. In 1954, it became part of the line spanning the Maghreb from Casablanca to Tunis. On railroad construction in the Bône region, see Chapter 4.

45 *La Seybouse*, 18 avril 1868; Emerit, *Les Saint-Simoniens*, p. 186. Algeria was administered by the Ministry of War at this time.

46 The standard study is René Passeron, *Les grandes sociétés de colonisation en Afrique du Nord* (Algiers: Typo-Litho, 1925), pp. 85–129. See also Emerit, *Les Saint-Simoniens*, pp. 305–13; Julien, *Histoire*, pp. 437–8; and TEFA (1865–6), pp. 245, 463–83.

47 On the construction of the Bône port, see the discussion in Chapter 4 and the references cited there.

48 Tomas, *Annaba*, p. 202. See also TEFA (1865–6), p. 245.

49 SGA (1867–72), p. 309.

50 In 1843, the population appeared to decline, but this was due to the manner in which the census of that year was carried out. What happened was that first the houses of Bône had to be numbered – an indication in itself of how new this frontier community still was – before the population could be counted. This meant that the census could not be carried out simultaneously everywhere, the result of which was an apparent population decline when compared to the previous year. See TEFA (1843–4), p. 55.

51 TEFA (1846–9), p. 89.

52 APCA, Etats récapitulatifs 1840–1869: Dr. Moreau, "Notice sur l'état sanitaire de Bône et de ses environs en 1847." On death and epidemic disease, see also TEFA (1837), p. 299; TEFA (1846–9), p. 89; TEFA (1850–2), p. 84; Maurice-Marcel Grimal, *L'évolution du paludisme dans la région de Bône de 1830 à nos jours*, thèse de médecine (Paris, 1934); Nouschi, *Enquête*, pp. 29–30; Nouschi, "La crise économique de 1866 à 1869 dans le Constantinois: Aspect démographique," *Hespéris* (1959): 105–23; Lucette Valensi, "Calamités démographiques en Tunisie et en Méditerranée orientale aux XVIIIe et XIXe siècles," *Annales ESC* 24 (1969): 1540–61; and Nancy Gallagher, *Medicine and Power in Tunisia, 1780–1900* (Cambridge: Cambridge University Press, 1983).

53 To compare Bône with Paris is instructive. In 1842, thirty-three of every 1,000 Parisians died versus fifty-one of every 1,000 Bônois. And remember that this is the period in Paris when, according to Louis Chevalier, demographic conditions were so bad that the laboring classes were transformed into dangerous classes, at least in the minds of the middle classes. Yet the European death rate in Bône – as high as it was – was significantly lower than that of the Algerians. See TEFA (1843–4), p. 60; Louis Chevalier, *Laboring Classes and Dangerous Classes in Paris during the First Half of the Nineteenth Century*, trans. Frank Jellinek (New York: Fertig, 1973).

54 Daniel Headrick, *The Tools of Empire* (New York: Oxford University Press, 1981), p. 67; Grimal, *Paludisme*, p. 21. On the cinchona transfer from the Andes to India and Indonesia, see Lucile Brockway, *Science and Colonial Expansion* (New York: Academic Press, 1979).

55 The Scientific Congress of Algiers, quoted in Headrick, *Tools of Empire*, p. 67.

56 Between 1833 and 1851, 2,299 French died compared to 2,019 other Europeans (TEFA [1850–2], pp. 106–7). While neither the Maltese nor the Italians died at the same high rate the French did, the Maltese death rate was considerably lower than that of the Italians. (Based on data for 1853–55 not presented here.)

57 Pronounced population mobility is one of the chief discoveries of the so-called new urban history. The key study is Stephen Thernstrom and Peter Knights, "Men in Motion: Some Data and Speculations about Urban Population Mobility in Nineteenth Century America," in Tamara K. Hareven, ed., *Anonymous Americans: Explorations in Nineteenth-Century Social History* (Englewood Cliffs, NJ: Prentice-Hall, 1971), pp. 17–47.

58 Large jumps in the male/female ratio (1844, 1849, 1853) can be attributed largely to different mortality rates between men and women. Most male/

female ratios in Figure 3.4 are based on European adults rather than all Europeans, because this is the way the French recorded the data. While it would be more accurate to have ratios for the entire population instead of adults only, the difference is not large. For example, 1848 is one year for which we can calculate both ratios, and the difference – 1.61 for adults compared to 1.53 for everyone – is slight.

59 Furthermore, this ratio of mineral production to mineral export holds throughout the history of colonial Bône. For example, in 1955, 2,748,000 tons of iron ore were mined in Constantine department, and 2,683,000 tons were exported from the port of Bône. Tomas, *Annaba*, p. 198.

60 Arnaud, *Bône*, p. 86.

Chapter 4

1 Gilbert Meynier, *L'Algérie révélée. La guerre de 1914–1918 et le premier quart du XXe siècle* (Geneva: Droz, 1981), pp. 54–6. Meynier is referring to the years immediately prior to the First World War. I would argue that his characterization of the economy holds for the entire period 1870–1920, and well beyond for that matter.

2 *Ibid.*, p. 71.

3 François Tomas, *Annaba et sa région. Organisation de l'espace dans l'extrême-est algérien* (Saint Etienne: Guichard, 1977), pp. 196, 198.

4 Roger Dumoulin, *La structure asymétrique de l'économie algérienne d'après une analyse de la région de Bône* (Paris: Genin, 1959), pp. 92, 102. What Dumoulin calls asymmetry, other writers term dependency.

5 See Tony Hodges, *Spanish Sahara* (Westport, CN: Lawrence Hill, 1983).

6 On the Tébessa phosphates, see Dumoulin, *La structure asymétrique*, pp. 92–103; Désiré Dussert, "Les gisements algériens de phosphates de chaux," *Annales des Mines*, thirteenth series, Vol. 6 (1924), pp. 135–221, 229–325, 333–98, 407–51; Dussert, *Les mines at les carrières en Algérie* (Paris: Larose, 1931); Tomas, *Annaba*, pp. 180–205; Tomas, "Les Mines et la région d'Annaba," *Revue de Géographie de Lyon* 45 (1970): 31–59; and René Lespès, "Le port de Bône et les mines de l'Est Constantinois," *Annales de Géographie* 32 (1923): 526–41.

7 Tomas, *Annaba*, p. 196. For example, production dropped significantly during the 1930s due not to technical problems at the mine, but to the Great Depression.

8 *Ibid.*, p. 193. On the labor force, see Dussert, "Les gisements . . . de chaux," p. 428.

9 Tomas, *Annaba*, pp. 195, 425.

10 On the Djebel Onk phosphates, see, in addition to the references cited above for the Tébessa phosphates, APCA, Monographie économique de la Wilaya de Annaba (May 1976, mimeographed).

11 On the Ouenza affair, see in addition to the references cited above on the Tébessa phosphates, Dussert, "Etude sur les gisements de fer de l'Algérie," *Annales des Mines*, eleventh series, 1 (1912): 69–133, 135–256; Emile-Félix Gautier, "L'Ouenza," in *L'Algérie et la métropole* (Paris: Payot, 1920), pp.

99–129; Meynier, *L'Algérie révélée*, pp. 68–71; C. Bartuel and H. Rullière, *La mine et les mineurs* (Paris: Doin, 1923), pp. 159–77; and J. Barral, *Etude sur la question de l'Ouenza* (Paris: Ste. Sirey, 1912). A first-rate overview is Aimé Baldacci, *L'Algérie et la société de l'Ouenza* (Algiers, 1947). The views of two contemporary Bône politicians are presented in Fernand Marchis, *La question de l'Ouenza* (Bône: Mariani, 1907); and Charles de Peretti, *L'Ouenza devant le Conseil Général de Constantine* (Bône: Mariani, 1908).

12 Gautier, "L'Ouenza," p. 103.
13 *Ibid.*, p. 102.
14 Tomas, *Annaba*, p. 196.
15 For a complete breakdown of shareholders, see Barral, *La question de l'Ouenza*, pp. 97–8.
16 Gautier, "L'Ouenza," p. 110.
17 *Loc. cit.*
18 *Ibid.*, p. 120.
19 Meynier, *L'Algérie révélée*, p. 69.
20 *Loc. cit.*; Tomas, *Annaba*, p. 200; Bartuel and Rullière, *La mine*, p. 172; and Marchis, *La question de l'Ouenza*.
21 On the events in Bône, see the documents in AN, BB 18 2394 2199 Ouenza, and the newspaper clippings in AOM, AGGA 5 X 1.
22 *Le Matin*, 10 March 1909; *La Dépêche Algérienne*, 11 March 1909. Gaston Thomson was Bône's representative in the National Assembly. See Chapter 6.
23 AN, BB 18 2394 2199, report of Capt. Serraz, 17 April 1909.
24 *Ibid.* The composition of the crowd is uncertain; at least some Algerians took part but in the main it was made up of European settlers and French at that. The printers' union, coorganizers of the later demonstrations, were entirely French in membership. The other main organizer of the demonstrations, the "Committee of Bône youth," was headed by one Gabriel Abbo, whose own background is indicative if not entirely representative. Abbo's grandfather arrived in Algeria with a French admiral and founded a village later named Abboville. Abbo's father was in charge of the Bône vineyards of the *Banque de l'Algérie*, one of the largest owners of Algerian vineyards. And Gabriel Abbo himself later became president of the mayors of Algeria in the 1930s. (Louis Montoy, "La presse dans le département de Constantine (1870–1918)," 4 vols., unpublished thèse de doctorat [Aix-en-Provence: Université de Provence, 1982], p. 676.)
25 Gautier, *L'Ouenza*, p. 114. See also Meynier, *L'Algérie révélée*, p. 69; and Baldacci, *La société de l'Ouenza*, p. 36. Eighty percent of the shares were held by the old Société concessionnaire, ten percent by Algerian banks, and ten percent by new steelmaking interests. Krupp no longer figured in the enterprise, but French interests no longer dominated either since Le Creusot was no longer the majority shareholder. Instead, it was Muller who emerged stronger than ever.
26 This is also the conclusion which Meynier draws. See his *L'Algérie révélée*, pp. 69–70.
27 Tomas, *Annaba*, p. 199. On railroads in the Bône region, see APCA, Al-

gérie. Département de Constantine. Ville de Bône. *Renseignements généraux* (1902); Louis Arnaud, *Bône. Son histoire, ses histoires* (Constantine: Damrémont, 1960), pp. 89–100, 124–7; and Tomas, *Annaba*, pp. 198–201.

28 De Cerner, an Opportunist Republican, was linked closely to Mayor Jérome Bertagna, and played an active role in local politics, acting at one time or another as a member of the Bône municipal council, the Constantine departmental council, and as a delegate to the Délégations financières, a budget advisory body. On de Cerner, see APCA, Opérations électorales; and Montoy, "La presse," pp. 65–6, 139, 144, 217, 227, 231, 433, 578, 609, 614, 632, 660, 1450.

29 Arnaud, *Bône*, p. 91. Even without accepting the ludicrously high cost differential put forward by Arnaud – 50,000 vs. 1,000,000 francs per kilometer – it is clear that the difference in cost was considerable.

30 AN, AD XIX Z 478, Chambre de Commerce de Bône, *Compte-rendu des travaux pendant l'année 1897*, quoted in Tomas, *Annaba*, p. 199.

31 With this investment already made, the government built an additional line when the phosphates of Djebel Onk were discovered to link it to Tébessa. Successor to the Kouif phosphates, those of Djebel Onk began production in 1966 and today supply the superphosphates factory in Annaba. See APCA, Monographie économique (May 1976, mimeographed); and Tomas, *Annaba*, p. 201.

32 Lespès, "Le port de Bône," p. 526.

33 Lespès, "Bône, Port minier," *Revue africaine* (1930): 128–53.

34 On construction of the port of Bône, see in addition to Lespès, "Port minier," "Le port de Bône," and Chapter 3, M. Burger, *Notice sur le port de Bône* (Paris: Imprimerie Nationale, 1892); Gouvernement Général de l'Algérie, *Notice sur les routes et ports de l'Algérie* (Algiers: Giralt, 1900); Jérome Bertagna, *Le port de Bône. Compte Rendu de la séance de la Chambre de commerce du 3 septembre 1894. Rapport de Bertagna* (Bône, 1894); Ponts et Chaussées. Département de Constantine. Circonscription de Bône. *Statistique des Ports Maritimes de Commerce. Année 1937. Ports de Bône, de La Calle, et Herbillon* (Bône: Bouchet, 1938); Arnaud, *Bône*, pp. 17–28; and Tomas, *Annaba*, pp. 201–5.

35 Arnaud, *Bône*, p. 117.

36 *Ibid.*, pp. 117–18.

37 AN, AD XIX Z 478, Chambre de Commerce de Bône, *Compte-rendu des travaux pendant l'année 1899*, p. 53, quoted in Tomas, *Annaba*, p. 204, emphasis added.

38 Tomas, *Annaba*, p. 205.

39 APCA, Algérie. Département de Constantine. Ville de Bône, *Renseignements Généraux* (1902).

40 APCA, Etats Récapitulatifs 1901–48 (1932) (untitled, handwritten).

41 David Landes, *The Unbound Prometheus* (Cambridge: Cambridge University Press, 1969), p. 235.

42 For an analysis of Algeria from this theoretical perspective, see René Gallissot, "L'Algérie précoloniale," in Gallissot et al., *Sur le féodalisme*, Cahiers du Centre d'Etudes et de Recherches Marxistes (Paris: Editions Sociales,

1971), pp. 147–79. For a critique of Gallissot from an *Annales* viewpoint, see Lucette Valensi, "Archaisme de la société maghrébine," in *Sur le féodalisme* pp. 223–32.

43 Following Eric Wolf, I would term this precapitalist mode a tributary mode of production, and argue that it constitutes a theoretical continuum encompassing the so-called Asiatic mode at one extreme and a feudal mode derived primarily from Europe at the other. See Wolf, *Europe and the People Without History* (Berkeley: University of California Press, 1982), pp. 73–100. Wolf borrows the term "tributary mode" from Samir Amin, but defines it differently and more carefully. See Amin, *Le développement inégal* (Paris: Editions de Minuit, 1973), chap. 1. Wolf's tributary mode encompasses Gallissot's notion of a mode of command feudalism which he argues characterizes precolonial Algeria, since surplus extraction took the form of tribute not rent. See Gallissot, *Sur le féodalisme*, pp. 147–79. In any case, what is at issue here is the distinction between a precapitalist and a capitalist mode in Annaba/Algeria, not the specific form which the former takes.

44 The process is clear in Vincent Darasse, "Paysans en communauté et colporteurs émigrants de Tabou-Douch-el-Baar (Grande Kabylie) (Province d'Alger)," *Les ouvriers des deux mondes* 5 (1885): 459–502. On the articulation of modes of production, see Aidan Foster-Carter, "The Modes of Production Controversy," *New Left Review* 107 (1978): 47–78.

45 For Annaba, see Dumoulin, *La structure asymétrique*; and for Algeria, Meynier, *L'Algérie révélée,* esp. pp. 54–9. What Dumoulin calls "asymmetry," others term "dependency." Meynier uses "dependency" more in a descriptive than analytical sense.

46 The number of wholesale and retail businessmen has been adjusted in Table 4.1 to reflect the different numbers of Europeans and Algerians living in Bône at the time. Thus, the number of businessmen involved in a particular type of business is expressed in terms of the number of businessmen per 15,000 population of the respective ethnic group in question.

47 Harold Brookfield, *Interdependent Development* (Pittsburgh: University of Pittsburgh Press, 1975), p. 54. Although referring to postcolonial cities and societies, I would argue that the same argument can be made for colonial cities and societies. See Chapter 1.

48 For a discussion of the literature on the dual economy, see *ibid.*, Chapter 3. See also Bryan Roberts, *Cities of Peasants: The Political Economy of Urbanization in the Third World* (Beverly Hills: Sage, 1978), chap. 5. The desuetude into which the dual economy approach has fallen is strikingly apparent in the work of Clifford Geertz. In *Peddlers and Princes* (Chicago: University of Chicago Press, 1963), he used it as the framework in which he described the bazaar economy of two Indonesian towns (see Chapter 1). In his study fifteen years later of a Moroccan bazaar he replaced it with an interpretation of the bazaar as an information network in which he drew on semiotics and communications theory. See his "*Suq*: the bazaar economy in Sefrou," in Geertz, Hildred Geertz, and Lawrence Rosen, *Meaning and Order in Moroccan Society* (Cambridge: Cambridge University Press, 1979), pp. 123–313.

49 David M. Gordon, Richard Edwards, and Michael Reich, *Segmented Work, Divided Workers* (Cambridge: Cambridge University Press, 1982); Suzanne Berger and Michael Piore, *Dualism and Discontinuity in Industrial Societies* (Cambridge: Cambridge University Press, 1980); and William Reddy, *The Rise of Market Culture* (Cambridge: Cambridge University Press, 1984).

50 Chris Gerry, *Petty Producers and the Urban Economy: A Case Study in Dakar* (Geneva: International Labor Office, 1974); Keith Hart, "Informal Income Opportunities and Urban Employment in Ghana," *Journal of Modern African Studies* 11 (1973): 61–89; and Alejandro Portes and John Walton, *Labor, Class, and the International System* (New York: Academic Press, 1981).

51 Portes and Walton, *Labor, Class*, p. 64. See also p. 63, and Chapter 6.

52 *Ibid.*, pp. 69, 116–7. See also Portes, *Latin Journey* (Berkeley: University of California Press, 1985), p. 203.

53 Although the models discussed above are found mostly in the sociology of development literature, and have been developed primarily for what I would call postcolonial cities, it can be shown that the bifurcation found in the postcolonial economy corresponds to an earlier division of the colonial urban economy into colonizer and colonized sectors.

54 See Chapter 5.

55 Traditionally, a *funduq* is an establishment that provides commercial travelers lodging, sleeping quarters, stables, and storage facilities; this is the sense in which it was used in Table 4.1. However, the *Situation Industrielle* for 1883 employed it both in the sense of a business, and also to denote the location of the various Algerian retailers grouped together here in Table 4.3.

56 Arnaud, *Bône*, p. 179.

57 Lea Jellinek, "The Life of a Jakarta Street Trader," in Janet Abu-Lughod and Richard Hay, Jr., eds., *Third World Urbanization* (Chicago: Maroufa Press, 1977), pp. 244–56.

58 AN, F 80 1751, *Dénombrement de la population en 1891. Nomenclature alphabétique des professions* (Paris, 1891).

59 APCA, *Affaires Indigènes*, Bertagna to subprefect, May 25, 1895.

60 Archives de la Wilaya de Constantine [hereafter AWC], *El Hack*, August 27, 1893.

61 AWC, *El Hack*, 3 September 1893.

62 A. Blanc, *Tableautins sur l'Extrême-Orient algérien* (Bône: Puccini, 1887), p. 42.

63 Arnaud, *Bône*, p. 45. *Yaouled* is formed from *Ya ouled!* which means "hey, kid!" In Algiers, *yaouleds* were also called *ouled-plaça*, children of the place, referring to the large Place du Gouvernement. See Musette, *Cagayous. Ses meilleures histoires* (Paris: Librairie Gallimard, 1931), p. 260.

64 Louis Chevalier, *Laboring Classes and Dangerous Classes in Paris During the First Half of the Nineteenth Century*, trans. Frank Jellinek (New York: H. Fertig, 1973). On Algerian violence, see the thought-provoking comments by Frantz Fanon, *The Wretched of the Earth* (New York: Grove Press, 1968), pp. 307–9.

65 Arnaud, *Bône*, p. 178.
66 Blanc, *Tableautins*, pp. 19–20.
67 APCA, *Situation Industrielle* (1909), *Situation Administrative* (1883); Blanc, *Tableautins*, p. 16.

Chapter 5

1 Stephen Thernstrom and Peter Knights, "Men in Motion: Some Data and Speculations about Urban Population Mobility in the Nineteenth Century," in Tamara K. Hareven, ed., *Anonymous Americans: Explorations in Nineteenth-Century Social History* (Englewood Cliffs, NJ: Prentice-Hall, 1971), pp. 17–47.
2 In *Peasants into Frenchmen* (Stanford: Stanford Universty Press, 1976), Eugen Weber discusses the transformation of peasants into Frenchmen in terms of colonization and colonialism borrowing extensively from none other than Frantz Fanon to characterize the process. See esp. pp. 485–6, 489, 491–2.
3 Charles-Robert Ageron, "Gambetta et la reprise de l'expansion coloniale," *Revue français d'histoire d'outre-mer* 59 (1972): 165–204; and Jacques Binoche, "Les élus d'outre-mer au Parlement de 1871 à 1914," *Revue français d'histoire d'outre-mer* 58 (1971): 82–115. See also Sanford Elwitt, *The Making of the Third Republic: Class and Politics in France, 1868–1884* (Baton Rouge: Louisiana State University Press, 1975).
4 On the Jews in Algeria during this period, see Richard Ayoun and Bernard Cohen, *Les juifs d'Algérie* (Paris: Lattes, 1982); Michel Abitbol, ed., *Judaïsme d'Afrique du Nord au XIXe-XXe siècles* (Jerusalem: Institut Ben Zvi, 1980); and Centre National de la Recherche Scientifique, *Les relations entre juifs et musulmans en Afrique du Nord XIXe-XXe siècles* (Paris: Editions du CNRS, 1980).
5 R. Attal, "Croyances et préjugés. Image du juif dans l'expression populaire arabe du Maghreb," in CNRS, *Relations*, p. 57. See also Attal, p. 58; and Morton Rosenstock, "Economic and Social Conditions among the Jews of Algeria, 1790–1848," *Historia Judaica* 18 (1956): 6.
6 Scholars debate whether relations between Jews and Muslims were good (Lawrence Rosen, "Muslim-Jewish Relations in a Moroccan City," *International Journal of Middle East Studies* 3 [1972]: 435–49) or bad (Norman Stillman, "L'expérience judéo-marocaine. Un point de vue révisionniste," in Abitbol, *Iudaïsme*, pp. 5–24). For bibliographical orientation, see P. Shinar, "La recherche relative aux rapports judéo-musulmans dans le Maghreb contemporain", in CNRS, *Relations*, pp. 1–31.
7 E. Sivan, "Stéréotypes antijuifs dans la mentalité pied-noir," in CNRS, *Relations*, p. 161; Rosenstock, "Economic and Social Conditions," pp. 19, 21–2, 25–6; and I. Ben-Ami, "Le culte des saints chez les juifs et les musulmans au Maroc," in CNRS, *Relations*, pp. 104–9.
8 Simon Schwarzfuchs, "Colonialisme français et colonialisme juif en Algérie (1830–1845)," in Abitbol, *Judaïsme*, pp. 37–48.
9 Rosenstock, "Economic and Social Conditions," pp. 7, 9.
10 On the Jews of Leghorn, see J. P. Filippini, "Livourne et l'Afrique du Nord

au XVIIIe siècle," *Revue d'histoire maghrébine* 7–8 (1977): pp. 125–50; on the Jews of Tunis, known as *israélites livournais*, see Gaston Loth, *Le peuplement italien en Tunisie et en Algérie* (Paris: Colin, 1905), pp. 319–24. See also Fernand Braudel and Ruggiero Romano, *Navires et marchandises à l'entrée du port de Livourne (1547–1611)* (Paris: Colin, 1951).

11 See, in addition to the works cited above on the Jews, Sivan, "Stéréotypes antijuifs dans la mentalité pied-noir."

12 Victor Demontès, *Le peuple algérien. Essai de démographie algérienne* (Algiers: Imprimerie Algérienne, 1906), p. 107.

13 Janet Abu-Lughod, *Cairo: One Thousand years of the City Victorious* (Princeton: Princeton University Press, 1971), p. 98.

14 Data not presented here, but conclusions based on SGA, 1867–87; APCA, *Listes nominatives*, 1866–1911; and M. Eisenbeth, *Le judaïsme nord-africain. Etudes démographiques sur les Israélites du département de Constantine* (Paris: Natanson, 1932), pp. 181–7.

15 The naturalized French, a legal construct rather than a naturally occurring demographic population has been eliminated from the analysis. See the discussion concerning residential segregation in this chapter.

16 The decrease in the percentage of other Europeans born in Algeria in 1911 is due to the 1889 naturalization law which made the children of other Europeans automatically French at age twenty-one, transferred them from the other European category to the French, and thus reduced the number of other Europeans actually born in Algeria.

17 The naturalized French have been excluded because the 1889 naturalization law caused the naturalized French to be defined differently in 1876 than in 1891 and 1911. See text for discussion.

18 The small Jewish sample size (11 women and 15 children in 1876, 8 women and 21 children in 1891, and 12 women and 31 children in 1911) accounts in part for the wide fluctuation in Jewish fertility rates.

19 This and the following paragraphs on the Maltese in Algeria are based primarily on Jacques Godechot, *Histoire de Malte* (Paris: Presses Universitaires de France, 1970); and O. Vidala, *Les maltais hors de Malte. Etude sur l'émigration maltaise* (Paris: Rousseau, 1911).

20 This and the following paragraphs on the Italians in Bône are based primarily on Loth, *Le peuplement italien*; Jeanne Maguelonne, "Le peuplement italien et la propriété foncière italienne en Algérie," *Revue algérienne, tunisienne et marocaine* (1931): 56–79; and Demontès, *Le peuple algérien*, chaps. 2, 4–6. See also the *Lega italiana*, 1896–7 (BNV), a newspaper published in Italian for Bône's Italian community. For a comparative perspective on Italian migration, see, among others, Josef Barton, *Peasants and Strangers: Italians, Rumanians and Slovaks in an American City* (Cambridge: Harvard University Press, 1975); and Samuel Baily, "The Adjustment of Italian Immigrants in Buenos Aires and New York, 1870–1914," *American Historical Review* 88 (1983): 281–305.

21 *Bollettino Consolare*, 1870, p. 417, quoted in Loth, *Le peuplement italien*, p. 136.

22 Loth, *Le peuplement italien*, pp. 123–5, 129–30.

23 *Ibid.*, p. 123; and Maguelonne, *Le peuplement italien*, p. 56.

24 Loth, *Le peuplement italien*, p. 292. See also p. 127.

25 Report of 1881, quoted in *ibid.*, p. 126.

26 *Bollettino Consolare*, 1870, p. 448, quoted in *ibid.*, pp. 136–7.

27 *Bollettino Consolare*, 1881, p. 241, quoted in *ibid.*, pp. 158–9.

28 See Figure 5.6; and Loth, *Le peuplement italien*, p. 118.

29 Demontès, *Le peuple algérien*, p. 183. See also, SGA, 1900, pp. 24–5, 35.

30 Maguelonne, *Le peuplement italien*, p. 63.

31 Marc Baroli, *La vie quotidienne des français en Algérie, 1830–1914" (Paris: Hachette, 1967); and Pierre Boyer, La vie quotidienne à Alger à la veille de l'intervention français* (Paris: Hachette, 1963).

32 Michael Banton, "Urbanization and the Color Line in Africa," in Victor Turner, ed., *Colonialism in Africa* (Cambridge: Cambridge University Press, 1969), pp. 256–85.

33 Janet Abu-Lughod, *Rabat: Urban Apartheid in Morocco* (Princeton: Princeton University Press, 1980), p. 172. See also Hildred Geertz, "Appendix: A Statistical Profile of the population of the town of Sefrou in 1960," in Geertz, Clifford Geertz, and Lawrence Rosen, *Meaning and Order in Moroccan Society* (Cambridge: Cambridge University Press, 1979), pp. 393–506. This view of Maghribi social structure is shared as well by others. For example, Grandguillaume writes about "the double contrast existing in Algerian society in 1950. First of all, there was the contrast between Europeans and Algerians; between the colonizer and the colonized. There was a secondary contrast due to the internal stratification within either group. This social stratification can be expressed in terms of class (as long as the term is not too restrictive)." Gilbert Grandguillaume, "Algeria," in C. A. O. Nieuwenhuijze, ed., *Commoners, Climbers and Notables* (Leiden: Brill, 1977), p. 176. See also Raymond Barbé, "Les classes sociales en Algérie," *Economie et Politique* 62 (1959): 7–23 and 63 (1959): 22–46.

34 APCA, *Listes nominatives*, 1926, 1931, 1936. See also André Nouschi, "Le sens de certains chiffres. Croissance urbaine et vie politique en Algérie (1926–1936)," pp. 199–210 in *Etudes Maghrébines. Mélanges Charles-André Julien* (Paris: Presses Universitaires de France, 1964).

35 Abu-Lughod, *Rabat*, p. 173. See also among many others, David Landes, *Bankers and Pashas* (Cambridge: Harvard University Press, 1958), pp. 89–90; and Herbert Luethy, *France Against Herself* (New York: Praeger, 1955), pt. 3.

36 *The Wretched of the Earth* (New York: Grove Press, 1963), p. 40.

37 Pierre Bourdieu, *The Algerians* (New York: Beacon, 1962), pp. 152, 161. See also Bourdieu, *Outline of a Theory of Practice* (Cambridge: Cambridge University Press, 1977).

38 The standard study of the colonial policy of assimilation is Raymond Betts, *Assimilation and Association in French Colonial Theory, 1890–1914* (New York: Columbia University Press, 1961).

39 See Chapter 7.

40 Leo Kuper, Hilstan Watts, and Ronald Davies, *Durban: A Study in Racial Ecology* (London: Jonathan Cape, 1958); William J. Barber, "Urbanization

and Economic Growth: The Cases of Two White Settler Territories," in Horace Miner, ed., *The City in Modern Africa* (New York: Praeger, 1967); Anthony King, *Colonial Urban Development* (London: Routledge & Kegan Paul, 1976); Rhoads Murphey, *The Outsiders* (Ann Arbor, MI: University of Michigan Press, 1977); Janet Abu-Lughod, "Moroccan Cities: Apartheid and the Serendipity of Conservation," in Ibrahim Abu-Lughod, ed., *African Themes* (Ann Arbor, MI: Edwards Brothers, 1975).

41 See Chapter 1, pp. 33–4.

42 The index of relative concentration is calculated by dividing the percentage of a given city area comprised of a given population group by the percentage of the same ethnic group in the total Bône population. The percentages on which Table 5.4 is based are not given here.

43 APCA, *Liste nominative*, 1954. See also my article, "La ségrégation résidentielle en société coloniale: le cas de Bône (Algérie), 1872–1954," *Cahiers d'histoire* 25 (1980): 149–76.

44 Based on computerized manuscript census sample data of major city areas and various occupational measures not included here.

45 APCA, *Listes nominatives*, 1926, 1931, 1936, 1954. See also the important article by Nouschi, "Le sens de certains chiffres."

46 Data on which percentages are calculated are not presented here.

47 The fact that the Jews are overrepresented in the old city more between 1901 and 1911 than between 1872 and 1876 is somwhat deceptive, because the absolute number of individuals involved is relatively small. Jewish population growth generally kept pace with Bône's overall growth, but it appears greater in the old city because the old city scarcely grew during this period. Otherwise, the Jewish indexes of relative concentration and the percentage of all Jews in each census district display a consistent pattern.

48 See Ageron, *Les algériens musulmans et la France (1871–1919)*, 2 vols. (Paris: Presses Universitaires de France, 1968), pp. 588–90; Claude Martin, *Les Israélites algériens de 1830 à 1902* (Paris: Herakles, 1936), pp. 38–9, 169–72, 243–5, 288–91; and this chapter.

49 The fact that there was a higher percentage of first generation naturalized Jews in the old city and a lower percentage in the new city in 1911 than in 1906 is more likely attributable to census inaccuracies than to actual population shifts. After having worked with both the 1906 and 1911 manuscript censuses, I have serious reservations about the validity of comparing them. In the present case, I believe that the discrepancies are due to varying interpretations of the 1889 naturalization law. Since naturalization was virtually automatic for the children of Europeans, it was left up to the census taker to determine whether a person was, for example, Maltese or Maltese naturalized French. Ageron contends that there were similar inaccuracies in the Algerian censuses of 1901 and 1906. See his *Les Algériens musulmans*, pp. 578–9. Here, however, the 1906 and 1911 censuses can be treated separately because what is important is the geographical distributions of the two generations. In this respect the data is unequivocally clear.

50 After 1911, the residential pattern of Jews is unfortunately not tabulated separately from the French. *Faute des sources*, I would speculate that the

Notes

Jews of Bône continued to have a distinctly different housing distribution while at the same time moving closer to the European pattern.

51 Richard Lawless and Gerald Blake, *Tlemcen: Continuity and Change in an Algerian Islamic Town* (London: Bowker, 1976), p. 90.

52 On socioeconomic differences, see the discussion in this chapter on occupation and ethnicity; on the formation of a settler colonial society, see Chapter 7.

53 The problem is complicated by deficiencies in the available data. The necessary information exists for only three censuses, those of 1876, 1906, and 1911. However, the number of naturalized French in 1876 (149) is too small to yield reliable results. Moreover, the 1906 and 1911 census information is contradictory for reasons discussed above. Generally, however, comparisons within each census are more accurate than comparisons between the two censuses.

54 APCA, *Listes nominatives*, 1906, 1911. Again, I believe that percentage fluctuations between 1906 and 1911 are due to census inaccuracies, and that comparisons between population groups for the same point in time are generally accurate.

55 The best sociological study that uses this index is Karl E. Taeuber and Alma F. Taeuber, *Negroes in Cities* (Chicago: Aldine Publishing Co., 1965). Historical studies of residential segregation that employ the same measure include Howard P. Chudacoff, *Mobile Americans: Residential and Social Mobility in Omaha, 1880–1920* (New York, 1972); Nathan Kantrowitz, "The Index of Dissimilarity: A Measurement of Residential Segregation for Historical Analysis," *Historical Methods Newsletter* 7 (1974): 285–9; Leo F. Schnore and Peter R. Knights, "Residence and Social Structure: Boston in the Ante-Bellum Period," in Stephen Thernstrom and Richard Sennett, eds., *Nineteenth Century Cities: Essays in the New Urban History* (New Haven: Yale University Press, 1969); Thernstrom, *The Other Bostonians* (Cambridge: Harvard University Press, 1973); Olivier Zunz, "Detroit en 1880: espace et ségrégation," *Annales: ESC* 32 (1977): 106–36; Barton, *Peasants and Strangers*, pp. 20–2; and Stephanie Greenberg, "Industrial Location and Ethnic Residential Patterns in an Industrializing City: Philadelphia, 1880," in Theodore Hershberg, ed., *Philadelphia: Work, Space, Family, and Group Experience in the Nineteenth Century* (New York: Oxford University Press, 1981), pp. 204–32. See also the discussions by Hershberg, "The Historical Study of Urban Space: An Introduction," and Alan N. Burstein, "Patterns of Segregation and the Residential Experience," pp. 99–104 and 105–13, respectively, *Historical Methods Newletter* (1976); and Zunz, *The Changing Face of Inequality: Urbanization, Industrial Development, and Immigrants in Detroit, 1880–1920* (Chicago: University of Chicago Press, 1982), app. 4.

Although the index of dissimilarity is the preferred social statistic for studying residential segregation, other measures are available and have been used. For example, Taeuber and Taeuber discuss several others – the Gini index, ghetto index, Cowgill index – all of which can be adapted from a Lorenz curve of inequality to make a segregation curve. For the most penetrating and comprehensive study of these and related issues, see *Negroes in Cities*, "Appendix A: The Measurement of Residential Segregation," pp. 195–245.

56 See my "La ségrégation résidentielle."

57 It would be highly interesting to know whether and to what extent the Jewish situation improved after 1911. However, the Jews are lumped together with all French citizens in censuses conducted after 1911.

58 For a discusion of the problems and methods of occupational classification, see among others, Stuart Blumin, "The Historical Study of Vertical Mobility," *Historical Methods Newsletter* 1 (1968): 1–13; Clyde Griffin, "Occupational Mobility in Nineteenth Century America: Problems and Possibilities," *Journal of Social History* 5 (1972): 310–30; Michael Katz, "Occupational Classification in History," *Journal of Interdisciplinary History* 3 (1972): 68–88; and Theodore Hershberg and Robert Dockhorn, "Occupational Classification," *Historical Methods Newsletter* 9 (1976): 59–77. For a discussion of the problems and methods of occupational classification, see among others, Stuart Blumin, "The Historical Study of Vertical Mobility," *Historical Methods Newsletter* 1 (1968): 1–13; Clyde Griffin, "Occupational Mobility in Nineteenth Century America: Problems and Possibilities," *Journal of Social History* 5 (1972): 310–30; Michael Katz, "Occupational Classification in History," *Journal of Interdisciplinary History* 3 (1972): 68–88; and Theodore Hershberg and Robert Dockhorn, "Occupational Classification," *Historical Methods Newsletter* 9 (1976): 59–77.

59 The schema utilized here was developed by the Philadelphia Social History Project (PSHP). It is possible to use others; for example, the schema devised for the 1891 French census is essentially an industrial one. But where this latter occupational code mixes in elements of vertical schemas indiscriminately as well, the PSHP industry code is considerably more rigorous. It is also more detailed and nuanced. For an overview of the PSHP, see the special issue of *Historical Methods Newsletter* 9 (1976): 43–181; and Herschberg, ed., *Philadelphia*. On the 1891 French census, see AOM, F 80 1751, Dénombrement de la population en 1891. Nomenclature alphabétique des professions (Paris, 1891).

60 Based on computerized manuscript census sample data not presented here.

61 Michael Hechter, *Internal Colonialism* (Berkeley: University of California Press, 1975), pp. 30–40.

62 The main problem with vertical codes is that you tend to assume that a person with a given job fits into a given position in the occupational hierarchy when in fact this is precisely what you want to determine. The problem is exacerbated by the fact that rankings by occupation coincide generally but not always with rankings by property holding, personal wealth, or other criteria. The more empirically based the code, therefore, the better. The code used here is patterned again after that utilized by the Philadelphia Social History Project, which itself has been refined and redefined on empirical grounds, in particular through a comparative analysis of occupation and ethnicity in five North American cities. See Theodore Hershberg, Michael Katz, Stuart Blumin, Laurence Glasco, and Clyde Griffin, "Occupation and Ethnicity in Five Nineteenth-Century Cities: A Collaborative Inquiry,"

Historical Methods Newsletter 7 (1973): 174–216; and Katz, Michael Doucet, and Mark Stern, *The Social Organization of Early Industrial Capitalism* (Cambridge: Harvard University Press, 1982).

63 Such vertical schemas of the sort utilized here have been criticized on the grounds that movement up or down indicates actual social mobility, because the four or five rungs of the theoretical occupational ladder do not correspond in fact to empirical occupational divisions. Here, however, I am not using such a vertical scheme to measure social mobility, but only to stratify in a rough-and-ready fashion the occupational hierarchy.

More recently, Michael Katz has proposed that a two-class schema of social stratification ought to be substituted in American history for the vertical schemas widely used by urban historians on the grounds that a two-class model conforms better to nineteenth-century North American social reality. Leaving aside the theoretical question of which schema mirrors more closely social reality, the main practical problem is that nineteenth-century censuses French or American do not differentiate explicitly between owners or master artisans and journeymen skilled workers, so it is generally not possible to know whether a "baker" or "tailor" or "shoemaker" is a worker or owner. In Table 5.12, I present data from a different source pertaining to job position which makes exactly these sorts of distinctions. Most important, however, is that whatever schema is employed, the Algerians come out worse compared to the Europeans, and the other Europeans worse than the native French. In short, these colonial relationships are so fundamental and pervasive that they emerge time and again from different data.

64 Griffen, "Occupational Mobility"; Katz, *Hamilton*, chaps. 2 and 3.

65 It should also be noted that the code used here was designed for nineteenth-century Philadelphia and the United States rather than for nineteenth-century Bône and Algeria. No code comparable in sophistication has been devised for colonial Algeria – or France either. Fanny Colonna provides the single best occupational classification for colonial Algeria, but although I have used it to inform my own research it falls far short of meeting my own needs. See her *Instituteurs algériens, 1883–1939* (Algiers: Office des publications universitaires, 1975), Annexe IX. Correspondance entre la nomenclature des secteurs économiques en usage avant 1939 et la classification utilisée dans l'enquête, pp. 237–9. What I have done is to use the PSHP vertical code as a starting point and have modified it according to my own sense of the Bône past.

66 The jobs in the *Statistique Industrielle* are divided into fifteen main industries, and within each category separate data is provided on all firms of the same type. For each type of business salary ranges are provided for each job position. The mean salary for each group of workers in each job category have been added together to arrive at the data presented here. That the French or other Europeans are not apparently the highest paid in some categories is misleading, and is due to the way the wage data has been averaged. Within each of the 15 individual industrial subcategories, the French rank highest followed by the other Europeans.

67 The distribution of French, Europeans, and Algerians by position in job is

constant for 1904, 1905, and 1907, and the data have been pooled, therefore, in a single distribution presented in Figure 5.13.

68 Lespès, *Alger. Etude de géographie et d'histoire urbaines* (Paris: Alcan, 1930); and *Oran. Etude de géographie et d'histoire urbaines* (Paris: Alcan, 1938).

69 Abu-Lughod, *Rabat*, p. 278. The results of her factorial ecology appear on pp. 275–331.

70 Geertz, "A Statistical Profile of the Population," in Geertz, Geertz, and Rosen, *Meaning and Order in Moroccan Society*, pp. 393–506.

71 Colonna, *Instituteurs algériens*, pp. 237–9.

72 Peter Laslett and Richard wall, eds., *Household and Family in Past Time* (Cambridge: Cambridge University Press, 1972).

73 Katz, "Occupational Classification;" Herschberg et al., *Philadelphia*; and Herschberg et al., "Occupation and Ethnicity."

Chapter 6

1 René Bouyac, *Histoire de Bône* (Paris: 1980), pp. 246–9; Albert-Charles Maitrot, *Bône militaire* (Bône: Mariani, 1934), pp. 285–7, 320–4; Louis Arnaud, *Bône. Son histoire, ses histoires* (Constantine: Imprimerie Damrémont, 1960), p. 60; Ministère de la Guerre, *Tableau de l'établissement français en Algérie* (Paris: 1837), p. 262. .

2 Arnaud, *Bône*, p. 46; Bouyac, *Bône*, pp. 320–1; Maitrot, *Bône militaire*, pp. 367–70.

3 Charles-Robert Ageron, *Les Algériens musulmans et la France 1870–1919*, 2 vols. (Paris: Presses Universitaires de France, 1968), p. 430; Jacques Binoche, "Les élus d'outre-mer au Parlement de 1871 à 1914," unpublished thèse de troisième cycle (Toulouse: Université de Toulouse, 1970), pp. 88–90, 107. All but four of the 102 deputies and senators elected from overseas 1871–1914 were leftists or extreme leftists.

Although the Muqrani uprising of 1871 – the largest Algerian revolt prior to the Algerian Revolution – did not affect Bône directly, the defeat of the Algerians strengthened the settlers' position very substantially. The best general discussion remains Ageron, *Les Algériens musulmans*, pp. 3–36.

4 Ageron, *Les Algériens musulmans*, pp. 151, 163; APCA, Ville de Bône. Renseignements généraux (1932).

5 Ageron, *Les Algériens musulmans*, p. 365. Algerian municipal council members could no longer vote for mayor, and those businessmen paying the commercial tax (*patente*) were deprived of the vote.

6 *Ibid.*, pp. 630ff.

7 Claude Bontems, *Manuel des institutions algériennes de la domination turque à l'indépendance, Vol. 1: La domination turque et le régime militaire, 1518–1870* (Paris: Editions Cujas, 1975), p. 366; Ageron, *Les Algériens musulmans*, pp. 190–1, 627.

8 APCA, Etat nominatif du personnel de la Mairie (1878); Etat du personnel communal actuellement en fonctions (ca. 1910–11); Listes nominatives, 1876, 1911.

9 Cited in Ageron, *Les Algériens musulmans*, p. 190, note 7. Operating costs

ranged from 25 to 35 percent in all *communes de pleine exercice.* Ageron, p. 628.

10 Quoted in *ibid.*, pp. 452, 191.
11 Charles-Robert Ageron, *Histoire de l'Algérie contemporaine (1830–1973)* (Paris: Presses Universitaires de France, 1974), p. 49.
12 It may be objected that the partisan complaints of electoral fraud on which the following account is based cannot be taken at face value, that what the prefectoral administration rejected as "false" (usually for lack of evidence), I cannot accept as "true." But this is to miss the point, because my purpose is different from that of the French administration. The French authoritie had to decide whether there was sufficient evidence to prove that an isolated violation of the electoral regulations had occurred, whereas I have to determine whether the repeated references over time to the same or similar practice, and lacking compelling evidence to the contrary, demonstrate that this practice was in fact characteristic of a Bône election. In fact, I would argue that to consider the veracity of these complaints one after another in isolation is to miss the fact that they recur and are interconnected; in short, to miss a sense of how together they constitute one of the primary historical facts of the political culture of Bône.
13 APCA, Liste électorale, 1900; Liste nominative, 1901.
14 Arnaud, *Bône*, p. 110.
15 *Ibid.*, p. 92.
16 Louis P. Montoy, "La presse dans le département de Constantine (1870–1918)," 3 vols., unpublished thèse de doctorat (Aix-en-Provence: Université de Provence, 1982).
17 APCA, Opérations électorales, Conseil Municipal (hereafter Ops. élecs. C.M.), 1896. See also those for 1908 and 1919.
18 In the words of their opponents. APCA, Ops. élecs. C.M., 1904. Cf. 1892.
19 APCA, Ops. élecs. C.M., 1919, 1908. This was a major reason why the election was annulled by the *Conseil d'Etat* in Paris.
20 APCA, Ops. élecs. C.M., 1892, 1896, 1897, 1904, 1908.
21 APCA, Ops. élecs. C.M., 1910, 1896, 1892; Ops. élecs. Conseil Général (hereafter C.G.), 1895.
22 APCA, Ops. élecs. C.M., 1896, 1910, 1919; Arnaud, *Bône*, p. 100.
23 APCA, Ops. élecs. C.M., 1896, 1908. The disingenuous excuse offered was that it was customary to hire more workers after the rains to clean the streets.
24 APCA, Ops. élecs. C.M., 1896; AN, BB 18 2006 dossier 1846 A 95: Procureur Général Broussard to Minister of Justice, July 6, 1896. It is a fact that 189 francs was distributed to 292 individuals April 28 and May 8, 1896.
25 APCA, Ops. élecs. C.M., 1910. The (Radical) candidate's limp explanation was that he employed numerous dockers who happened to be paid on Saturdays and Sundays, and that "it is likely that in electoral matters these voters took their cue [*s'inspirent*] from the preferences of their *patron.*"
26 APCA, Ops. élecs. C.M., 1919. Large numbers of voters were thus "conducted" to the polls. See also Ops. élecs. C.G., 1895; Ops. élecs. C.M., 1980, 1896, 1878.
27 Arnaud, *Bône*, p. 110.

28 APCA, Ops. élecs. C.M., 1870, 1904, 1908. In 1885 Thomson was accused of buying Jewish votes. In 1893 the *préfet*, the *Compagnie de l'Est algérienne*, and Forcioli, the other deputy representing Constantine department, all were alleged to have pressured voters to vote for him. And in 1898 an inquest into his election was ordered despite the fact that Eugène Etienne, his friend and leader of the *parti colonial*, came to his defense. Binoche, *Les élus*, pp. 141–2, 233, 248–9, 307; Ageron, *Les Algériens musulmans*, p. 436, note 1.

29 James C. Scott, *Comparative Political Corruption* (Englewood Cliffs, NJ: Prentice-Hall, 1972), pp. 108–9. It can be shown that several features of societies in which machine politics thrive – poverty, large-scale immigration, ethnic cleavage, not to mention universal suffrage and parliamentary elections – are found also in colonial Bône. See Chapter 5.

30 Ageron, *Les Algériens musulmans*, pp. 506, note 3, 531. Mauguin represented Algiers in the *Sénat*.

31 Arnaud, *Bône*, pp. 112, 111.

32 Scott, *Political Corruption*, p. 98.

33 *Ibid.*, p. 108.

34 Marc Baroli *La vie quotidienne des français en Algérie, 1830–1914* (Paris: Hachette, 1967), p. 240.

35 Scott, *Political Corruption*, pp. 112, 114, 150.

36 It is not possible to correlate ethnicity or socioeconomic position from the manuscript censuses (*listes nominatives*) with precinct vote totals, because in Bône the polling places were organized in alphabetical clusters by the voters' last names rather than by areas of town. Nor do the *listes électorales* indicate political party preference. So far as I know, the necessary information does not exist for any major city in colonial Algeria.

37 On the *parti colonial*, see C. M. Andrew and A. S. Kanya-Forstner, "The French 'Colonial Party': Its Composition, Aims and Influence, 1885–1914," *Historical Journal* 14 (1971): 99–128; *idem.*, "French Business and the French Colonialists," *Historical Journal* 19 (1976): 981–1000; *idem.*, *The Climax of French Imperial Expansion, 1914–1924* (Stanford: Stanford University Press, 1981), chap. 1; Andrew, Kanya-Forstner and P. Grupp, "Le Mouvement colonial français et ses principales personnalités 1890–1914," *Revue française d'histoire d'outre-mer* 62 (1975): 640–73; Andrew, "The French Colonialist Movement during the Third Republic: The Unofficial Mind of Imperialism," *Transactions of the Royal Historical Society*, 5th series, 26 (1976): 143–66; Ageron, *France coloniale ou parti colonial?* (Paris: Presses Universitaires de France, 1978); and Larry Abrams and D. J. Miller, "Who were the French Colonialists? A Reassessment of the Parti Colonial, 1890–1914," *Historical Journal* 19 (1976): 685–725. See also Stuart Michael Persell, *The French Colonial Lobby, 1889–1938* (Stanford: Hoover Institution Press, 1983). On the *groupe colonial*, see Andrew and Kanya-Forstner, "The Groupe Colonial in the French Chamber of Deputies, 1892–1932," *Historical Journal* 17 (1974): 837–66. On the *élus algériens*, see Jacques Binoche, "Les élus d'outre-mer au Parlement de 1871 à 1914," *Revue française d'histoire d'outre-mer* 58 (1971): 82–115; and *idem.*, *Les élus*.

38 J. Davis, *People of the Mediterranean* (London: Routledge & Kegan Paul, 1977), p. 138.

39 Jeremy Boissevain, "Poverty and Politics in a Sicilian Agro-Town," *International Archives of Ethnography* 50 (1966): 218. I find this view congenial because it corresponds to my own experience in Algeria (and elsewhere in the Third World).

40 Alex Weingrod, "Patrons, Patronage, and Political Parties," *Comparative Studies in Society and History* 10 (1968): 398; Eric Wolf, "Kinship, Friendship, and Patron-Client Relations in Complex Societies," in Michael Banton, ed., *The Social Anthropology of Complex Societies*, Vol. 4 (London: Tavistock, 1966), p. 18; and Boissevain, "Patronage in Sicily," *Man*, new series, 1 (1966): 29.

41 Robert K. Merton, *Social Theory and Social Structure* (New York: The Free Press, 1957), cited in Alexander B. Callow, ed., *American Urban History* (New York: Oxford University Press, 1973), p. 222, writing about political machines.

42 Scott, *Political Corruption*, p. 115.

43 Is it necessary to point out that cash is not the only currency of corruption, that the political loyalty of clients strengthens and extends a patron's power base in the most efficacious way possible?

44 AN, BB 18 2006, Broussard to Min. Justice, June 12, 1896.

45 AN, F 80 1837, Broussard to Min. Justice, January 4, 1896; BB 18 2006, Broussard to Min. Justice, February 19, 1896.

46 Arnaud, *Bône*, pp. 117–8; AWC, Gouvernement Général de l'Algérie, *Notice sur les routes et ports de l'Algérie* (Algiers: Giralt Imprimeur, 1900), pp. 58–60. On port construction, see Chapter 4.

47 AN, BB 18 2006, Broussard to Min. Justice, July 6, 1896; F 80 1837, Gouverneur Général Cambon to Constantine Préfet, September 12, 1896. It was these "voluntary gifts" that allegedly comprised an election slush fund. See p. 233.

48 Arnaud, *Bône*, p. 119.

49 AN, BB 18 2006, Broussard to Min. Justice, February 25, February 19, July 11, and March 16, 1896; Ageron, *Les Algériens musulmans*, p. 474.

50 AN, BB 18 2006, Broussard to Min. Justice, January 28, and June 12, 1896.

51 AN, BB 18 2006, Inspecteur des Finances Blondel, quoted in Broussard to Min. Justice, July 11, 1896. Blondel's investigation covered the period 1890–5. In 1910–1 Barriol was still in the accounting department. APCA, Etat du personnel communal. . . . (ca. 1910–11).

52 AN, BB 18 2006, Inspecteur Général des Ponts et Chaussées Flamant, reported in Broussard to Min. Justice, February 25, 1896; Broussard to Min. Justice, June 12, 1896. Burger was transferred at the conclusion of Flamant's administrative inquest.

53 AN, BB 18 2006, Flamant reported in Broussard to Min. Justice, February 25, 1896; Broussard to Min. Justice, June 19, 1896. Dormoy later became Inspecteur Général de la Colonisation in Algeria.

54 AN, BB 18 2006, Broussard to Min. Justice, June 12, and January 28, 1896.

55 AN, BB 18 2006, Blondel quoted in Broussard to Min. Justice, July 11, 1896.

56 APCA, Administration communale. Circulaire au sujet de perceptions ir-régulièrement ou illégalement faîtes par des Agents des divers Services mun-icipaux (1903).

57 AN, BB 18 2006, Cellerin to Min. Justice, September 16, 1895; Broussard to Min. Justice, March 16, 1896.

58 Baroli, *La vie quotidienne*, p. 242; Ageron, *Histoire de l'Algérie*, p. 48.

59 Baroli, *La vie quotidienne*, p. 243.

60 AN, BB 18 2006, Broussard to Min. Justice, November 28, 1895.

61 Baroli, *La vie quotidienne*, pp. 243–4.

62 AN, BB 18 2006, Maxime Rasteil to Min. Justice, December 24, 1895; Broussard to Min. Justice, February 19, February 25, and July 11, 1896. But there is more. Malassis, pressed by his creditors, asked Burger for his money, who asked Bertagna to lend Malassis 6,000 francs. This Bertagna did, but it was insufficient, because Malassis saw Burger again and told him he was afraid of going bankrupt. Thereupon Burger made out a false invoice charg-ing the Bône-Guelma for the work Malassis had done, but Duportal refused to pay, saying that the Bône-Guelma "did not want to make any more advances." Malassis then declared bankruptcy. Burger's final act was to transfer another note, which he had made out stating that the *département* owed Malassis for this work, from Malassis to one of Malassis's creditors!

63 AN, BB 18 2006, Broussard to Min. Justice, February 19, 1896.

64 Ageron, *Histoire de l'Algérie*, p. 48; Ageron, *Les Algériens musulmans*, p. 504.

65 On the phosphates of Tébessa, see Chapter 4.

66 AN, BB 18 2006, Broussard to Min. Justice, March 16 and June 19, 1896.

67 AN, BB 18 2006, Engineer quoted in Broussard to Min. Justice, June 19, 1896; Roger Dumoulin, *La structure asymétrique de l'économie algérienne d'après une analyse de la région de Bône* (Paris: Editions Genin, 1959), pp. 93, 96–8.

68 Binoche, *Les élus*, p. 333; AN, BB 18 2006, confidential note from Senator Pauliat, July 21, 1895.

69 AN, BB 18 2006, Broussard to Min. Justice, March 16 and June 19, 1896. See also Ageron, *Les Algériens musulmans*, pp. 504–5.

70 *Loc. cit.*

71 AN, BB 18 2006, Broussard to Min. Justice, March 16, 1896. Cf. June 19, 1896.

72 Quoted in *Réveil Bônois*, May 18, 1896; APCA, Ops. élecs. C.M., 1896.

73 AN, BB 18 2006, Broussard to Min. Justice, June 19, 1896. Broussard had foreseen just such an outcome if the Bône judiciary were entrusted with the investigation. See his report to the Minister of Justice, December 4, 1895.

74 Ageron, *Les Algériens musulmans*, pp. 505, 531.

75 *Ibid.*, pp. 479, 531. Ageron feels it is "more than likely" that Morinaud, another Constantine politician, was right when he claimed that Cambon was removed at the instigation of Thomson and Etienne.

Notes

76 Speech to Parliament, quoted in *Réveil Bônois*, January 3, 1896.
77 Ageron, *Histoire de l'Algérie*, pp. 39–40. The terms *antijuif/antijudaïsme* and anti-semite/anti-semitism are used interchangeably in the Algerian case. *Antijuidaïsme* is technically more accurate, since the Algerians are also Semitic peoples, but anti-semitism has the advantage of explicitly linking anti-semitism in Algeria to anti-semitism elsewhere.
78 Ageron, *Les Algériens musulmans*, p. 594. On Algerian anti-semitism, see esp. *ibid.*, pp. 583–608; C. Iancu, "Du nouveau sur les troubles antijuifs en Algerie à la fin du XIXème siècle," in Centre National de la Recherche Scientifique, *Relations entre juifs et musulmans en Afrique du Nord XIXe-XXe siècles* (Paris: Editions du CNRS, 1980), pp. 173–87; and Geneviève Dermenjian, *La crise anti-juive oranaise (1895–1905)* (Paris: L'Harmattan, 1986). On Jewish electors, see APCA, *Liste électorale*, 1870; Dermenjian, *La crise anti-juive*, pp. 36–7; and Iancu, "Du nouveau sur les troubles antijuifs," p. 183, note 8.
79 Ageron, *Les algériens musulmans*, p. 595; Iancu, "Du nouveau sur les troubles antijuifs," pp. 180–1; and Dermenjian, *La crise antijuive*, pp. 74–89.
80 Jacques Bouveresse and Louis P. Montoy, *Les maires des agglomérations urbaines du Département de Constantine (1884–1941)* (Rouen: Publications du Centre de Recherches d'Histoire du Droit et de Droit Romain, 1984), p. 28. On Bône Jews, see Richard Ayoun, "Les Juifs de Bône," in Jean Laloum and Jean-Luc Alloch, eds., *Les Juifs d'Algérie* (Paris: Editions du Scribe, 1987), pp. 148–53.
81 Bône's leading Radical newspaper, *Le Réveil Bônois*, took an increasingly anti-semitic line from 1895; *L'Avant-Garde* published six issues in 1898 attacking Thomson, and constituted a simple electoral supplement to *Le Réveil Bônois*; *Le Français* and *L'Express Algérien* appeared in 1896 only; and *L'Antijuif Bônois* (1898–1900) succeeded the Radical *Courrier de Bône*, and was the organ of the local *Ligue antijuive*. Moreover, *Le Tocsin* appeared in 1896 specifically to combat the anti-semitic press. See Montoy, "La presse," pp. 318, 330–6, 342–6, 1363–71, 1373–5, 1413–20.
82 Former Archives du Gouvernement Général de l'Algérie (hereafter AGGA), 7 G 9, Bône. Cabinet du Commissaire central to Gouverneur Général, February 26, 1899.
83 AGGA, 7 G 9, Bône. Cabinet du Commissaire central to Gouverneur Général, November 14, 1898.
84 Former Archives Départementales de Constantine (hereafter ADC), 1 B 7, Rapport du Commissariat spécial de la police des chemins de fer et des ports (gare de Bône) to Préfet, June 16, 1898, and marked "Très confidentiel."
85 ADC, 1 B 8bis, sous-préfet to préfet, May 7, 1900. Vote totals for the Opportunists ranged from 2904 to 1867, those for the Radicals from 1076 to 907.
86 Ageron, *Les Algériens musulmans*, p. 588.
87 Iancu, "Du nouveau sur les troubles antijuifs," p. 175.
88 Lys du Pac, quoted in Dermenjian, *La crise anti-juive*, p. 230.
89 Dermenjian and Iancu contend that he was, Ageron defends him. See Dermenjian, *La crise antijuive*, pp. 88, 177, 202; Iancu, "Du nouveau sur les

troubles antijuifs," p. 179; and Ageron, *Les Algériens musulmans*, pp. 531–2. On the revision of Jewish electoral lists, see Dermenjian, *La crise antijuive*, pp. 67 ff.; and Ageron, *Les Algériens musulmans*, p. 587.

90 Ageron recognizes Cambon failed to achieve anything, but argues he prefigured the 1919 reforms. But just as settlers stymied Cambon in the 1890s, so they prevented France from enacting meaningful reforms in 1919, and again in 1936. Where Ageron interprets the history of colonial Algeria as a series of missed opportunities, therefore, I contend that it constitutes a classic case of settler colonialism in which the settlers consistently prevailed over the *métropole* – until the Algerians forced the Fifth Republic to jettison them. See Ageron, *Les Algériens musulmans*, pp. 489, 491, 511–2, 527.

91 Ageron, *Histoire de l'Algérie*, p. 133. He concludes, "This chanting of separatism was one of the constants of the Algerian [i.e., European] *mentalité*."

92 *Ibid.*, pp. 39–40.

Chapter 7

1 Quoted in Marc Baroli, *La vie quotidienne des français en Algérie, 1830–1914* (Paris: Hachette, 1967), pp. 173, 175–6.

2 Quoted in Charles-Robert Ageron, *Histoire de l'Algérie contemporaine*, Vol. 2 (1871–1954) (Paris: Presses Universitaires de France, 1979), pp. 129, 131.

3 *Ibid.*, pp. 128, 131.

4 Emanuel Sivan, "Colonialism and Popular Culture in Algeria," *Journal of Contemporary History* 14 (1979): 24.

5 Baroli, *La vie quotidienne*, pp. 213, 261.

6 John Waterbury, *North for the Trade: The Life and Times of a Berber Merchant* (Berkeley: University of California Press, 1972), p. 116.

7 Among other commentaries, see Sivan, "Colonialism and Popular Culture."

8 Anthony King, *Colonial Urban Development* (London: Routledge & Kegan Paul, 1976), p. 167.

9 Arnaud, *Bône militaire*, pp. 177–80.

10 Gaston Loth, *Le peuplement italien en Tunisie et en Algérie* (Paris: Armand Colin, 1905).

11 Frantz Fanon, *The Wretched of the Earth* (New York: Grove Press, 1968), pp. 51–2.

12 Other suggestive examples of "reading" aspects of colonialism in the built environment include Thomas R. Metcalf, "Architecture and Empire," *History Today* 32 (1982): 40–5; Metcalf, "Architecture and the Representation of Empire: India, 1860–1910," *Representations* 6 (1984); Paul Rabinow, "Ordonnance, Discipline, Regulation: Some Reflections on Urbanism," *Humanities in Society* 5 (1982): 267–78; and Gwendolyn Wright and Paul Rabinow, "Savoir et pouvoir dans l'urbanisme moderne colonial d'Ernest Hébrard," *Les cahiers de la recherche architecturale* 9 (1982): 26–43. More broadly, an example of the sort of cultural analysis of the colonial situation that I have in mind here is Bernard Cohn, "Representing Authority in Victorian India," in E. J. Hobsbawm and Terence Ranger, eds., *The In-*

vention of Tradition (New York: Cambridge University Press, 1983), pp. 165–209.

13 Maitrot, "Les rues du vieux Bône et l'histoire," *Bulletin de l'Académie d'Hippone* 32 (1912–13): 149–69.

14 *Ibid.*, pp. 156–69.

15 On the Mediterranean in the sixteenth century, see Fernand Braudel's masterwork, *The Mediterranean and the Mediterranean World in the Age of Philip II*, trans. Sian Reynolds (New York: Harper & Row, 1972). The Spanish–Turkish confrontation in North Africa is discussed on pp. 661–81, 854–9, 1189–95. See also his "Les Espagnols et l'Afrique du Nord de 1492 à 1577," *Revue Africaine* 69 (1928): 184–233, 351–428.

16 APCA, "Dénomination des rues" (s.d.; mimeographed).

17 The following discussion is based on my collection of more than 150 postcards of Bône printed in the first decades of the twentieth century, and obtained from public archives (Bibliothèque Nationale) and private sellers (booksellers and kiosks in Annaba to flea markets in Tunis, Aix-en-Provence, and Paris). While by no means complete, I would argue that it is large enough to obtain a general sense of the most photographed buildings and views of colonial Bône.

18 Quoted in Ageron, *Histoire de l'Algerie*, p. 128.

19 Pierre Mille, quoted in Musette [pseud. Auguste Robinet], introduction and lexicon by Gabriel Audisio, *Cagayous. Ses meilleures histoires* (Paris: Gallimard, 1931), p. 7.

20 Audisio in Musette, *Cagayous*, p. 9.

21 Albert Lanly, *Le français d'Afrique du Nord. Etude linguistique* (Paris: Bordas, 1962), p. 328. According to the historian of this dialect, it had grown out of and away from French in the same way that French had grown out of and away from Latin centuries earlier. See pp. 328–32 and Audisio in Musette, *Cagayous*, p. 22.

22 Lanly, *Le français*, p. 160. This and the paragraphs that follow concerning the Italian influence on the French dialect spoken in Bône are based largely on Lanly, *Le français*, pp. 158–70. See also Audisio in Musette, *Cagayous*, pp. 7–40, 251–65.

23 Musette, *Cagayous*, p. 65.

24 Quoted in Lanly, *Le français*, p. 166.

25 From Edmond Brua, *Histoires Bônoises*, quoted in Lanly, *Le français*, p. 163. *Salaouetche* is a corruption from the Arabic for face, *al-ouedj*, plus *sale tête*, *sale individu*, dirty individual.

26 Camus quoted in Lanly, *Le français*, p. 161.

27 Lanly, *Le français*, p. 162.

28 *Le Réveil Bônois*, 27 juillet 1895 (BNV).

29 Louis Arnaud, *Bône. Son histoire, ses histoires* (Constantine, Algeria: Damrémont, 1960), p. 129. I am indebted to M. Merad, my former landlord in Annaba, for giving me a now unavailable postcard depicting the statue that clearly shows Carloutch doffing his hat to Bertagna.

30 Arnaud, *Bône*, p. 92.

31 Musette, *Cagayous*, pp. 116–9.

32 David Prochaska, "Cagayous of Algiers" (mss.).
33 Eighteen "Croquis naturalistes" by Pepino appeared in *Les Clochettes Bô-noises* between 4 mai 1895 and 6 juin 1897 (AWC). Another five "Croquis naturalistes" were published in *Les Gaités Bônoises* between 21 février and 21 mars 1897 (BNV). Only one issue of *Le Diocane Bônois* appeared due to the scandal, that of 31 decembre 1898 (BNV). The name was changed to *Le Scandale Bônoise*, which was published 7 and 14 janvier 1899 (BNV).
34 Edmond Brua, *Fables Bônoises* (Algiers: Type-Lithos, 1938); Brua, *La parodie du Cid* (Algiers: Collections du Cactus, 1941); Louis Lafourcade, *Harmonies Bônoises* (Algiers: Baconnier, s.d.) (this latter is conserved only in the Bibliothèque Nationale in Tunis). I have been unable to locate another work entitled *Moi et Augu. Histoires Bônoises* (Bône: Imprimerie Centrale, s.d.).
35 Albert-Paul Lentin, "El Cid: Portrait d'Edmond Brua," in Emmanuel Robles, *Les Pieds-Noirs* (Paris: Philippe Lebaud, 1982), p. 100.
36 *Ibid.* The best study of this literature is Hubert Gourdon, Jean-Robert Henry, and Françoise Henry-Lorcerie, "Roman colonial et idéologie colonial en Algérie," *Revue algérienne des sciences juridiques, économiques et politiques* 11 (1974): 7–252. An Algerian figure analogous in many ways to Cagayous is Djoha, a trickster known throughout the Middle East as J'ha. On Djoha, see Auguste Mouliéras, *Les Fourberies de Si Djeh'a* (Paris: E. Leroux, 1892); and Jean Déjeux, *Djoh'a hier et aujourd'hui* (Sherbrooke, Canada: Naaman, 1978).

Conclusion

1 APCA, *Liste nominative* 1876, p. 285.
2 The name is the same and the leading contemporary local historian of Annaba, H'sen Derdour, told me he was, but I have no conclusive evidence linking the two. See H'sen Derdour, *Annaba. 25 siècles de vie quotidienne et de luttes*, 2 vols. (Algiers: SNED, 1982–3).
3 *L'Islam*, 30 decembre 1909 (AWC). Charles-Robert Ageron points out that this was very likely the first mass meeting of Algerians, and that it followed soon after the 1908 Young Turk revolution in Turkey plus a 1908 visit of *Jeunes Algériens* who met with Clemenceau in Paris. See Ageron, *Les Algériens musulmans et la France (1870–1919)*, 2 vols. (Paris: Presses Universitaires de France, 1968), pp. 1037–8; Ageron, *Histoire de l'Algérie contemporaine*, Vol. 2: 1871–1954 (Paris: Presses Universitaires de France, 1979), p. 235. On *L'Islam*, see Louis Montoy, "La presse dans le département de Constantine (1870–1918)," 4 vols., unpublished thèse de doctorat (Aix-en-Provence: Université de Provence, 1982), pp. 662–3, 1515–21. The first director of *L'Islam*, 'Abd al Aziz Tebibel, founded a second *Jeune Algérien* paper in Bône, *L'Etendard Algérien*, which appeared from 22 novembre 1910 to 29 janvier 1911 (Hoover Institution, Stanford, California). See Montoy, *La Presse*, pp. 663–4, 1529–30.
4 On Denden, see APCA, *Liste nominative*, 1876, p. 285; Montoy, *La presse*,

pp. 639, 662, 670, 759, 1515. He died penniless in 1938, despite modest financial support from H'Sen Derdour's father among others (interview with H'Sen Derdour, July 1983). See Ageron, *Les Algériens musulmans*, pp. 1040, 1049, 1050–2; Ageron, *Histoire de l'Algérie*, p. 234; Mahfoud Kaddache, *La vie politique à Alger de 1919 à 1939* (Algiers: SNED, 1970), p. 42.

5 On Kaid Layoun, see Montoy, "La presse," pp. 468, 1347.

6 *El Hack*, 30 juillet 1893–25 mars 1894 (AWC). See Montoy, "La presse," pp. 468–75, 1347–50; Ageron, *Histoire de l'Algérie*, p. 233. A year later many of the same editorial staff launched *L'Eclair*, which soon changed its name to *La Bataille Algérienne*. See *L'Eclair/La Bataille Algérienne*, 24 mars 1895–30 juin 1895 (BNV); Montoy, "La Presse," pp. 475–6, 1353–5; *Les Algériens musulmans*, p. 1036; Ageron, *Histoire de l'Algérie*, p. 234.

7 *Procès-verbaux de la sous-commission d'étude et de la législation civile en Algérie*. Annexe no. 1840 au procès-verbal de la 2e séance du 9 juillet 1900. Tome XXXI (Paris: Imprimerie de la Chambre des Députés, 1901), pp. 661–3. See Ageron, *Les Algériens musulmans*, p. 1031.

8 APCA, Affaires Indigènes. Folder on Société Djemâ'a El Kheiria El Arabia, 1900. On Hassam, see APCA, *Liste électorale*, 1912.

9 Ageron, *Les Algériens musulmans*, p. 1031.

10 Bône and Algiers were "the two *Jeunes Algériens* capitals." Ageron, *Histoire de l'Algérie*, p. 232.

11 See the important articles by Joseph Desparmet, "La réaction linguistique en Algérie," *Bulletin de la Société Géographique d'Alger* 36 (1931): 1–33; "Les réactions nationalitaires en Algérie," *Bulletin de la Société Géographique d'Alger* 37 (1932): 173–84; "La conquête racontée par les indigènes," *Bulletin de la Société Géographique d'Alger* 37 (1932): 437–546; and "Elégies et satires politiques de 1830 à 1914," *Bulletin de la Société Géographique d'Alger* 38 (1933): 35–64.

12 Hadj Omar Bengui's son, Sliman, was director of *El Hack*. See APCA, *Situation Industrielle*, 1883; Montoy, "La Presse," pp. 468, 1349. The main members of the Benyacoub family are Hamidou (1858–99), Tahar (1876–?), Amar (1875–1928), Ali (1855–1927), and Mihoub (1887–1948). See APCA, *Liste nominative*, 1911, pp. 1180, 1182–3, 1188; *Listes électorales*, 1908, 1912; Conseil Municipal. Opérations électorales, 1900; AOM, 6 H 33, 16 H 31.

13 APCA, Affaires Indigènes. Société Djemâ'a El Kheiria El Arabia. Bertagna's Algerian collaborator, Mohammed Tahar Boumaiza (1832–1920), was the head of the other leading Algerian family in Bône. See APCA, *Liste nominative*, 1911, p. 246; *Listes électorales*, 1908, 1912; AOM, 6H 33, 16H 31; Montoy, "La presse," pp. 231, 733, 905.

14 Algerian voluntary associations formed in Bône included *la Sadikiya, Société islamique constantinoise, le Croissant*, and *le Cercle du Progrès*. Thus, Bône was again precocious in this regard.See Ageron, *Les Algériens musulmans*, p. 1034; and *Histoire de l'Algérie*, p. 234.

15 On Algiers, see Kaddache, *La vie politique*, pp. 41–3. On Bône, see APCA, Opérations électorales. Conseil Municipal, 1919. See also Ageron, *Histoire de l'Algérie*, p. 282. In Bône, on a slate headed by Ali and Mihoub Beny-

acoub, Mahmoud Hassam, Kaid Layoun's coorganizer of the Djemâ'a El Kheiria El Arabia, was the top vote-getter.

16 Abd al-Hamid Ben Badis, quoted in Derdour, *Annaba*, Vol. 2, p. 462.

17 See esp. Ali Merad, *Le réformisme musulman en Algérie de 1925 à 1940. Essai d'histoire religieuse et sociale* (Paris-La Haye: Mouton, 1967).

18 Salah el Din el Zein el Tayeb, "The Europeanized Algerians and the Emancipation of Algeria," *Middle Eastern Studies* 22 (1986): 206–35.

19 Jacques Berque, *French North Africa: The Maghrib Between Two World Wars* (New York: Praeger, 1967), p. 383.

20 Derdour, *Annaba*, Vol. 2, pp. 505–11.

21 Derdour, *Annaba*, Vol. 2, p. 507.

22 Henri Alleg et al., *La Guerre d'Algérie*, 3 vols. (Paris: Temps Actuel, 1981), Vol. 1, pp. 256–69; and Alistair Horne, *A Savage War of Peace: Algeria 1954–1962* (New York: Viking, 1978), pp. 26–7. On the Algerian revolution, see also René Gallissot, "La guerre d'Algérie: La fin des secrets et le secret d'une guerre doublement nationale," *Le mouvement social* 138 (1987): 69–109; Bernard Droz and Evelyne Lever, *Histoire de la guerre d'Algérie (1954–1962)* (Paris: Seuil, 1982); Pierre Montagnon, *Histoire de la guerre d'Algérie* (Paris: Pygmalion-Gerard Watelet, 1984); Harbi Mohamed, *Le FLN mirage et realité, des origines à la prise du pouvoir* (Paris: Editions Jeune Afrique, 1960); *idem.*, *Les Archives de la révolution algérienne, 1945–1962* (Paris: Editions Jeune Afrique, 1981); *idem.*, *La guerre commence en Algérie, 1954* (Paris: Editions Complexe, 1984); Slimane Chikh, *L'Algérie en armes ou le temps des certitudes* (Algiers: Office des publications universitaires, 1981); Teguia Mohamed, *L'Algérie en guerre* (Algiers: Office des publications universitaires, 1981); and Remi Kauffer, *OAS, histoire d'une organisation secrète* (Paris: Fayard, 1986).

23 Ageron, *Histoire de l'Algérie contemporaine*, p. 612. See also Alleg, *La Guerre d'Algérie*, Vol. 1, p. 273.

24 On post-World War I Bône political culture, see Jean Peroni, *Bône, tu te rappelles* (Grenoble: Dardelet, 1979).

25 Alleg, *La Guerre d'Algérie*, Vol. 1, p. 350; Vol. 3, p. 496, O.S. Composition Socio-professionnelle.

26 Benjamin Stora, *Dictionnaire biographique de militants nationalistes algériens E.N.A., P.P.A., M.T.L.D. (1926–1954)* (Paris: L'Harmattan, 1985), pp. 322–3; Alleg, *La Guerre d'Algérie*, Vol. 1, p. 331; Vol. 2, p. 218.

27 Alleg, *La guerre d'Algérie*, Vol. 3, pp. 494–5, Organigramme de l'O.S. Section d'Annaba (Bône), Fin 1949.

28 Stora, *Dictionnaire biographique des militants*, p. 321; Derdour, *Annaba*, Vol. 2, p. 442.

29 Stora, *Dictionnaire biographique des militants*, p. 332.

30 Alleg, *La guerre d'Algérie*, Vol. 1, p. 556.

31 Quoted in Horne, *A Savage War of Peace*, p. 119.

32 Derdour, *Annaba*, Vol. 2, p. 519.

33 Horne, *A Savage War of Peace*, p. 121.

34 Derdour, *Annaba*, Vol. 2, p. 521. In a note, Derdour adds, "These scenes

Notes

appear unbelievable, but not for those who witnessed them. The inhabitants of these neighborhoods, today more than 40 years old, can confirm them and even disclose others even more painful."

35 *Ibid.*, pp. 529–31.
36 *Ibid.*, pp. 515, 557–8.
37 Alain Amato, *Monuments en exil* (Paris: Editions de l'Atlanthrope, 1979), pp. 174–6. In a note, Amato adds, "At the request of M. Claude Bertagna I have not mentioned the exact location of the statue."
38 *Ibid.*, pp. 33–4, 39–41, 194–7.
39 Quoted in Horne, *A Savage War of Peace*, p. 531.
40 APCA,"Dénomination des rues." (s.d.; mimeographed).

Epilogue

1 Erwan Marec quoted in Louis Arnaud, *Bône. Son histoire, ses histoires* (Constantine: Damrémont, 1960), p. 1.
2 Emile-Félix Gautier, *Les siècles obscurs* (Paris: Alcan, 1930).
3 Georges Marçais, "La Mosquée de Sidi Bou Marwan de Bône," in *Mélanges d'histoire et d'archéologie de l'Occident musulman*, 2 vols. (Algiers, 1957), pp. 225–36. Derdour, *Annaba*, Vol. 1, pp. 179–85; Vol. 2, pp. 570–3. In 1832, the French converted the mosque into a military hospital; not until 1947 did it serve again as a mosque. In 1968 Annaba celebrated its 1,000-year anniversary (*hegiran*).
4 For accounts of Annaba, see Ibn Hauqal, *Configuration de la terre* (Paris: Maisonneuve et Larose, 1964); Al-Bakri, *Description de l'Afrique septentrionale* (Algiers: Jourdan, 1913), pp. 116–7; Al-Idrisi, *Description de l'Afrique et de l'Espagne* (Leiden: Brill, 1866), p. 136; H. A. R. Gibb, *The Travels of Ibn Battuta*, 3 vols. (Cambridge: Cambridge for the Hakluyt Society, 1958–71), Vol. 1, p. 12; Ross Dunn, *The Adventures of Ibn Battuta* (London: Croom Helm, 1986), p. 35; and Leo Africanus, *The History and Description of Africa* (London: Bedford, 1896), pp. 708–10.
5 Thomas Shaw, "Travels or observations relating to several parts of Barbary and the Levant," in John Pinkerton, ed., *A General Collection of the Best and Most Interesting Voyages and Travels in all Parts of the World* (London, 1814); Jean André Peyssonnel, "Relation d'un voyage sur les côtes de Barbarie (1724–25)," in Dureau de la Malle, ed., *Voyages dans les régence de Tunis et d'Alger*, 2 vols. (Paris: Gide, 1838); Louis René Desfontaines, "Fragments d'un voyage dans les régences de Tunis et d'Alger fait de 1783 à 1786," in de la Malle, ed., *Voyages*; L'abbé Poiret, *Voyage en Barbarie, ou lettres écrites de l'ancienne Numidie en 1785 et 1786 sur la religion, les coutumes et les moeurs des Maures et des Arabes Bédouins* (Paris: Rochelle, 1789); L'abbé de Pietri, *Détails sur Bône et ses environs et divers autres sujets* (Algiers: Philippe, 1836); Grenville Temple, *Excursions in the Mediterranean: Algiers and Tunis* (London: Saunders and Otley, 1835); Abbé Suchet, *Lettres édifiants et curieuses sur l'Afrique* (Tours: Mame, 1840); and C.-A. Rozet, *Voyage dans la Régence d'Alger* (Paris: Arthus Bernard, 1833).

6 Poiret, *Voyage en Barbarie*, p. 133.

7 Alexandre Dumas, *Impressions de voyage. Le véloce*, Vol. 2 (Paris: Levy, 1871), p. 45. On Eugène Giraud and Louis Boulanger, see Philippe Jullian, *The Orientalists* (Oxford: Phaidon, 1977), pp. 63, 94, 116; and Lynne Thornton, *The Orientalists* (Paris: ACR, 1983), pp. 257, 260.

8 Gustave Flaubert, *Voyages*, ed. René Dumesnil, 2 vols. (Paris: Société les Belles Lettres, 1948), Vol. 2, p. 547. Cf. Arnaud, *Bône*, pp. 64, 84.

9 He wrote about Tahiti in *Le mariage de Loti* (1880), and Senegal in *Le roman d'un spahi* (1881). In 1891, Loti was elected to the Académie Française.

10 Pierre Loti, *Journal intime*, 2 vols. (Paris: Calmann-Levy, 1929), Vol. 1, pp. 141, 148–53. See also Lesley Blanch, *Pierre Loti* (New York: Harcourt Brace Jovanovich, 1983), pp. 151–2. Blanch does not make it clear that the scene she describes occurred in Bône rather than Algiers.

11 Quoted in Arnaud, *Bône*, p. 71, and Derdour, *Annaba*, Vol. 2, p. 385. See also AOM, former Gouvernement Général d'Algérie, 23 X 11: Isabelle Eberhardt, *Notes journalières*.

12 Louis P. Montoy, "La presse dans le département de Constantine (1870–1918)," 3 vols., unpublished thèse de doctorat (Aix-en-Provence: Université de Provence, 1982), Vol. 1, p. 889; Cecily Mackworth, *The Destiny of Isabelle Eberhardt* (New York: Ecco Press, 1975), p. 40. Among other works, see Simone Rezzoug, "Etat présent des travaux sur Isabelle Eberhardt," *Annuaire de l'Afrique du Nord* (Aix-en-Provence: CNRS, 1982), pp. 841–7; Lesley Blanch, *The Wilder Shores of Love* (New York: Simon & Schuster, 1954); Ursula Kingsmill Hart, *Two Ladies of Colonial Algeria* (Athens, OH: Ohio University, 1987); Isabelle Eberhardt, *The Oblivion Seekers*, trans. Paul Bowles (San Francisco: City Lights, 1972); and *idem.*, *The Passionate Nomad: The Diary of Isabelle Eberhardt*, trans. Nina de Voogd, preface by Rana Kabbani (Boston: Beacon Press, 1988).

13 In her novel, *La vandale*, Magali Boisnard, a Bônoise and practitioner of the *roman colonial*, also recounted the history of the siege of Hippo.

14 Elie de la Primaudaie, "Documents inédits sur l'histoire de l'occupation espagnole en Afrique," *Revue africaine* (1875–7); *Les Estraines royales...* (1608); Comte de Cornulier-Lucinière, *La prise de Bône et Bougie d'après des documents inédits (1832–1835)* (Paris: Lethielleux, 1895); and L.-Charles Féraud, "Documents pour servir à l'histoire de Bône," *Revue africaine* 17 (1873): 4–23, 81–103, 165–86, 254–74, 341–51. See Bouyac, *Bône*, pp. 48, 87, 153, 163–4, 205, 207.

15 Bouyac, Bône, pp. 30, 33, respectively.

16 *Ibid.*, pp. 213, 249, respectively.

17 Bouyac, 235–42. See also Maitrot, *Bône militaire*, pp. 295–300, 292–4.

18 Bouyac, Bône, p. 352.

19 Albert-Charles Maitrot, *Bône militaire. 44 siècles de luttes* (Bône: Mariani, 1934); *idem.*, *Bône anecdotique* (Bône: Mariani, 1912); *idem.*, *Bône à travers les siècles* (Bône: Mariani); *idem.*, "Les rues du vieux Bône et l'histoire," *Bulletin de l'Académie d'Hippone* 32 (1912–19): 149–69; *idem.*, "Les petits métiers à Hippone," *Bulletin de l'Académie d'Hippone* 37 (1930–5): 91–6;

and *idem.*, "La question de la Basilique de la Paix," *Bulletin de l'Académie d'Hippone.*

20 Maitrot, *Bône militaire*, p. 425.

21 De Mas Latrie, *Les traités de paix et de commerce* (Paris: Plon, 1866); Sanson d'Abbeville, *L'Afrique en plusieurs cartes...* (Paris: chez l'auteur, 1656); and Sidi Hamdan ben Othman Khodja, *Le Miroir* (Paris: Goetscy, 1833). See Maitrot, *Bône militaire*, pp. 54, 123, 184–7.

22 *Ibid.*, p. 315.

23 *Ibid.*, pp. 360, 374–5. See also pp. 312, 352–7.

24 *Ibid.*, pp. 380–1, 385. See also p. 283.

25 He was defeated along with Marchis in 1910 and 1912, but elected *conseiller général* in 1926. APCA, *Opérations électorales*, 1908, 1910, 1912.

26 Arnaud, *Bône*, pp. 53–7, 183–9, 158–60, respectively.

27 Arnaud, *Bône*, pp. 156–7.

28 *Ibid.*, p. 45. See Chapter 4, page 131.

29 *Ibid.*, pp. 59–60, 82, 84, 107.

30 *Ibid.*, p. 77. As Frantz Fanon correctly put it, "Hostile nature, obstinate and fundamentally rebellious, is in fact represented in the colonies by the bush, by mosquitos, natives, and fever, and colonization is a success when all this indocile nature has been finally tamed. Railways across the bush, the draining of swamps and a native population which is nonexistent politically and economically are in fact one and the same thing" (Fanon, *The Wretched of the Earth* [New York: Grove Press, 1968], p. 250).

31 Arnaud, *Bône*, p. 145; Loti, *Journal*, Vol. 1, pp. 142–3.

32 Another Bônois, Jean Peroni, writes in a similar tale-telling vein, relating such stories as how Gaston Thomson's death in Bône in 1932 was kept secret until the polling places closed. See Peroni, *Bône, tu te rappelles* (Grenoble: Dardelet, 1973).

33 Derdour, *Annaba*, Vol. 2, pp. 447–8. See also pp. 467–80.

34 *Ibid.*, Vol. 1, pp. 51, 122, 150, 315; Vol. 2, pp. 224, 239.

35 *Ibid.*, Vol. 2, p. 352. Derdour mentions other informants at pp. 264, 273, 276, 313, 335, 357, 370–1, 388, and 436.

36 *Ibid.*, Vol. 2, pp. 225, 244, 267. "For greater factual authenticity, we will follow the account of Mme. Bir-rais in preference to the diverse accounts of French chroniclers" (p. 258). Derdour mentions two additional manuscripts at Vol. 1, p. 261 and Vol. 2, p. 108.

37 *Ibid.*, Vol. 2, pp. 321, 357–60, 395–6, 397, 428, 513, respectively.

38 *Ibid.*, Vol. 2, p. 126. The case in point concerns the 1694 attack on the Bey of Tunis, Mohammed, by Hadj Chaaban, Dey of Algiers, who used Annaba as a staging ground. See Maitrot, *Bône militaire*, pp. 125–6. Derdour also criticizes Maitrot in Vol. 2, pp. 209, 371.

39 Abdelhakim Meziani, *El Moudjahid* (3 juin 1982), and quoted on cover of Derdour, *Annaba.*

40 Derdour, *Annaba*, Vol. 2, p. 430. See also pp. 388, 461.

41 *Ibid.*, Vol. 2, pp. 431–3.

42 *Ibid.*, Vol. 2, p. 567.

43 *Ibid.*, Vol. 2, pp. 365, 366, 435, 367, 394, respectively. See also pp. 295, 301–2, 351–3, 389–93.
44 *Ibid.*, Vol. 2, pp. 384–5.
45 Examples are found in Vol. 2, pp. 47, 378, 404, and 568.

Sources and bibliography

Archives

The primary archival sources for this study are those of the Assemblée Populaire et Communale de Annaba, the former Archives Municipales de Bône. I am the first person to use these archives since at least 1962 so far as I know, and therefore, it might be useful to provide an overview of the Annaba archives as I found them. Since no inventory exists that I was ever able to discover, I provide below a cursory survey of archival series organized by the cabinets in which they are stored.

Cabinet 1: Politique générale. Conseil général.
Cabinet 2: Administration municipale. Services municipaux. Maires et Adjoints. Impôts arabes.
Cabinet 3: Sociétés de secours mutuels et autres. Consulats. Banques.
Cabinet 4: Budgets. Comptabilité général.
Cabinet 5: Contentieux. Actions judiciaires. Avocats de la commune.
Cabinets 6–7: Instruction publique.
Cabinet 8: Port de Bône. Pêche.
Cabinet 9: Affaires militaires et indigènes. Constitution de la propriété individuelle. Sociétés secrètes des indigènes. Demandes de secours.
Cabinet 11: Culte. Catholique. Protestant. Hébraïque. Musulman.
Cabinet 12: Conseil Muncipal. Procès-verbaux des séances.
Cabinet 18: Milices.
Cabinet 19: Taxes municipales.
Cabinet 20: Affaires indigènes. Secours aux indigènes. Renseignements et affaires indigènes divers, 1868–1900.
Cabinet 22: Police générale, 1836–1949.
Cabinet 29: Personnel.
Cabinet 38: Coup d'état, 1851.
Cabinets 40–41: Conseil Municipal. Déliberations (1849 on).
Cabinet 41: États Récapitulatifs, 1840–1948. Statistique agricole. Statistique industrielle. Dénombrements.
Cabinet 46: Recrutement registres, 1884–1912, 1914–1917. Naturalisation (1849 on).
Maitrices cadastres des propriétés baties.

308

Listes nominatives, 1848, 1861, 1866, 1872, 1876, 1881, 1886, 1891, 1896, 1901, 1906, 1911, 1926, 1931, 1936, 1948.
Mouvement de la population, 1853–4.
Actes de naissance (1830s on). Actes de mariages (1833 on). Migration (1874–1912).

Newspapers

Newspaper research is tedious, time-consuming, and dirty. Furthermore, colonial Bône newspapers are scattered widely between Paris, Constantine, and Annaba. For orientation, far and away the best study is Montoy, La presse dans le département de Constantine, (1870–1918) which appeared after research for this study was virtually completed (see bibliography below for full citation). Also useful are three manuscripts by Montoy deposited in AWC: "La presse du Constantinois: 1830–1962," 9 pp. (1977); "*Le Réveil Bônois*, 1890–1918. Grands thémes traités (index des principaux articles)," 149 pp. (1976); and "Le mouvement ouvrier dans le Constantinois (1870–1954). Répertoire de quelques informations parues dans la presse regionale," 2 vols. 52 and 37 pp. (1979).

L'Antijuif bônois, 1898–9.
La Bataille Algérienne, 1895. Successor to *L'Éclair* (11 issues).
Bône-Exposition, 1890. Issued during two-month long colonial exhibition in Bône.
Bône-Illustration, 1891 (2 issues).
Le Charivari Bônois, 1896 (2 issues).
Le Chêne-Liège, 1895–7, 1907–9. Economic journal founded to promote local cork oak industry.
Les Clochettes Bônoises, 1894–8.
Le Courrier de Bône, 1880–98.
La Démocratie Algérienne, 1886–1913. One of two leading papers in colonial Bône; Opportunist Republican. After 1913 becomes *La Dépêche de l'Est*.
Le Diocane Bônois, 1898 (1 issue). After one issue forced to change name to *Le Scandale Bônois*.
L'Echo de Bône, 1896–7.
L'Eclair, 1895 (10 issues). Later becomes *La Bataille Algérienne*.
L'Est Algérien, 1868, 1871–2.
L'Etendard Algérien, 1910–1, reappears 1919–20. One of earliest Jeune-Algérien papers.
L'Express Algérien, 1899–1900.
La Fronde, 1882–3.
Les Gaités Bônoises, 1897 (9 issues).
La Gazette Algérienne, 1885–6, 1891–1901.
El Hack, 1893–4 (26 issues). One of earliest Muslim papers in Algeria.
L'Islam, 1909–12 (Bône), 1912–14 (Algiers). The leading Jeune-Algérien paper, founded in Bône.
Lega Franco-Italiano, 1896–7 (7 issues). Published in Italian for Bône's Italian community.

Sources and bibliography

El Montakheb, 1882–3 (40 issues). One of earliest Muslim papers published in Algeria.
Le Petit Bônois, 1882–8.
Le Phare de l'Algérie, 1874.
Le Phare de l'Est, 1885–6.
Le Radical Algérien, 1881.
Le Réveil Bônois, 1890–1915. Second leading paper in colonial Bône along with *La Démocratie Algérienne*; Radical Republican.
La Revue de l'Exposition, 1890 (13 issues). Published on occasion of Bône's colonial exposition.
Le Scandale Bônois, 1899 (2 issues). Successor to *Le Diocane Bônois*.
La Seybouse, 1851–87. Most important early Bône paper, one of first in Algeria.
Le Simoun, 1880–4.
La Torpille, 1884–5.

Printed primary sources

Anon. *Annuaire général administratif de l'Algérie*. Algiers: Bouyer, 1864.
—. *Annuaire de l'Algérie et des colonies*. Paris: Hachette, 1859.
British Parliamentary Papers, Accounts and Papers. *Commercial Reports. Algeria*. London. Volumes for 1857–86, 1888–1900, 1902–9, 1912–6.
Faure, Casimir. *Annuaire-Almanach administratif, commercial, industriel et agricole de l'Algérie*. APCA.
Gomot, F. *Annuaire de l'Algérie*. Paris: Magen, 1842.
Gouillon, Charles. *Annuaire administratif et commercial des trois départements de l'Algérie*. Algiers: Imprimerie de l'Association ouvrière, 1877.
Gouvernement général de l'Algérie, *Statistique générale de l'Algérie*. Algiers: Imprimerie Algérienne. Volumes for 1867–72, 1876–1900, 1914, 1916–25.
—. *Tableau générale des communes de l'Algérie*. Algiers: Imprimerie Algérienne. Volumes for 1875, 1876, 1884, 1892, 1897, 1907.
—. *Notice sur les routes et ports de l'Algérie*. Algiers: Giralt, 1900.
—. *Le Bône-Guelma. L'Ouenza. Janvier 1913*. Algiers: Heintz, 1913.
Mines d'Ouenza. *Plaidorie et réplique de M. Colin. La société concessionnaire des mines d'Ouenza demanderesse contre M. Carbonnel défendeur*. Paris: Skipper & East, 1906.
Ministère de l'agriculture, du commerce et des travaux publics. *Enquête agricole. Algérie. Alger-Oran-Constantine*. Paris: Imprimerie nationale, 1870.
Ministère du commerce, Office du travail. *Statistique des grèves et des recours à la conciliation et à l'arbitrage*. Paris: Imprimerie nationale. Volumes for 1893–1905, 1907.
Ministère de la guerre. *Le tableau de la situation des établissements français dans l'Algérie*, 19 vols. Paris: Imprimerie royale, 1838–68.
Procès-verbaux de la sous-commission d'étude et de la législation civile en Algérie. Annexe no. 1840 au procès-verbal de la 2e séance du 9 juillet 1900. Tome XXXI. Paris: Imprimerie de la Chambre des Députés, 1901.
Revue algérienne, tunisienne et marocaine de législation et de jurisprudence. Algiers: Jourdan. Volumes for 1885–1925.

310

Select bibliography

Bône and the region

Alquier. "Notices concernant les communes du département," *Recueil officiel des actes de la préfecture de Constantine*, 74 (année 1927).

Anon. *Bône et l'Est Algérien*. Bône: Imprimerie Centrale, 1959.

—. *Quatre villes d'Algérie (Alger, Oran, Constantine, Bône)*. Algiers: Imprimerie officielle, 1954.

Arnaud, Louis. *Bône. Son histoire, ses histoires*. Constantine: Damrémont, 1960.

Bel, Alfred. "Les bibliothèques des medersas algériennes, bibliothèque arabe de Bône, bibliothèque arabe de Bougie," 459–84. In Henri Lemaitre, *La lecture publique. Mémoirs et voeux du congrès international d'Alger*. Paris: Droz, 1931.

Bertagna, Jérome. *Le Port de Bône. Compte-rendu de la séance de la Chambre de commerce du 3 septembre 1894. Rapport de Bertagna. Bône, 1894.*

Blanc, A. *Tableautins sur l'Extrême-Orient algérien*. Bône: Puccini, 1887.

Bouyac, René. *Histoire de Bône*. Paris: Lecene, Oudin et Cie, 1892.

Brua, Edmond. *Fables, dites bônoises*. Algiers: Charlot, 1946.

Burger, M. *Notice sur le port de Bône*. Paris: Imprimerie Nationale, 1892.

Cambon, Jules. *Le Gouvernement Général de l'Algérie (1891–1897)*. Paris: Champion, 1918.

Cambon, Victor. *De Bône à Tunis, Sousse et Kairouan*. Lyon: chez l'auteur, 1885.

Chollet. "Bône, 1830–1881." Unpublished Diplôme d'études supérieures, Université d'Alger, 1952.

Conseil Municipal de la ville de Bône, *Enquête sur le projet de création du département de la Seybouse ayant Bône pour chef-lieu*. Bône: Carle, 1883.

Cornulier-Lucinière, Comte de. *La prise de Bône et de Bougie, d'après des documents inédits*. Paris: Lethielleux, 1895.

Del, Eugene. *Coups de pinceau sur Blida, Bône, Tlemcen, Oran et Constantine, suivi de l'éloge de Lamartine*. Paris: Challamel, 1885.

Derdour, H'sen. *Annaba. 25 siècles de vie quotidienne et de luttes*, 2 vols. Algiers: SNED, 1982–3.

Desfontaines, Louis René. "Fragments d'un voyage dans les régences de Tunis et d'Alger fait de 1783 à 1786." In Dureau de la Malle, ed., *Voyages dans les régences de Tunis et d'Alger*, 2 vols. Paris: Gide, 1838.

Dumoulin, Roger. *La structure asymétrique de l'économie algérienne d'après une analyse de la région de Bône*. Paris: Genin, 1959.

Eisenbeth, M. *Le Judaïsme Nord-Africain. Études démographiques sur les Israélites du département de Constantine*. Paris: Natanson, 1932.

Feraud, Charles. "Documents pour servir à l'histoire de Bône," *Revue africaine* 17 (1873): 4–23, 81–103, 165–86, 254–74, 341–51.

Fischer, Theobaldi. "Le golfe de Bône," *Bulletin de l'Académie d'Hippône* 26 (1894): 63–103.

311

Sources and bibliography

Grimal, Maurice-Marcel. *L'évolution du paludisme dans la région de Bône de 1830 à nos jours.* Thèse de médecine. Paris, 1934.

Khoudja, Louis. *La question indigène par un français d'adoption.* Bône, 1891.

Lafourcade, Louis. *Harmonies Bônoises.* Algiers: Baconnier, n.d.

Africanus, Leo. *The History and Description of Africa,* trans. John Pory, ed. Robert Brown, 3 vols. London: Bedford Press, 1896.

Maitrot, Albert-Charles. *Bône anecdotique.* Bône: Mariani, 1912.

—. *Bône militaire.* Bône: Mariani, 1934.

—. "Les rues du vieux Bône et l'Histoire," *Bulletin de l'Académie d'Hippone,* 32 (1912–13): 149–169.

—. and O. Damichel. *Fêtes du Cinquantenaire d'Hippone (1863–1913). Guide-Programme.* Bône: Xerri, 1913.

Marçais, Georges. "La Mosquée de Sidi Bou Marwan de Bône," in *Mélanges d'histoire et d'archéologie de l'Occident musulman,* 2 vols. Algiers: 1957, pp. 225–36.

Marchis, Fernand. *La Question de l'Ouenza.* Bône: Mariani, 1907.

Marec, Erwan. *Hippône la royale. Antique Hippo Regius.* Algiers: Imprimerie officielle, 1954.

Martel, André. *A l'arrière-plan des relations franco-maghrébines (1830–1881). Luis-Arnold et Joseph Allegro, consuls du Bey de Tunis à Bône.* Paris: Presses Universitaires de France, 1967.

Noireterre, Jumel de. *Contre la compagnie de Mokta-el-Hadid.* AWC: Ak 86.

Papier, Alexandre. *Lettres sur Hippone.* Bône: Carle, 1887.

—. "La mousquée de Bône," *Revue africaine* 33 (1889): 312–20.

Peretti, Charles de. *L'Ouenza devant le Conseil général de Constantine.* Bône: Mariani, 1908.

Peroni, Jean. *Bône, tu te rappelles.* Grenoble: Dardelet, 1979.

Peyssonnel, Jean André. "Relation d'un voyage sur les côtes de Barbarie (1724–25)," in Dureau de la Malle, ed., *Voyages dans la régence de Tunis et d'Alger,* 2 vols. Paris: Gide, 1838.

Pietri, L'abbé de. *Détails sur Bône et ses environs et divers autres sujets.* Algiers: Philippe, 1836.

Poiret, L'abbé. *Voyage en Barbarie, ou lettres écrites de l'ancienne Numidie en 1785 et 1786 sur la religion, les coutumes et les moeurs des Maures et des Arabes Bédouins.* Paris: Rochelle, 1789.

Prax, Victoriano. *Etude sur la question algérienne.* Bône: Lampronti, 1892.

Quillié, Joseph. *Le typhus examthematique à Bône, épidémie de 1909.* Montpellier, 1910.

Rasteil, Maxime. *A l'aube de l'Algérie française: Le calvaire des colons de 1848.* Paris: Figuiere, 1930.

Shaw, Thomas. "Travels or observations relating to several parts of Barbary and the Levant." In John Pinkerton, ed., *A General Collection of the Best and Most Interesting Voyages and Travels in all Parts of the World.* London, 1814.

Siari-Tengour, Ouanassa. "Les populations rurales des communes mixtes de l'arrondissement de Bône (Annaba) de la fin du XIXe siècle à 1914." Unpublished Thèse de 3e cycle, Université de Paris VII, Jussieu, 1981.

312

Travers, Lucette. "Bône. La Formation de la ville et les facteurs de son évolution," *Annales de Géographie* 67 (1958): 498–520.

—. "La mise en valeur du lac Fetzara," *Annales de géographie* 67 (1958): 260–2.

Algeria and beyond

Abitbol, Michel, ed. *Judaïsme d'Afrique du Nord aux XIXe-XXe siècles*. Jerusalem: Institut Ben Zvi, 1980.

Abrams, Larry, and D. J. Miller. "Who were the French Colonialists? A Reassessment of the *Parti Colonial*, 1890–1914," *Historical Journal* 19 (1976): 685–725.

Abu-Lughod, Janet. *Cairo*. Princeton: Princeton University Press, 1971.

—. *Rabat: Urban Apartheid in Morocco*, Princeton: Princeton University Press, 1980.

Abun-Nasr, J. *A History of the Maghrib*. Cambridge: Cambridge University Press, 1971.

Adam, André. *Casablanca. Essai sur la transformation de la société marocaine au contact de l'Occident*, 2 vols. Paris: Editions du Centre National de la Recherche Scientifique: 1968.

Ageron, Charles-Robert. *L'Algérie algérienne de Napoléon III à de Gaulle*. Paris: Sindbad, 1980.

—. "Le mouvement 'Jeune-Algérien' de 1900 à 1923" in *Etudes Maghrébines. Mélanges Charles-André Julien*, 217–43. Paris: Presses Universitaires de France, 1964.

—. *Histoire de l'Algérie contemporaine*, Vol. 2 (1871–1954). Paris: Presses Universitaires de France, 1979.

—. *Politiques coloniales au Maghreb*, Paris: Presses Universitaires de France, 1973.

—. "Brève histoire de la politique d'assimilation en Algérie," *Revue Socialiste* 95 (1956): 225–36.

—. *Les Algériens musulmans et la France (1870–1919)*, 2 vols. Paris: Presses Universitaires de France, 1968.

—. *France coloniale ou parti colonial?* Paris: Presses Universitaires de France, 1978.

—. "Gambetta et la reprise de l'expansion coloniale," *Revue français d'histoire d'outre-mer* 59 (1972): 165–204.

Amin, Samir. *L'Economie du Maghreb*, 2 vols. Paris: Editions de minuit, 1976.

Andrew, Christopher. "The French Colonialist Movement during the Third Republic: the Unofficial Mind of Imperialism," *Transactions of the Royal Historical Society*, fifth series, 26 (1976): 143–66.

Andrew, Christopher, P. Grupp and A. S. Kanya-Forstner. "Le mouvement colonial français et ses principales personnalités (1890–1914)," *Revue français d'histoire d'outre-mer* 62 (1975): 640–73.

Andrew, Christopher, and Sidney Kanya-Forstner. "The *Groupe Colonial* in the French Chamber of Deputies, 1892–1932," *Historical Journal* 17 (1974): 837–66.

313

Sources and bibliography

—. *The Climax of French Imperial Expansion, 1914–1924*. Stanford: Stanford University Press, 1981.

—. "French Business and the French Colonialists," *Historical Journal* 19 (1976): 981–1000.

—. "The French 'Colonial Party': Its Composition, Aims and Influence, 1885–1914," *Historical Journal* 14 (1971): 91–128.

Anon. "Note sur la Compagnie des phosphates de Constantine," *Revue de l'Industrie Minérale* (1931): 97–104.

—. *Le mal de voir. Ethnologie et orientalisme: politique et épistemologie, critique et autocritique*, Cahiers Jussieu No. 2, Université de Paris VII. Paris: Collection, 10/18, 1976.

—. *Les influences occidentales dans les villes maghrébines à l'époque contemporaine*. Aix-en-Provence: Centre de recherches et d'études sur les sociétés méditerranéennes, 1974.

—. "Le mouvement ouvrier français et l'Afrique du Nord (1920–1939)," *Le mouvement social*, special issue, 78 (1972).

Ayoun, Richard, and Bernard Cohen. *Les Juifs d'Algérie*. Paris: Lattes, 1982.

Azoulay, Paul. *La Nostalgérie français*. Paris: Baschet, 1980.

Bacri, Roland. *Trésors des racines pataouètes*. Paris: Belin, 1983.

Baldacci, Aimé. "L'Algérie et la société de l'Ouenza." Thèse. Algiers, 1947.

Balandier, Georges. "The Colonial Situation," in Pierre L. Van den Berghe, ed., *Africa: Social Problems of Change and Conflict*. San Francisco: Chandler, 1965.

Baroli, Marc. *La vie quotidienne des français en Algérie 1830–1914*. Paris: Hachette, 1967.

Barral, J. "Étude sur la question de l'Ouenza." Thèse pour le Doctorat de Droit. Paris: Libraire de la Ste. Sirey, 1912.

Bartuel, C., and H. Rulliére. *La mine et les mineurs*. Paris: Doin, 1923.

Battistini, Eugène. *Les Fôrets de chêne-liège de l'Algérie*. Algiers: Heintz, 1937.

Beguin, François. *Arabisances. Décor architectural et tracé urbain en Afrique du Nord, 1830–1950*. Paris: Bordas, 1983.

Bencheneb, S. "Quelques historiens modernes arabes en Algérie," *Revue Africaine* 100 (1956): 475–99.

Benhabiles, Cherif. *L'Algérie français vue par un indigène*. Algiers: Fontana, 1914.

Berbrugger, A. "M. Marion," *Revue africaine* 12 (1868): 139–43.

Berque, Augustin. "Esquisse d'une historie de la seigneurie algérienne," *Revue de la Méditerranée* (1949): 18–34, 168–180.

—. "La bourgeoisie algérienne," *Hesperis* 35 (1948): 1–29.

—. "Essai d'une bibliographie critique des confréries musulmanes algériennes," *Bulletin de la société d'archéologie et de géographie d'Oran* 39 (1919): 135–174, 193–233.

Berque, Jacques. *Le Maghrib entre deux guerres*, Paris: Seuil, 1962.

—. "Qu'est-ce qu'une tribu nord africaine?" in *Eventail de l'histoire vivante. Hommage à Lucien Febvre*, Vol. 1. Paris: Colin 1953, pp. 261–71.

—. "Médinas, villeneuves et bidonvilles," *Cahiers de Tunisie* 21–22 (1958): 5–42.

Betts, Raymond F. "The Architecture of French African Empire: A Neglected History," in *Études africaines offertes à Henri Brunschwig*. Paris: Editions de l'école des hautes études en sciences sociales, 1982, pp. 307–15.

—. *Assimilation and Association in French Colonial Theory, 1890–1914*. New York: Columbia University Press, 1961.

Binoche, Jacques. "Les élus d'outre-mer au Parlement de 1871 à 1914," *Revue français d'histoire d'outre-mer* 58 (1971): 82–115.

—. "Les élus d'outre-mer au Parlement de 1871 à 1914," unpublished thèse de Troisième cycle, Université de Toulouse, 1970.

Blanch, Lesley. *The Wilder Shores of Love*. London: John Murray, 1954.

Bontems, Claude. *Manuel des institutions algériennes de la domination turque à l'indépendance, Vol. 1: La domination turque et le régime militaire 1518–1870*. Paris: Cujas, 1975.

Bordas, Jeannine. *Le peuplement algérien. Essai démographique*. Oran: Fonque, 1958.

Boujedra, Rachid. *La vie quotidienne en Algérie*. Paris: Hachette, 1971.

Bourdieu, Pierre. "Le champ scientifique," in *Actes de la recherche en sciences sociales*. Paris: Service des publications de la Maison de l'Homme, 1977, pp. 88–104.

—. *Algeria 1960*. Cambridge: Cambridge University Press, 1979.

—. *Sociologie de l'Algérie*. Paris: Presses Universitaires de France, 1958.

—. *Outline of a Theory of Practice*. Cambridge: Cambridge University Press, 1977.

Boyer, Pierre. *La vie quotidienne à Alger à la veille de l'intervention française*. Paris, Hachette, 1963.

Braudel, Fernand. "Les Espagnols et l'Afrique du Nord de 1492 à 1577," *Revue africaine* 69 (1968): 184–233, 351–428.

—. *The Mediterranean and the Mediterranean World in the Age of Philip II*, trans. Sian Reynolds, 2 vols,. New York: Harper and Row, 1972.

Brett, Michael. "Problems in the Interpretation of the History of the Maghrib in the Light of Some Recent Publications," *Journal of African History* 13 (1972): 489–506.

Brochier, J., and A. Brochier. *Livre d'or de l'Algérie. Dictionnaire des personnalités passées et contemporaines*. Algiers: 1937.

Brown, Kenneth. *People of Salé*. Cambridge: Harvard University Press, 1976.

Brown, Leon Carl, ed. *From Madina to Metropolis*. Princeton: Darwin Press, 1973.

—. "The Many Faces of Colonial Rule in French North Africa," *Revue de l'occident musulman et de la Méditerranée* 13–14 (1973): 171–191.

—. *The Tunisia of Ahmad Bey, 1837–1855*. Princeton: Princeton University Press, 1974.

Brunot, L. "Sabirs," *Journal des Instituteurs de l'Afrique du Nord* 1 (April 1948): 209–10.

Brunschwig, Henri. *French Colonialism, 1871–1914: Myths and Realities*. London: Pall Mall, 1966.

Burke, Edmund. "Fez, the Setting Sun of Islam: A Study of the Politics of Colonial Ethnography," *Maghreb Review* 2 (1977): 1–7.

—. "Pan-Islam and Moroccan Resistance to French Colonial Penetration," *Journal of African History* 13 (1972): 97–118.

—. "The Sociology of Islam: The French Tradition," in Malcolm Kerr, ed., *Islamic Studies: A Tradition and its Problems*. Malibu, California, 1980, pp. 73–88.

—. *Prelude to Protectorate in Morocco: Precolonial Protest and Resistance, 1860–1912*. Chicago: University of Chicago Press, 1976.

—. "Towards a History of the Maghrib," *Middle Eastern Studies* 11 (1975): 306–23.

—. "Recent Books on Colonial Algerian History," *Middle Eastern Studies* 7 (1971): 241–50.

Cat, Edouard. *Biographies algériennes, 1830–1900*. Algiers: Imprimerie de l'Algérie nouvelle, n.d.

Centre national de la recherche scientifique, *Les relations entre juifs et musulmans en Afrique du Nord XIXe-XXe siècles*. Paris: Editions du CNRS, 1980.

Charnay, Jean-Paul. *La vie musulmane en Algérie d'après la jurisprudence de la première moitié du XXe siècle*. Paris: Presses Universitaires de France, 1965.

Chombart de Lauwe, J. "Tableau des syndicats indigènes d'Algérie et de Tunisie," *Revue des études islamiques*, cahier II (1935): 187–94.

—. "L'organisation ouvrière et artisanale des indigènes dans les principales villes et les mines d'Algérie et de Tunisie," *Renseignements coloniaux de l'Afrique française* (1936): 74–9, 81–6.

Chouraqui, André. *Les Juifs de l'Afrique du Nord*. Paris: Presses Universitaires de France, 1952.

Colonna, Fanny. "Saints furieux et saints studieux ou, dans l'Aurès, comment la religion vient aux tribus," *Annales E.S.C.* 35 (1980): 642–62.

—. *Instituteurs algériens (1883–1939)*. Algiers: Office des publications universitaires, 1975.

—. "Questions à propos de la littérature orale comme savoir," *Revue de l'occident musulman et de la Méditerranée* 21 (1976): 17–26.

—. "Cultural resistance and religious legitimacy in colonial Algeria," *Economy and Society* 3 (1974): 233–52.

Coppolani, Xavier. *Confrérie religieuse musulmane de Sidi Ammar bou Senna ou l'Ammaria*. Algiers: Jourdan, 1894.

—. and Depont, Octave. *Les confréries religieuses musulmanes*. Algiers: Jourdan, 1897.

Cousteix, P. "Les financiers sous le Second Empire," *1848: revue des révolutions contemporaines* 43 (1950): 105–35.

Crapanzano, Vincent. *Tuhami: Portrait of a Moroccan*. Chicago: University of Chicago Press, 1980.

Dachot, Léon. *La fabrication du tabac en Algérie*. Algiers: Giralt, 1900.

Danziger, Raphael. *Abd al-Qadir and the Algérians*. New York: Holmes and Meier, 1977.

Darasse, Vincent. "Paysans en communauté et colporteurs émigrants de Tabou-Douchd-el-Baar (Grande Kabylie) (Province d'Alger)," *Les ouvriers des deux mondes* 5 (1885): 459–502.

316

Déjeux, Jean. *Djoha hier et aujourd'hui*. Sherbrooke, Canada: Naaman, 1978.

Demontès, Victor. *Le peuple algérien. Essai de démographie algérienne*. Algiers: Imprimerie Algérienne, 1906.

Desparmet, Joseph. "La réaction linguistique en Algérie," *Bulletin de la Société Géographique d'Alger* 36 (1931): 1–33.

—. "Les réactions nationalitaires en Algérie," *Bulletin de la Société Géographique d'Alger* 37 (1932): 173–84.

—. "La conquête racontée par les indigènes," *Bulletin de la Société Géographique d'Alger* 37 (1932): 437–546.

—. "Elégies et satires politiques de 1830 à 1914," *Bulletin de la Société Géographique d'Alger* 38 (1933): 35–64.

Djender, Mahieddine. *Introduction à l'histoire de l'Algérie*. Algiers: SNED, 1972.

Duboucher, Georges. *L'Algérie 1870–1930*. Toulouse: Milan, 1983.

Dumoulin, Roger. *La structure asymétrique de l'économie algérienne d'après une analyse de la région de Bône*. Paris: Génin, 1959.

Dussert, Désiré. "Étude sur les gisements métallifères de l'Algérie," *Annales des Mines*, tenth series, 17 (1910): 24–84, 91–203.

—. "Étude sur les gisements de fer de l'Algérie," *Annales des Mines*, eleventh series, 1 (1912): 69–133, 135–256.

—. "Les gisements algériens de phosphates de chaux," *Annales des Mines*, thirteenth series, 6 (1924): 135–221, 229–325, 333–98, 407–51.

—. *Les Mines et les carrières en Algérie*. Paris: Larose, 1931.

Duvignaud, Jean. *Change at Shebika*. New York: Randon House, 1970.

Eickelman, Dale. "Ideological Change and Regional Cults: Maraboutism and Ties of 'Closeness' in Western Morocco," in R. P. Werbner, ed., *Regional Cults*. London: Academic Press, 1977, pp. 3–28.

—. *The Middle East: An Anthropological Approach*. Englewood-Cliffs, New Jersey: Prentice-Hall, 1981.

—. "Is There an Islamic City? The Making of a quarter in a Moroccan Town," *International Journal of Middle East Studies* 5 (1974): 274–94.

Eisenbeth, Maurice. *Les Juifs de l'Afrique du Nord*. Algiers: Imprimerie du Lycée, 1936.

—. "Les Juifs en Algérie et en Tunisie à l'époque turque (1516–1830)," *Revue africaine* 96 (1952): 114–87, 344–84.

Emerit, Marcel. "L'état d'esprit des musulmans d'Algérie de 1847 à 1870," *Revue d'histoire moderne et contemporaine* 8 (1961): 103–120.

—. "La question algérienne en 1871," *Revue d'histoire moderne et contemporaine* 19 (1972): 256–64.

—. *Les Saint-Simoniens en Algérie*. Paris: Belles Lettres 1941.

—. "Le mystère Yusuf," *Revue africaine* 96 (1952): 385–98.

—. "Les liaisons terrestres entre le Soudan et l'Afrique du Nord au XVIIIe et au début du XIXe siècle," *Travaux de l'institut des recherches sahariennes* 11 (1954): 29–47.

Ernouf, A. *Paulin Talabot: sa vie et son oeuvre, 1799–1885*. Paris, 1886.

Esquer, Gabriel. *Iconographie historique de l'Algérie depuis le XVIe siècle jusqu'à 1870*, 3 vols. Paris: Plon, 1929.

Sources and bibliography

Evans-Pritchard, E.E. *The Sanusi of Cyrenaica*. Oxford: Clarendon Press, 1949.

Fauçon, Narcisse. *Le livre d'or de l'Algérie (1830–89)*. Paris: Challamel, 1889.

Filippini, J.P. "Livourne et l'Afrique du Nord au XVIIIe siècle," *Revue d'histoire Maghrébine* 7–8 (1977): 125–50.

Fitzgerald, Peter. "The Political Consequences of Economic Failure: An Interpretation of Colonial Algeria (ca. 1880–1950)." Unpublished paper presented at annual meeting, Society for French Historical Studies, Los Angeles, 1985.

—. "Algerian Farmers and Agricultural Modernization in the Colonial Era: Market Opportunities vs. Market Avoidance Strategies." Unpublished paper presented at annual meeting, French Colonial History Society, Evanston, IL, 1982.

Gallagher, Nancy. *Medicine and Power in Tunisia, 1780–1900*, Cambridge: Cambridge University Press, 1983.

Gallissot, René. "Precolonial Algeria," *Economy and Society* 4 (1975): 418–445.

— et al. *Sur le féodalisme*. Cahiers du Centre d'études et de recherches marxistes. Paris: Editions sociales, 1971.

—, ed. *Structures et cultures precapitalistes*. Actes de colloque tenu à l'Université de Paris VIII-Vincennes, decembre 1976. Paris: Ed. Anthropos, 1981.

Gautier, Emile-Félix. *L'Algérie et la métropole* Paris: Payot, 1920.

—. *Un siècle de colonisation*. Paris: Alcan, 1930.

Geertz, Clifford. *Islam Observed*. New Haven: Yale University Press, 1968.

—. "In Search of North Africa," *New York Review of Books* (April 22, 1971): 10–24.

—. "Centers, Kings, and Charisma: Reflections on the Symbolics of Power," in *Local Knowledge*. New York: Basic Books, 1983, pp. 150–71.

—. Hildred Geertz and Lawrence Rosen. *Meaning and Order in Moroccan Society*. Cambridge: Cambridge University Press, 1979.

Gellner, Ernest. *Saints of the Atlas*. Chicago: University of Chicago Press, 1969.

—. *Muslim Society*. Cambridge: Cambridge University Press, 1981.

—. and Charles Micaud, eds. *Arabs and Berbers*. London: Duckworth, 1973.

—. and Jean-Claude Vatin, eds., *Islam et Politique au Maghreb*. Paris: Centre national de la recherche scientifique, 1981.

Geoffrey, Auguste. "Arabes pasteurs nomades de la tribu des Larbas (Région saharienne de l'Algérie)," *Les ouvriers des deux mondes*, second series, 1 (1887): 409–64.

—. "Bordier (fellah) berbère de la Grande Kabylie (Province d'Alger)," *Les ouvriers des deux mondes*, second series, 2 (1888): 53–92.

van Gennep, Arnold. *En Algérie*. Paris: Mercure de France, 1914.

Gille, Bertrand. "Minérais algériens et sidérurgie métropolitaine," *Revue d'histoire de la Sidérurgie* 1 (1960): 37–55.

Gilsenan, Michael. *Recognizing Islam*. New York: Random House, 1982.

Gordon, David. *The Passing of French Algeria*. New York: Oxford University Press, 1966.

318

Gourdon, Hubert, Jean-Robert Henry, and Françoise Henry-Lorcerie. "Roman colonial et idéologie colonial en Algérie," *Revue algérienne des sciences juridiques, économiques et politiques* 11 (1974): 7–252.

Gouvion, Marthe and Edmond. *Kitab Aayane el-Marhariba (Livre des notables maghrébins)*. Paris: Genthner, 1929.

Gran, Peter. *Islamic Roots of Capitalism: Egypt, 1760–1840*. Austin: University of Texas Press, 1979.

Grandguillaume, Gilbert. *Nédroma, l'évolution d'une medina*. Leiden: E. J. Brill, 1976.

Hadj-Sadok, Mahammed. "Dialectes arabes et francisation linguistique de l'Algérie," *Annales de l'institut d'études orientales* (1955): 61–97.

Hammoudi, A. "Segmentarity, social stratification, political power and sainthood: Reflections on Gellner's theses," *Economy and Society* 9 (1980): 279–303.

Hanoteau, Adolphe, and A. Letourneau. *La Kabylie et les coutumes kabyles*, 3 vols. Paris: Imprimerie nationale, 1872–3.

Heggoy, Alf Andrew. "The Origins of Algerian nationalism in the colony and in France," *Muslim World* 58 (1968): 128–40.

Hirschberg, Haim Zeev. *A History of the Jews in North Africa*, Vol. 2: *From the Ottoman Conquest to the Present Time*. Leiden: E. J. Brill, 1981.

Horne, Alistair. *A Savage War of Peace*. London: Macmillan, 1977.

Hourani, Albert. *Arabic Thought in the Liberal Age, 1798–1939*. London: Oxford University Press, 1962.

—. and S. Stern, eds. *The Islamic City*. Oxford, 1970.

Isnard, Hildebert. *La vigne en Algérie*, 2 vols. Gap: Ophrys, 1951–4.

—. "La vigne en Algérie," Vol. 3. AOM, typescript, no date.

Julien, Charles-André. "Colons français et Jeunes-Tunisiens," *Revue française d'histoire d'outre-mer* 54 (1967): 87–150.

—. *L'Afrique du Nord en marche*, third revised edition. Paris: Julliard, 1972.

—. *Histoire de l'Algérie contemporaine. Les débuts 1830–70*, Vol. 1. Paris: Presses Universitaires de France, 1964.

Juving, Alexandre. *Le socialisme en Algerie*. Algiers, 1924.

Kaddache, Mahfoud. *La vie politique à Algiers de 1919 à 1939*. Algiers: SNED, 1970.

—. *Histoire du nationalisme algérien*, 2 vols. Algiers: SNED, 1980.

Keddie, Nikki., ed. *Scholars, Saints and Sufis*. Berkeley: University of California Press, 1972.

Kramer, Jane. *Unsettling Europe*. New York: Random House, 1980.

Lacheraf, Mostefa. *L'Algérie. Nation et société*. Paris: Maspero, 1965.

Laffont, Pierre. *L'Algérie des français*. Paris: Bordas, 1981.

Lanly, A. *Le français d'Afrique du Nord*, 2nd ed. Paris: Bordas, 1970.

Lapidus, Ira M. *Contemporary Islamic Movements in Historical Perspective*. Berkeley: Institute of International Studies, University of California, Berkeley, 1983.

—. "The Evolution of Muslim Urban Society," *Comparative Studies in Society and History* 15 (1973): 21–50.

Sources and bibliography

Laroui, Abdallah. *L'histoire du Maghreb, un essai de synthèse*, 2 vols. Paris: Maspero, 1970.

Lawless, Richard, and Gerald Blake. *Tlemcen: Continuity and Change in an Algerian Islamic Town*. London: Bowker, 1976.

Leconte, Daniel. *Les pieds noirs. Histoire et portrait d'une communauté*. Paris: Seuil, 1980.

Lespès, René. "Le Port de Bône et les mines de l'Est Constantinois," *Annales de Géographie* 32 (1923): 526–41.

—. *Oran. Etude de géographie et d'histoire urbaines*. Paris: Alcan, 1938.

—. *Alger. Etude de géographie et d'histoire urbaines*. Paris: Alcan, 1930.

Le Tourneau, Roger. *Fès avant le protectorat*. Casablanca: Société marocaine de librairie et d'édition, 1949.

Loth, Gaston. *Le peuplement italien en Tunisie et en Algérie*. Paris: Colin, 1905.

Lucas, Philippe, and Jean-Claude Vatin, eds. *L'Algérie des anthropologues*. Paris: Maspero, 1975.

McCarthy, Patrick. *Camus: A Critical Study of His Life and Work*. New York: Random House, 1982.

Maguelonne, Jeanne. "Le peuplement italien et la propriété foncière italienne en Algérie," *Revue algérienne, tunisienne et marocaine* (1931): 56–79.

Marc, H. *Notes sur les fôrets de l'Algérie*. Paris: Larose, 1930.

Mammeri, Mouloud, and Pierre Bourdieu. "Dialogue sur la poésie orale en Kabylie," *Actes de la recherche en sciences sociales* 23 (1978): 51–66.

Martin, B. G. *Muslim Brotherhoods in Nineteenth Century Africa*. New York: Cambridge University Press, 1976.

Masquéray, Emile. *Formation des cités chez les populations sedentaires de l'Algérie: Kabyles du Djurdjura, Chaouia de l'Aurès, Beni-Mezab 1886*, introduction Fanny Colonna. Paris: Edisud, 1886, 1983.

Merad, Ali. *Le réformisme musulman en Algérie de 1925 à 1940. Essai d'histoire religiense et sociale*. Paris-La Haye: Mouton, 1967.

Meynier, Gilbert. *L'Algérie révélée. La guerre de 1914–1918 et le premier quart du XXe siècle*. Geneva: Droz, 1981.

—. "Aspects de l'économie de l'Est algérien pendant la guerre de 1914–1918," *Revue historique* 501 (1972): 81–116.

Micaud, Ellen. "Urbanization, Urbanism, and the Medina of Tunis," *International Journal of Middle East Studies* 9 (1978): 433–49.

Miège, Jean-Louis. "Corailleurs italiens en Algérie au XIXe siècle," in *Minorités, techniques et métiers*, Institut de recherches méditerranéennes. Aix-en-Provence: Centre National de le Recherche Scientifique, 1980.

—. "Algiers: Colonial Metropolis (1830–1961)," in Robert Ross and Gerard Telkamp, eds., *Colonial Cities*. Dordrecht: Martinus Nijhoff, 1985, pp. 171–9.

Millet, Philippe. "Les jeunes algériens," *Revue de Paris* 20 (1913): 158–90.

Si Mohand-ou-Mhand. *Les esefra, poèmes de Si Mohand-ou-Mhand*, trans. Mouloud Mammeri. Paris: Maspero, 1969.

Montoy, Louis. "Un journal algérien au XIXe siècle. *La Démocratie Algérienne* de Bône (1886–1913)," *Revue de l'occident musulman et de la Méditerranée* 26 (1978): 105–20.

—. La presse dans le département de Constantine (1870–1918), 3 vols. Unpublished thèse de doctorat, Université de Provence, 1982.

Morsly, Taieb-Ould. *Contribution à la question indigène en Algérie*. Constantine: Marle et Biron, 1894.

Musette [pseud. Auguste Robinet], *Cagayous. Ses meilleures histoires*. Paris: Gallimard, 1931.

Musso, Fréderic. *L'Algérie d'autrefois*. Paris: La Table Ronde, 1976.

Neveu, François de. *Les khouan. Ordres religieux chez les Musulmans*. Algiers, 1846.

Nouschi, André. "Le travail à Alger dans la première moitié du XIXe siècle," in Université de Nice, *La force de travail dans les cités méditerranéenes du milieu du XVIIIe au milieu du XIXe siècle*. Nice, 1975, pp. 169–75.

—. *La naissance du nationalisme algérien*. Paris: Editions de Minuit, 1962.

—. "Un cas ambigu: le Maghreb," in Madeleine Reberioux and Georges Haupt, eds., *La Deuxième Internationale et l'Orient*. Paris: Cujas, 1967, pp. 439–71.

—. "La crise commerciale et financière de 1875 en Algérie et dans le Constantinois." *Revue d'histoire économique et sociale* 36 (1958): 412–31.

—. "La crise économique de 1866 à 1869 dans le Constantinois: Aspect démographique," *Hespéris* (1959): 105–23.

—. *Enquête sur le niveau de vie des populations rurales constantinoises de la conquête jusqu'en 1919*. Paris: Presses Universitaires de France, 1961.

—. "Notes sur la vie traditionnelle des populations forestières algériennes," *Annales de géographie* 68 (1959): 525–35.

—. "Constantine à la veille de la conquête française," *Les Cahiers de Tunisie* 3 (1955): 371–87.

—. "Le sens de certains chiffres. Croissance urbaine et vie politique en Algérie (1926–1936)," in *Études Maghrébines. Mélanges Charles-André Julien*, pp. 199–210. Paris: Presses Universitaires de France, 1964.

O'Brien, Conor Cruise. *Albert Camus of Europe and Africa*. New York: Viking Press, 1970.

Papier, Alexandre. *Question des tabacs en Algérie*. Algiers: Duclaux, 1862.

Passeron, René. *Les grandes sociétés de colonisation en Afrique du Nord*. Algiers: Typo-Litho, 1925.

Pensa, H. *Voyage de la délégation de la commission sénatoriale d'études des questions algériennes présidée par Jules Ferry*. Paris, 1894.

Peristiany, J. G., ed. *Mediterranean Family Structures*. Cambridge: Cambridge University Press, 1976.

—. ed. *Honor & Shame: The Values of Mediterranean Society*. London: Weidenfield & Nicolson, 1965.

Perkins, Kenneth. *Qaids, Captains, and Colons: French Military Administration in the Colonial Maghreb, 1884–1934*. New York, 1981.

Persell, Stuart. *The French Colonial Lobby, 1889–1938*. Stanford: Hoover Institution Press, 1983.

Peyerimhoff, Henri de. *Enquête sur les résultats de la colonisation officielle de 1871 à 1895*, 2 vols. Algiers: Torrent, 1906.

321

Sources and bibliography

Peyronnet, Raymond. *Livre d'or des officiers des affaires indigènes (1830–1930)*, 2 vols. Algiers: Imprimerie algérienne, 1930.

Prenant, André. "La propriété foncière des citadins dans les régions de Tlemcen et Sidi bel Abbès," *Annales algériennes de géographie* 2 (1967): 2–94.

—. "Rapports villes-campagnes dans le Maghreb: l'exemple de l'Algérie," *Revue tunisienne de sciences sociales* 15 (1968): 191–216.

Prochaska, David. "The Political Culture of Settler Colonialism in Algeria: Politics in Bône, 1870–1920," *Revue de l'Occident Musulman et de la Méditerranée* 48–49 (1988): 293–311.

—. "Fire on the Mountain: Resisting Colonialism in Algeria," in Donald Crummey, ed., *Banditry, Rebellion and Social Protest in Africa*. Portsmouth, NH: Heinemann, 1986.

—. "Reconstructing *L'Algérie Française*," in Jean-Claude Vatin, ed., *Connaissances du Maghreb*, pp. 65–78. Paris: Centre National de la Recherche Scientifique, 1984.

—. "La ségrégation résidentielle en société coloniale. Le cas de Bône (Algérie) de 1872 à 1954," *Cahiers d'Histoire* 25 (1980): 53–74.

Rabinow, Paul. "Ordonnance, Discipline, Regulation: Some Reflections on Urbanism," *Humanities in Society* 5 (1982): 267–78.

—. *Reflections on Fieldwork in Morocco*. Berkeley: University of California Press, 1979.

Renaudot, Françoise. *L'histoire des Français en Algérie, 1830–1962*. Paris: Robert Laffont, 1979.

Rey-Goldzeiguer, Annie. *Le royaume arabe. La politique algérienne de Napoléon III, 1861–1870*. Algiers: SNED, 1977.

Ricoux, René. *La population européenne en Algérie pendant l'année 1884. Etude statistique*. Philippeville: Feuille, 1885.

Rinn, Louis. *Marabouts et khouan. Etude sur l'Islam en Algérie*. Algiers, 1884.

Robles, Emmanuel, ed. *Les pieds-noirs*. Paris: Lebaud, 1982.

Rosen, Lawrence. "Muslim-Jewish Relations in a Moroccan City," *International Journal of Middle East Studies* 3 (1972): 435–49.

Ruedy, John. *Land Policy in Colonial Algeria*. Berkeley: University of California Press, 1967.

Sahli, Mohamed. *Décoloniser l'histoire: Introduction à l'histoire du Maghreb*. Paris: Maspero, 1965.

Sainte-Maire, A. "Etude des migrations dans la Régence d'Alger," in *Les migrations dans les pays méditerranéens au XVIIIe et au début du XIXe siècles*, pp. 158–73. Nice: Centre de la Méditerranée moderne et contemporaine, 1974.

Sari, Djilali. *L'insurrection de 1871*. Algiers: SNED, 1972.

—. *La dépossession des fellahs*. Algiers: SNED, 1975.

—. *Les villes précoloniales de l'Algérie occidentale*. Algiers: SNED, 1970.

Schwarzfuchs, Simon. *Les Juifs d'Algérie et la France (1830–1855)*. Jerusalem: Institut Ben-Zvi, 1981.

Seddon, David. "Economic Anthropology or Political Economy?: Approaches to the Analysis of Pre-Capitalist Formations in the Maghreb," in John

Clammer, ed. *The New Economic Anthropology*, pp. 61–109. New York: St. Martin's Press, 1978.

Sivan, Emmanuel. *Communisme et nationalisme en Algérie, 1920–1962*. Paris: Fondation Nationale des Sciences Politiques, 1976.

—. "Colonialism and Popular Culture in Algeria," *Journal of Contemporary History* 14 (1979): 21–53.

Sivers, Peter von. "Family Budgets and Subsistence Minima in Rural Households of French Colonial Algeria, 1880–1914," *Peasant Studies* 10 (1982): 35–48.

—. "The realm of justice: Apocalyptic revolts in Algeria (1849–1879)," *Humaniora Islamica* 1 (1973): 47–60.

—. "Les plaisirs du collectionneur: capitalisme fiscal et chefs indigènes en Algérie (1840–1860)," *Annales ESC* 35 (1980): 679–699.

—. "Algerian Landownership and Rural Leadership, 1860–1914: A Quantitative Approach," *Maghreb Review* 4 (1979): 58–62.

—. "Insurrection and Accommodation: Tribal Leadership in Eastern Algeria, 1840–1900," *International Journal of Middle East Studies* 6 (1975): 259–75.

Slim. *Zid Ya Bouzid. Les meilleures bandes dessines de Slim*. Algiers: SNED, 1980.

Smith, Tony. "Muslim Impoverishment in Colonial Algeria," *Revue de l'Occident Musulman et de la Méditerranée* 17 (1974): 139–62.

—. *The French Stake in Algeria, 1945–1962*. Ithaca: Cornell University Press, 1978.

Stambouli, F. "Système social et urbanisation: Aspects de la dynamique globale de l'urbanisation de le ville de Tunis," *Revue tunisienne de sciences sociales* 8 (1971): 31–63.

—. and A. Zghal. "Urban life in pre-colonial North Africa," *British Journal of Sociology* 27 (1976): 1–20.

Tomas, François. *Annaba et sa région. Organisation de l'espace dans l'extrême-est algérien*. Saint-Etienne: Guichard, 1977.

—. "Les mines et la région d'Annaba," *Revue de géographie de Lyon* 45 (1970): 31–59.

—. "Annaba et sa région agricole," *Revue de géographie de Lyon* 44 (1969): 37–74.

Turin, Yvonne. *Affrontements culturels dans l'Algérie coloniale. Ecoles, médecines, religion, 1830–1880*. Paris: Maspero, 1971.

Udovitch, Avram, and Lucette Valensi. *The Last Arab Jews: The Communities of Jerba, Tunisia*. New York: Harwood, 1984.

Valensi, Lucette. "Calamités démographiques en Tunisie et en méditerranée orientale aux XVIIIe et XIXe siècles," *Annales ESC* 24 (1969): 1540–61.

—. *Fellahs tunisiens*. Paris: Mouton, 1977.

—. "Islam et capitalisme: Production et commerce des chéchias en Tunisie et en France aux XVIIIe et XIXe siècles," *Revue d'histoire moderne et contemporaine* 16 (1969): 376–400.

—. *Le Maghreb avant la prise d'Alger (1790–1830)*. Paris: Flammarion, 1969.

Vatin, Jean-Claude, et al. *Connaissances du Maghreb*. Paris: Centre national de la recherche scientifique, 1984.

Sources and bibliography

—. "Religious Resistance and State Power in Algeria," in A. E. Cudsi and A. Dessouki, eds., *Islam and Power*, pp. 119–57. London: Croom Helm, 1981.

—. "Popular Puritanism versus State Reformism: Islam in Algeria," in James Piscatori, ed., *Islam in the Political Process*, pp. 98–121. Cambridge: Cambridge University Press, 1983.

—. *L'Algérie politique. Histoire et société*. Paris: Armand Colin, 1974.

Vayssettes, M. "Histoire de Constantine sous la domination turque de 1517 à 1837," *Revue de la société archéologique de Constantine* 11 (1807): 241–352; 12 (1868): 255–392; 13 (1869): 453–620.

Vidala, R. *Les maltais hors de malte. Etude sur l'émigration maltaise*. Paris: Rousseau, 1911.

Wansbrough, John. "The Decolonization of North African History," *Journal of African History* 9 (1968): 643–50.

—. "On Recomposing the Islamic History of North Africa," *Journal of the Royal Asiatic Society* (1969): 161–70.

Wright, Gwendolyn, and Paul Rabinow. "Savoir et pouvoir dans l'urbanisme moderne colonial d'Ernest Hébrard," *Les cahiers de la recherche architecturale* 9 (1982): 26–43.

Yacono, Xavier. *La colonisation des plaines du Chélif*, 2 vols. Algiers: Imbert, 1955–6.

—. "La Recherche et les livres sur l'histoire contemporarine de l'Algérie au cours des dernières années (1962–1970)," *Comptes rendus mensuels de l'Académie des sciences d'outre-mer* 30 (séance du 18 decembre 1970): 429–55.

Index

Abbas, Ferhat, 237, 240
Abd al-Qadir, Amir, 211, 215, 232, 237
Abu-Lughod, Janet, 11, 154–5, 179
Adjoint indigène, 24, 183, 252
Ageron, Charles-Robert, 1, 3–5, 202, 204, 206, 234
Ahmed Bey, 62–3
Ain Mokra (Berrahal), 77–8, 81, 83–4, 93, 109, 111, 152. *See also* Mokta el Hadid
Algeria, historiography of, 1–6, 25; precolonial mode of production in, 54; 1832 land law in, 65, 70, 181
Algerian nationalism, 10–11, 26–7, 236. *See also Jeunes Algériens*; Islamic Reformism; Messali Hadj
Algerian Revolution, 2, 26, 80, 115, 209, 215, 238, 253, 255–6
Algérie française, 1, 3–4, 27, 237. *See also* Algeria
Algiers, 11, 19, 22, 44, 51, 53, 62, 83–4, 111, 136, 140, 152, 192, 202–3, 224, 232–3, 236, 241–2, 257
Algiers, Regency of, 50, 57
Annaba, 26, 247; coral fishing in, 35, 45, 53; demography of, 41–7; disease in, 45–6; economy of, 47–54; geography of, 32–41; plain of, 32–3, 36, 42; politics in, 57–9; port of, 35; religion in, 59–61; society in, 54–7. *See also* Bône
Anti-semitism, 202–5, 256
Arabs, 2–4, 6, 41, 43–4, 47, 50–2, 56, 59, 124, 153–4, 213–5, 237, 247; in Bône, 27, 136, 167–8, 170, 173, 182, 254–5. *See also* individual groups
Arnaud, Louis, 253–4
Assemblée Nationale, Paris, 113, 190, 216, 226
Assimilation, policy of, 155, 183–4, 198, 232–3

Baroli, Marc, 197, 206
Bassano, marquis de, 78–9, 81, 92, 242
Benaouda, Benmostefa, 238–9, 242
Ben Badis, Abd al-Hamid, 236–7, 244, 256–8
Ben Bella, Ahmed, 238, 256
Bengui, Hadj Omar, 133, 222, 234
Beni Salah, 42–3, 50, 71
Beni Salah forest, 26, 33, 48, 73–5
Beni Urgine, 42, 44, 47, 61, 120, 167
Benyacoub, Belkassem, 253, 256
Benyacoub family, 56, 223, 235, 252–4
Benzaim, Mohammed, 238–9
Berbers, 2–4, 41, 43–4, 47, 50–2, 56, 58, 73, 124, 136, 153–4, 181–2, 213, 215, 237, 247, 250, 252; in Bône, 27, 173, 255. *See also* Kabyles
Bertagna, Dominique, 197–200
Bertagna, Jérome, mayor, 66–7, 70–1, 99, 112–13, 130, 181, 186, 188–9, 192–205, 209, 216, 223, 226, 229–31, 233–4, 238, 243–4, 252–3, 255, 258
Bizerte, 105–9
Blum-Violette reforms, 2–3, 237
Bône, 11, 22–6; commerce in, 115–17, 123; demography of, 142–9; disease in, 45–6; elections in, 27, 184–8, 192; industry in, 115–17, 123; *mairie* (city hall), 115, 133, 207; *mellah*, 41, 138, 162, 223; new city (*nouvelle ville*), 157, 159–60, 207–8, 222, 242; old city (*vieille ville*), 157, 160–3, 165, 207–8, 212, 222, 242, 254; Opportunist Republicans in, 185, 187–9, 200, 202–4; outskirts (*banlieue*), 71, 157, 159, 163, 165, 222; port of, 84–5, 111–15, 193, 216, 222; Radical Republicans in, 185–6, 188–9, 200, 202–4
Bône *département*, 109–11
Bône-Guelma railroad, 105, 107, 109–11, 125–6, 197–8

325

Index

Boudjimah River, 34, 36, 135
Bou Hamra mine, 77, 125
Boumaiza, Mohammed Tahar, 252
Boumaiza family, 56, 252, 254
Bourdieu, Pierre, 3, 28, 155
Bouyac, René, 249–51
Broussard, state prosecutor, 194–6, 200
Brua, Edmund, 229
Bugeaud. *See* Seraidi
Bugeaud, marshal, 211, 215
Burger, Bône employee, 193–8

Cairo, 19, 22, 85, 141
Cambon, Jules, governor general, 199,
   201–2, 204–5, 223, 233
Camus, Albert, 70, 228–31, 240–4, 256
Carloutche, Bône fisherman, 226, 229,
   253
Carthage, 247–8
Casablanca, 19, 22, 109, 207
Casbah in Bône/Annaba, 36, 44, 57, 62,
   210, 238, 248
Cerner, Philippe de, 109
Cès-Caupenne, forest concessionaire,
   74–5
Charles X, 62
Clemenceau, Georges, 105–6
Colonial situation, 7–9
Colonial urbanism, colonial cities, 11–14,
   16–20, 26; protocolonial cities, 14–16,
   26; postcolonial cities, 12, 21; settler
   colonial cities, 21–5. *See also* individual
   cities
Colonne Randon, 69, 72, 121, 127, 157,
   159, 162–3, 165, 181, 207, 220, 222,
   242, 244, 254
Colons, 5–6, 11, 25, 139–40, 152, 180,
   202, 243. *See also* pieds noirs; Settlers
Compagnie d'Afrique, 40, 45, 53, 58,
   212, 250
Constantine, 36–7, 51–5, 62–3, 66, 109–
   11, 136, 196, 200–1, 203, 211, 224,
   240–1, 252, 257–8
Constantinople. *See* Istanbul
Cours Bertagna, 106–7, 120, 132, 207–8,
   215–16, 220, 222–3, 226, 237, 241–4,
   258
Cours de la Révolution, 215
Crémieux Decree, 202
Çuff-s (çoffs), 57, 188
Cultural division of labor, 8; in Bône,
   170, 176–8

Delhi, 19, 22, 156, 208
Denden, Sadek, 230–2, 249
Denden, Sidi, 61, 230–2

Dependency theory, 78, 98, 108, 114,
   117, 133
Derdour, H'Sen, 254–7
Djebel Onk, 101–2
Djemâ'a El Kheiria El Arabia (Muslim
   Benevolent Society), 233–5
Dréan. *See* Mondovi
Dreyfus Affair, 107, 138, 202, 204
Dual economy, 7, 18, 122
Dubourg, Prosper, 71
Dumas, Alexandre, 248, 254
Duvignaud, Jean, 27
Duwar-s (douars), 41–2, 182
Duzerville (El Hadjar), 66, 71, 80, 102,
   238

Eberhardt, Isabelle, 249, 254, 256
Economic dualism, 18–19, 26, 117, 120,
   122–4, 126–7, 133, 166
Edough Mountains, 33, 36, 42, 48, 50,
   72–5, 77, 79, 92, 121, 125, 133, 211,
   240, 244, 252
Egypt, 41, 80, 85, 141, 149–50, 209, 248
El Hack, 233–5
El Hadjar. *See* Duzerville
El Kala (La Calle), 53, 152, 239, 245–6
Enclave economy, 18, 123
Enfantin, Père, 67, 80–1, 83–5
Etienne, Eugène, 188, 190, 196, 203
Evolués, 2, 10, 235. *See also Jeunes
   Algériens*

Fanon, Frantz, 21–2, 155–6, 209
Fellah, 3, 48
Ferry, Jules, 6, 183, 198
Fetzara, Lake, 33, 56, 135
Flaubert, Gustave, 248, 254
Forest, cork oak, 26, 33, 78, 245; conces-
   sionaires of, 121, 133; capitalizing on,
   71–7
Fort Cigogne, 36, 213, 222
Fort Génois, 35, 150
Fourierists, 67–8
Fournel, Henri, 77–8, 81, 92, 103
Foucault, Michel, 3–4, 28
Français d'Algérie, 6, 10. *See also Colons;
   Pieds noirs*; Settlers
France, 1789 Revolution in, 53–4, 66;
   July Monarchy in, 67, 210; 1830 Revo-
   lution in, 62; 1848 Revolution in, 69,
   79, 87; Second Republic in, 72; Second
   Empire in, 26, 74, 76, 78, 81–2, 138,
   182, 242; Third Republic in, 26, 85,
   138, 140, 182, 188, 204; Fourth Repub-
   lic in, 2, 4, 241. *See also Métropole*.
François family, 69–70

Index

Oran, 11, 22, 83–4, 111, 140, 151–2, 190, 196, 202–4, 233, 239, 242, 257–8
Organisation Armée Secrète (OAS), 242
Ottoman Empire, 57, 80
Ouenza iron ore, 78, 98, 102–3, 108, 110, 113, 133, 242; affair of, 103–8

Parti colonial, 190, 192
Pataouète, 224–6, 228–9
Patron-client relations, 24, 56, 123, 190. *See also* Patronage politics
Patronage politics, 24, 27, 180, 182, 188–92, 196–8, 201, 205. *See also* Patron-client relations
Pereire family, 78, 80
Petits blancs, 10, 124, 154, 172, 202, 204
Philippeville, 109–10, 152, 224, 252
Pieds noirs, 4, 6, 8, 11, 23, 25, 139, 153–5, 160, 162, 206–8, 220, 224, 238, 240–1, 244, 254. *See also Colons*; Settlers
Plan de Constantine, 80, 242, 244
Plural society, 7–8, 15, 18, 20–4, 122
Poor whites. *See Petits blancs*

Qūbba, 36, 60, 220, 230

Race and ethnicity, 10
Radical Republican party, 133
Randon, marshal, 72, 74, 181–2, 207, 211, 252
Residential segregation, 15, 19–21, 23, 26, 208; in Bône, 156–65, 242
Romans, 1, 36, 48, 77, 102, 210, 213, 222

Sahara desert, 32, 42, 45, 53, 114, 120, 140
Said, Edward, 4
St. Augustine, 35–6, 102, 213, 215, 219, 222, 229, 244, 249. *See also* Hippo
Saint-Saens, Camille, 249, 254, 256
Saint-Simonians, 68–9, 77–8, 80–1
Salafiyya. *See* Islamic Reformism
Salah Bey, 38, 60, 213, 220, 222
Salah Bey mosque, 38–9
Schneider family, 81–2, 103–8
Segmented labor markets, 18, 122
Senhadja, 44, 48, 50
Seraidi (Bugeaud), 23, 208, 240
Sétif riots, 237–8
Seybouse River, 34–6, 71, 83–4, 113, 135, 248

Settler colonialism, 6–11, 25, 116; in Algeria, 23
Settlers, 5, 7, 11, 21, 184. *See also Colons; Pieds noirs*
Sidi Bou Merouane mosque, 38–40, 64, 213, 222, 247
Sidi Brahim tomb, 36–7, 220–2
Social networks, 56
Social stratification, 10, 20–2, 26, 54–6, 153–6, 191
Société Générale Algérienne (SGA), 83–5, 132
Société Nationale de la Sidérurgie (SNS), 102, 242
Spanish, 124, 138, 145, 151, 153–4, 178, 202, 206, 224
Souk Ahras, 102, 110, 152, 239, 247
Suez Canal, 84, 141, 149
Sufi brotherhoods, 58–60, 236, 249, 256
Suq (souk), 39, 51–2, 114

Tabarka, 33, 212, 245–6
Talabot, Paulin, 80, 92, 242
Talabot family, 78, 81–5, 103
Taxes, 50, 183
Tébessa affair of 1950, 239
Tébessa phosphates, 78, 98–102, 110, 133, 152, 216; scandal of, 199–201
Thomson, Gaston, 182, 187–90, 196, 199–204
Tunis, 19, 36, 43–4, 53, 58, 109, 139, 150, 245, 247, 253
Tunisia, 33, 43, 67, 87, 105–6, 121, 141, 150, 245, 250
Turks, Turkish, 2, 43–4, 49, 52, 54–5, 57, 62, 70, 73, 138, 210, 213, 222, 250–2, 255. *See also Koulougli-s*

Utopian socialists, 67–9

Vatin, Jean-Claude, 5

Wallerstein, Immanuel, 78
World systems theory, 117

Yacono, Xavier, 4–5
Youcef, Zighout, 209, 238, 240, 244

Zawiyas, 36, 39, 49, 60
Zeghdoud, cheikh, 252, 255

328